10,000
DREAMS
AND THEIR
TRADITIONAL
MEANINGS

10,000
DREAMS
AND THEIR
TRADITIONAL
MEANINGS

foulsham

LONDON · NEW YORK · TORONTO · SYDNEY

foulsham

The Publishing House, Bennetts Close,
Cippenham, Berkshire SL1 5AP

ISBN 0-572-02144-5

Copyright © 1995 W. Foulsham & Co.

Printed in Great Britain by
The Guernsey Press Co. Ltd.,
Guernsey, Channel Islands.

CONTENTS

DREAMS

A.

12

J.

K.

L.

M.

19

PREFACE.

"Dreams are rudiments of the great state to come.
We dream what is about to happen."—BAILEY.

The Bible, as well as other great books of historical and revealed religion, shows traces of a general and substantial belief in dreams. Plato, Goethe, Shakespeare and Napoleon assigned to certain dreams prophetic value. Joseph saw eleven stars of the Zodiac bow to himself, the twelfth star. The famine of Egypt was revealed by a vision of fat and lean cattle. The parents of Christ were warned of the cruel edict of Herod, and fled with the Divine Child into Egypt.

Pilate's wife, through the influence of a dream, advised her husband to have nothing to do with the conviction of Christ. But the gross materialism of the day laughed at dreams, as it echoed the voice and verdict of the multitude, "Crucify the Spirit, but let the flesh live." Barabbas, the robber, was set at liberty.

The ultimatum of all human decrees and wisdom is to gratify the passions of the flesh at the expense of the spirit. The prophets and those who have stood nearest the fountain of universal knowledge used dreams with more frequency than any other mode of divination.

Profane, as well as sacred, history is threaded with incidents of dream prophecy. Ancient history relates that Gennadius was convinced of the immortality of his soul by conversing with an apparition in his dream.

Through the dream of Cecilia Metella, the wife of a Consul, the Roman Senate was induced to order the temple of Juno Sospita rebuilt.

The Emperor Marcian dreamed he saw the bow of the Hunnish conqueror break on the same night that Attila died.

23

Plutarch relates how Augustus, while ill, through the dream of a friend, was persuaded to leave his tent, which a few hours after was captured by the enemy, and the bed whereon he had lain was pierced with the enemies' swords.

If Julius Cæsar had been less incredulous about dreams he would have listened to the warning which Calpurnia, his wife, received in a dream.

Crœsus saw his son killed in a dream.

Petrarch saw his beloved Laura, in a dream, on the day she died, after which he wrote his beautiful poem, "The Triumph of Death."

Cicero relates the story of two traveling Arcadians who went to different lodgings—one to an inn, and the other to a private house. During the night the latter dreamed that his friend was begging for help. The dreamer awoke; but, thinking the matter unworthy of notice, went to sleep again. The second time he dreamed his friend appeared, saying it would be too late, for he had already been murdered and his body hid in a cart, under manure. The cart was afterward sought for and the body found. Cicero also wrote, "If the gods love men they will certainly disclose their purposes to them in sleep."

Chrysippus wrote a volume on dreams as divine portent. He refers to the skilled interpretations of dreams as a true divination; but adds that, like all other arts in which men have to proceed on conjecture and on artificial rules, it is not infallible.

Plato concurred in the general idea prevailing in his day, that there were divine manifestations to the soul in sleep. Condorcet thought and wrote with greater fluency in his dreams than in waking life.

Tartini, a distinguished violinist, composed his "Devil's Sonata" under the inspiration of a dream. Coleridge, through dream influence, composed his "Kubla Khan."

The writers of Greek and Latin classics relate many instances of dream experiences. Homer accorded to some dreams divine origin. During the third and fourth centuries, the supernatural origin of dreams was so generally accepted that the fathers, relying upon the classics and the Bible as authority, made this belief a doctrine of the Christian Church.

Synesius placed dreaming above all methods of divining the future; he thought it the surest, and open to the poor and rich alike.

Aristotle wrote: "There is a divination concerning some things in dreams not incredible." Camille Flammarion, in his great book on "Premonitory Dreams and Divination of the Future," says: "I do not hesitate to affirm at the outset that occurrence of dreams foretelling future events with accuracy must be accepted as certain."

Joan of Arc predicted her death.

Cazotte, the French philosopher and transcendentalist, warned Condorcet against the manner of his death.

People dream now, the same as they did in medieval and ancient times.

The following excerpt from "The Unknown,"* a recent book by Flammarion, the French astronomer, supplemented with a few of my own thoughts and collections, will answer the purposes intended for this book.

"We may see without eyes and hear without ears, not by unnatural excitement of our sense of vision or of hearing, for these accounts prove the contrary, but by some interior sense, psychic and mental.

"The soul, by its interior vision, may see not only what is passing at a great distance, but it may also know in advance what is to happen in the future. The future exists potentially, determined by causes which bring to pass successive events.

"POSITIVE OBSERVATION PROVES THE EXISTENCE OF A PSYCHIC WORLD, as real as the world known to our physical senses.

"And now, because the soul acts at a distance by some power that belongs to it, are we authorized to conclude that it exists as something real, and that it is not the result of functions of the brain?

"Does light really exist?

"Does heat exist?

"Does sound exist?

"No.

"They are only manifestations produced by movement.

"What we call light is a sensation produced upon our optic nerve by the vibrations of ether, comprising between 400 and 756

---

*"From 'The Unknown.' Published by Harper & Brothers. Copyright, 1900, by Camille Flammarion."

trillions per second, undulations that are themselves very obscure.

"What we call heat is a sensation produced by vibrations between 350 and and 600 trillions.

"The sun lights up space, as much at midnight as at midday. Its temperature is nearly 270 degrees below zero.

"What we call sound is a sensation produced upon our auditory nerve by silent vibrations of the air, themselves comprising between 32,000 and 36,000 a second.

. . . .

"Very many scientific terms represent only results, not causes.

"The soul may be in the same case.

"The observations given in this work, the sensations, the impressions, the visions, things heard, etc., may indicate physical effects produced without the brain.

"Yes, no doubt, but it does not seem so.

"Let us examine one instance.

"A young woman, adored by her husband, dies at Moscow. Her father-in-law, at Pulkowo, near St. Petersburg, saw her that same hour by his side. She walked with him along the street; then she disappeared. Surprised, startled, and terrified, he telegraphed to his son, and learned both the sickness and the death of his daughter-in-law.

"We are absolutely obliged to admit that SOMETHING emanated from the dying woman and touched her father-in-law. This *thing unknown* may have been an ethereal movement, as in the case of light, and may have been only an effect, a product, a result; but this effect must have had a cause, and this cause evidently proceeded from the woman who was dying. Can the constitution of the brain explain this projection? I do not think that any anatomist or physiologist will give this question an affirmative answer. One feels that there is a force unknown, proceeding, not from our physical organization, but from that in us which can think.

"Take another example.

"A lady in her own house hears a voice singing. It is the voice of a friend now in a convent, and she faints, because she is sure it is the voice of the dead. At the same moment that friend does really die, twenty miles away from her.

"Does not this give us the impression that one soul holds communication with another?

"The wife of a captain who has gone out to the Indian mutiny sees one night her husband standing before her with his hands pressed to his breast, and a look of suffering on his face. The agitation that she feels convinces her that he is either killed or badly wounded. It was November 14th. The War Office subsequently publishes his death as having taken place on November 15th. She endeavors to have the true date ascertained. The War Office was wrong. He died on the 14th.

"A child six years old stops in the middle of his play and cries out, frightened: "Mamma, I have seen Mamma." At that moment his mother was dying far away from him.

"A young girl at a ball stops short in the middle of a dance and cries, bursting into tears. 'My father is dead; I have just seen him.' At that moment her father died. She did not even know he was ill.

"All these things present themselves to us as indicating not physiological operations of one brain acting on another, but psychic actions of spirit upon spirit. We feel that they indicate to us some power unknown.

"No doubt it is difficult to apportion what belongs to the spirit, the soul, and what belongs to the brain. We can only let ourselves be guided in our judgment and our appreciations by the same feeling that is created in us by the discussion of phenomena. This is how all science has been started. Well, and does not every one feel that we have here to do with manifestations from beings capable of thought, and not with material physiological facts only?

"This impression is superabundantly confirmed by investigation concerning the unknown faculties of the soul, when active in dreams and somnambulism.

"A brother learns the death of his young sister by a terrible nightmare.

"A young girl sees beforehand, in a dream, the man whom she will marry.

"A mother sees her child lying in a road, covered with blood.

"A lady goes, in a dream, to visit her husband on a distant steamer, and her husband really receives this visit, which is seen by a third person.

"A magnetized lady sees and describes the interior of the body of her dying mother; what she said is confirmed by the autopsy.

"A gentleman sees, in a dream, a lady whom he knows arriving at night in a railroad station, her journey having been undertaken suddenly.

"A magistrate sees three years in advance the commission of a crime, down to its smallest details.

"Several persons report that they have seen towns and landscapes before they ever visited them, and have seen themselves in situations in which they found themselves long after.

"A mother hears her daughter announce her intended marriage six months before it has been thought of.

"Frequent cases of death are foretold with precision.

"A theft is seen by a somnambulist, and the execution of the criminal is foretold.

"A young girl sees her fiancé, or an intimate friend dying (these are frequent cases), etc.

"All these show unknown faculties in the soul. Such at least is my own impression. It seems to me that we cannot reasonably attribute the prevision of the future and mental sight to a nervous action of the brain.

"I think we must either deny these facts or admit that they must have had an intellectual and spiritual cause of the psychic order, and I recommend sceptics who do not desire to be convinced, to deny them outright; to treat them as illusions and cases of a fortuitous coincidence of circumstances. They will find this easier. Uncompromising deniers of facts, rebels against evidence, may be all the more positive, and may declare that the writers of these extraordinary narratives are persons fond of a joke, who have written them to hoax me, and that there have been persons in all ages who have done the same thing to mystify thinkers who have taken up such questions.

"These phenomena prove, I think, that the soul exists, and that it is endowed with faculties at present unknown. That is the logical way of commencing our study, which in the end may lead us to the problem of the after-life and immortality. A thought can be transmitted to the mind of another. There are mental transmissions, communications of thoughts, and psychic currents between human souls. Space appears to be no obstacle in these cases, and time sometimes seems to be annihilated."

A few years ago a person whom I will designate as "A" related a dream to me as follows: "I take no interest in pugilism or pugilists, but I saw, in a dream, every detail of the Corbett and Fitzsimmons mill, four days before it took place out West. Two nights before the fight I had a second dream in which a favorite horse was running, but suddenly, just before the judge's stand was passed, a hitherto unobserved little black horse ran ahead and the crowd shouted in my ears, 'Fitzsimmons wins!' "

"B" relates the following as a dream: "I saw the American soldiers, in clay-colored uniform, bearing the flag of victory two weeks before the Spanish-American war was declared, and of course before any living being could have known the uniform to be adopted. Later I saw, several days before the actual occurrence happened, the destruction of Cervera's fleet by the American navy." Signed "B."

"Just after the South African hostilities began, I saw in a dream a fierce struggle between the British and Boers, in which the former suffered severe losses. A few nights after I had a second dream in which I saw the contending forces in a long-drawn contest, very disastrous to both, and in which neither could claim a victory. They seemed to be fighting to a frazzle." Signed "C."

"D" related to me at the time of the occurrence of the dream the following: "It had been suggested to me that the two cereals, corn and wheat, were too far apart, and that I ought to buy corn. At noon I lay down on a lounge to await luncheon; I had barely closed my eyes before a voice whispered: 'Don't buy, but sell that corn.' 'What do you mean?' I asked. 'Sell at the present price, and buy at 23⅞.' " The foregoing dream was related to me by a practical, successful business man who never speculates. I watched the corn market and know it took the turns indicated in the dream.

In this dream we find the dreamer conversing with some strange intelligence possessed of knowledge unknown to objective reason. It could not, therefore, have been the waking thoughts of the dreamer, for he possessed no such information. Was the message superinduced through the energies and activities of the waking mind on the subjective mind? This could not have been, because he had no such thoughts; besides, the intelligence given was free from the errors of the calculating and anxious waking mind.

We must therefore look to other sources for an explanation. Was it the higher self that manifested to Abraham in the dim ages of the world? Was it the Divine Voice that gave solace to Krishna in his abstraction? Was it the unerring light that preceded Gautama into the strange solitudes of Asia? Was it the small voice that Elijah heard in the desert of Shurr? Was it the Comforter of Jesus in the wilderness and the garden of distress? Or, was it Paul's indwelling spirit of this earthly tabernacle? One thing we may truthfully affirm—that it did not proceed from the rational, objective mind of the rank materialist, who would close all doors to that inner life and consciousness where all true religion finds its birthmark, its hope, its promises and its faith; which, rightly understood, will leave to the horrors of the Roman crucifixion the twin thieves, superstition and scepticism, while the angel of "Goodwill" will go free to solace the world with the fruit and fragrance of enduring power and promise The steel chains that fasten these hydra-headed crocodiles of sensuous poison around love and destiny can only be severed by the diamond of wisdom and knowledge.

A citizen worthy of confidence relates the following dream: "In December, 1878, I saw in a dream my brother-in-law, Henry Yarnell, suffering from a bloody knife wound; after this I awoke, but soon fell asleep again. The second time I dreamed of a similar scene, except that the wound was the result of a shotgun. After this I did not go to sleep again. I was much troubled about my dream, and soon started in the direction of my brother-in-law's house. I had not gone far, when I met an acquaintance who promptly informed me that my brother-in-law had been shot."   Signed "E."

A well-known resident of Chattanooga, Tenn., formerly of New York City, will vouch for the accuracy of the following incident in his life:

"On February 19, 1878, I was boarding with a family on Christopher street, New York, while my wife and baby were visiting my parents in the country, a short distance from the city. Our baby was taken sick. The malady developed into brain fever, followed by water on the brain, causing the little one's death.

"At our boarding-place there was at the time a quartette of us grass widowers, as we called ourselves, and in order to pass away the time pleasantly we had organized a 'grass widowers' euchre club.' We used to meet almost every evening after dinner in the dining-room, and play until about eleven o'clock, when we would retire. On the above date I dreamed that after playing our usual evening games we took our departure for our rooms, and on the way up the second flight of stairs I heard a slight movement behind me; on looking around I found I was being followed by a tall figure robed in a long, loose white gown, which came down to the floor. The figure seemed to be that of a man—I would say, about seven feet tall— who followed me up the second flight and along the hallway, entering my room. After coming in the door he made a circle of the room and seemed to be looking for something, and when he approached the door to make his exit he stopped still, and with a gesture of his hand remarked, 'I have taken all you have.' On the following morning, about 9:30 o'clock, I received a telegram from my wife announcing the death of our only baby."   Signed "F."

A well-known citizen of Chattanooga, Tenn., relates and vouches for the truth of the following occurrence:

"Several years ago, when a boy, I had a schoolmate and friend, Willie T., between whom and myself there sprung up a mutual feeling of high regard. We were chums in the sense that we were almost constantly together, both at school and at home, and among the partnerships we formed was one of having amàteur shadowgraph and panoramic shows in the basement of Willie's home. This much to show the mental and social relationship that existed between us. Some time during this association (I cannot recall the exact night now) I had a strange dream, in which my chum appeared to me with outstretched hand, asking me to shake, saying, 'I shall not see you any more.' With that, the dream lapsed and was over. I thought nothing of the occurrence, and had almost forgotten it, when one day, about a week later, during which time I had not had a glimpse of my chum, while he was out hunting with another friend, W. McC., in following him over a rail fence. the latter's gun was accidentally discharged in Willie's face and neck, resulting in instant death. With this shocking news the memory of the dream I had had came back to me vividly and puzzled me very greatly, and indeed has puzzled me to this day."   Signed "G."

The recipients of the above dreams are living to-day and their names and address may be obtained, none of them are credulous fanatics or predisposed to a belief in psychic or spirit phenomena.

The above dreams, except two, cannot be explained by telepathy, because the mental picture cast on the dream mind had not in either instance taken place in waking life. This would account for the dream perception of "D," which did not, in all probability, take place until after the murder had been committed.

The vision of "F" might be disposed of in the same way. In this instance "F" saw the white-robed specter open the door, walk around the room and finally, taking his position as if to depart, say: "I have taken all you have." No doubt this vision took place at the exact moment of the child's death.

There are thousands of similar experiences occurring daily in the lives of honest, healthy and sane human beings, that rival the psychic manifestations of Indian Yogism or Hebrew records.

Still men go on doubting this true and loving subjective intelligence that is constantly wooing for entrance into the soul and is ever vigilant in warning the material life of approaching evils. They prefer the Witch of Endor, and the Black Magicians of ancient Egypt to the higher, or Christ self, that has been seen and heard by the sages and saints of all ages, assuming appropriate symbols, as in the case of the vision of "F," where the angel of death was assumed.

To Paul it appeared as a great personal truth whom he was relentlessly persecuting. To many a wayward son or daughter of the present time, it appears as a dead relative or friend, in order to approach the material mind and make its warning more effective.

To those who were interested in the teachings of Christ, but who after his death were inclined to doubt him, this higher self materialized in the form of the Great Master in order to impress on their material minds the spiritual import of his teachings. So, to this day, when doubt and temptation mar the moral instinct, God, through the spiritual self, as Job says, approaches man while in deep sleep upon the bed to impress his instructions that he may change man from his purpose.

The spiritual world always fixes its orbit upon a straight line, while the material world is fonder of curves. We find man struggling through dreadful marshes and deserts of char-latanism in order to get a glimpse into his future, instead of solicitously following the straight line of inner consciousness that connects with the infinite mind, from which, aided by his Church and the healthy action of his own judgment, he may re-ceive those helpful spiritual impressions and messages necessary to solace the longings of the searching soul.

The philosophy of the True Master is the straight line. Pythagoras, Plato and Christ created angles by running ver-tical lines through the ecclesiastical and hypocritical conven-tionalities of their day. The new angles and curves thus pro-duced by the bold philosophy of the humble Nazarene have confronted with impregnable firmness during the intervening ages the sophistry of the Pharisees.

"In a dream, in a vision of the night, when deep sleep falleth upon men, in slumberings upon the bed; then he openeth the ears of men and sealeth their instruction. That he may with-draw man from his purpose and hide pride from man."—JOB 33:15.

"Man cannot contradict the laws of Nature. But, are all the laws of Nature yet understood?"

"Real philosophy seeks rather to solve than to deny."— LYTTON.

Those who live active lives exclude spiritual thought and fill their minds with the fascinations of worldly affairs, pleasure and business, dream with less frequency than those who regard objective matters with lighter concern. The former depend alone upon the voluptuous warmth of the world for content-ment; they look to money, the presence of some one, or to other external sources for happiness, and are often disappointed; while the latter, with a just appreciation of temporal wants, depend alone upon the inner consciousness for that peace which passeth all carnal understanding.

They are strengthened, as were Buddha and Christ, by sup-pressing the sensual fires for forty days and nights in the wilderness of trial and temptation. They number a few, and are never disappointed, while the former number millions.

Nature is three-fold, so is man; male and female, son or soul. The union of one and two produce the triad or the trinity which underlies the philosophy of the ancients.

Man has a physical or visible body, an atom of the physical or visible earth. He has a soul the exact counterpart of his body, but invisible and subjective; incomplete and imperfect as the external man, or *vice versa*.

The soul is not only the son or creation of man, but it is the real man. It is the inner imperishable double or imprint of what has outwardly and inwardly transpired. All thoughts, desires and actions enter the soul through the objective mind.

The automaton of the body responds as quickly to the bat of the eye as it does to the movement of the whole body. By it the foot-steps of man and the very hairs of his head are numbered. Thus it becomes his invisible counterpart. It is therefore the book of life or death, and by it he judges himself or is already judged. When it is complete nothing can be added or taken from its personnel. It is sometimes partly opened to him in his dreams, but in death is clearly revealed.

Man has also a spiritual body, subjective to, and more ethereal than the soul. It is an infinitesimal atom, and is related in substance to the spiritual or infinite mind of the universe. Just as the great physical sun, the center of visible light, life and heat, is striving to purify the foul miasma of the marsh and send its luminous messages of love into the dark crevices of the earth. so the Great Spiritual Sun, of which the former is a visible prototype or reflection, is striving to illuminate with Divine Wisdom the personal soul and mind of man, thus enabling him to become cognizant of the spiritual or Christ presence within.

The heresy and Herod of wanton flesh, degenerate victim of the sensuous filth and fermentation of self-indulgence, is ever striving to exile and suppress, from the wilderness of sin, the warning cry of the Nazarite voice by intriguing with the cunning, incestuous daughters of unholy thoughts and desires.

The objective mind is most active when the body is awake. The subjective influences are most active, and often fill the mind with impressions, while the physical body is asleep. The spiritual intelligence can only intrude itself when the human

34

will is suspended, or passive to external states. A man who lives only on the sensual plane will receive his knowledge through the senses, and will not, while in that state, receive spiritual impressions or warning dreams.

Men and women rarely ever degrade themselves so low that the small voice of the desert does not bring them a message. Sodom and Gomorrah, vile with the debauchery of a nameless crime, were not deserted by the angel of love until the fire which they had lighted in their souls had consumed them. The walls of Jericho did not fall until Rahab, the harlot, had been saved and the inmates had heard for several days the ram's-horn and the tramp of Joshua's infantry.

The evangelist Jonah, the Sam Jones of Hebrew theology, exhorted the adulterous Nineveh many times to repentance before it fell.

David, while intoxicated with the wine of love, from languishing in the seductive embrace of the beautiful bathing nymph, Bathsheba, heard the voice of Nathan. Surely God is no respecter of persons, and will speak to all classes if the people will not stiffen their necks or harden their hearts.

Women dream more often and more vividly than men, because their dream composition is less influenced and allied to external environments.

All dreams possess an element of warning or prescience; some more than others. This is unknown to the many, but is known to the observing few. There are many people who have no natural taste for music, and who do not know one note from another. There are also those who cannot distinguish one color from another. To the former there is no harmony of sound, and to the latter there is no blending of colors.

They are heard and seen, but there is no artistic recognition of the same. Still it would be absurd to say to either the musician or the artist: your art is false and is only an illusion of the senses.

One man apparently never dreams; another dreams occasionally, and still another more frequently; none atttempt to interpret their dream, or to observe what follows; therefore, the verdict is, "There is nothing in dreams." (Schopenhauer aptly says: "No man can see over his own height. . . . Intellect is invisible to the man who has none.") The first is like the blind man who denies the existence of light, because he does not perceive it. The second and third resemble the color-blind man, who sees but who persists in calling green blue, and *vice versa*.

A fourth man sees in a dream a friend walking in his room; the vision is so vivid he instantly gets up and strikes a match. After making sure there is no intruder about the room he looks at his watch and goes back to bed. The next day he receives the unwelcome tidings that his friend died at the exact moment of the vision.

At another time he hears in his dream a familiar voice cry out in agony. Soon he hears of a shocking accident or distressing illness befalling the one whose voice he recognized in the dream.*

The third man, already referred to, has about the same dream experiences, but calls them strange coincidences or unconscious cerebration, etc.

Again, the fourth man dreams of walking through green fields of corn, grass or wheat. He notes after such dreams prosperous conditions follow for at least a few days. He also notes, if the area over which he passes is interspersed with rocks or other adverse signs, good and bad follow in the wake of the dream. If he succeeds in climbing a mountain and finds the top barren he will accomplish his object, but the deal will prove unprofitable. If it is green and spring-like in appearance, it will yield good results. If he sees muddy water, sickness, business depression or causes for jealousy may develop.

A nightmare suggests to the dreamer to be careful of health and diet, to relax his whole body, to sleep with his arms down and keep plenty of fresh air in the room.

He sums up the foregoing with a thousand similar dream incidents, and is led to believe certain dreams possess an element of warning.

There are three pure types of dreams, namely, *subjective, physical* and *spiritual*. They relate to the past, present and future, and are influenced by past or subjective, physical and spiritual causes. The latter is always deeply prophetic, especially when it leaves a vivid impression on the conscious mind. The former, too, possesses an element of warning and prophecy,

---

* For authentic records, see Flammarion's "Unknown."

36

though the true meaning is hidden in symbols or allegory. They are due to contingent mental pictures of the past falling upon the conscious mind of the dreamer. Thus he is back at the old home, and finds mother pale and aged, or ruddy and healthy, and the lawn withered or green. It all augurs, according to the aspect the picture assumes, ill or good fortune.

Physical dreams are more or less unimportant. They are usually superinduced by the anxious waking mind, and when this is so they possess no prophetic significance.

Dreams induced by opiates, fevers, mesmerism and ill health come under this class. A man who gambles is liable to dream of cards; if he dreams of them in deep sleep the warning is to be heeded; but if it comes as a reverie while he sleeps lightly he should regard it as worthless. Such dreams reflect only the present condition of the body and mind of the dreamer; but as the past and present enter into shaping the future, the reflections thus left on the waking mind should not go by unheeded.

We often observe matters of dress and exterior appearance through mirrors, and we soon make the necessary alterations to put our bodies in harmony with existing formalities. Then, why not study more seriously the mental images reflected from the mirror of the soul upon our minds through the occult processes within us?

Thirdly, the spiritual dreams are brought about by the higher self penetrating the soul realm, and reflecting upon the waking mind approaching events. When we put our animal mind and soul in harmony with our higher self we become one with it, and, therefore, one with the universal mind or will by becoming a part of it. It is through the higher self we reach the infinite. It is through the lower self we fall into the whirlpool of matter.

10,000 DREAMS
INTERPRETED

WHAT'S IN A DREAM.

A.

"When he was set down on the Judgment seat, his wife sent unto him, saying, 'Have thou nothing to do with that just man; for I have suffered many things this day in a dream, because of him.'"—Matthew xxvii, 19.

Abandon.

To dream that you are abandoned, denotes that you will have difficulty in framing your plans for future success.

To abandon others, you will see unhappy conditions piled thick around you, leaving little hope of surmounting them.

If it is your house that you abandon, you will soon come to grief in experimenting with fortune.

If you abandon your sweetheart, you will fail to recover lost valuables, and friends will turn aside from your favors.

If you abandon a mistress, you will unexpectedly come into a goodly inheritance.

If it is religion you abandon, you will come to grief by your attacks on prominent people.

To abandon children, denotes that you will lose your fortune by lack of calmness and judgment.

To abandon your business, indicates distressing circumstances in which there will be quarrels and suspicion. (This dream may have a literal fulfilment if it is impressed on your waking mind, whether you abandon a person, or that person abandons you, or, as indicated, it denotes other worries.)

To see yourself or friend abandon a ship, suggests your possible entanglement in some business failure, but if you escape to shore your interests will remain secure.

Abbey.*

To see an abbey in ruins, foretells that your hopes and schemes will fall into ignoble incompletion.

To dream that a priest bars your entrance into an abbey, denotes that you will be saved from a ruinous state by enemies mistaking your embarrassment for progress.

For a young woman to get into an abbey, foretells her violent illness. If she converses with a priest in an abbey, she will incur the censure of true friends for indiscretion.

Abbess.

For a young woman to dream that she sees an abbess, denotes that she will be compelled to perform distasteful tasks, and will submit to authority only after unsuccessful rebellion.

To dream of an abbess smiling and benignant, denotes you will be surrounded by true friends and pleasing prospects.

Abbot.*

To dream that you are an abbot, warns you that treacherous plots are being laid for your downfall.

If you see this pious man in devotional exercises, it forewarns you of smooth flattery and deceit pulling you a willing victim into the meshes of artful bewilderment.

For a young woman to talk with an abbot, portends that she will yield to insinuating flatteries, and in yielding she will besmirch her reputation. If she marries one, she will

* See similar words in connection with churches, priests, etc.

uphold her name and honor despite poverty and temptation.

Abdomen.*

To see your abdomen in a dream, foretells that you will have great expectations, but you must curb hardheadedness and redouble your energies on your labor, as pleasure is approaching to your hurt.

To see your abdomen shriveled, foretells that you will be persecuted and defied by false friends.

To see it swollen, you will have tribulations, but you will overcome them and enjoy the fruits of your labor.

To see blood oozing from the abdomen, foretells an accident or tragedy in your family.

The abdomen of children in an unhealthy state, portends that contagion will pursue you.

Abhor.

To dream that you abhor a person, denotes that you will entertain strange dislike for some person, and your suspicion of his honesty will prove correct.

To think yourself held in abhorrence by others, predicts that your good intentions to others will subside into selfishness.

For a young woman to dream that her lover abhors her, foretells that she will love a man who is in no sense congenial.

Abject.

To dream that you are abject, denotes that you will be the recipient of gloomy tidings, which will cause a relaxation in your strenuous efforts to climb the heights of prosperity.

---

* See Belly.

To see others abject, is a sign of bickerings and false dealings among your friends.

Abode.*

To dream that you can't find your abode, you will completely lose faith in the integrity of others.

If you have no abode in your dreams, you will be unfortunate in your affairs, and lose by speculation.

To change your abode, signifies hurried tidings and that hasty journeys will be made by you.

For a young woman to dream that she has left her abode, is significant of slander and falsehoods being perpetrated against her.

Abortion.

For a woman to dream that she assents to abortion being committed on her, is a warning that she is contemplating some enterprise which if carried out will steep her in disgrace and unhappiness.

For a doctor to dream that he is a party to an abortion, foretells that his practice will suffer from his inattention to duty, which will cause much trouble.

Above.

To see anything hanging above you, and about to fall, implies danger; if it falls upon you it may be ruin or sudden disappointment. If it falls near, but misses you, it is a sign that you will have a narrow escape from loss of money, or other misfortunes may follow.

Should it be securely fixed above you, so as not to imply danger, your condition will improve after threatened loss.

---

* See Home.

Abroad.

To dream that you are abroad, or going abroad, foretells that you will soon, in company with a party, make a pleasant trip, and you will find it necessary to absent yourself from your native country for a sojourn in a different climate.

Absalom.

To dream of Absalom, is significant of distressing incidents. You may unconsciously fall a victim to error, and penetrate some well beloved heart with keen anguish and pain over the committal of immoral actions and the outraging of innocence. No flower of purity will ever be too sacred for you to breathe a passionate breath upon. To dream of this, or any other disobedient character, is a warning against immoral tendencies. A father is warned by this dream to be careful of his children.

Absence.

To grieve over the absence of any one in your dreams, denotes that repentance for some hasty action will be the means of securing you life-long friendships.

If you rejoice over the absence of friends, it denotes that you will soon be well rid of an enemy.

Abscess.

To dream that you have an abscess which seems to have reached a chronic stage, you will be overwhelmed with misfortune of your own; at the same time your deepest sympathies will be enlisted for the sorrows of others.

Absinthe.

To come under the influence of absinthe in dreams, denotes that you will lead a merry and foolish pace with innocent companions, and waste your inheritance in prodigal lavishness on the siren, selfish fancy.

For a young woman to dream that she drinks absinthe with her lover warns her to resist his persuasions to illicit consummation of their love. If she dreams she is drunk, she will yield up her favors without strong persuasion. (This dream typifies that you are likely to waste your energies in pleasure.)

Abundance.

To dream that you are possessed with an abundance foretells that you will have no occasion to reproach Fortune, and that you will be independent of her future favors; but your domestic happiness may suffer a collapse under the strain you are likely to put upon it by your infidelity.

Abuse.

To dream of abusing a person, means that you will be unfortunate in your affairs, losing good money through over-bearing persistency in business relations with others.

To feel yourself abused, you will be molested in your daily pursuits by the enmity of others.

For a young woman to dream that she hears abusive language, foretells that she will fall under the ban of some person's jealousy and envy. If she uses the language herself, she will meet with unexpected rebuffs, that may fill her with mortification and remorse for her past unworthy conduct toward friends.

Abyss.

To dream of looking into an abyss, means that you will be confronted by threats of seizure of property, and that there will be quarrels and reproaches of a personal nature which will unfit you to meet the problems of life.

For a woman to be looking into an abyss, foretells that

she will burden herself with unwelcome cares. If she falls into the abyss her disappointment will be complete; but if she succeeds in crossing, or avoiding it, she will reinstate herself.

Academy.

To visit an academy in your dreams, denotes that you will regret opportunities that you have let pass through sheer idleness and indifference.

To think you own, or are an inmate of one, you will find that you are to meet easy defeat of aspirations. You will take on knowledge, but be unable to rightly assimilate and apply it.

For a young woman or any person to return to an academy after having finished there, signifies that demands will be made which the dreamer may find himself or herself unable to meet.

Accepted.*

For a business man to dream that his proposition has been accepted, foretells that he will succeed in making a trade, which heretofore looked as if it would prove a failure.

For a lover to dream that he has been accepted by his sweetheart, denotes that he will happily wed the object of his own and others' admiration.

Accident.

To dream of an accident is a warning to avoid any mode of travel for a short period, as you are threatened with loss of life.

---

* If this dream has been occasioned by overanxiety and weakness, the contrary may be expected. The elementary influences often play pranks upon weak and credulous minds by lying, and deceptive utterances. Therefore the dreamer should live a pure life, fortified by a strong will, thus controlling his destiny by expelling from it involuntary intrusions.

For an accident to befall stock, denotes that you will struggle with all your might to gain some object and then see some friend lose property of the same value in aiding your cause.

Accordion.

To dream of hearing the music of an accordion, denotes that you will engage in amusement which will win you from sadness and retrospection. You will by this means be enabled to take up your burden more cheerfully.

For a young woman to dream that she is playing an accordion, portends that she will win her lover by some sad occurrence; but, notwithstanding which, the same will confer lasting happiness upon her union. If the accordion gets out of tune, she will be saddened by the illness or trouble of her lover.

Accounts.

To dream of having accounts presented to you for payment, you will be in a dangerous position. You may have recourse to law to disentangle yourself. If you pay the accounts, you will soon effect a compromise in some serious dispute.

To hold accounts against others, foretells that disagreeable contingencies will arise in your business, marring the smoothness of its management.

For a young woman book-keeper to dream of footing up accounts, denotes that she will have trouble in business, and in her love affairs; but some worthy person will persuade her to account for his happiness. She will be much respected by her present employers.

Accuse.*

To dream that you accuse any one of a mean action,

* See similar words in following chapters.

denotes that you will have quarrels with those under you, and your dignity will be thrown from a high pedestal.

If you are accused, you are in danger of being guilty of distributing scandal in a sly and malicious way.

Aches.*

To dream that you have aches, denotes that you are halting too much in your business, and that some other person is profiting by your ideas.

For a young woman to dream that she has the heart-ache, foretells that she will be in sore distress over the laggardly way her lover prosecutes his suit. If it is the backache, she will encounter illness through careless exposure. If she has the headache, there will be much disquietude of mind for the risk she has taken to rid herself of rivalry.

Acid.

To drink any acid is an adverse dream, bringing you much anxiety.

For a woman to drink aciduous liquors, denotes that she may ensnare herself with compromising situations; even health may be involved.

To see poisonous acids, some treachery against you may be discovered.

Acorn.

Seeing acorns in dreams, is portent of pleasant things ahead, and much gain is to be expected.

To pick them from the ground, foretells success after weary labors.

For a woman to eat them, denotes that she will rise

---

* This dream is usually due to physical causes and is of little significance.

from a station of labor to a position of ease and pleasure.

To shake them from the trees, denotes that you will rapidly attain your wishes in business or love.

To see green-growing acorns, or to see them scattered over the ground, affairs will change for the better. Decayed or blasted acorns have import of disappointments and reverses.

To pull them green from the trees, you will injure your interests by haste and indiscretion.

Acquaintance.*

To meet an acquaintance, and converse pleasantly with him, foretells that your business will run smoothly, and there will be but little discord in your domestic affairs.

If you seem to be disputing, or engaged in loud talk, humiliations and embarrassments will whirl seethingly around you.

If you feel ashamed of meeting an acquaintance, or meet him at an inopportune time, it denotes that you will be guilty of illicitly conducting yourself, and other parties will let the secret out.

For a young woman to think that she has an extensive acquaintance, signifies that she will be the possessor of vast interests, and her love will be worthy the winning. If her circle of acquaintances is small, she will be unlucky in gaining social favors.

Acquit.

To dream that you are acquitted of a crime, denotes that you are about to come into possession of valuable property, but there is danger of a law suit before obtaining possession.

---

* After dreaming of acquaintances, you may see or hear from them.

To see others acquitted, foretells that your friends will add pleasure to your labors.

Acrobat.

To dream of seeing acrobats, denotes that you will be prevented from carrying out hazardous schemes by the foolish fears of others.

To see yourself acrobating, you will have a sensation to answer for, and your existence will be made almost unendurable by the guying of your enemies.

To see women acrobating, denotes that your name will be maliciously and slanderously handled. Also your business interests will be hindered.

For a young woman to dream that she sees acrobats in tights, signifies that she will court favor of men.

Actor and Actress.

To see in your dreams an actress, denotes that your present state will be one of unbroken pleasure and favor.

To see one in distress, you will gladly contribute your means and influence to raise a friend from misfortune and indebtedness.

If you think yourself one, you will have to work for subsistence, but your labors will be pleasantly attended.

If you dream of being in love with one, your inclination and talent will be allied with pleasure and opposed to downright toil.

To see a dead actor, or actress, your good luck will be overwhelmed in violent and insubordinate misery.

To see them wandering and penniless, foretells that your affairs will undergo a change from promise to threatenings of failure. To those enjoying domestic comforts, it is a warning of revolution and faithless vows.

For a young woman to dream that she is engaged to an actor, or about to marry one, foretells that her fancy will bring remorse after the glamor of pleasure has vanished.

If a man dreams that he is sporting with an actress, it foretells that private broils with his wife, or sweetheart, will make him more misery than enjoyment.

Adam and Eve.

To dream of Adam and Eve, foretells that some eventful occasion will rob you of the hope of success in your affairs.

To see them in the garden, Adam dressed in his fig leaf, but Eve perfectly nude save for an Oriental colored serpent ornamenting her waist and abdomen, signifies that treachery and ill faith will combine to overthrow your fortune.

To see or hear Eve conversing with the serpent, foretells that artful women will reduce you to the loss of fortune and reputation.

Adamant.

To dream of adamant, denotes that you will be troubled and defeated in some desire that you held as your life.

Adder.

To dream of seeing an adder strike, and a friend, who is dead but seems to be lying down and breathing, rises partly to a sitting position when the adder strikes at him, and then both disappearing into some bushes nearby, denotes that you will be greatly distressed over the ill luck of friends, and a loss threatened to yourself.

For a young woman to see an adder, foretells a deceitful person is going to cause her trouble. If it runs from her, she will be able to defend her character in attacks made on her.

Addition.

To dream of pondering over addition, denotes that you will have a struggle to overcome difficult situations, which will soon prominently assume formidable shapes in your business transactions.

To find some error in addition, shows that you will be able to overcome enemies by fortunately discerning their intention before they have executed their design.

To add figures with a machine, foretells that you will have a powerful ally who will save you from much oppression.

If you fail to read the figures, you will lose fortune by blind speculation.

Adieu.

To dream of bidding cheerful adieus to people, denotes that you will make pleasant visits and enjoy much social festivity; but if they are made in a sad or doleful strain, you will endure loss and bereaving sorrow.

If you bid adieu to home and country, you will travel in the nature of an exile from fortune and love.

To throw kisses of adieu to loved ones, or children, foretells that you will soon have a journey to make, but there will be no unpleasant accidents or happenings attending your trip.

Admire.

To dream that you are an object of admiration, denotes that you will retain the love of former associates, though your position will take you above their circle.

Admonish.

To admonish your child, or son, or some young person,

denotes that your generous principles will keep you in favor, and fortune will be added to your gifts.

Adopted.

To see your adopted child, or parent, in your dreams, indicates that you will amass fortune through the schemes and speculations of strangers.

To dream that you or others are adopting a child, you will make an unfortunate change in your abode.

Adultery.*

To dream that you commit adultery, foretells that you will be arrainged for some illegal action. If a woman has this dream, she will fail to hold her husband's affections, letting her temper and spite overwhelm her at the least provocation. If it is with her husband's friend, she will be unjustly ignored by her husband. Her rights will be cruelly trampled upon by him. If she thinks she is enticing a youth into this act, she will be in danger of desertion and divorced for her open intriguing.

For a young woman this implies abasement and low desires, in which she will find strange adventures afford her pleasure.

Adulation.

To dream that you seek adulation, foretells that you will pompously fill unmerited positions of honor.

---

* It is always good to dream that you have successfully resisted any temptation. To yield, is bad. If a man chooses low ideals, vampirish influences will swarm around him ready to help him in his nefarious designs. Such dreams may only be the result of depraved elementary influences. If a man chooses high ideals, he will be illuminated by the deific principle within him, and will be exempt from lascivious dreams. The man who denies the existence and power of evil spirits has no arcana or occult knowledge. Did not the black magicians of Pharaoh's time, and Simon Magnus, the Sorcerer, rival the men of God? The dreamer of amorous sweets is warned to beware of scandal.

If you offer adulation, you will expressly part with some dear belonging in the hope of furthering material interests.

Advancement.

To dream of advancing in any engagement, denotes your rapid ascendency to preferment and to the consummation of affairs of the heart.

To see others advancing, foretells that friends will hold positions of favor near you.

Adversary.*

To dream that you meet or engage with an adversary, denotes that you will promptly defend any attacks on your interest. Sickness may also threaten you after this dream.

If you overcome an adversary, you will escape the effect of some serious disaster.

Adventurer.

To dream that you are victimized by an adventurer, proves that you will be an easy prey for flatterers and designing villains. You will be unfortunate in manipulating your affairs to a smooth consistency.

For a young woman to think she is an adventuress, portends that she will be too wrapped up in her own conduct to see that she is being flattered into exchanging her favors for disgrace.

Adversity.

To dream that you are in the clutches of adversity, denotes that you will have failures and continued bad prospects.

To see others in adversity, portends gloomy surround-

* See Enemies.

55

ings, and the illness of some one will produce grave fears of the successful working of plans.*

Advertisement.

To dream that you are getting out advertisements, denotes that you will have to resort to physical labor to promote your interest, or establish your fortune.

To read advertisements, denotes that enemies will overtake you, and defeat you in rivalry.

Advice.

To dream that you receive advice, denotes that you will be enabled to raise your standard of integrity, and strive by honest means to reach independent competency and moral altitude.

To dream that you seek legal advice, foretells that there will be some transactions in your affairs which will create doubt of their merits and legality.

Advocate.

To dream that you advocate any cause, denotes that you will be faithful to your interests, and endeavor to deal honestly with the public, as your interests affect it, and be loyal to your promises to friends.

---

* The old dream books give this as a sign of coming prosperity. This definition is untrue. There are two forces at work in man, one from within and the other from without. They are from two distinct spheres; the animal mind influenced by the personal world of carnal appetites, and the spiritual mind from the realm of universal Brotherhood, present antagonistic motives on the dream consciousness. If these two forces were in harmony, the spirit or mental picture from the dream mind would find a literal fulfilment in the life of the dreamer. The pleasurable sensations of the body cause the spirit anguish. The selfish enrichment of the body impoverishes the spirit influence upon the Soul. The trials of adversity often cause the spirit to rejoice and the flesh to weep. If the cry of the grieved spirit is left on the dream mind it may indicate to the dreamer worldly advancement, but it is hardly the theory of the occult forces, which have contributed to the contents of this book.

Afraid.

To feel that you are afraid to proceed with some affair, or continue a journey, denotes that you will find trouble in your household, and enterprises will be unsuccessful.

To see others afraid, denotes that some friend will be deterred from performing some favor for you because of his own difficulties.

For a young woman to dream that she is afraid of a dog, there will be a possibility of her doubting a true friend.

Africa.

To dream that you are in Africa surrounded by Cannibals, foretells that you will be oppressed by enemies and quarrelsome persons.

For a woman to dream of African scenes, denotes she will make journeys which will prove lonesome and devoid of pleasure or profit.

Afternoon.

For a woman to dream of an afternoon, denotes she will form friendships which will be lasting and entertaining. A cloudy, rainy afternoon, implies disappointment and displeasure.

Affliction.

To dream that affliction lays a heavy hand upon you and calls your energy to a halt, foretells that some disaster is surely approaching you.

To see others afflicted, foretells that you will be surrounded by many ills and misfortunes.

Affrighted.

To dream that you are affrighted, foretells that you will sustain an injury through an accident.

To see others affrighted, brings you close to misery and distressing scenes. Dreams of this nature are frequently caused by nervous and feverish conditions, either from malaria or excitement. When such is the case, the dreamer is warned to take immediate steps to remove the cause. Such dreams or reveries only occur when sleep is disturbed.

Affront.

This is a bad dream. The dreamer is sure to shed tears and weep. For a young woman to dream that she is affronted, denotes that some unfriendly person will take advantage of her ignorance to place her in a compromising situation with a stranger, or to jeopardize her interests with a friend.

Affluence.*

To dream that you are in affluence, foretells that you will make fortunate ventures, and will be pleasantly associated with people of wealth. To young women, a vision of weird and fairy affluence is ominous of illusive and evanescent pleasure. They should study more closely their duty to friends and parents. After dreams of this nature they are warned to cultivate a love for home life.

Agate.

To see agate in a dream, signifies a slight advancement in business affairs.

Age.

To dream of age, portends failures in any kind of undertaking.

To dream of your own age, indicates that perversity of opinion will bring down upon you the indignation of relatives.

---

* See Wealth.

For a young woman to dream of being accused of being older than she is, denotes that she will fall into bad companionship, and her denial of stated things will be brought to scorn. To see herself looking aged, intimates possible sickness, or unsatisfactory ventures. If it is her lover she sees aged, she will be in danger of losing him.

Agony.*

This is not as good a dream, as some would wish you to believe. It portends worry and pleasure intermingled, more of the former than of the latter.

To be in agony over the loss of money, or property, denotes that disturbing and imaginary fears will rack you over the critical condition of affairs, or the illness of some dear relative.

Ague.

A sickly condition of the dreamer is sometimes implied by this dream. To dream that you are shaking with an ague, signifies that you will suffer from some physical disorder, and that fluctuating opinions of your own affairs may bring you to the borders of prostration.

To see others thus affected, denotes that you will offend people by your supreme indifference to the influences of others.

Air.

This dream denotes a withering state of things, and bodes no good to the dreamer.

To dream of breathing hot air suggests that you will be influenced to evil by oppression.

To feel cold air, denotes discrepancies in your business, and incompatibility in domestic relations.

To feel oppressed with humidity, some curse will fall

---

* See Weeping.

on you that will prostrate and close down on your optimistical views of the future.

Alabaster.

To dream of alabaster, foretells success in marriage and all legitimate affairs. To break an alabaster figure or vessel, denotes sorrow and repentence. For a young woman to lose an alabaster box containing incense, signifies that she will lose her lover or property through carelessness of her reputation.

Alarm Bell.

To hear a bell in your sleep, denotes that you will have cause for anxiety.

Album.

To dream of an album, denotes you will have success and true friends.

For a young woman to dream of looking at photographs in an album, foretells that she will soon have a new lover who will be very agreeable to her.

Ale-house.

The dreamer of an ale-house should be very cautious of his affairs. Enemies are watching him.

Alien.

To dream of a stranger pleasing you, denotes good health and pleasant surroundings; if he displeases you, look for disappointments.

To dream you are an alien, denotes abiding friendships.

Alley.

To dream of an alley, denotes your fortune will not be so pleasing or promising as formerly. Many vexing cares will present themselves to you.

For a young woman to wander through an alley after dark, warns her of disreputable friendships and a stigma on her character.

Alligator.

To dream of an alligator, unless you kill it, is unfavorable to all persons connected with the dream. It is a dream of caution.

Alloy.

To dream of alloy, denotes your business will vex you in its complications. For a woman to dream of alloy, is significant of sorrow and trouble completely hiding pleasure.

Almanac.

To dream of an almanac, means variable fortunes and illusive pleasures. To be studying the signs, foretells that you will be harassed by small matters taking up your time.

Almonds.

This is a good omen. It has wealth in store. However, sorrow will go with it for a short while. If the almonds are defective, your disappointment in obtaining a certain wish will be complete until new conditions are brought about.

Alms.

Alms will bring evil if given or taken unwillingly. Otherwise, a good dream.

Alms-house.

For a young woman to dream of an alms-house, denotes she will meet failure in her efforts to contract a worldly marriage.

Altar.

To dream of seeing a priest at the altar, denotes quarrels and unsatisfactory states in your business and home. To see a marriage, sorrow to friends, and death to old age.

An altar would hardly be shown you in a dream, except to warn you against the commission of error. Repentance is also implied.

Alum.

Alum seen in a dream, portends frustration of well laid plans. To taste alum, denotes secret remorse over some evil work by you upon some innocent person.

For a woman to dream of quantities of alum, foretells disappointment in her marriage and loss of affection.

Aluminum.

To dream of aluminum, denotes contentment with any fortune, however small. For a woman to see her aluminum ornaments or vessels tarnished, foretells strange and unexpected sorrow, and loss will befall her.

Amateur.

To dream of seeing an amateur actor on the stage, denotes that you will see your hopes pleasantly and satisfactorily fulfilled. If they play a tragedy, evil will be disseminated through your happiness. If there is an indistinctness or distorted images in the dream, you are likely to meet with quick and decided defeat in some enterprise apart from your regular business.

Ambush.

To dream that your are atacked from ambush, denotes that you have lurking secretly near you a danger, which will soon set upon and overthrow you if you are heedless of warnings.

If you lie in ambush to revenge yourself on others, you will unhesitatingly stoop to debasing actions to defraud your friends.

America.

High officials should be careful of State affairs, others will do well to look after their own person, for some trouble is at hand after this dream.

Amethyst.

Amethyst seen in a dream, represents contentment with fair business.

For a young woman to lose an amethyst, fortells broken engagements and slights in love.

Ammonia.

Ammonia seen in a dream, means displeasure will be felt by the dreamer at the conduct of a friend. Quarrels and disruptions of friendships will follow this dream.

For a young woman to see clear bottles of ammonia, foretells she will be deceived in the character and intentions of some person whom she considers friendly.

Ammunition.

To dream of ammunition, foretells the undertaking of some work, which promises fruitful completion. To dream your ammunition is exhausted, denotes fruitless struggles and endeavors.

Amorous.

To dream you are amorous, warns you against personal desires and pleasures, as they are threatening to engulf you in scandal.

For a young woman it portends illicit engagements, unless she chooses staid and moral companions. For a married woman, it foreshadows discontent and desire for pleasure outside the home.

To see others amorous, foretells that you will be persuaded to neglect your moral obligations. To see animals thus, denotes you will engage in degrading pleasures with fast men or women.

Amputation.

Ordinary amputation of limbs, denotes small offices lost; the loss of entire legs or arms, unusual depression in trade. To seamen, storm and loss of property. Afflicted persons should be warned to watchfulness after this dream.

Anchor.

To dream of an anchor is favorable to sailors, if seas are calm. To others it portends separation from friends, change of residence, and foreign travel. Sweethearts are soon to quarrel if either sees an anchor.

Andirons.

Andirons seen in a dream, denotes good will among friends, if the irons support burning logs; if they are in an empty fireplace, loss of property and death are signified.

Anecdote.

To dream of relating an anecdote, signifies that you will greatly prefer gay companionship to that of intellect, and that your affairs will prove as unstable as yourself.

For a young woman to hear anecdotes related, denotes that she will be one of a merry party of pleasure-seekers.

Angels.

To dream of angels is prophetic of disturbing influences in the soul. It brings a changed condition of the person's lot. If the dream is unusually pleasing, you will hear of the health of friends, and receive a legacy from unknown relatives.

If the dream comes as a token of warning, the dreamer may expect threats of scandal about love or money matters. To wicked people, it is a demand to repent; to good people it should be a consolation.

Anger.

To dream of anger, denotes that some awful trial awaits you. Disappointments in loved ones, and broken ties, or enemies may make new attacks upon your property or character.

To dreams that friends or relatives are angry with you, while you meet their anger with composure, denotes you will mediate between opposing friends, and gain their lasting favor and gratitude.

Angling.

To dream of catching fish is good. If you fail to catch any, it will be bad for you.

Annoy.

This dream denotes that you have enemies who are at work against you. Annoyances experienced in dreams are apt to find speedy fulfilment in the trifling incidents of the following day.

Antelope.

Seeing antelopes in a dream, foretells your ambitions will be high, but may be realized by putting forth great energy.

For a young woman to see an antelope miss its footing and fall from a height, denotes the love she aspires to will prove her undoing.

Ants.

The dreamer of ants should expect many petty annoyances during the day; chasing little worries, and finding general dissatisfaction in all things.

Anvil.

To see hot iron with sparks flying, is significant of a pleasing work; to the farmer, an abundant crop; favorable indeed to women. Cold, or small, favors may be expected from those in power. The means of success is in your power, but in order to obtain it you will have to labor under difficulty. If the anvil is broken, it foretells that you have, through your own neglect, thrown away promising opportunities that cannot be recalled.

Anxiety.

A dream of this kind is occasionally a good omen, denoting, after threatening states, success and rejuvenation of mind; but if the dreamer is anxious about some momentous affair, it indicates a disastrous combination of business and social states.

Apes.

This dream brings humiliation and disease to some dear friend.

To see a small ape cling to a tree, warns the dreamer to beware; a false person is close to you and will cause unpleasantness in your circle. Deceit goes with this dream.

Apparel.*

Dreams of apparel, denote that enterprises will be

* See Clothes and Coat.

successes or failures, as the apparel seems to be whole and clean, or soiled and threadbare.

To see fine apparel, but out of date, foretells that you will have fortune, but you will scorn progressive ideas.

If you reject out-of-date apparel, you will outgrow present environments and enter into new relations, new enterprises and new loves, which will transform you into a different person.

To see yourself or others appareled in white, denotes eventful changes, and you will nearly always find the change bearing sadness.

To walk with a person wearing white, proclaims that person's illness or distress, unless it be a young woman or child, then you will have pleasing surroundings for a season at least.

To see yourself, or others, dressed in black, portends quarrels, disappointments, and disagreeable companions; or, if it refers to business, the business will fall short of expectations.

To see yellow apparel, foretells approaching gaieties and financial progress. Seen as a flitting spectre, in an unnatural light, the reverse may be expected. You will be fortunate if you dream of yellow cloth.

To dream of blue apparel, signifies carrying forward to victory your aspirations, through energetic, insistent efforts. Friends will loyally support you.

To dream of crimson apparel, foretells that you will escape formidable enemies by a timely cnange in your expressed intention.

To see green apparel, is a hopeful sign of prosperity and happiness.

To see many colored apparel, foretells swift changes, and intermingling of good and bad influences in your future.

To dream of misfitting apparel, intimates crosses in your affections, and that you are likely to make a mistake in some enterprise.

To see old or young in appropriate apparel, denotes that you will undertake some engagement for which you will have no liking, and which will give rise to many cares.

For a woman to dream that she is displeased with her apparel, foretells that she will find many vexatious rivalries in her quest for social distinction.

To admire the apparel of others, denotes that she will have jealous fears of her friends.

To dream of the loss of any article of apparel, denotes disturbances in your business and love affairs.

For a young woman to dream of being attired in a gauzy black costume, foretells she will undergo chastening sorrow and disappointment.

For a young woman to dream that she meets another attired in a crimson dress with a crepe mourning veil over her face, foretells she will be outrivaled by one she hardly considers her equal, and bitter disappointment will sour her against women generally.

The dreamer interpreting the dream of apparel should be careful to note whether the objects are looking natural. If the faces are distorted and the light unearthly, though the colors are bright, beware; the miscarriage of some worthy plan will work you harm. There are few dreams in which the element of evil is wanting, as there are few enterprises in waking life from which the element of chance is obviated.

Apparition.

Take unusual care of all depending upon you. Calamity awaits you and yours. Both property and life are in danger. Young people should be decidedly upright in their communications with the opposite sex. Character is likely to be rated at a discount.

Apples.

This is a very good dream to the majority of people.

To see red apples on trees with green foliage is exceedingly propitious to the dreamer.

To eat them is not as good, unless they be faultless. A friend who interprets dreams says: " Ripe apples on a tree, denotes that the time has arrived for you to realize your hopes; think over what you intend to do, and go fearlessly ahead. Ripe on the top of the tree, warns you not to aim too high. Apples on the ground imply that false friends, and flatterers are working you harm. Decayed apples typify hopeless efforts."

Apprentice.

To dream that you serve as an apprentice, foretells you will have a struggle to win a place among your companions.

Apricot.

Dreams of seeing apricots growing, denote that the future, though seemingly rosy hued, holds masked bitterness and sorrow for you.

To eat them signifies the near approach of calamitous influences. If others eat them, your surroundings will be unpleasant and disagreeable to your fancies. A friend says: " Apricots denote that you have been wasting time over trifles or small things of no value."

April.

To dream of the month of April, signifies that much pleasure and profit will be your allotment. If the weather is miserable, it is a sign of passing ill luck.

Apron.

To dream of an apron, signifies a zigzag course, for a young woman. For a school girl to dream that her apron is loosened, or torn, implies bad lessons, and lectures in propriety from parents and teachers.

Arch.

An arch in a dream, denotes your rise to distinction and the gaining of wealth by persistent effort. To pass under one, foretells that many will seek you who formerly ignored your position.

For a young woman to see a fallen arch, denotes the destruction of her hopes, and she will be miserable in her new situation.

Archbishop.

To dream of seeing an archbishop, foretells you will have many obstacles to resist in your attempt to master fortune or rise to public honor. To see one in the every day dress of a common citizen, denotes you will have aid and encouragement from those in prominent positions and will succeed in your enterprises.

For a young woman to dream that an archbishop is kindly directing her, foretells she will be fortunate in forming her friendships.

Architect.

Architects drawing plans in your dreams, denotes a change in your business, which will be likely to result in loss to you.

For a young woman to see an architect, foretells she will meet rebuffs in her aspirations and maneuvers to make a favorable marriage.

Arm.

To dream of seeing an arm amputated, means separation or divorce. Mutual dissatisfaction will occur between husband and wife. It is a dream of sinister import. Beware of deceitfulness and fraud.

Aroma.

For a young woman to dream of a sweet aroma, denotes she will soon be the recipient of some pleasure or present.

Arrested.*

To see respectable-looking strangers arrested, foretells that you desire to make changes, and new speculations will be subordinated by the fear of failure. If they resist the officers, you will have great delight in pushing to completion the new enterprise.

Arrow.

Pleasure follows this dream. Entertainments, festivals and pleasant journeys may be expected. Suffering will cease.

An old or broken arrow, portends disappointments in love or business.

Art Gallery.

To visit an art gallery, portends unfortunate unions in domestic circles. You will struggle to put forth an appearance of happiness, but will secretly care for other associations.

Ascend.

If you reach the extreme point of ascent, or top of steps, without stumbling, it is good; otherwise, you will have obstacles to overcome before the good of the day is found.

Asceticism.

To dream of asceticism, denotes that you will cultivate

---

* See Prisoner.

71

strange principles and views, rendering yourself fascinating to strangers, but repulsive to friends.

Ashes.

Dreaming of ashes omens woe, and many bitter changes are sure to come to the dreamer. Blasted crops to the farmer. Unsuccessful deals for the trader. Parents will reap the sorrows of wayward children.

Asia.

To dream of visiting Asia is assurance of change, but no material benefits from fortune will follow.

Asp.

This is an unfortunate dream. Females may lose the respect of honorable and virtuous people. Deadly enemies are at work to defame character. Sweethearts will wrong each other.

Asparagus.

To dream of asparagus, signifies prosperous surroundings and obedience from servants and children. To eat it, denotes interrupted success.

Ass.*

To see an ass in a dream, you will meet many annoyances, and delays will accrue in receiving news or goods.

To see donkeys carrying burdens, denotes that, after patience and toil, you will succeed in your undertakings, whether of travel or love.

If an ass pursues you, and you are afraid of it, you will be the victim of scandal or other displeasing reports.

---

* See Donkey.

If you unwillingly ride on one, or, as jockey, unnecessary quarrels may follow.

Assassin.

If you are the one to receive the assassin's blow, you will not surmount all your trials.

To see another, with the assassin standing over him with blood stains, portends that misfortune will come to the dreamer.

To see an assassin under any condition is a warning that losses may befall you through secret enemies.

Assistance.

Giving assistance to any one in a dream, foretells you will be favored in your efforts to rise to higher position.

If any one assists you, you will be pleasantly situated, and loving friends will be near you.

Asylum.

To dream of an asylum, denotes sickness and unlucky dealings, which cannot be overcome without great mental struggle.

Astral.

Dreams of the astral, denote that your efforts and plans will culminate in worldly success and distinction. A spectre or picture of your astral self brings heart-rending tribulation.

Atlas.

To dream you are looking at an atlas, denotes that you will carefully study interests before making changes or journeys.

Atonement.

Means joyous communing with friends, and speculators

need not fear any drop in stocks. Courting among the young will meet with happy consummation. The sacrifice or atonement of another for your waywardness, is portentous of the humiliation of self or friends through your open or secret disregard of duty. A woman after this dream is warned of approaching disappointment.

Attic.

To dream that you are in an attic, denotes that you are entertaining hopes which will fail of materialization.

For a young woman to dream that she is sleeping in an attic, foretells that she will fail to find contentment in her present occupation.

Attorney.

To see an attorney at the bar, denotes that disputes of a serious nature will arise between parties interested in worldly things. Enemies are stealing upon you with false claims. If you see an attorney defending you, your friends will assist you in coming trouble, but they will cause you more worry than enemies.

Auction.

To dream of an auction in a general way, is good. If you hear the auctioneer crying his sales, it means bright prospects and fair treatment from business ventures.

To dream of buying at an auction, signifies close deals to tradesmen, and good luck in live stock to the farmer. Plenty, to the housewife is the omen for women. If there is a feeling of regret about the dream, you are warned to be careful of your business affairs.

August.

To dream of the month of August, denotes unfortunate deals, and misunderstandings in love affairs.

For a young woman to dream that she is going to be

married in August, is an omen of sorrow in her early
wedded life.

Augur.

To see augurs in your dreams, is a forecast of labor
and toil.

Aunt.

For a young woman to dream of seeing her aunt, denotes she will receive sharp censure for some action, which
will cause her much distress.

If this relative appears smiling and happy, slight differ-
ence will soon give way to pleasure.

Aura.

To dream of discussing any subject relating to aura,
denotes that you will reach states of mental unrest, and
work to discover the power which influences you from
within.

Autumn.

For a woman to dream of Autumn, denotes she will
obtain property through the struggles of others. If she
thinks of marrying in Autumn, she will be likely to contract a favorable marriage and possess a cheerful home.

Automobile.

To dream that you ride in an automobile, denotes that
you will be restless under pleasant conditions, and will
make a change in your affairs. There is grave danger
of impolitic conduct intimated through a dream of this
nature.

If one breaks down with you, the enjoyment of a pleasure will not extend to the heights you contemplate.

To find yourself escaping from the path of one, signifies
that you will do well to avoid some rival as much as you
can honestly allow.

For a young woman to look for one, she will be disappointed in her aims to entice some one into her favor.

Author.

For an author to dream that his manuscript has been rejected by the publisher, denotes some doubt at first, but finally his work will be accepted as authentic and original.

To dream of seeing an author over his work, perusing it with anxiety, denotes that you will be worried over some literary work either of your own or that of some other person.

Awake.

To dream that you are awake, denotes that you will experience strange happenings which will throw you into gloom.

To pass through green, growing fields, and look upon landscape, in your dreams, and feel that it is an awaking experience, signifies that there is some good and brightness in store for you, but there will be disappointments intermingled between the present and that time.

Axe.

Seeing an axe in a dream, foretells that what enjoyment you may have will depend on your struggles and energy. To see others using an axe, foretells, your friends will be energetic and lively, making existence a pleasure when near them.

For a young woman to see one, portends her lover will be worthy, but not possessed with much wealth. A broken or rusty axe, indicates illness and loss of money and property.

B.

"God came to Abimelech in a dream by night, and said to him, 'Behold, thou art but a dead man, for the woman thou hast taken; for she is a man's wife."—Gen. xx., 3rd.

Baby.

To dream of crying babies, is indicative of ill health and disappointments.

A bright, clean baby, denotes love requited, and many warm friends. Walking alone, it is a sure sign of independence and a total ignoring of smaller spirits. If a woman dream she is nursing a baby, she will be deceived by the one she trusts most.

It is a bad sign to dream that you take your baby if sick with fever. You will have many sorrows of mind.

Baby Carriages.

To dream of a baby carriage, denotes that you will have a congenial friend who will devise many pleasurable surprises for you.

Bachelor.

For a man to dream that he is a bachelor, is a warning for him to keep clear of women.

For a woman to dream of a bachelor, denotes love not born of purity. Justice goes awry. Politicians lose honor.

Back.

To dream of seeing a nude back, denotes loss of power. Lending advice or money is dangerous. Sickness often attends this dream.

To see a person turn and walk away from you, you may be sure envy and jealousy are working to your hurt.

To dream of your own back, bodes no good to the dreamer.

Back-bite.

Conditions will change from good to bad if you are joined with others in back-biting.

For your friends to back-bite you, indicates worriment by servants and children.

Backgammon.

To dream of playing backgammon, denotes that you will, while visiting, meet with unfriendly hospitality, but will unconsciously win friendships which will endure much straining.

If you are defeated in the game, you will be unfortunate in bestowing your affections, and your affairs will remain in an unsettled condition.

Bacon.

To dream of eating bacon is good, if some one is eating with you and hands are clean.

Rancid bacon, is dullness of perception and unsatisfactory states will worry you.

To dream of curing bacon is bad, if not clear of salt and smoke. If clear, it is good.

Badger.

To dream of a badger, is a sign of luck after battles with hardships.

Bag-Pipe.

This is not a bad dream, unless the music be harsh and the player in rags.

Baghavad Ghitta.

To dream of the Baghavad, foretells for you a season of seclusion; also rest to the exhausted faculties. A pleasant journey for your advancement will be planned by your friends. Little financial advancement is promised in this dream.

Bail.

If the dreamer is seeking bail, unforeseen troubles will

arise; accidents are likely to occur; unfortunate alliances
may be made.

If you go bail for another, about the same conditions,
though hardly as bad.

Bailiff.

Shows a striving for a higher place, and a deficiency in
intellect. If the bailiff comes to arrest, or make love, false
friends are trying to work for your money.

Bake-house.

To dream of a bake-house, demands caution in making
changes in one's career. Pitfalls may reveal themselves
on every hand.

For a young woman to dream that she is in a bake-
house, portends that her character wil be assailed. She
should exercise great care in her social affairs.

Baking.

Baking is unpropitious for a woman. Ill health and the
care of many children; meanness and poverty of sup-
porters are indicated.

Balcony.

For lovers to dream of making sad adieus on a bal-
cony, long and perhaps final separation may follow. Bal-
cony also denotes unpleasant news of absent friends.

Bald.

To see a bald-headed man, denotes that sharpers are to
make a deal adverse to your interests, but by keeping wide
awake, you will outwit them.

For a man to dream of a bald-headed woman, insures
him to have a vixen for wife.

A bald hill, or mountain, indicates famine and suffering in various forms.

For a young woman to dream of a bald-headed man, is a warning to her to use her intelligence against listening to her next marriage offer.

Bald-headed babies signify a happy home, a loving companion, and obedient children.

Ball.

A very satisfactory omen, if beautiful and gaily-dressed people are dancing to the strains of entrancing music. If you feel gloomy and distressed at the inattention of others, a death in the family may be expected soon.

Ballet.

Indicates infidelity in the marriage state; also failures in business, and quarrels and jealousies among sweethearts.

Balloon.

Blighted hopes and adversity come with this dream. Business of every character will sustain an apparent falling off.

To ascend in a balloon, denotes an unfortunate journey.

Banishment.

Evil pursues the unfortunate dreamer. If you are banished to foreign lands, death will be your portion at an early date. To banish a child, means perjury of business allies. It is a dream of fatality.

Banjo.

To dream of a banjo, denotes that pleasant amusements will be enjoyed. To see a busker playing one, denotes that you will have slight worries, but no serious vexation for a season.

For a young woman to see busker with their banjos,

foretells that she will fail in some anticipated amusement. She will have misunderstandings with her lover.

Bank.

To see vacant tellers, foretells business losses. Giving out gold money, denotes carelessness; receiving it, great gain and prosperity.

To see silver and bank-notes accumulated, increase of honor and fortune. You will enjoy the highest respect of all classes.

Bankrupt.

Denotes partial collapse in business, and weakening of the brain faculties. A warning to leave speculations alone.

Banana.

To dream of bananas, foretells that you will be mated to an uninteresting and an unloved companion.

To eat them, foretells a tiresome venture in business, and self-inflicted duty.

To see them decaying, you are soon to fall into some disagreeable enterprise.

To trade in them, non-productive interests will accumulate around you.

Banner.

To see one's country's banner floating in a clear sky, denotes triumph over foreign foes. To see it battered, is significant of wars and loss of military honors on land and sea.

Banquet.

It is good to dream of a banquet. Friends will wait to do you favors. To dream of yourself, together with many gaily-attired guests, eating from costly plate and drinking wine of fabulous price and age, foretells enormous gain in enterprises of every nature, and happiness among friends.

To see inharmonious influences, strange and grotesque faces or empty tables, is ominous of grave misunderstandings or disappointments.

Bantam.

To see bantam chickens in your dream, denotes your fortune will be small, yet you will enjoy contentment. If they appear sickly, or exposed to wintry storms, your interests will be impaired.

Baptism.

To dream of baptism, signifies that your character needs strengthening by the practice of temperance in advocating your opinions to the disparagement of your friends.

To dream that you are an applicant, signifies that you will humiliate your inward self for public favor.

To dream that you see John the Baptist baptizing Christ in the Jordan, denotes that you will have a desperate mental struggle between yielding yourself to labor in meagre capacity for the sustenance of others, or follow desires which might lead you into wealth and exclusiveness.

To see the Holy Ghost descending on Christ, is significant of resignation to duty and abnegation of self.

If you are being baptized with the Holy Ghost and fire, means that you will be thrown into a state of terror over being discovered in some lustful engagement.

Bar.

To dream of tending a bar, denotes that you will resort to some questionable mode of advancement.

Seeing a bar, denotes activity in communities, quick

uplifting of fortunes, and the consummation of illicit desires.

Barber.

To dream of a barber, denotes that success will come through struggling and close attention to business. For a young woman to dream of a barber, foretells that her fortune will increase, though meagerly.

Barefoot.

To wander in the night barefoot with torn garments, denotes that you will be crushed in expectation, and evil influences will surround your every effort.

Barley-field.

The dreamer will obtain his highest desires, and every effort will be crowned with success. Decay in anything denotes loss.

Barmaid.

For a man to dream of a barmaid, denotes that his desires run to low pleasures, and he will scorn purity.

For a young woman to dream that she is a barmaid, foretells that she will be attracted to fast men, and that she will prefer irregular pleasures to propriety.

Barn.

If well filled with ripe and matured grain, and perfect ears of corn, with fat stock surrounding it, it is an omen of great prosperity. If empty, the reverse may be expected.

Barrel.*

Barometer.

To see a barometer in a dream, foretells a change will

---

* See Cask.

soon take place in your affairs, which will prove profitable to you. If it is broken, you will find displeasing incidents in your business, arising unexpectedly.

Baseball.

To see baseball in your dream, denotes you will be easily contented, and your cheerfulness will make you a popular companion.

For a young woman to dream that she is playing baseball, means much pleasure for her, but no real profit or comfort.

Basement.*

To dream that you are in a basement, foretells that you will see prosperous opportunities abating, and with them, pleasure will dwindle into trouble and care.

Basin.

For a young woman to dream of bathing in a basin, foretells her womanly graces will win her real friendships and elevations.

Basket.

To dream of seeing or carrying a basket, signifies that you will meet unqualified success, if the basket is full; but empty baskets indicate discontent and sorrow.

Baste.

To dream of basting meats while cooking, denotes you will undermine your own expectations by folly and selfishness. For a woman to baste her sewing, omens much vexation owing to her extravagance.

Bass Voice.

To dream that you have a bass voice denotes you will

---

* See Cellar.

detect some discrepancy in your business, brought about by the deceit of some one in your employ. For the lover, this foretells estrangements and quarrels.

Bath.

For a young person to dream of taking a bath, means much solicitude for one of the opposite sex, fearing to lose his good opinion through the influence of others.

For a pregnant woman to dream this, denotes miscarriage or accident. For a man, adultery. Dealings of all kinds should be carried on with discretion after this dream.

To go in bathing with others, evil companions should be avoided. Defamation of character is likely to follow. If the water is muddy, evil, indeed death, and enemies are near you.

For a widow to dream of her bath, she has forgotten her former ties, and is hurrying on to earthly loves. Girls should shun male companions. Men will engage in intrigues of salacious character.

A warm bath is generally significant of evil. A cold, clear bath is the fore-runner of joyful tidings and a long period of excellent health. Bathing in a clear sea, denotes expansion of business and satisfying research after knowledge.

Bathroom.

To see white roses in a bathroom, and yellow ones in a box, denote that sickness will interfere with pleasure; but more lasting joys will result from this disappointment.

For a young woman to dream of a bathroom, foretells that her inclinations trend too much toward light pleasures and frivolities.

Bats.

Awful is the fate of the unfortunate dreamer of this ugly

animal. Sorrows and calamities from hosts of evil work against you. Death of parents and friends, loss of limbs or sight, may follow after a dream of these ghoulish monsters. A white bat is almost a sure sign of death. Often the death of a child follows this dream.

Battle.

Battle signifies striving with difficulties, but a final victory over the same.

If you are defeated in battle, it denotes that bad deals made by others will mar your prospects for good.

Bayonet.

To dream of a bayonet, signifies that enemies will hold you in their power, unless you get possession of the bayonet.

Bay Tree.

A palmy leisure awaits you in which you will meet many pleasing varieties of diversions. Much knowledge will be reaped in the rest from work. It is generally a good dream for everybody.

Beacon-light.

For a sailor to see a beacon-light, portends fair seas and a prosperous voyage.

For persons in distress, warm attachments and unbroken, will arise among the young.

To the sick, speedy recovery and continued health. Business will gain new impetus. To see it go out in time of storm or distress, indicates reverses at the time when you thought Fortune was deciding in your favor.

Beads.

To dream of beads, foretells attention from those in

elevated position will be shown you. To count beads, portends immaculate joy and contentment. To string them, you will obtain the favor of the rich.

To scatter them, signifies loss of caste among your acquaintances.

Beans.

This is a bad dream. To see them growing, omens worries and sickness among children.

Dried beans, means much disappointment in worldly affairs. Care should be taken to prevent contagious diseases from spreading.

To dream of eating them, implies the misfortune or illness of a well loved friend.

Bear.

Bear is significant of overwhelming competition in pursuits of every kind.

To kill a bear, portends extrication from former entanglements.

A young woman who dreams of a bear will have a threatening rival or some misfortune.

Beard.

To dream of seeing a beard, denotes that some uncongenial person will oppose his will against yours, and there will be a fierce struggle for mastery, and you are likely to lose some money in the combat.

Gray beard, signifies hard luck and quarrels.

To see beard on women, foretells unpleasant associations and lingering illness.

For some one to pull your beard, denotes that you will run a narrow risk if you do not lose property.

To comb and admire it, shows that your vanity will

grow with prosperity, making you detestable in the sight of many of your former companions.

For a young woman to admire a beard, intimates her desire to leave celibacy; but she is threatened with an unfortunate marriage.

Beat.

It bodes no good to dream of being beaten by an angry person; family jars and discord are signified.

To beat a child, ungenerous advantage is taken by you of another; perhaps the tendency will be to cruelly treat a child.

Beauty.

Beauty in any form is pre-eminently good. A beautiful woman brings pleasure and profitable business. A well formed and beautiful child, indicates love reciprocated and a happy union.

Beaver.

To dream of seeing beavers, foretells that you will obtain comfortable circumstances by patient striving. If you dream of killing them for their skins, you will be accused of fraud and improper conduct toward the innocent.

Bed.

A bed, clean and white, denotes peaceful surcease of worries. For a woman to dream of making a bed, signifies a new lover and pleasant occupation.

To dream of being in bed, if in a strange room, unexpected friends will visit you. If a sick person dreams of being in bed, new complications will arise, and, perhaps, death.

To dream that you are sleeping on a bed in the open air, foretells that you will have delightful experiences, and opportunity for improving your fortune. For you to see negroes passing by your bed, denotes exasperating circumstances arising, which will interfere with your plans.

To see a friend looking very pale, lying in bed, signifies strange and woeful complications will oppress your friends, bringing discontent to yourself.

For a mother to dream that her child wets a bed, foretells she will have unusual anxiety, and persons sick, will not reach recovery as early as may be expected. For persons to dream that they wet the bed, denotes sickness, or a tragedy will interfere with their daily routine of business.

Bedbugs.

Seen in your dreams, they indicate continued sickness and unhappy states. Fatalities are intimated if you see them in profusion.

To see bedbugs simulating death, foretells unhappiness caused by illness. To mash them, and water appears instead of blood, denotes alarming but not fatal illness or accident. To see bedbugs crawling up white walls, and you throw scalding water upon them, denotes grave illness will distress you, but there will be useless fear of fatality.

If the water fails to destroy them, some serious complication with fatal results is not improbable.

Bed Fellow.

To dream that you do not like your bed fellow, foretells that some person who has claims upon you, will censure and make your surroundings unpleasant generally.

If you have a strange bed fellow, your discontent will worry all who come near you. If you think you have any kind of animal in bed with you, there will be unbounded ill luck overhanging you.

Bed-chamber.

To see one newly furnished, a happy change for the dreamer. Journeys to distant places, and pleasant companions.

Beef.

If raw and bloody, cancers and tumors of a malignant nature will attack the subject. Be on your guard as to bruises and hurts of any kind.

To see, or eat cooked beef, anguish surpassing human aid is before you. Loss of life by horrible means will occur. Beef properly served under pleasing surroundings denotes harmonious states in love and business, if otherwise, evil is foreboded, though it may be of a trifling nature.

Beer.

Fateful of disappointments if drinking from a bar. To see others drinking, work of designing intriguers will displace your fairest hopes.

To habitués of this beverage, harmonious prospectives are foreshadowed, if pleasing, natural and cleanly conditions survive. The dream occurrences frequently follow in the actual.

Bees.

Bees signify pleasant and profitable engagements.

For an officer, it brings obedient subjects and healthful environments.

To a preacher, many new members and a praying congregation.

To business men, increase in trade. To parents, much pleasure from dutiful children. If one stings, loss or injury will bear upon you from a friendly source.

Beetles.

To dream of seeing them on your person, denotes poverty and small ills. To kill them is good.

Beets.

To see them growing abundantly, harvest and peace will obtain in the land; eating them with others, is full of good tidings.

If they are served in soiled or impure dishes, distressful awakenings will disturb you.

Beggar.

To see an old, decrepit beggar, is a sign of bad management, and unless you are economical, you will lose much property. Scandalous reports will prove detrimental to your fame.

To give to a beggar, denotes dissatisfaction with present surroundings.

To dream that you refuse to give to a beggar is altogether bad.

Beheading.

To dream of being beheaded, overwhelming defeat or failure in some undertaking will soon follow.

To see others beheaded, if accompanied by a large flow of blood, death and exile are portended.

Bier.

To see one, indicates disastrous losses and the early dissolution of a dear relative.

To see one, strewn with flowers in a church, denotes an unfortunate marriage.

Belladonna.

Strategic moves will bring success in commercial

circles. Women will find rivals in society; vain and fruitless efforts will be made for places in men's affections.

Taking it, denotes misery and failure to meet past debts.

Bell-boy.

Fortune is aurrying after you. Questions of importance will be settled amicably among disputants. To see him looking sad some sorrowful event or misfortune may soon follow.

Bellows.

Working a bellows, denotes a struggle, but a final triumph over poverty and fate by energy and perseverance.

To dream of seeing a bellows, distant friends are longing to see you.

To hear one, occult knowledge will be obtained by the help of powerful means. One fallen into disuse, portends you have wasted energies under misguiding impulses.

Bells.

To hear bells tolling in your dreams, death of distant friends will occur, and intelligence of wrong will worry you.

Liberty bells, indicate a joyous victory over an opponent.

Belly.*

It is bad to dream of seeing a swollen mortifying belly, it indicates desperate sickness.

To see anything moving on the belly, prognosticates humiliation and hard labor.

To see a healthy belly, denotes insane desires.

Belt.

To dream that you have a new style belt, denotes you

---

* See Abdomen.

are soon to meet and make engagements with a stranger, which will demoralize your prosperity. If it is out of date, you will be meritedly censured for rudeness.

Bench.

Distrust debtors and confidants if you dream of sitting on one.

If you see others doing so, happy reunions between friends who have been separated through misunderstandings are suggested.

Bequest.

After this dream, pleasures of consolation from the knowledge of duties well performed, and the health of the young is assured.

Bereavement.

To dream of the bereavement of a child, warns you that your plans will meet with quick frustration, and where you expect success there will be failure.

Bereavement of relatives, or friends, denotes disappointment in well matured plans and a poor outlook for the future.

Bet.

Betting on races, beware of engaging in new undertakings. Enemies are trying to divert your attention from legitimate business.

Betting at gaming tables, denotes that immoral devices will be used to wring money from you.

Bible.

To dream of the Bible, foretells that innocent and disillusioned enjoyment will be proffered for your acceptance.

To dream that you villify the teachings of the Bible,

forewarns you that you are about to succumb to resisted temptations through the seductive persuasiveness of a friend.

Bigamy.

For a man to commit bigamy, denotes loss of manhood and failing mentality. To a woman, it predicts that she will suffer dishonor unless very discreet.

Bicycle.

To dream of riding a bicycle up hill, signifies bright prospects. Riding it down hill, if the rider be a woman, calls for care regarding her good name and health; misfortune hovers near.

Billiards.

Billiards, foretell coming troubles to the dreamer. Law suits and contentions over property. Slander will get in her work to your detriment. If you see table and balls idle, deceitful comrades are undermining you

Birds.

It is a favorable dream to see birds of beautiful plumage. A wealthy and happy partner is near if a woman has dreams of this nature.

Moulting and songless birds, denotes merciless and inhuman treatment of the outcast and fallen by people of wealth.

To see a wounded bird, is fateful of deep sorrow caused by erring offspring.

To see flying birds, is a sign of prosperity to the dreamer. All disagreeable environments will vanish before the wave of prospective good.

To catch birds, is not at all bad. To hear them speak, is owning one's inability to perform tasks that demand great clearness of perception.

To kill them with a gun, is disaster from dearth of harvest.

Bird's Nest.

To see an empty bird's nest, denotes gloom and a dull outlook for business. With eggs in the nest, good results will follow all engagements. If young ones are in the nest, it denotes successful journeys and satisfactory dealings. If they are lonely and deserted, sorrow, and folly of yours will cause you anxiety.

Birth.

For a married woman to dream of giving birth to a child, great joy and a handsome legacy is foretold.

For a single woman, loss of virtue and abandonment by her lover.

Birthday.

To dream of a birthday is a signal of poverty and falsehood to the young, to the old, long trouble and desolation.

Birthday Presents.

Receiving happy surprises, means a multitude of high accomplishments. Working people will advance in their trades.

Giving birthday presents, denotes small deferences, if given at a fête or reception.

Biscuits.

Eating or baking them, indicates ill health and family peace ruptured over silly disputes.

Bishop.

To dream of a bishop, teachers and authors will suffer great mental worries, caused from delving into intricate subjects.

To the tradesman, foolish buying, in which he is likely to incur loss of good money.

For one to see a bishop in his dreams, hard work will be his patrimony, with chills and ague as attendant. If you meet the approval of a much admired bishop, you will be successful in your undertakings in love or business.

Bite.

This dream omens ill.

It implies a wish to undo work that is past undoing. You are also likely to suffer losses through some enemy.

Blackberries.

To dream of blackberries denotes many ills. To gather them is unlucky. Eating them denotes losses.

Blackboard.

To see in your dreams writing in white chalk on a blackboard, denotes ill tidings of some person prostrated with some severe malady, or your financial security will be swayed by the panicky condition of commerce.

Blacksmith.

To see a blacksmith in a dream, means laborious undertakings will soon work to your advantage.

Bladder.

To dream of your bladder, denotes you will have heavy trouble in your business if you are not careful of your health and the way you spend your energies.

To see children blowing up bladders, foretells your expectations will fail to give you much comfort.

Blanket.

Blankets in your dream means treachery if soiled. If

new and white, success where failure is feared, and a fatal sickness will be avoided through unseen agencies.

Blasphemy.*

Blasphemy, denotes an enemy creeping into your life, who under assumed friendship will do you great harm.

To dream you are cursing yourself, means evil fortune. To dream you are cursed by others, signifies relief through affection and prosperity.

The interpretation of this dream here given is not satisfactory.

Bleating.

To hear young animals bleating in your dreams, foretells that you will have new duties and cares, though not necessarily unpleasant ones.

Bleeding.

To dream of bleeding, denotes death by horrible accidents and malicious reports about you. Fortune will turn against you.

Blind.

To dream of being blind, denotes a sudden change from affluence to almost abject poverty.

To see others blind, denotes that some worthy person will call on you for aid.

Blindfold.

For a woman to dream that she is blindfolded, means that disturbing elements are rising around to distress and trouble her. Disappointment will be felt by others through her.

Blind Man's Buff.

To dream that you are playing at blind man's buff,

---

* See Profanity.

denotes that you are about to engage in some weak enterprise which will likely humiliate you, besides losing money for you.

Blood.

Blood-stained garments, indicate enemies who seek to tear down a successful career that is opening up before you.

The dreamer should beware of strange friendships.

To see blood flowing from a wound, physical ailments and worry. Bad business caused from disastrous dealings with foreign combines.

To see blood on your hands, immediate bad luck, if not careful of your person and your own affairs.

Blood Stone.

To dream of seeing a blood stone, denotes that you will be unfortunate in your engagements. For a young woman to receive one as a gift, denotes she will suffer estrangement from one friend, but will, by this, gain one more worthy of her.

Blossoms.

To dream of seeing trees and shrubs in blossom, denotes a time of pleasing prosperity is nearing you.

Blows.

Denotes injury to yourself. If you receive a blow, brain trouble will threaten you.

If you defend yourself, a rise in business will follow.

Blotting Paper.

To dream of using blotting paper, signifies you will be deceived into the betrayal of secrets which will seriously involve a friend.

To see worn blotting paper, denotes continued disagreements in the home or among friends.

Blushing.

For a young woman to dream of blushing, denotes she will be worried and humiliated by false accusations. If she sees others blush, she will be given to flippant railery which will make her unpleasing to her friends.

Boarding House.

To dream of a boarding house, foretells that you will suffer entanglement and disorder in your enterprises, and you are likely to change your residence.

Boa-Constrictor.

To dream of this is just about the same as to dream of the devil; it indicates stormy times and much bad fortune. Disenchantment with humanity will follow. To kill one is good.

Boasting.

To hear boasting in your dreams, you will sincerely regret an impulsive act, which will cause trouble to your friends. To boast to a competitor, foretells that you will be unjust, and will use dishonest means to overcome competition.

Boat.

Boat signals forecast bright prospects, if upon clear water. If the water is unsettled and turbulent, cares and unhappy changes threaten the dreamer. If with a gay party you board a boat without an accident, many favors will be showered upon you. Unlucky the dreamer who falls overboard while sailing upon stormy waters.

Bobbin.

To dream of bobbins, denotes that important work will

devolve on you, and your interests will be adversely affected if you are negligent in dispatching the same work.

Bog.*

Bogs, denotes burdens under whose weight you feel that endeavors to rise are useless. Illness and other worries may oppress you.

Boiler.

To dream of seeing a boiler out of repair, signifies you will suffer from bad management or disappointment. For a woman to dream that she goes into a cellar to see about a boiler foretells that sickness and losses will surround her.

Boils.

To dream of a boil running pus and blood, you will have unpleasant things to meet in your immediate future. May be that the insincerity of friends will cause you great inconvenience.

To dream of boils on your forehead, is significant of the sickness of some one near you.

Bolts.

To dream of bolts, signifies that formidable obstacles will oppose your progress.

If the bolts are old or broken, your expectations will be eclipsed by failures.

Bomb Shell.

To dream of bomb shells, foretells anger and disputes, ending in law suits. Many displeasing incidents follow this dream.

---

* See Swamp.

Bones.

To see your bones protruding from the flesh, denotes that treachery is working to ensnare you.

To see a pile of bones, famine and contaminating influences surround you.

Bonnet.

Bonnet, denotes much gossiping and slanderous insinuations, from which a woman should carefully defend herself.

For a man to see a woman tying her bonnet, denotes unforeseen good luck near by. His friends will be faithful and true.

A young woman is likely to engage in pleasant and harmless flirtations if her bonnet is new and of any color except black.

Black bonnets, denote false friends of the opposite sex.

Books.

Pleasant pursuits, honor and riches to dream of studying them. For an author to dream of his works going to press, is a dream of caution; he will have much trouble in placing them before the public.

To dream of spending great study and time in solving some intricate subjects, and the hidden meaning of learned authors, is significant of honors well earned.

To see children at their books, denotes harmony and good conduct of the young.

To dream of old books, is a warning to shun evil in any form.

Bookcase.

To see a bookcase in your dreams, signifies that you will associate knowledge with your work and pleasure.

Empty bookcases, imply that you will be put out because of lack of means or facility for work.

Book Store.

To visit a book store in your dream, foretells you will be filled with literary aspirations, which will interfere with your other works and labors.

Boots.

To see your boots on another, your place will be usurped in the affections of your sweetheart.

To wear new boots, you will be lucky in your dealings. Bread winners will command higher wages.

Old and torn boots, indicate sickness and snares before you.

Borrowing.

Borrowing is a sign of loss and meagre support. For a banker to dream of borrowing from another bank, a run on his own will leave him in a state of collapse, unless he accepts this warning. If another borrows from you, help in time of need will be extended or offered you. True friends will attend you.

Bosom.

For a young woman to dream that her bosom is wounded, foretells that some affliction is threatening her.

To see it soiled or shrunken, she will have a great disappointment in love and many rivals will vex her. If it is white and full she is soon to be possessed of fortune. If her lover is slyly observing it through her sheer corsage, she is about to come under the soft persuasive influence of a too ardent wooer.

Bottles.

Bottles are good to dream of if well filled with transparent liquid. You will overcome all obstacles in affairs of the heart, prosperous engagements will ensue. If empty, coming trouble will envelop you in meshes of sinister design, from which you will be forced to use strategy to disengage yourself.

Bouquet.

To dream of a bouquet beautifully and richly colored, denotes a legacy from some wealthy and unknown relative; also, pleasant, joyous gatherings among young folks.

To see a withered bouquet, signifies sickness and death.

Bow and Arrow.

Bow and arrow in a dream, denotes great gain reaped from the inability of others to carry out plans.

To make a bad shot means disappointed hopes in carrying forward successfully business affairs.

Box.

Opening a goods box in your dream, signifies untold wealth and that delightful journeys to distant places may be made with happy results. If the box is empty disappointment in works of all kinds will follow.

To see full money boxes, augurs cessation from business cares and a pleasant retirement.

Bracelet.

To see in your dreams a bracelet encircling your arm, the gift of lover or friend, is assurance of an early marriage and a happy union.

If a young woman lose her bracelet she will meet with sundry losses and vexations.

To find one, good property will come into her possession.

Brain.

To see your own brain in a dream, denotes uncongenial surroundings will irritate and dwarf you into an unpleasant companion. To see the brains of animals, foretells that you will suffer mental trouble.

If you eat them, you will gain knowledge, and profit unexpectedly.

Brambles.

To dream of brambles entangling you, is a messenger of evil. Law suits will go against you, and malignant sickness attack you, or some of your family.

Brandy.

To dream of brandy, foretells that while you may reach heights of distinction and wealth, you will lack that innate refinement which wins true friendship from people whom you most wish to please.

Branch.

It betokens, if full of fruit and green leaves, wealth, many delightful hours with friends. If they are dried, sorrowful news of the absent.

Brass.

To dream of brass, denotes that you will rise rapidly in your profession, but while of apparently solid elevation you will secretly fear a downfall of fortune.

Bray.

Hearing an ass bray, is significant of unwelcome tidings or intrusions.

Bread.*

For a woman to dream of eating bread, denotes that

---

* See Baking and Crust.

she will be afflicted with children of stubborn will, for whom she will spend many days of useless labor and worry.

To dream of breaking bread with others, indicates an assured competence through life.

To see a lot of impure bread, want and misery will burden the dreamer. If the bread is good and you have access to it, it is a favorable dream.

Break.

Breakage is a bad dream. To dream of breaking any of your limbs, denotes bad management and probable failures. To break furniture, denotes domestic quarrels and an unquiet state of the mind.

To break a window, signifies bereavement. To see a broken ring order will be displaced by furious and dangerous uprisings, such as jealous contentions often cause.

Breakfast.*

Is favorable to persons engaged in mental work. To see a breakfast of fresh milk and eggs and a well filled dish of ripe fruit, indicates hasty, but favorable changes.

If you are eating alone, it means you will fall into your enemies' trap. If you are eating with others it is good.

Breath.

To come close to a person in your dreaming with a pure and sweet breath, commendable will be your conduct, and a profitable consummation of business deals will follow.

Breath if fetid, indicates sickness and snares.

Losing one's breath, denotes signal failure where success seemed assured.

---

* See Meals.

Brewing.

To dream of being in a vast brewing establishment, means unjust persecution by public officials, but you will eventually prove your innocence and will rise far above your persecutors.

Brewing in any way in your dreams, denotes anxiety at the outset, but usually ends in profit and satisfaction.

Briars.

To see yourself caught among briars, black enemies are weaving cords of calumny and perjury intricately around you and will cause you great distress, but if you succeed in disengaging yourself from the briars, loyal friends will come to your assistance in every emergency.

Brick.

Brick in a dream, indicates unsettled business and disagreements in love affairs. To make them you will doubtless fail in your efforts to amass great wealth.

Bride.*

For a young woman to dream that she is a bride, foretells that she will shortly come into an inheritance which will please her exceedingly, if she is pleased in making her bridal toilet. If displeasure is felt she will suffer disappointments in her anticipations.

To dream that you kiss a bride, denotes a happy reconciliation between friends. For a bride to kiss others, foretells for you many friends and pleasures; to kiss you, denotes you will enjoy health and find that your sweetheart will inherit unexpected fortune.

To kiss a bride and find that she looks careworn and

---

* See Wedding.

ill, denotes you will be displeased with your success and the action of your friends.

If a bride dreams that she is indifferent to her husband, it foretells that many unhappy circumstances will pollute her pleasures.

Bridge.

To see a long bridge dilapidated, and mysteriously winding into darkness, profound melancholy over the loss of dearest possessions and dismal situations will fall upon you. To the young and those in love, disappointment in the heart's fondest hopes, as the loved one will fall below your ideal.

To cross a bridge safely, a final surmounting of difficulties, though the means seem hardly safe to use. Any obstacle or delay denotes disaster.

To see a bridge give way before you, beware of treachery and false admirers. Affluence comes with clear waters. Sorrowful returns of best efforts are experienced after looking upon or coming in contact with muddy or turbid water in dreams.

Bridle.

To dream of a bridle, denotes you will engage in some enterprise which will afford much worry, but will eventually terminate in pleasure and gain. If it is old or broken you will have difficulties to encounter, and the probabilities are that you will go down before them.

A blind bridle signifies you will be deceived by some wily enemy, or some woman will entangle you in an intrigue.

Bridle Bits.

To see bridle bits in your dreams, foretells you will subdue and overcome any obstacle opposing your advancement or happiness. If they break or are broken you will be surprised into making concessions to enemies.

Brimstone (Sulphur).

To dream of brimstone (sulphur), foretells that discreditable dealings will lose you many friends, if you fail to rectify the mistakes you are making.

To see fires of brimstone (sulphur), denotes you will be threatened with loss by contagion in your vicinity.

Bronchitis.

To dream that you are affected with bronchitis, foretells you will be detained from pursuing your views and plans by unfortunate complications of sickness in your home.

To suffer with bronchitis in a dream, denotes that discouraging prospects of winning desired objects will soon loom up before you.

Bronze.

For a woman to dream of a bronze statue, signifies that she will fail in her efforts to win the person she has determined on for a husband.

If the statue simulates life, or moves, she will be involved in a love affair, but no marriage will occur. Disappointment to some person may follow the dream.

To dream of bronze serpents or insects, foretells you will be pursued by envy and ruin. To see bronze metals, denotes your fortune will be uncertain and unsatisfactory.

Brood.

To see a fowl with her brood, denotes that, if you are a woman, your cares will be varied and irksome. Many children will be in your care, and some of them will prove wayward and unruly.

Brood, to others, denotes accumulation of wealth.

Broom.

To dream of brooms, denotes thrift and rapid improvement in your fortune, if the brooms are new. If they are seen in use, you will lose in speculation. For a woman to lose a broom, foretells that she will prove a disagreeable and slovenly wife and housekeeper.

Broth.

Broth denotes the sincerity of friends. They will uphold you in all instances. If you need pecuniary aid it will be forthcoming. To lovers, it promises a strong and lasting attachment.

To make broth, you will rule your own and others' fate.

Brothel.

To dream of being in a brothel, denotes you will encounter disgrace through your material indulgence.

Brothers.

To see your brothers, while dreaming, full of energy, you will have cause to rejoice at your own, or their good fortune; but if they are poor and in distress, or begging for assistance, you will be called to a deathbed soon, or some dire loss will overwhelm you or them.

Brush.

To dream of using a hair-brush, denotes you will suffer misfortune from your mismanagement. To see old hair brushes, denotes sickness and ill health. To see clothes brushes, indicates a heavy task is pending over you.

If you are busy brushing your clothes, you will soon receive reimbursement for laborious work. To see miscellaneous brushes, foretells a varied line of work, yet withal, rather pleasing and remunerative.

Buckle.

To dream of buckles, foretells that you will be beset

with invitations to places of pleasure, and your affairs will be in danger of chaotic confusion.

Buffalo.

If a woman dreams that she kills a lot of buffaloes, she will undertake a stupendous enterprise, but by enforcing will power and leaving off material pleasures, she will win commendation from men, and may receive long wished for favors. Buffalo, seen in a dream, augurs obstinate and powerful but stupid enemies. They will boldly declare against you but by diplomacy you will escape much misfortune.

Bugle.

To hear joyous blasts from a bugle, prepare for some unusual happiness, as a harmony of good things for you is being formed by unseen powers.

Blowing a bugle, denotes fortunate dealings.

Bugs.

To dream of bugs denotes that some disgustingly revolting complications will rise in your daily life. Families will suffer from the carelessness of servants, and sickness may follow.

Buildings.

To see large and magnificent buildings, with green lawns stretching out before them, is significant of a long life of plenty, and travels and explorations into distant countries.

Small and newly built houses, denote happy homes and profitable undertakings; but, if old and filthy buildings, ill health and decay of love and business will follow.

Bull.

To see one pursuing you, business trouble, through envious and jealous competitors, will harass you.

If a young woman meets a bull, she will have an offer of marriage, but, by declining this offer, she will better her fortune.

To see a bull goring a person, misfortune from unwisely using another's possessions will overtake you.

To dream of a white bull, denotes that you will lift yourself up to a higher plane of life than those who persist in making material things their God. It usually denotes gain.

Bulldog.*

To dream of entering strange premises and have a bulldog attack you, you will be in danger of transgressing the laws of your country by using perjury to obtain your desires.

If one meets you in a friendly way, you will rise in life, regardless of adverse criticisms and seditious interference of enemies.

Bullock.†

Denotes that kind friends will surround you, if you are in danger from enemies. Good health is promised you.

Burden.

To dream that you carry a heavy burden, signifies that you will be tied down by oppressive weights of care and injustice, caused from favoritism shown your enemies by those in power. But to struggle free from it, you will climb to the topmost heights of success.

Burr.

To dream of burrs, denotes that you will struggle to free self from some unpleasant burden, and will seek a change of surroundings.

---

* See Dog.
† See Bull.

111

Burglars.

To dream that they are searching your person, you will have dangerous enemies to contend with, who will destroy you if extreme carefulness is not practised in your dealings with strangers.

If you dream of your home, or place of business, being burglarized, your good standing in business or society will be assailed, but courage in meeting these difficulties will defend you. Accidents may happen to the careless after this dream.

Burial.*

To attend the burial of a relative, if the sun is shining on the procession, is a sign of the good health of relations, and perhaps the happy marriage of some one of them is about to occur. But if rain and dismal weather prevails, sickness and bad news of the absent will soon come, and depressions in business circles will be felt.

A burial where there are sad rites performed, or sorrowing faces, is indicative of adverse surroundings or their speedy approach.

Buried Alive.

To dream that you are buried alive. denotes that you are about to make a great mistake, which your opponents will quickly turn to your injury. If you are rescued from the grave, your struggle will eventually correct your misadventure.

Burns.

Burns stand for tidings of good. To burn your hand in a clear and flowing fire, denotes purity of purpose and the approbation of friends. To burn your feet in walking

---

* See Funeral.

through coals, or beds of fire, denotes your ability to accomplish any endeavor, however impossible it may be to others. Your usual good health will remain with you, but, if you are overcome in the fire, it represents that your interests will suffer through treachery of supposed friends.

Butcher.

To see them slaughtering cattle and much blood, you may expect long and fatal sickness in your family. To see a butcher cutting meat, your character will be dissected by society to your detriment. Beware of writing letters or documents.

Butter.

To dream of eating fresh, golden butter, is a sign of good health and plans well carried out; it will bring unto you possessions, wealth and knowledge.

To eat rancid butter, denotes a competency acquired through struggles of manual labor.

To sell butter, denotes small gain.

Butterfly.

To see a butterfly among flowers and green grasses, indicates prosperity and fair attainments.

To see them flying about, denotes news from absent friends by letter, or from some one who has seen them. To a young woman, a happy love, culminating in a life union.

Buttons.

To dream of sewing bright shining buttons on a uniform, betokens to a young woman the warm affection of a fine looking and wealthy partner in marriage. To a youth, it signifies admittance to military honors and a bright career.

Dull, or cloth buttons, denotes disappointments and systematic losses and ill health.

The loss of a button, and the consequent anxiety as to losing a garment, denotes prospective losses in trade.

Buttermilk.

Drinking buttermilk, denotes sorrow will follow some worldly pleasure, and some imprudence will impair the general health of the dreamer.

To give it away, or feed it to pigs, is bad still.

To dream that you are drinking buttermilk made into oyster soup, denotes that you will be called on to do some very repulsive thing, and ill luck will confront you. There are quarrels brewing and friendships threatened. It you awaken while you are drinking it, by discreet maneuvering you may effect a pleasant understanding of disagreements.

Buzzard.

To dream that you hear a buzzard talking, foretells that some old scandal will arise and work you injury by your connection with it.

To see one sitting on a railroad, denotes some accident or loss is about to descend upon you. To see them fly away as you approach, foretells that you will be able to smooth over some scandalous disagreement among your friends, or even appertaining to yourself.

To see buzzards in a dream, portends generally salacious gossip or that unusual scandal will disturb you.

C.

"And the Angel of God spoke unto me in a dream, saying, Ja-cob; and I said, here am I."—Gen. xxxi., 11.

Cab.

To ride in a cab in dreams, is significant of pleasant avocations, and average prosperity you will enjoy.

To ride in a cab at night, with others, indicates that you will have a secret that you will endeavor to keep from your friends.

To ride in a cab with a woman, scandal will couple your name with others of bad repute.

To dream of driving a public cab, denotes manual labor, with little chance of advancement.

Cabbage.

It is bad to dream of cabbage. Disorders may run riot in all forms. To dream of seeing cabbage green, means unfaithfulness in love and infidelity in wedlock.

To cut heads of cabbage, denotes that you are tighten-ing the cords of calamity around you by lavish expendi-ture.

Cable.

To dream of a cable, foretells the undertaking of a decidedly hazardous work, which, if successfully carried to completion, will abound in riches and honor to you.

To dream of receiving cablegrams, denotes that a mes-sage of importance will reach you soon, and will cause disagreeable comments.

Cabin.

The cabin of a ship is rather unfortunate to be in in a dream. Some mischief is brewing for you. You will most likely be engaged in a law suit, in which you will lose from the unstability of your witness.

For log cabin, see house.

Cackle.

To hear the cackling of hens denotes a sudden shock produced by the news of an unexpected death in your neighborhood. Sickness will cause poverty.

Cage.

In your dreaming if you see a cageful of birds, you will be the happy possessor of immense wealth and many beautiful and charming children. To see only one bird, you will contract a desirable and wealthy marriage. No bird indicates a member of the family lost, either by elopement or death.

To see wild animals caged, denotes that you will triumph over your enemies and misfortunes. If you are in the cage with them, it denotes harrowing scenes from accidents while traveling.

Cakes.

Batter or pancakes, denote that the affections of the dreamer are well placed, and a home will be bequeathed to him or her.

To dream of sweet cakes, is gain for the laboring and a favorable opportunity for the enterprising. Those in love will prosper.

Pound cake is significant of much pleasure either from society or business. For a young woman to dream of her wedding cake is the only bad luck cake in the category. Baking them is not so good an omen as seeing them or eating them.

Calomel.

To dream of calomel shows some person is seeking to

deceive and injure you through the unconscious abetting of friends. For a young woman to dream of taking it, foretells that she will be victimized through the artful designing of persons whom she trusts. If it is applied externally, she will close her eyes to deceit in order to enjoy a short season of pleasure.

Calves.*

To dream of calves peacefully grazing on a velvety lawn, foretells to the young, happy, festive gatherings and enjoyment. Those engaged in seeking wealth will see it rapidly increasing.

Called.

To hear your name called in a dream by strange voices, denotes that your business will fall into a precarious state, and that strangers may lend you assistance, or you may fail to meet your obligations.

To hear the voice of a friend or relative, denotes the desperate illness of some one of them, and may be death; in the latter case you may be called upon to stand as guardian over some one, in governing whom you should use much discretion.

Lovers hearing the voice of their affianced should heed the warning. If they have been negligent in attention they should make amends. Otherwise they may suffer separation from misunderstanding.

To hear the voice of the dead may be a warning of your own serious illness or some business worry from bad judgment may ensue. The voice is an echo thrown back from the future on the subjective mind, taking the sound of your ancestor's voice from coming in contact with that part of your ancestor which remains with you.

*See Cattle.

A certain portion of mind matter remains the same in lines of family descent.

Calendar.

To dream of keeping a calendar, indicates that you will be very orderly and systematic in habits throughout the year.

To see a calendar, denotes disappointment in your calculations.

Calm.

To see calm seas, denotes successful ending of doubtful undertaking.

To feel calm and happy, is a sign of a long and well-spent life and a vigorous old age.

Calumny.

To dream that you are the subject of calumny, denotes that your interests will suffer at the hands of evil-minded gossips. For a young woman, it warns her to be careful of her conduct, as her movements are being critically observed by persons who claim to be her friends.

Camera.

To dream of a camera, signifies that changes will bring undeserved environments. For a young woman to dream that she is taking pictures with a camera, foretells that her immediate future will have much that is displeasing and that a friend will subject her to acute disappointment.

Cameo Brooch.

To dream of a cameo brooch, denotes some sad occurrence will soon claim your attention.

Camels.

To see this beast of burden, signifies that you will entertain great patience and fortitude in time of almost unbearable anguish and failures that will seemingly sweep every vestige of hope from you.

To own a camel, is a sign that you will possess rich mining property.

To see a herd of camels on the desert, denotes assistance when all human aid seems at a low ebb, and of sickness from which you will arise, contrary to all expectations.

Camp.

To dream of camping in the open air, you may expect a change in your affairs, also prepare to make a long and wearisome journey.

To see a camping settlement, many of your companions will remove to new estates and your own prospects will appear gloomy.

For a young woman to dream that she is in a camp, denotes that her lover will have trouble in getting her to name a day for their wedding, and that he will prove a kind husband. If in a military camp she will marry the first time she has a chance.

A married woman after dreaming of being in a soldier's camp is in danger of having her husband's name sullied, and divorce courts may be her destination.

Campaign.

To dream of making a political one, signifies your opposition to approved ways of conducting business, and you will set up original plans for yourself regardless of enemies' working against you. Those in power will lose.

If it is a religious people conducting a campaign against sin, it denotes that you will be called upon to contribute from your private means to sustain charitable institutions.

For a woman to dream that she is interested in a campaign against fallen women, denotes that she will surmount obstacles and prove courageous in time of need.

Cane.

To see cane growing in your dream, foretells favorable advancement will be made toward fortune. To see it cut, denotes absolute failure in all undertakings.

Cancer.

To have one successfully treated in a dream, denotes a sudden rise from obscure poverty to wealthy surroundings.

To dream of a cancer, denotes illness of some one near you, and quarrels with those you love. Depressions may follow to the man of affairs after this dream.

To dream of a cancer, foretells sorrow in its ugliest phase. Love will resolve itself into cold formality, and business will be worrying and profitless.

Canal.

To see the water of a canal muddy and stagnant-looking, portends sickness and disorders of the stomach and dark designs of enemies. But if its waters are clear a placid life and the devotion of friends is before you.

For a young woman to glide in a canoe across a canal, denotes a chaste life and an adoring husband. If she crossed the canal on a bridge over clear water and gathers ferns and other greens on the banks, she will enjoy a life of ceaseless rounds of pleasure and attain to high social distinction. But if the water be turbid she will often find herself tangled in meshes of perplexity and will be the victim of nervous troubles.

Canary Birds.

To dream of this sweet songster, denotes unexpected

pleasures. For the young to dream of possessing a beautiful canary, denotes high class honors and a successful passage through the literary world, or a happy termination of love's young dream.

To dream one is given you, indicates a welcome legacy. To give away a canary, denotes that you will suffer disappointment in your dearest wishes.

To dream that one dies, denotes the unfaithfulness of dear friends.

Advancing, fluttering, and singing canaries, in luxurious apartments, denotes feasting and a life of exquisite refinement, wealth, and satisfying friendships. If the light is weird or unnaturally bright, it augurs that you are entertaining illusive hopes. Your over-confidence is your worst enemy. A young woman after this dream should beware, lest flattering promises react upon her in disappointment. Fairy-like scenes in a dream are peculiarly misleading and treacherous to women.

Candles.

To see them burning with a clear and steady flame, denotes the constancy of those about you and a well-grounded fortune.

For a maiden to dream that she is molding candles, denotes that she will have an unexpected offer of marriage and a pleasant visit to distant relatives. If she is lighting a candle, she will meet her lover clandestinely because of parental objections.

To see a candle wasting in a draught, enemies are circulating detrimental reports about you.

To snuff a candle, portends sorowful news. Friends are dead or in distressful straits.

Candlestick.

To see a candlestick bearing a whole candle, denotes

that a bright future lies before you filled with health, happiness and loving companions. If empty, the reverse.

Canker.*

To dream of seeing canker on anything, is an omen of evil. It foretells death and treacherous companions for the young. Sorrow and loneliness to the aged.

Cankerous growths in the flesh, denote future distinctions either as head of State or stage life.

Cannon.

This dream denotes that one's home and country are in danger of foreign intrusion, from which our youth will suffer from the perils of war.

For a young woman to hear or see cannons, denotes she will be a soldier's wife and will have to bid him godspeed as he marches in defense of her and honor.

The reader will have to interpret dreams of this character by the influences surrounding him, and by the experiences stored away in his subjective mind. If you have thought about cannons a great deal and you dream of them when there is no war, they are most likely to warn you against struggle and probable defeat. Or if business is manipulated by yourself successful engagements after much worry and ill luck may ensue.

Cannon-Ball.

This means that secret enemies are uniting against you. For a maid to see a cannon-ball, denotes that she will have a soldier sweetheart. For a youth to see a cannon-ball, denotes that he will be called upon to defend his country.

* The last definition is not consistent with other parts of this book, but I let it stand, as I find it among my automatic writings.

Canoe.

To paddle a canoe on a calm stream, denotes your perfect confidence in your own ability to conduct your business in a profitable way.

To row with a sweetheart, means an early marriage and fidelity. To row on rough waters you will have to tame a shrew before you attain connubial bliss. Affairs in the business world will prove disappointing after you dream of rowing in muddy waters. If the waters are shallow and swift, a hasty courtship or stolen pleasures, from which there can be no lasting good, are indicated.

Shallow, clear and calm waters in rowing, signifies happiness of a pleasing character, but of short duration.

Water is typical of futurity in the dream realms. If a pleasant immediate future awaits the dreamer he will come in close proximity with clear water. Or if he emerges from disturbed watery elements into waking life the near future is filled with crosses for him.

Candy.

To dream of making candy, denotes profit accruing from industry.

To dream of eating crisp, new candy, implies social pleasures and much love-making among the young and old. Sour candy is a sign of illness or that disgusting annoyances will grow out of confidences too long kept.

To receive a box of bonbons, signifies to a young person that he or she will be the recipient of much adulation. It generally means prosperity. If you send a box you will make a proposition, but will meet with disappointment.

Canopy.

To dream of a canopy or of being beneath one, denotes that false friends are influencing you to undesirable ways

123

of securing gain. You will do well to protect those in your care.

Cap.

For a woman to dream of seeing a cap, she will be invited to take part in some festivity.

For a girl to dream that she sees her sweetheart with a cap on, denotes that she will be bashful and shy in his presence.

To see a prisoner's cap, denotes that your courage is failing you in time of danger.

To see a miner's cap, you will inherit a substantial competency.

Captive.

To dream that you are a captive, denotes that you may have treachery to deal with, and if you cannot escape, that injury and misfortune will befall you.

To dream of taking any one captive, you will join yourself to pursuits and persons of lowest status.

For a young woman to dream that she is a captive, denotes that she will have a husband who will be jealous of her confidence in others; or she may be censured for her indiscretion.

Captain.

To dream of seeing a captain of any company, denotes your noblest aspirations will be realized. If a woman dreams that her lover is a captain, she will be much harassed in mind from jealousy and rivalry.

Cars.

To dream of seeing cars, denotes journeying and changing in quick succession. To get on one shows that travel which you held in contemplation will be made under different auspices than had been calculated upon.

To miss one, foretells that you will be foiled in an attempt to forward your prospects.

To get off of one, denotes that you will succeed with some interesting schemes which will fill you with self congratulations.

To dream of sleeping-cars, indicates that your struggles to amass wealth is animated by the desire of gratifying selfish and lewd principles which should be mastered and controlled.

To see street-cars in your dreams, denotes that some person is actively interested in causing you malicious trouble and disquiet.

To ride on a car, foretells that rivalry and jealousy will enthrall your happiness.

To stand on the platform of a street-car while it is running, denotes you will attempt to carry on an affair which will be extremely dangerous, but if you ride without accident you will be successful.

If the platform is up high, your danger will be more apparent, but if low, you will barely accomplish your purpose.

Cardinal.

It is unlucky to dream you see a cardinal in his robes. You will meet such misfortunes as will necessitate your removal to distant or foreign lands to begin anew your ruined fortune. For a woman to dream this is a sign of her downfall through false promises. If priest or preacher is a spiritual adviser and his services are supposed to be needed, especially in the hour of temptation, then we find ourselves dreaming of him as a warning against approaching evil.

Cards.

If playing them in your dreams with others for social

pastime, you will meet with fair realization of hopes that have long buoyed you up. Small ills will vanish. But playing for stakes will involve you in difficulties of a serious nature.

If you lose at cards you will encounter enemies. If you win you will justify yourself in the eyes of the law, but will have trouble in so doing.

If a young woman dreams that her sweetheart is playing at cards, she will have cause to question his good intentions.

In social games, seeing diamonds indicate wealth; clubs, that your partner in life will be exacting, and that you may have trouble in explaining your absence at times; hearts denote fidelity and cosy surroundings; spades signify that you will be a widow and encumbered with a large estate.

Carnival.

To dream that you are participating in a carnival, portends that you are soon to enjoy some unusual pleasure or recreation. A carnival when masks are used, or when incongruous or clownish figures are seen, implies discord in the home; business will be unsatisfactory and love unrequited.

Cart.

To dream of riding in a cart, ill luck and constant work will employ your time if you would keep supplies for your family.

To see a cart, denotes bad news from kindred or friends.

To dream of driving a cart, you will meet with merited success in business and other aspirations.

For lovers to ride together in a cart, they will be true in spite of the machinations of rivals.

Cartridge.

To dream of cartridges, foretells unhappy quarrels and dissensions.

Some untoward fate threatens you or some one closely allied to you.

If they are empty, there will be foolish variances in your associations.

Carving.

To dream of carving a fowl, indicates you will be poorly off in a worldly way. Companions will cause you vexation from continued ill temper.

Carving meat, denotes bad investments, but, if a change is made, prospects will be brighter.

Carpet.

To see a carpet in a dream, denotes profit, and wealthy friends to aid you in need.

To walk on a carpet, you will be prosperous and happy.

To dream that you buy carpets, denotes great gain. If selling them, you will have cause to go on a pleasant journey, as well as a profitable one.

For a young woman to dream of carpets, shows she will own a beautiful home and servants will wait upon her.

Carpenter.

To see carpenters at their labor, foretells you will engage in honest endeavors to raise your fortune, to the exclusion of selfish pastime or so-called recreation.

Carriage.

To see a carriage, implies that you will be gratified, and that you will make visits.

To ride in one, you will have a sickness that will soon

pass, and you will enjoy health and advantageous positions.

To dream that you are looking for a carriage, you will have to labor hard, but will eventually be possessed with a fair competency.

Carrot.

To dream of carrots, portends prosperity and health. For a young woman to eat them, denotes that she will contract an early marriage and be the mother of several hardy children.

Cask.

To see one filled, denotes prosperous times and feastings. If empty, your life will be void of any joy or consolation from outward influences.

Cash.*

To dream that you have plenty of cash, but that it has been borrowed, portends that you will be looked upon as a worthy man, but that those who come in close contact with you will find that you are mercenary and unfeeling.

For a young woman to dream that she is spending borrowed money, foretells that she will be found out in her practice of deceit, and through this lose a prized friend.

Cash Box.

To dream of a full cash box, denotes that favorable prospects will open around you. If empty, you will experience meager reimbursements.

Cashier.

To see a cashier in your dream, denotes that others will claim your possessions. If you owe any one, you will practice deceit in your designs upon some wealthy person.

---

* See Money.

Castle.

To dream of being in a castle, you will be possessed of sufficient wealth to make life as you wish. You have prospects of being a great traveler, enjoying contact with people of many nations.

To see an old and vine-covered castle, you are likely to become romantic in your tastes, and care should be taken that you do not contract an undesirable marriage or engagement. Business is depressed after this dream.

To dream that you are leaving a castle, you will be robbed of your possessions, or lose your lover or some dear one by death.

Castor Oil.

To dream of castor oil, denotes that you will seek to overthrow a friend who is secretly abetting your advancement.

Castoria.

To dream of castoria, denotes that you will fail to discharge some important duty, and your fortune will seemingly decline to low stages.

Cats.

To dream of a cat, denotes ill luck, if you do not succeed in killing it or driving it from your sight. If the cat attacks you, you will have enemies who will go to any extreme to blacken your reputation and to cause you loss of property. But if you succeed in banishing it, you will overcome great obstacles and rise in fortune and fame.

If you meet a thin, mean and dirty-looking cat, you will have bad news from the absent. Some friend lies at death's door; but if you chase it out of sight, your friend will recover after a long and lingering sickness.

To hear the scream or the mewing of a cat, some false

friend is using all the words and work at his command to do you harm.

To dream that a cat scratches you, an enemy will succeed in wrenching from you the profits of a deal that you have spent many days making.

If a young woman dreams that she is holding a cat, or kitten, she will be influenced into some impropriety through the treachery of others.

To dream of a clean white cat, denotes entanglements which, while seemingly harmless, will prove a source of sorrow and loss of wealth.

When a merchant dreams of a cat, he should put his best energies to work, as his competitors are about to succeed in demolishing his standard of dealing, and he will be forced to other measures if he undersells others and still succeeds.

To dream of seeing a cat and snake on friendly terms signifies the beginning of an angry struggle. It denotes that an enemy is being entertained by you with the intention of using him to find out some secret which you believe concerns yourself; uneasy of his confidences given, you will endeavor to disclaim all knowledge of his actions, as you are fearful that things divulged, concerning your private life, may become public.

Catechism.

To dream of the catechism, foretells that you will be offered a lucrative position, but the strictures will be such that you will be worried as to accepting it.

Caterpillar.

To see a caterpillar in a dream, denotes that low and hypocritical people are in your immediate future, and you will do well to keep clear of deceitful appearances. You may suffer a loss in love or business.

To dream of a caterpillar, foretells you will be placed in embarrassing situations, and there will be small honor or gain to be expected.

Cattle.*

To dream of seeing good-looking and fat cattle contentedly grazing in green pastures, denotes prosperity and happiness through a congenial and pleasant companion.

To see cattle lean and shaggy, and poorly fed, you will be likely to toil all your life because of misspent energy and dislike of details of work. Correct your habits after this dream.

To see cattle stampeding, means that you will have to exert all the powers of command you have to keep your career in a profitable channel.

To see a herd of cows at milking time, you will be the successful owner of wealth that many have worked to obtain. To a young woman this means that her affections will not suffer from the one of her choice.

To dream of milking cows with udders well filled, great good fortune is in store for you. If the calf has stolen the milk, it signifies that you are about to lose your lover by slowness to show your reciprocity, or your property from neglect of business.

To see young calves in your dream, you will become a great favorite in society and win the heart of a loyal person. For business, this dream indicates profit from sales. For a lover, the entering into bonds that will be respected. If the calves are poor, look for about the same, except that the object sought will be much harder to obtain.

Long-horned and dark, vicious cattle, denote enemies.

* See Calves.

Cathedral.

To dream of a vast cathedral with its domes rising into space, denotes that you will be possessed with an envious nature and unhappy longings for the unattainable, both mental and physical; but if you enter you will be elevated in life, having for your companions the learned and wise.

Cauliflower.

To dream of eating it, you will be taken to task for neglect of duty. To see it growing, your prospects will brighten after a period of loss.

For a young woman to see this vegetable in a garden, denotes that she will marry to please her parents and not herself.

Cavalry.

To dream that you see a division of cavalry, denotes personal advancement and distinction. Some little sensation may accompany your elevation.

Cavern or Cave.

To dream of seeing a cavern yawning in the weird moonlight before you, many perplexities will assail you, and doubtful advancement because of adversaries. Work and health is threatened.

To be in a cave foreshadows change. You will probably be estranged from those who are very dear to you.

For a young woman to walk in a cave with her lover or friend, denotes she will fall in love with a villain and will suffer the loss of true friends.

Cedars.

To dream of seeing them green and shapely, denotes pleasing success in an undertaking.

To see them dead or blighted, signifies despair. No object will be attained from seeing them thus.

Celestial Signs.*

To dream of celestial signs, foretells unhappy occurrences will cause you to make unseasonable journeys. Love or business may go awry, quarrels in the house are also predicted if you are not discreet with your engagements.

Celery.

To dream of seeing fresh, crisp stalks of celery, you will be prosperous and influential beyond your highest hopes.

To see it decaying, a death in your family will soon occur.

To eat it, boundless love and affection will be heaped upon you.

For a young woman to eat it with her lover, denotes she will come into rich possessions.

Cellar.

To dream of being in a cold, damp cellar, you will be oppressed by doubts. You will lose confidence in all things and suffer gloomy forebodings from which you will fail to escape unless you control your will. It also indicates loss of property.

To see a cellar stored with wines and table stores, you will be offered a share in profits coming from a doubtful source. If a young woman dreams of this she will have an offer of marriage from a speculator or gambler.

Cemetery.

To dream of being in a beautiful and well-kept cemetery, you will have unexpected news of the recovery of one whom you had mourned as dead, and you will have your title good to lands occupied by usurpers.

---

* See Illumination.

To see an old bramble grown and forgotten cemetery, you will live to see all your loved ones leave you, and you will be left to a stranger's care.

For young people to dream of wandering through the silent avenues of the dead foreshows they will meet with tender and loving responses from friends, but will have to meet sorrows that friends are powerless to avert.

Brides dreaming of passing a cemetery on their way to the wedding ceremony, will be bereft of their husbands by fatal accidents occurring on journeys.

For a mother to carry fresh flowers to a cemetery, indicates she may expect the continued good health of her family.

For a young widow to visit a cemetery means she will soon throw aside her weeds for robes of matrimony. If she feels sad and depressed she will have new cares and regrets.

Old people dreaming of a cemetery, shows they will soon make other journeys where they will find perfect rest.

To see little children gathering flowers and chasing butterflies among the graves, denotes prosperous changes and no graves of any of your friends to weep over. Good health will hold high carnival.

Chaff.

To see chaff, denotes an empty and fruitless undertaking and ill health causing much anxiety.

Women dreaming of piles of chaff, portends many hours spent in useless and degrading gossip, bringing them into notoriety and causing them to lose husbands who would have maintained them without work on their part.

Chains.

To dream of being bound in chains, denotes that unjust burdens are about to be thrown upon your shoulders; but if you succeed in breaking them you will free yourself from some unpleasant business or social engagement.

To see chains, brings calumny and treacherous designs of the envious.

Seeing others in chains, denotes bad fortunes for them.

Chair.

To see a chair in your dream, denotes failure to meet some obligation. If you are not careful you will also vacate your most profitable places.

To see a friend sitting on a chair and remaining motionless, signifies news of his death or illness.

Chair Maker.

To dream of seeing a chair maker, denotes that worry from apparently pleasant labor will confront you.

Chairman.

To dream that you see the chairman of any public body, foretells you will seek elevation and be recompensed by receiving a high position of trust. To see one looking out of humor you are threatened with unsatisfactory states.

If you are a chairman, you will be distinguished for your justice and kindness to others.

Chalk.

For a woman to dream of chalking her face, denotes that she will scheme to obtain admirers.

To dream of using chalk on a board, you will attain public honors, unless it is the blackboard; then it indicates ill luck.

To hold hands full of chalk, disappointment is foretold.

Chalice.

To dream of a chalice, denotes pleasure will be gained by you to the sorrow of others. To break one foretells your failure to obtain power over some friend.

Challenge.

If you are challenged to fight a duel, you will become involved in a social difficulty wherein you will be compelled to make apologies or else lose friendships.

To accept a challenge of any character, denotes that you will bear many ills yourself in your endeavor to shield others from dishonor.

Chamber.

To find yourself in a beautiful and richly furnished chamber implies sudden fortune, either through legacies from unknown relatives or through speculation. For a young woman, it denotes that a wealthy stranger will offer her marriage and a fine establishment. If the chamber is plainly furnished, it denotes that a small competency and frugality will be her portion.

Chambermaid.

To see a chambermaid, denotes bad fortune and decided changes will be made.

For a man to dream of making love to a chambermaid, shows he is likely to find himself an object of derision on account of indiscreet conduct and want of tact.

Chameleon.

To dream of seeing your sweetheart wearing a chameleon chained to her, shows she will prove faithless to you if by changing she can better her fortune. Ordinarily chameleons signify deceit and self advancement, even though others suffer.

Champion.

To dream of a champion, denotes you will win the warmest friendship of some person by your dignity and moral conduct.

Chandelier.

To dream of a chandelier, portends that unhoped-for success will make it possible for you to enjoy pleasure and luxury at your caprice.

To see a broken or ill-kept one, denotes that unfortunate speculation will depress your seemingly substantial fortune. To see the light in one go out, foretells that sickness and distress will cloud a promising future.

Chapel.

To dream of a chapel, denotes dissension in social circles and unsettled business.

To be in a chapel, denotes disappointment and change of business.

For young people to dream of entering a chapel, implies false loves and enemies. Unlucky unions may entangle them.

Charity.

To dream of giving charity, denotes that you will be harassed with supplications for help from the poor and your business will be at standstill.

To dream of giving to charitable institutions, your right of possession to paying property will be disputed. Worries and ill health will threaten you.

For young persons to dream of giving charity, foreshows they will be annoyed by deceitful rivals.

To dream that you are an object of charity, omens that

you will succeed in life after hard times with misfortunes.

Charcoal.

To dream of charcoal unlighted, denotes miserable situations and bleak unhappiness. If it is burning with glowing coals, there is prospects of great enhancement of fortune, and possession of unalloyed joys.

Chariot.

To dream of riding in a chariot, foretells that favorable opportunities will present themselves resulting in your good if rightly used by you.

To fall or see others fall from one, denotes displacement from high positions.

Chastise.

To dream of being chastised, denotes that you have not been prudent in conducting your affairs.

To dream that you administer chastisement to another, signifies that you will have an ill-tempered partner either in business or marriage.

For parents to dream of chastising their children, indicates they will be loose in their manner of correcting them, but they will succeed in bringing them up honorably.

Cheated.

To dream of being cheated in business, you will meet designing people who will seek to close your avenues to fortune.

For young persons to dream that they are being cheated in games, portend they will lose their sweethearts through quarrels and misunderstandings.

Checks.

To dream of palming off false checks on your friends, denotes that you will resort to subterfuge in order to carry forward your plans.

To receive checks you will be able to meet your payments and will inherit money.

To dream that you pay out checks, denotes depression and loss in business.

Checkers.

To dream of playing checkers, you will be involved in difficulties of a serious character, and strange people will come into your life, working you harm.

To dream that you win the game, you will succeed in some doubtful enterprise.

Cheese.

To dream of eating cheese, denotes great disappointments and sorrow. No good of any nature can be hoped for. Cheese is generally a bad dream.

Chemise.

For a woman to dream of a chemise, denotes she will hear unfavorable gossip about herself.

Cherries.

To dream of cherries, denotes you will gain popularity by your amiability and unselfishness. To eat them, portends possession of some much desired object. To see green ones, indicates approaching good fortune.

Cherubs.

To dream you see cherubs, foretells you will have some distinct joy, which will leave an impression of lasting good upon your life.

To see them looking sorrowful or reproachful, foretells that distress will come unexpectedly upon you.

Chess.

To dream of playing chess, denotes stagnation of business, dull companions, and poor health.

To dream that you lose at chess, worries from mean sources will ensue; but if you win, disagreeable influences may be surmounted.

Chestnuts.

To dream of handling chestnuts, foretells losses in a business way, but indicates an agreeable companion through life.

Eating them, denotes sorrow for a time, but final happiness.

For a young woman to dream of eating or trying her fortune with them, she will have a well-to-do lover and comparative plenty.

Chickens.

To dream of seeing a brood of chickens, denotes worry from many cares, some of which will prove to your profit.

Young or half grown chickens, signify fortunate enterprises, but to make them so you will have to exert your physical strength.

To see chickens going to roost, enemies are planning to work you evil.

To eat them, denotes that selfishness will detract from your otherwise good name. Business and love will remain in precarious states.

Chiffonier.

To see or search through a chiffonier, denotes you will

have disappointing anticipations. To see one in order, indicates pleasant friends and entertainments.

Chilblain.

To dream of suffering with chilblains, denotes that you will be driven into some bad dealing through over-anxity of a friend or partner. This dream also portends your own illness or an accident.

Childbed.

To dream of giving child birth, denotes fortunate circumstances and safe delivery of a handsome child.

For an unmarried woman to dream of being in childbed, denotes unhappy changes from honor to evil and low estates.

Children.

"Dream of children sweet and fair,
To you will come suave debonair,
Fortune robed in shining dress,
Bearing wealth and happiness."

To dream of seeing many beautiful children is portentous of great prosperity and blessings.

For a mother to dream of seeing her child sick from slight cause, she may see it enjoying robust health, but trifles of another nature may harass her.

To see children working or studying, denotes peaceful times and general prosperity.

To dream of seeing your child desperately ill or dead, you have much to fear, for its welfare is sadly threatened.

To dream of your dead child, denotes worry and disappointment in the near future.

To dream of seeing disappointed children, denotes

trouble from enemies, and anxious forebodings from underhanded work of seemingly friendly people.

To romp and play with children, denotes that all your speculating and love enterprises will prevail.

Chimes.

To dream of Christmas chimes, denotes fair prospects for business men and farmers.

For the young, happy anticipations fulfilled. Ordinary chimes, denotes some small anxiety will soon be displaced by news of distant friends.

Chimney.

To dream of seeing chimneys, denotes a very displeasing incident will occur in your life. Hasty intelligence of sickness will be borne you. A tumble down chimney, denotes sorrow and likely death in your family. To see one overgrown with ivy or other vines, foretells that happiness will result from sorrow or loss of relatives.

To see a fire burning in a chimney, denotes much good is approaching you. To hide in a chimney corner, denotes distress and doubt will assail you. Business will appear gloomy.

For a young woman to dream that she is going down a chimney, foretells she will be guilty of some impropriety which will cause consternation among her associates. To ascend a chimney, shows that she will escape trouble which will be planned for her.

China.

For a woman to dream of painting or arranging her china, foretells she will have a pleasant home and be a thrifty and economical matron.

China Store.*

For a china merchant to dream that his store looks empty, foretells he will have reverses in his business, and withal a gloomy period will follow.

Chocolate.

To dream of chocolate, denotes you will provide abundantly for those who are dependent on you. To see chocolate candy, indicates agreeable companions and employments. If sour, illness or other disappointments will follow. To drink chocolate, foretells you will prosper after a short period of unfavorable reverses.

Choir.

To dream of a choir, foretells you may expect cheerful surroundings to replace gloom and discontent. For a young woman to sing in a choir, denotes she will be miserable over the attention paid others by her lover.

Cholera.

To dream of this dread disease devastating the country, portends sickness of virulent type will rage and many disappointments will follow.

To dream that you are attacked by it, denotes your own sickness.

Christ.

To dream of beholding Christ, the young child, worshiped by the wise men, denotes many peaceful days, full of wealth and knowledge, abundant with joy, and content.

If in the garden of the Gethsemane, sorrowing adversity will fill your soul, great longings for change and absent objects of love will be felt.

To see him in the temple scourging the traders, denotes

* See Crockery.

143

that evil enemies will be defeated and honest endeavors
will prevail.

Christmas Tree.

To dream of a Christmas tree, denotes joyful occasions
and auspicious fortune. To see one dismantled, foretells
some painful incident will follow occasions of festivity.

Chrysanthemum.

To dream that you gather white chrysanthemums, signifies loss and much perplexity; colored ones, betokens
pleasant engagements.

To see them in bouquets, denotes that love will be offered you, but a foolish ambition will cause you to put
it aside. To pass down an avenue of white chrysanthemums, with here and there a yellow one showing
among the white, foretells a strange sense of loss and
sadness, from which the sensibilities will expand and take
on new powers. While looking on these white flowers
as you pass, and you suddenly feel your spirit leave your
body and a voice shouts aloud "Glory to God, my Cre-
ator," foretells that a crisis is pending in your near
future. If some of your friends pass out, and others take
up true ideas in connection with spiritual and earthly
needs, you will enjoy life in its deepest meaning. Often
death is near you in these dreams.

Church.*

To dream of seeing a church in the distance, denotes
disappointment in pleasures long anticipated.

To enter one wrapt in gloom, you will participate in a
funeral. Dull prospects of better times are portended.

Churchyard.

To dream of walking in a churchyard, if in winter,

* See Chapel.

144

denotes that you are to have a long and bitter struggle with poverty, and you will reside far from the home of your childhood, and friends will be separated from you; but if you see the signs of springtime, you will walk up in into pleasant places and enjoy the society of friends.

For lovers to dream of being in a churchyard means they will never marry each other, but will see others fill their places.

Churning.

To dream of churning, you will have difficult tasks set you, but by diligence and industry you will accomplish them and be very prosperous. To the farmer, it denotes profit from a plenteous harvest; to a young woman, it denotes a thrifty and energetic husband.

Cider.

To dream of cider, denotes fortune may be won by you if your time is not squandered upon material pleasure. To see people drinking it, you will be under the influence of unfaithful friends.

Cipher.

To dream of reading cipher, indicates that you are interested in literary researches, and by constant study you will become well acquainted with the habits and lives of the ancients.

Circle.

To dream of a circle, denotes that your affairs will deceive you in their proportions of gain. For a young woman to dream of a circle, warns her of indiscreet involvement to the exclusion of marriage.

Cistern.

To dream of a cistern, denotes you are in danger of

trespassing upon the pleasures and rights of your friends. To draw from one, foretells that you will enlarge in your pastime and enjoyment in a manner which may be questioned by propriety.

To see an empty one, foretells despairing change from happiness to sorrow.

City.

To dream that you are in a strange city, denotes you will have sorrowful occasion to change your abode or mode of living.

City Council.

To dream of a city council, foretells that your interests will clash with public institutions and there will be discouraging outlooks for you.

City Hall.

To dream of a city hall, denotes contentions and threatened law suits.

To a young woman this dream is a foreboding of unhappy estrangement from her lover by her failure to keep virtue inviolate.

Clams.

To dream of clams, denotes you will have dealings with an obstinate but honest person. To eat them, foretells you will enjoy another's prosperity.

For a young woman to dream of eating baked clams with her sweetheart, foretells that she will enjoy his money as well as his confidence.

Clay.

To dream of clay, denotes isolation of interest and probable insolvency. To dig in a clay bank, foretells you will submit to extraordinary demands of enemies. If you dig in an ash bank and find clay, unfortunate surprises will combat progressive enterprises or new work. Your efforts are likely to be misdirected after this dream.

Women will find this dream unfavorable in love, social and business states, and misrepresentations will overwhelm them.

Claret.

To dream of drinking claret, denotes you will come under the influence of ennobling association. To dream of seeing broken bottles of claret, portends you will be induced to commit immoralities by the false persuasions of deceitful persons.

Claret Cup and Punch.

To dream of claret cup or punch, foretells that you will be much pleased with the attention shown you by new acquaintances.

Clarinet.

To dream of a clarinet, foretells that you will indulge in frivolity beneath your usual dignity. If it is broken, you will incur the displeasure of a close friend.

Clairvoyance.

To dream of being a clairvoyant and seeing yourself in the future, denotes signal changes in your present occupation, followed by a series of unhappy conflicts with designing people.

To dream of visiting a clairvoyant, foretells unprosperous commercial states and unhappy unions.

Clergyman.*

To dream that you send for a clergyman to preach a funeral sermon, denotes that you will vainly strive against

* See Minister.

sickness and to ward off evil influences, but they will prevail in spite of your earnest endeavors.

If a young woman marries a clergyman in her dream, she will be the object of much mental distress, and the wayward hand of fortune will lead her into the morass of adversity.

Climbing.*

To dream of climbing up a hill or mountain and reaching the top, you will overcome the most formidable obstacles between you and a prosperous future; but if you should fail to reach the top, your dearest plans will suffer being wrecked.

To climb a ladder to the last rung, you will succeed in business; but if the ladder breaks, you will be plunged into unexpected straits, and accidents may happen to you.

To see yourself climbing the side of a house in some mysterious way in a dream, and to have a window suddenly open to let you in, foretells that you will make or have made extraordinary ventures against the approbation of friends, but success will eventually crown your efforts, though there will be times when despair will almost enshroud you.

Clock.

To dream that you see a clock, denotes danger from a foe. To hear one strike, you will receive unpleasant news. The death of some friend is implied.

Cloister.

To dream of a cloister, omens dissatisfaction with present surroundings, and you will soon seek new environments. For a young woman to dream of a cloister, fore-

* See Ascend Hill and Mountain.

tells that her life will be made unselfish by the chastening of sorrow.

Clothes.*

To dream of seeing clothes soiled and torn, denotes that deceit will be practised to your harm. Beware of friendly dealings with strangers.

For a woman to dream that her clothing is soiled or torn, her virtue will be dragged in the mire if she is not careful of her associates. Clean new clothes, denotes prosperity.

To dream that you have plenty, or an assortment of clothes, is a doubtful omen; you may want the necessaries of life. To a young person, this dream denotes unsatisfied hopes and disappointments.

Clouds.

To dream of seeing dark heavy clouds, portends misfortune and bad management. If rain is falling, it denotes troubles and sickness.

To see bright transparent clouds with the sun shining through them, you will be successful after trouble has been your companion.

To see them with the stars shining, denotes fleeting joys and small advancements.

Clover.

Walking through fields of fragrant clover is a propitious dream. It brings all objects desired into the reach of the dreamer. Fine crops is portended for the farmer and wealth for the young. Blasted fields of clover brings harrowing and regretful sighs.

To dream of clover, foretells prosperity will soon enfold you. For a young woman to dream of seeing a snake

* See Apparel.

crawling through blossoming clover, foretells she will be early disappointed in love, and her surroundings will be gloomy and discouraging, though to her friends she seems peculiarly fortunate.

Cloven Foot.

To dream of a cloven foot, portends some unusual ill luck is threatening you, and you will do well to avoid the friendship of strange persons.

Club.

To dream of being approached by a person bearing a club, denotes that you will be assailed by your adversaries, but you will overcome them and be unusually happy and prosperous; but if you club any one, you will undergo a rough and profitless journey.

Coach.

To dream of riding in a coach, denotes continued losses and depressions in business. Driving one implies removal or business changes.

Coals.

To see bright coals of fire, denotes pleasure and many pleasant changes.

To dream you handle them yourself, denotes unmitigated joy. To see dead coals implies trouble and disappointments.

Coal-scuttle

To dream of a coal-scuttle, denotes that grief will be likely to fill a vacancy made by reckless extravagance. To see your neighbor carrying in hods, foretells your surroundings will be decidedly distasteful and inharmonious.

Coat.*

To dream of wearing another's coat, signifies that you will ask some friend to go security for you. To see your coat torn, denotes the loss of a close friend and dreary business.

To see a new coat, portends for you some literary honor.

To lose your coat, you will have to rebuild your fortune lost through being over-confident in speculations.

Coat-of-Arms.

To dream of seeing your coat-of-arms, is a dream of ill luck. You will never possess a title.

Cocoa.

To dream of cocoa, denotes you will cultivate distasteful friends for your own advancement and pleasure.

Cocoanut.

Cocoanuts in dreams, warns you of fatalities in your expectations, as sly enemies are encroaching upon your rights in the guise of ardent friends. Dead cocoanut trees are a sign of loss and sorrow. The death of some one near you may follow.

Cock-Crowing.

To dream of hearing a cock crowing in the morning, is significant of good. If you be single, it denotes an early marriage and a luxurious home.

To hear one at night is despair, and cause for tears you will have.

To dream of seeing cocks fight, you will leave your family because of quarrels and infidelity. This dream usually announces some unexpected and sorrowful

---

* See Apparel and Clothes.

events. The cock warned the Apostle Peter when he was about to perjure himself. It may also warn you in a dream when the meshes of the world are swaying you from "the straight line" of spiritual wisdom.

Cockade.

This dream denotes that foes will bring disastrous suits against you. Beware of titles.

Cocktail.

To drink a cocktail while dreaming, denotes that you will deceive your friends as to your inclinations and enjoy the companionship of fast men and women while posing as a serious student and staid home lover. For a woman, this dream portends fast living and an ignoring of moral and set rules.

Cola.

For a woman to dream that she is drinking cola signifies that she will lose health and a chance for marrying a wealthy man by her abandonment to material delights.

Coffin.

This dream is unlucky. You will, if you are a farmer, see your crops blasted and your cattle lean and unhealthy. To business men it means debts whose accumulation they are powerless to avoid. To the young it denotes unhappy unions and death of loved ones.

To see your own coffin in a dream, business defeat and domestic sorrow may be expected.

To dream of a coffin moving of itself, denotes sickness and marriage in close conjunction. Sorrow and pleasure intermingled. Death may follow this dream, but there will also be good.

To see your corpse in a coffin, signifies brave efforts will be crushed in defeat and ignominy.

To dream that you find yourself sitting on a coffin in a moving hearse, denotes desperate if not fatal illness for you or some person closely allied to you.

Quarrels with the opposite sex is also indicated. You will remorsefully consider your conduct toward a friend.

Coffee.

To dream of drinking coffee, denotes the disapproval of friends toward your marriage intentions. If married, disagreements and frequent quarrels are implied.

To dream of dealing in coffee, portends business failures. If selling, sure loss. Buying it, you may with ease retain your credit.

For a young woman to see or handle coffee she will be made a by-word if she is not discreet in her actions.

To dream of roasting coffee, for a young woman it denotes escape from evil by luckily marrying a stranger.

To see ground coffee, foretells successful struggles with adversity. Parched coffee, warns you of the evil attentions of strangers.

Green coffee, denotes you have bold enemies who will show you no quarter, but will fight for your overthrow.

Coffee Mill.

To see a coffee mill in your dreams, denotes you are approaching a critical danger, and all your energy and alertness will have to stand up with obduracy to avert its disastrous consequences. To hear it grinding, signifies you will hardly overthrow some evil pitted against your interest.

Coffee House.

To see or visit a coffee house in your dreams, foretells

that you will unwisely entertain friendly relations with persons known to be your enemies. Designing women may intrigue against your morality and possessions.

Coins.

To dream of gold, denotes great prosperity and much pleasure derived from sight-seeing and ocean voyages.

Silver coin is unlucky to dream about. Dissensions will arise in the most orderly families.

For a maiden to dream that her lover gives her a silver coin, signifies she will be jilted by him.

Copper coins, denotes despair and physical burdens. Nickel coins, imply that work of the lowest nature will devolve upon you.

If silver coins are your ideal of money, and they are bright and clean, or seen distinctly in your possession, the dream will be a propitious one.

Coke.

To dream of coke, denotes affliction and discord will enter your near future.

Coke Oven.

To see coke ovens burning, foretells some unexpected good fortune will result from failure in some enterprise.

Cold.

To dream of suffering from cold, you are warned to look well to your affairs. There are enemies at work to destroy you. Your health is also menaced.

Colonel.

To dream of seeing or being commanded by a colonel, denotes you will fail to reach any prominence in social or business circles.

If you are a colonel, it denotes you will contrive to hold position above those of friends or acquaintances.

Collar.

To dream of wearing a collar, you will have high honors thrust upon you that you will hardly be worthy of. For a woman to dream of collars, she will have many admirers, but no sincere ones. She will be likely to remain single for a long while.

College.

To dream of a college, denotes you are soon to advance to a position long sought after. To dream that you are back in college, foretells you will receive distinction through some well favored work.

Colliery or Coal-Mine.

To dream of being in a coal-mine or colliery and seeing miners, denotes that some evil will assert its power for your downfall; but if you dream of holding a share in a coal-mine, it denotes your safe investment in some deal.

For a young woman to dream of mining coal, foreshows she will become the wife of a real-estate dealer or dentist.

Collision.

To dream of a collision, you will meet with an accident of a serious type and disappointments in business.

For a young woman to see a collision, denotes she will be unable to decide between lovers, and will be the cause of wrangles.

Combat.

To dream of engaging in combat, you will find yourself seeking to ingratiate your affections into the life and love of some one whom you know to be another's, and you will run great risks of losing your good reputation in business. It denotes struggles to keep on firm ground.

For a young woman to dream of seeing combatants, signifies that she will have choice between lovers, both of whom love her and would face death for her.

Combing.*

To dream of combing one's hair, denotes the illness or death of a friend or relative. Decay of friendship and loss of property is also indicated by this dream.

Comedy.

To dream of being at a light play, denotes that foolish and short-lived pleasures will be indulged in by the dreamer.

To dream of seeing a comedy, is significant of light pleasures and pleasant tasks.

Comet.

To dream of this heavenly awe-inspiring object sailing through the skies, you will have trials of an unexpected nature to beset you, but by bravely combating these foes you will rise above the mediocre in life to heights of fame.

For a young person, this dream portends bereavement and sorrow.

Comic Songs.

To hear comic songs in dreams, foretells you will disregard opportunity to advance your affairs and enjoy the companionship of the pleasure loving. To sing one, proves you will enjoy much pleasure for a time, but difficulties will overtake you.

---

* See Hair.

Command

To dream of being commanded, denotes that you will be humbled in some way by your associates for scorn shown your superiors.

To dream of giving a command, you will have some honor conferred upon you. If this is done in a tyrannical or boastful way disappointments will follow.

Commandment.

To dream of receiving commands, foretells you will be unwisely influenced by persons of stronger will than your own. To read or hear the Ten Commandments read, denotes you will fall into errors from which you will hardly escape, even with the counsels of friends of wise and unerring judgment.

Commerce.

To dream that you are engaged in commerce, denotes you will handle your opportunities wisely and advantageously. To dream of failures and gloomy outlooks in commercial circles, denotes trouble and ominous threatening of failure in real business life.

Committee.

To dream of a committee, foretells that you will be surprised into doing some distasteful work. For one to wait on you, foretells some unfruitful labor will be assigned you.

Companion.

To dream of seeing a wife or husband, signifies small anxieties and probable sickness.

To dream of social companions, denotes light and frivolous pastimes will engage your attention hindering you from performing your duties.

Compass.

To dream of a compass, denotes you will be forced to struggle in narrow limits, thus making elevation more toilsome but fuller of honor.

To dream of the compass or mariner's needle, foretells you will be surrounded by prosperous circumstances and honest people will favor you.

To see one pointing awry, foretells threatened loss and deception.

Completion.

To dream of completing a task or piece of work, denotes that you will have acquired a competency early in life, and that you can spend your days as you like and wherever you please.

For a young woman to dream that she has completed a garment, denotes that she will soon decide on a husband.

To dream of completing a journey, you will have the means to make one whenever you like.

Complexion.

To dream that you have a beautiful complexion is lucky. You will pass through pleasing incidents.

To dream that you have bad and dark complexion, denotes disappointment and sickness.

Composing.

To see in your dreams a composing stick, foretells that difficult problems will disclose themselves, and you will be at great trouble to meet them.

Concert.

To dream of a concert of a high musical order, denotes delightful seasons of pleasure, and literary work to the author. To the business man it portends successful trade, and to the young it signifies unalloyed bliss and faithful loves.

Ordinary concerts such as engage ballet singers, denote that disagreeable companions and ungrateful friends will be met with. Business will show a falling off.

Concubine.

For a man to dream that he is in company with a concubine, forecasts he is in danger of public disgrace, striving to keep from the world his true character and state of business.

For a woman to dream that she is a concubine, indicates that she will degrade herself by her own improprieties.

For a man to dream that his mistress is untrue, denotes that he has old enemies to encounter. Expected reverses will arise.

Confectionary.

To dream of impure confectionary, denotes that an enemy in the guise of a friend will enter your privacy and discover secrets of moment to your opponents.

Confetti.

To dream of confetti obstructing your view in a crowd of merry-makers, denotes that you will lose much by first seeking enjoyment, and later fulfil tasks set by duty.

Conjuror.

To dream of a conjuror, denotes unpleasant experience will beset you in your search for wealth and happiness.

Conjuring.

To dream that you are in a hypnotic state or under the

power of others, portends disastrous results, for your enemies will enthrall you; but if you hold others under a spell you will assert decided will power in governing your surroundings.

For a young woman to dream that she is under strange influences, denotes her immediate exposure to danger, and she should beware.

To dream of seeing hypnotic and slight-of-hand performances, signifies worries and perplexities in business and domestic circles, and unhealthy conditions of state.

Conflagration.*

To dream of a conflagration, denotes, if no lives are lost, changes in the future which will be beneficial to your interests and happiness.

Conspiracy

To dream that you are the object of a conspiracy, foretells you will make a wrong move in the directing of your affairs.

Conscience.

To dream that your conscience censures you for deceiving some one, denotes that you will be tempted to commit wrong and should be constantly on your guard.

To dream of having a quiet conscience, denotes that you will stand in high repute.

Consumption.

To dream that you have consumption, denotes that you are exposing yourself to danger. Remain with your friends.

Contempt.

To dream of being in contempt of court, denotes that

---

* See Fire.

you have committed business or social indiscretion and that it is unmerited.

To dream that you are held in contempt by others, you will succeed in winning their highest regard, and will find yourself prosperous and happy. But if the contempt is merited, your exile from business or social circles is intimated.

Convent.

To dream of seeking refuge in a convent, denotes that your future will be signally free from care and enemies, unless on entering the building you encounter a priest. If so, you will seek often and in vain for relief from worldly cares and mind worry.

For a young girl to dream of seeing a convent, her virtue and honestly will be questioned.

Convicts.

To dream of seeing convicts, denotes disasters and sad news. To dream that you are a convict, indicates that you will worry over some affair; but you will clear up all mistakes.

For a young woman to dream of seeing her lover in the garb of a convict, indicates she will have cause to question the character of his love.

Convicted.*

Convention.

To dream of a convention, denotes unusual activity in business affairs and final engagement in love. An inharmonious or displeasing convention brings you disappointment.

Cooking.

To cook a meal, denotes some pleasant duty will de-

---

* See Accuse.

volve on you. Many friends will visit you in the near future. If there is discord or a lack of cheerfulness you may expect harassing and disappointing events to happen.

Cooking Stove.

To see a cooking stove in a dream, denotes that much unpleasantness will be modified by your timely interference. For a young woman to dream of using a cooking stove, foretells she will be too hasty in showing her appreciation of the attention of some person and thereby lose a closer friendship.

Cooling Board.

For a young woman to see a cooling board in her dreams, foretells sickness and quarrels with her lover. To dream of some living person as dead and rising up from a cooling board, denotes she will be indirectly connected with that person in some trouble, but will find out that things will work out satisfactorily.

To see her brother, who has long since been dead, rising from a cooling board, warns her of complications which may be averted if she puts forth the proper will and energy in struggling against them.

Copper.

To dream of copper, denotes oppression from those above you in station.

Copperas (Fool's Gold).

To dream of copperas or Fool's Gold foretells unintential wrong will be done you which will be distressing and will cause you loss.

Copper Plate.

Copper plate seen in a dream, is a warning of discordant views causing unhappiness between members of the same household.

Coppersmith.

To dream of a coppersmith, denotes small returns for labor, but withal contentment.

Copying.

To dream of copying, denotes unfavorable workings of well tried plans.

For a young woman to dream that she is copying a letter, denotes she will be prejudiced into error by her love for a certain class of people.

Coral.

To dream of coral, is momentous of enduring friendship which will know no weariness in alleviating your trouble. Colored coral is meant in this dream.

White coral, foretells unfaithfulness and warning of love.

Cornet.

A cornet seen or heard in a dream, denotes kindly attentions from strangers.

Coronation.

To dream of a coronation, foretells you will enjoy acquaintances and friendships with prominent people. For a young woman to be participating in a coronation, foretells that she will come into some surprising favor with distinguished personages. But if the coronation presents disagreeable incoherence in her dreams, then she may expect unsatisfactory states growing out of anticipated pleasure.

Cords.*

---

* See Rope.

Cork.

To dream of drawing corks at a banquet, signifies that you will soon enter a state of prosperity, in which you will revel in happiness of the most select kind.

To dream of medicine corks, denotes sickness and wasted energies.

To dream of seeing a fishing cork resting on clear water, denotes success. If water is disturbed you will be annoyed by unprincipled persons.

To dream that you are corking bottles, denotes a well organized business and system in your living.

For a young woman to dream of drawing champagne corks, indicates she will have a gay and handsome lover who will lavish much attention and money on her. She should look well to her reputation and listen to the warning of parents after this dream.

Corn.

To dream of husking pied ears of corn, denotes you will enjoy varied success and pleasure. To see others gathering corn, foretells you will rejoice in the prosperity of friends or relatives.

Corn and Corn-Field.

To dream of passing through a green and luxurious corn-field, and seeing full ears hanging heavily, denotes great wealth for the farmer. It denotes fine crops and rich harvest and harmony in the home. To the young it promises much happiness and true friends, but to see the ears blasted, denotes disappointments and bereavements.

To see young corn newly ploughed, denotes favor with the powerful and coming success. To see it ripe, denotes fame and wealth. To see it cribbed, signifies that your highest desires will be realized.

To see shelled corn, denotes wealthy combines and unstinted favors.

To dream of eating green corn, denotes harmony among friends and happy unions for the young.

Corns.

To dream that your corns hurt your feet, denotes that some enemies are undermining you, and you will have much distress; but if you succeed in clearing your feet of corns, you will inherit a large estate from some unknown source.

For a young woman to dream of having corns on her feet, indicates she will have to bear many crosses and be coldly treated by her sex.

Corkscrew.

To dream of seeing a corkscrew, indicates an unsatisfied mind, and the dreamer should heed this as a warning to curb his desires, for it is likely they are on dangerous grounds.

To dream of breaking a corkscrew while using it, indicates to the dreamer perilous surroundings, and he should use force of will to abandon unhealthful inclinations.

Corpse.

To dream of a corpse is fatal to happiness, as this dream indicates sorrowful tidings of the absent, and gloomy business prospects. The young will suffer many disappointments and pleasure will vanish.

To see a corpse placed in its casket, denotes immediate troubles to the dreamer.

To see a corpse in black, denotes the violent death of

a friend or some desperate business entanglement.

To see a battle-field strewn with corpses, indicates war and general dissatisfaction between countries and political factions.

To see the corpse of an animal, denotes unhealthy situation, both as to business and health.

To see the corpse of any one of your immediate family, indicates death to that person, or to some member of the family, or a serious rupture of domestic relations, also unusual business depression. For lovers it is a sure sign of failure to keep promises of a sacred nature.

To put money on the eyes of a corpse in your dreams, denotes that you will see unscrupulous enemies robbing you while you are powerless to resent injury. If you only put it on one eye you will be able to recover lost property after an almost hopeless struggle. For a young woman this dream denotes distress and loss by unfortunately giving her confidence to designing persons.

For a young woman to dream that the proprietor of the store in which she works is a corpse, and she sees while sitting up with him that his face is clean shaven, foretells that she will fall below the standard of perfection in which she was held by her lover. If she sees the head of the corpse falling from the body, she is warned of secret enemies who, in harming her, will also detract from the interest of her employer. Seeing the corpse in the store, foretells that loss and unpleasantness will offset all concerned. There are those who are not conscientiously doing the right thing. There will be a gloomy outlook for peace and prosperous work.

Cornmeal.

To see cornmeal, foretells the consummation of ardent wishes. To eat it made into bread, denotes that you will unwittingly throw obstructions in the way of your own advancement.

Corner.

This is an unfavorable dream if the dreamer is frightened and secretes himself in a corner for safety.

To see persons talking in a corner, enemies are seeking to destroy you. The chances are that some one whom you consider a friend will prove a traitor to your interest.

Corpulence.

For a person to dream of being corpulent, indicates to the dreamer bountiful increase of wealth and pleasant abiding places.

To see others corpulent, denotes unusual activity and prosperous times.

If a man or woman sees himself or herself looking grossly corpulent, he or she should look well to their moral nature and impulses. Beware of either concave or convex telescopically or microscopically drawn pictures of yourself or others, as they forbode evil.

Corset.

To dream of a corset, denotes that you will be perplexed as to the meaning of attentions won by you. If a young woman is vexed over undoing or fastening her corset, she will be strongly inclined to quarrel with her friends under slight provocations.

Cossack.

To dream of a Cossack, denotes humiliation of a personal character, brought about by dissipation and wanton extravagance.

Cot.

To dream of a cot, foretells some affliction, either

through sickness or accident. Cots in rows signify you will not be alone in trouble, as friends will be afflicted also.

Cotton.

To dream of young growing cotton-fields, denotes great business and prosperous times. To see cotton ready for gathering, denotes wealth and abundance for farmers.

For manufacturers to dream of cotton, means that they will be benefited by the advancement of this article. For merchants, it denotes a change for the better in their line of business.

To see cotton in bales, is a favorable indication for better times.

To dream that cotton is advancing, denotes an immediate change from low to high prices, and all will be in better circumstances.

Cotton Cap.

It is a good dream, denoting many sincere friends.

Cotton Cloth.

To see cotton cloth in a dream, denotes easy circumstances. No great changes follow this dream.

For a young woman to dream of weaving cotton cloth, denotes that she will have a thrifty and enterprising husband. To the married it denotes a pleasant yet a humble abode.

Cotton Gin.

To dream of a cotton gin, foretells you will make some advancement toward fortune which will be very pleasing and satisfactory. To see a broken or dilapidated gin, signifies misfortune and trouble will overthrow success.

Couch.

To dream of reclining on a couch, indicates that false

hopes will be entertained. You should be alert to every change of your affairs, for only in this way will your hopes be realized.

Cough.

To dream that you are aggravated by a constant cough indicates a state of low health; but one from which you will recuperate if care is observed in your habits.

To dream of hearing others cough, indicates unpleasant surroundings from which you will ultimately emerge.

Counter.

To dream of counters, foretells that active interest will debar idleness from infecting your life with unhealthful desires. To dream of empty and soiled counters, foretells unfortunate engagements which will bring great uneasiness of mind lest your interest will be wholly swept away.

Counterfeit Money.

To dream of counterfeit money, denotes you will have trouble with some unruly and worthless person. This dream always omens evil, whether you receive it or pass it.

Counselor.

To dream of a counselor, you are likely to be possessed of some ability yourself, and you will usually prefer your own judgment to that of others. Be guarded in executing your ideas of right.

Countenance.

To dream of a beautiful and ingenuous countenance, you may safely look for some pleasure to fall to your lot in the near future; but to behold an ugly and scowling visage, portends unfavorable transactions.

Counterpane.

A counterpane is very good to dream of, if clean and white, denoting pleasant occupations for women; but if it be soiled you may expect harassing situations. Sickness usually follows this dream.

Counting.

To dream of counting your children, and they are merry and sweet-looking, denotes that you will have no trouble in controlling them, and they will attain honorable places.

To dream of counting money, you will be lucky and always able to pay your debts; but to count out money to another person, you will meet with loss of some kind. Such will be the case, also, in counting other things. If for yourself, good; if for others, usually bad luck will attend you.

Country.

To dream of being in a beautiful and fertile country, where abound rich fields of grain and running streams of pure water, denotes the very acme of good times is at hand. Wealth will pile in upon you, and you will be able to reign in state in any country. If the country be dry and bare, you will see and hear of troublous times. Famine and sickness will be in the land.

Courtship.

Bad, bad, will be the fate of the woman who dreams of being courted. She will often think that now he will propose, but often she will be disappointed. Disappointments will follow illusory hopes and fleeting pleasures.

For a man to dream of courting, implies that he is not worthy of a companion.

Cousin.

Dreaming of one's cousin, denotes disappointments and afflictions. Saddened lives are predicted by this dream.

To dream of an affectionate correspondence with one's cousin, denotes a fatal rupture between families.

Cows.*

To dream of seeing cows waiting for the milking hour, promises abundant fulfilment of hopes and desires.

Cowslip.

To dream of gathering cowslips, portends unhappy ending of seemingly close and warm friendships; but seeing them growing, denotes a limited competency for lovers. This is a sinister dream.

To see them in full bloom, denotes a crisis in your affairs. The breaking up of happy homes may follow this dream.

Coxcomb.

To dream of a coxcomb, denotes a low state of mind. The dreamer should endeavor to elevate his mind to nobler thoughts.

Cradle.

To dream of a cradle, with a beautiful infant occupying it, portends prosperity and the affections of beautiful children.

To rock your own baby in a cradle, denotes the serious illness of one of the family.

For a young woman to dream of rocking a cradle is portentous of her downfall. She should beware of gossiping.

Crabs.

To dream of crabs, indicates that you will have many

* See Cattle.

complicated affairs, for the solving of which you will be forced to exert the soundest judgment. This dream portends to lovers a long and difficult courtship.

Crane.

To dream of seeing a flight of cranes tending northward, indicates gloomy prospects for business. To a woman, it is significant of disappointment; but to see them flying southward, prognosticates a joyful meeting of absent friends, and that lovers will remain faithful.

To see them fly to the ground, events of unusual moment are at hand.

Crape.

To dream of seeing crape hanging from a door, denotes that you will hear of the sudden death of some relative or friend.

To see a person dressed in crape, indicates that sorrow, other than death, will possess you. It is bad for business and trade. To the young, it implies lovers' disputes and separations.

Crawfish.

Deceit is sure to assail you in your affairs of the heart, if you are young, after dreaming of this backward-going thing.

Crawl.

To dream that you are crawling on the ground, and hurt your hand, you may expect humiliating tasks to be placed on you.

To crawl over rough places and stones, indicates that you have not taken proper advantage of your opportunities. A young woman, after dreaming of crawling, if not very careful of her conduct, will lose the respect of her lover.

To crawl in mire with others, denotes depression in

business and loss of credit. Your friends will have cause to censure you.

Cream.

To dream of seeing cream served, denotes that you will be associated with wealth if you are engaged in business other than farming.

To the farmer, it indicates fine crops and pleasant family relations. To drink cream yourself, denotes immediate good fortune. To lovers, this is a happy omen, as they will soon be united.

Credit.

To dream of asking for credit, denotes that you will have cause to worry, although you may be inclined sometimes to think things look bright.

To credit another, warns you to be careful of your affairs, as you are likely to trust those who will eventually work you harm.

Creek.

To dream of a creek, denotes new experiences and short journeys. If it is overflowing, you will have sharp trouble, but of brief period.

If it is dry, disappointment will be felt by you, and you will see another obtain the things you intrigued to secure.

Cremate.

To dream of seeing bodies cremated, denotes enemies will reduce your influence in business circles. To think you are being cremated, portends distinct failure in enterprises, if you mind any but your own judgment in conducting them.

Crew.

To dream of seeing a crew getting ready to leave port, some unforseen circumstance will cause you to give up a journey from which you would have gained much.

To see a crew working to save a ship in a storm, denotes disaster on land and sea. To the young, this dream bodes evil.

Cricket.

To hear a cricket in one's dream, indicates melancholy news, and perhaps the death of some distant friend.

To see them, indicates hard struggles with poverty.

Cries.

To hear cries of distress, denotes that you will be engulfed in serious troubles, but by being alert you will finally emerge from these distressing straits and gain by this temporary gloom.

To hear a cry of surprise, you will receive aid from unexpected sources.

To hear the cries of wild beasts, denotes an accident of a serious nature.

To hear a cry for help from relatives, or friends, denotes that they are sick or in distress.

Criminal.

To dream of associating with a person who has committed a crime, denotes that you will be harassed with unscrupulous persons, who will try to use your friendship for their own advancement.

To see a criminal fleeing from justice, denotes that you will come into the possession of the secrets of others, and will therefore be in danger, for they will fear that you will betray them, and consequently will seek your removal.

Crippled.

To dream of the maimed and crippled, denotes famine and distress among the poor, and you should be willing to contribute to their store. It also indicates a temporary dulness in trade.

Crochet Work.

To dream of doing crochet work, foretells your entanglement in some silly affair growing out of a too great curiosity about other people's business. Beware of talking too frankly with over-confidential women.

Crockery.

To dream of having an abundance of nice, clean crockery, denotes that you will be a tidy and economical housekeeper.

To be in a crockery store, indicates, if you are a merchant or business man, that you will look well to the details of your business and thereby experience profit. To a young woman, this dream denotes that she will marry a sturdy and upright man. An untidy store, with empty shelves, implies loss.

Crocodile.

As sure as you dream of this creature, you will be deceived by your warmest friends. Enemies will assail you at every turn.

To dream of stepping on a crocodile's back, you may expect to fall into trouble, from which you will have to struggle mightily to extricate yourself. Heed this warning when dreams of this nature visit you. Avoid giving your confidence even to friends.

Cross.

To dream of seeing a cross, indicates trouble ahead for you. Shape your affairs accordingly.

To dream of seeing a person bearing a cross, you will be called on by missionaries to aid in charities.

Cross-bones.

To dream of cross-bones, foretells you will be troubled

by the evil influence of others, and prosperity will assume other than promising aspects.

To see cross-bones as a monogram on an invitation to a funeral, which was sent out by a secret order, denotes that unnecessary fears will be entertained for some person, and events will transpire seemingly harsh, but of good import to the dreamer.

Cross Roads.

To dream of cross roads, denotes you will be unable to hold some former favorable opportunity for reaching your desires. If you are undecided which one to take, you are likely to let unimportant matters irritate you in a distressing manner. You will be better favored by fortune if you decide on your route. It may be after this dream you will have some important matter of business or love to decide.

Croup.

To dream that your child has the croup, denotes slight illness, but useless fear for its safety. This is generally a good omen of health and domestic harmony.

Crow.*

To dream of seeing a crow, betokens misfortune and grief. To hear crows cawing, you will be influenced by others to make a bad disposal of property. To a young man, it is indicative of his succumbing to the wiles of designing women.

Crowd.

To dream of a large, handsomely dressed crowd of people at some entertainment, denotes pleasant association with friends; but anything occurring to mar the pleasure of the guests, denotes distress and loss of friend-

* See Raven.

ship, and unhappiness will be found where profit and congenial intercourse was expected. It also denotes dissatisfaction in government and family dissensions.

To see a crowd in a church, denotes that a death will be likely to affect you, or some slight unpleasantness may develop.

To see a crowd in the street, indicates unusual briskness in trade and a general air of prosperity will surround you.

To try to be heard in a crowd, foretells that you will push your interests ahead of all others.

To see a crowd is usually good, if too many are not wearing black or dull costumes.

To dream of seeing a hypnotist trying to hypnotize others, and then turn his attention on you, and fail to do so, indicates that a trouble is hanging above you which friends will not succeed in warding off. Yourself alone can avert the impending danger.

Crown.

To dream of a crown, prognosticates change of mode in the habit of one's life. The dreamer will travel a long distance from home and form new relations. Fatal illness may also be the sad omen of this dream.

To dream that you wear a crown, signifies loss of personal property.

To dream of crowning a person, denotes your own worthiness.

To dream of talking with a person of high authority, denotes that you are interested in affairs of state, and sometimes show a great longing to be a politician.

Crucifixion.

If you chance to dream of the crucifixion, you will see your opportunities slip away, tearing your hopes from your grasp, and leaving you wailing over the frustration of desires.

Crucifix.

To see a crucifix in a dream, is a warning of distress approaching, which will involve others beside yourself. To kiss one, foretells that trouble will be accepted by you with resignation.

For a young woman to possess one, foretells she will observe modesty and kindness in her deportment, and thus win the love of others and better her fortune.

Cruelty.

To dream of cruelty being shown you, foretells you will have trouble and disappointment in some dealings. If it is shown to others, there will be a disagreeable task set for others by you, which will contribute to your own loss.

Crust.

To dream of a crust of bread, denotes incompetency, and threatened misery through carelessness in appointed duties.

Crutches.

To dream that you go on crutches, denotes that you will depend largely on others for your support and advancement.

To see others on crutches, denotes unsatisfactory results from labors.

Crying.

To dream of crying, is a forerunner of illusory pleasures, which will subside into gloom, and distressing influences affecting for evil business engagements and domestic affairs.

To see others crying, forbodes unexpected calls for aid from you.

Crystal.

To dream of crystal in any form, is a fatal sign of coming depression either in social relations or business transactions. Electrical storms often attend this dream, doing damage to town and country.

For a woman to dream of seeing a dining-room furnished in crystal, even to the chairs, she will have cause to believe that those whom she holds in high regard no longer deserve this distinction, but she will find out that there were others in the crystal-furnished room, who were implicated also in this sinister dream.

Cuckoo.

To dream of a cuckoo, prognosticates a sudden ending of a happy life caused by the downfall of a dear friend.

To dream that you hear a cuckoo, denotes the painful illness of the death of some absent loved one, or accident to some one in your family.

Cucumber.

This is a dream of plenty, denoting health and prosperity. For the sick to dream of serving cucumbers, denotes their speedy recovery. For the married, a pleasant change.

Cunning.

To dream of being cunning, denotes you will assume happy cheerfulness to retain the friendship of prosperous and gay people. If you are associating with cunning people, it warns you that deceit is being practised upon you in order to use your means for their own advancement.

Cupboard.*

To see a cupboard in your dream, is significant of pleas-

* See Safe.

ure and comfort, or penury and distress, according as the cupboard is clean and full of shining ware, or empty and dirty.

Curbstone.

To dream of stepping on a curbstone, denotes your rapid rise in business circles, and that you will be held in high esteem by your friends and the public.

For lovers to dream of stepping together on a curb, denotes an early marriage and consequent fidelity; but if in your dream you step or fall from a curbstone your fortunes will be reversed.

Currycomb.

To dream of a currycomb foretells that great labors must be endured in order to obtain wealth and comfort.

Currying a Horse.

To dream of currying a horse, signifies that you will have a great many hard licks to make both with brain and hand before you attain to the heights of your ambition; but if you successfully curry him you will attain that height, whatever it may be.

Curtains.

To dream of curtains, foretells that unwelcome visitors will cause you worry and unhappiness. Soiled or torn curtains seen in a dream means disgraceful quarrels and reproaches.

Cushion.

To dream of reclining on silken cushions, foretells that your ease will be procured at the expense of others; but to see the cushions, denotes that you will prosper in business and love-making.

For a young woman to dream of making silken cushions, implies that she will be a bride before many months.

Cuspidor.

To see a cuspidor in a dream, signifies that an unworthy attachment will be formed by you, and that your work will be neglected.

To spit in one, foretells that reflections will be cast upon your conduct.

Custard.*

For a married woman to dream of making or eating custard, indicates she will be called upon to entertain an unexpected guest. A young woman will meet a stranger who will in time become a warm friend. If the custard has a sickening sweet taste, or is insipid, nothing but sorrow will intervene where you had expected a pleasant experience.

Custom-house.

To dream of a custom-house, denotes you will have rivalries and competition in your labors.

To enter a custom-house, foretells that you will strive for, or have offered you, a position which you have long desired.

To leave one, signifies loss of position, trade or failure of securing some desired object.

Cut.

To dream of a cut, denotes sickness or the treachery of a friend will frustrate your cheerfulness.

Cymbal.

Hearing a cymbal in your dreams, foretells the death of a very aged person of your acquaintance. The sun will shine, but you will see it darkly because of gloom.

---

* See Baking.

D.

"God came to Laban, the Syrian, by night, in a dream, and said unto him, take heed that thou speak not to Jacob, either good or bad."—Gen. xxxi., 24.

Dagger.

If seen in a dream, denotes threatening enemies. If you wrench the dagger from the hand of another, it denotes that you will be able to counteract the influence of your enemies and overcome misfortune.

Dahlia.*

To see dahlias in a dream, if they are fresh and bright, signifies good fortune to the dreamer.

Dairy.†

Dairy is a good dream both to the married and unmarried.

Daisy.

To dream of a bunch of daisys, implies sadness, but if you dream of being in a field where these lovely flowers are in bloom, with the sun shining and birds singing, happiness, health and prosperity will vie each with the other to lead you through the pleasantest avenues of life.

To dream of seeing them out of season, you will be assailed by evil in some guise.

Damask Rose.

To dream of seeing a damask rosebush in full foliage and bloom, denotes that a wedding will soon take place in your family, and great hopes will be fulfilled.

For a lover to place this rose in your hair, foretells that

---

*See Bouquet.
†See Churning Butter.

you will be deceived. If a woman receives a bouquet of damask roses in springtime, she will have a faithful lover; but if she received them in winter, she will cherish blasted hopes.

Damson.

This is a peculiarly good dream if one is so fortunate as to see these trees lifting their branches loaded with rich purple fruit and dainty foliage; one may expect riches compared with his present estate.

To dream of eating them at any time, forebodes grief.

Dance.*

To dream of seeing a crowd of merry children dancing, signifies to the married, loving, obedient and intelligent children and a cheerful and comfortable home. To young people, it denotes easy tasks and many pleasures.

To see older people dancing, denotes a brighter outlook for business.

To dream of dancing yourself, some unexpected good fortune will come to you.

Dancing Master.

To dream of a dancing master, foretells you will neglect important affairs to pursue frivolities. For a young woman to dream that her lover is a dancing master, portends that she will have a friend in accordance with her views of pleasure and life.

Dandelion.

Dandelions blossoming in green foliage, foretells happy unions and prosperous surroundings.

Danger.

To dream of being in a perilous situation, and death

---

*See Ball.

seems iminent, denotes that you will emerge from obscurity into places of distinction and honor; but if you should not escape the impending danger, and suffer death or a wound, you will lose in business and be annoyed in your home, and by others. If you are in love, your prospects will grow discouraging.

Dark.

To dream of darkness overtaking you on a journey, augurs ill for any work you may attempt, unless the sun breaks through before the journey ends, then faults will be overcome.

To lose your friend, or child, in the darkness, portends many provocations to wrath. Try to remain under control after dreaming of darkness, for trials in business and love will beset you.

Dates.

To dream of seeing them on their parent trees, signifies prosperity and happy union; but to eat them as prepared for commerce, they are omens of want and distress.

Daughter.

To dream of your daughter, signifies that many displeasing incidents will give way to pleasure and harmony. If in the dream, she fails to meet your wishes, through any cause, you will suffer vexation and discontent.

Daughter-in-law.

To dream of your daughter-in-law, indicates some unusual occurence will add to happiness, or disquiet, according as she is pleasant or unreasonable.

David.

To dream of David, of Bible fame, denotes divisions in

domestic circles, and unsettled affairs, will tax heavily your nerve force.

Day.

To dream of the day, denotes improvement in your situation, and pleasant associations. A gloomy or cloudy day, foretells loss and ill success in new enterprises.

Daybreak.

To watch the day break in a dream, omens successful undertakings, unless the scene is indistinct and weird; then it may imply disappointment when success in business or love seems assured.

Dead.*

To dream of the dead, is usually a dream of warning. If you see and talk with your father, some unlucky transaction is about to be made by you. Be careful how you enter into contracts, enemies are around you. Men and women are warned to look to their reputations after this dream.

To see your mother, warns you to control your inclina-

---

*Paracelsus says on this subject: "It may happen that the soul of persons who have died perhaps fifty years ago may appear to us in a dream, and if it speaks to us we should pay special attention to what it says, for such a vision is not an illusion or delusion, and it is possible that a man is as much able to use his reason during the sleep of his body as when the latter is awake; and if in such a case such a soul appears to him and he asks questions, he will then hear that which is true. Through these solicitous souls we may obtain a great deal of knowledge to good or to evil things if we ask them to reveal them to us. Many persons have had such prayers granted to them. Some people that were sick have been informed during their sleep what remedies they should use, and after using the remedies, they became cured, and such things have happened not only to Christians, but also to Jews, Persians, and heathens, to good and to bad persons."

The writer does not hold that such knowledge is obtained from external or excarnate spirits, but rather through the personal *Spirit Glimpses* that is in man.—AUTHOR.

tion to cultivate morbidness and ill will towards your fellow creatures. A brother, or other relatives or friends, denotes that you may be called on for charity or aid within a short time.

To dream of seeing the dead, living and happy, signifies you are letting wrong influences into your life, which will bring material loss if not corrected by the assumption of your own will force.

To dream that you are conversing with a dead relative, and that relative endeavors to extract a promise from you, warns you of coming distress, unless you follow the advice given you. Disastrous consequences could often be averted if minds could grasp the inner workings and sight of the higher or spiritual self. The voice of relatives is only that higher self taking form to approach more distinctly the mind that lives near the material plane. There is so little congeniality between common or material natures that persons should depend upon their own subjectivity for true contentment and pleasure.

Death.*

To dream of seeing any of your people dead, warns you of coming dissolution or sorrow. Disappointments always follow dreams of this nature.

To hear of any friend or relative being dead, you will soon have bad news from some of them.

Dreams relating to death or dying, unless they are due to spiritual causes, are misleading and very confusing to the novice in dream lore when he attempts to interpret them. A man who thinks intensely fills his aura with thought or subjective images active with the passions that gave them birth; by thinking and acting on other lines, he may supplant these images with others possessed of

*See Corpse.

a different form and nature. In his dreams he may see these images dying, dead or their burial, and mistake them for friends or enemies. In this way he may, while asleep, see himself or a relative die, when in reality he has been warned that some good thought or deed is to be supplanted by an evil one. To illustrate: If it is a dear friend or relative whom he sees in the agony of death, he is warned against immoral or other improper thought and action, but if it is an enemy or some repulsive object dismantled in death, he may overcome his evil ways and thus give himself or friends cause for joy. Often the end or beginning of suspense or trials are foretold by dreams of this nature. They also frequently occur when the dreamer is controlled by imaginary states of evil or good. A man in that state is not himself, but is what the dominating influences make him. He may be warned of approaching conditions or his extrication from the same. In our dreams we are closer to our real self than in waking life. The hideous or pleasing incidents seen and heard about us in our dreams are all of our own making, they reflect the true state of our soul and body, and we cannot flee from them unless we drive them out of our being by the use of good thoughts and deeds, by the power of the spirit within us.

Debt.

Debt is rather a bad dream, foretelling worries in business and love, and struggles for a competency; but if you have plenty to meet all your obligations, your affairs will assume a favorable turn.

December.

To dream of December, foretells accumulation of wealth, but loss of friendship. Strangers will occupy the position in the affections of some friend which was formerly held by you.

Deck.*

To dream of being on a ship and that a storm is raging, great disasters and unfortunate alliances will overtake you; but if the sea is calm and the light distinct, your way is clear to success. For lovers, this dream augurs happiness.

Decorate.

To dream of decorating a place with bright-hued flowers for some festive occasion, is significant of favorable turns in business, and, to the young, of continued rounds of social pleasures and fruitful study.

To see the graves or caskets of the dead decorated with white flowers, is unfavorable to pleasure and worldly pursuits.

To be decorating, or see others decorate for some heroic action, foretells that you will be worthy, but that few will recognize your ability.

Deed.†

To dream of seeing or signing deeds, portends a law suit, to gain which you should be careful in selecting your counsel, as you are likely to be the loser. To dream of signing any kind of a paper, is a bad omen for the dreamer.

Deer.

This is a favorable dream, denoting pure and deep friendships for the young and a quiet and even life for the married.

To kill a deer, denotes that you will be hounded by enemies. For farmers, or business people, to dream of hunting deer, denotes failure in their respective pursuits.

---

*See Boat.
† See Mortgage.

Delay.

To be delayed in a dream, warns you of the scheming of enemies to prevent your progress.

Delight.

To dream of experiencing delight over any event, signifies a favorable turn in affairs. For lovers to be delighted with the conduct of their sweethearts, denotes pleasant greetings.

To feel delight when looking on beautiful landscapes, prognosticates to the dreamer very great success and congenial associations.

Demand.

To dream that a demand for charity comes in upon you, denotes that you will be placed in embarrassing situations, but by your persistency you will fully restore your good standing. If the demand is unjust, you will become a leader in your profession. For a lover to command you adversely, implies his, or her, leniency.

Dentist.

To dream of a dentist working on your teeth, denotes that you will have occasion to doubt the sincerity and honor of some person with whom you have dealings.

To see him at work on a young woman's teeth, denotes that you will soon be shocked by a scandal in circles near you.

Derrick.

Derricks seen in a dream, indicate strife and obstruction in your way to success.

Desert.

To dream of wandering through a gloomy and barren desert, denotes famine and uprisal of races and great loss of life and property.

For a young woman to find herself alone in a desert, her health and reputation is being jeopardized by her indiscretion. She should be more cautious.

Desk.

To be using a desk in a dream, denotes unforeseen ill luck will rise before you. To see money on your desk, brings you unexpected extrication from private difficulties.

Despair.

To be in despair in dreams, denotes that you will have many and cruel vexations in the working world.

To see others in despair, foretells the distress and unhappy position of some relative or friend.

Detective.

To dream of a detective keeping in your wake when you are innocent of charges preferred, denotes that fortune and honor are drawing nearer to you each day; but if you feel yourself guilty, you are likely to find your reputation at stake, and friends will turn from you. For a young woman, this is not a fortunate dream.

Devotion.

For a farmer to dream of showing his devotion to God, or to his family, denotes plenteous crops and peaceful neighbors. To business people, this is a warning that nothing is to be gained by deceit.

For a young woman to dream of being devout, implies her chastity and an adoring husband.

Devil.

For farmers to dream of the devil, denotes blasted crops and death among stock, also family sickness. Sporting people should heed this dream as a warning to be careful of their affairs, as they are likely to venture beyond the laws of their area. For a preacher, this dream is undeniable proof that he is over-zealous, and should forebear worshiping God by tongue-lashing his neighbor.

To dream of the devil as being a large, imposingly dressed person, wearing many sparkling jewels on his body and hands, trying to persuade you to enter his abode, warns you that unscrupulous persons are seeking your ruin by the most ingenious flattery. Young and innocent women, should seek the stronghold of friends after this dream, and avoid strange attentions, especially from married men. Women of low character, are likely to be robbed of jewels and money by seeming strangers.

Beware of associating with the devil, even in dreams. He is always the forerunner of despair. If you dream of being pursued by his majesty, you will fall into snares set for you by enemies in the guise of friends. To a lover, this denotes that he will be won away from his allegiance by a wanton.

Dew.

To feel the dew falling on you in your dreams, portends that you will be attacked by fever or some malignant disease; but to see the dew sparkling through the grass in the sunlight, great honors and wealth are about to be heaped upon you. If you are single, a wealthy marriage will soon be your portion.

Diadem.

To dream of a diadem, denotes that some honor will be tendered you for acceptance.

Diamonds.

To dream of owning diamonds is a very propitious dream, signifying great honor and recognition from high places.

For a young woman to dream of her lover presenting her with diamonds, foreshows that she will make a great and honorable marriage, which will fill her people with honest pride; but to lose diamonds, and not find them again, is the most unlucky of dreams, foretelling disgrace, want and death.

For a sporting woman to dream of diamonds, foretells for her many prosperous days and magnificent presents. For a speculator, it denotes prosperous transactions. To dream of owning diamonds, portends the same for sporting men or women.

Diamonds are omens of good luck, unless stolen from the bodies of dead persons, when they foretell that your own unfaithfulness will be discovered by your friends.

Dice.

To dream of dice, is indicative of unfortunate speculations, and consequent misery and despair. It also foretells contagious sickness.

For a girl to dream that she sees her lover throwing dice, indicates his unworthiness.

Dictionary.

To dream that you are referring to a dictionary, signifies you will depend too much upon the opinion and suggestions of others for the clear management of your own affairs, which could be done with proper dispatch if your own will was given play.

Difficulty.

This dream signifies temporary embarrassment for business men of all classes, including soldiers and writers. But to extricate yourself from difficulties, foretells your prosperity.

For a woman to dream of being in difficulties, denotes

that she is threatened with ill health or enemies. For lovers, this is a dream of contrariety, denoting pleasant courtship.

Digging.

To dream of digging, denotes that you will never be in want, but life will be an uphill affair.

To dig a hole and find any glittering substance, denotes a favorable turn in fortune; but to dig and open up a vast area of hollow mist, you will be harrassed with real misfortunes and be filled with gloomy forebodings. Water filling the hole that you dig, denotes that in spite of your most strenuous efforts things will not bend to your will.

Dinner.

To dream that you eat your dinner alone, denotes that you will often have cause to think seriously of the necessaries of life.

For a young woman to dream of taking dinner with her lover, is indicative of a lovers' quarrel or a rupture, unless the affair is one of harmonious pleasure, when the reverse may be expected.

To be one of many invited guests at a dinner, denotes that you will enjoy the hospitalities of those who are able to extend to you many pleasant courtesies.

Dirt.

To dream of seeing freshly stirred dirt around flowers or trees, denotes thrift and healthful conditions abound for the dreamer.

To see your clothes soiled with unclean dirt, you will be forced to save yourself from contagious diseases by leaving your home or submitting to the strictures of the law.

To dream that some one throws dirt upon you, denotes that enemies will try to injure your character.

Disaster.

To dream of being in any disaster from public conveyance, you are in danger of losing property or of being maimed from some malarious disease.

For a young woman to dream of a disaster in which she is a participant, foretells that she will mourn the loss of her lover by death or desertion.

To dream of a disaster at sea, denotes unhappiness to sailors and loss of their gains. To others, it signifies loss by death; but if you dream that you are rescued, you will be placed in trying situations, but will come out unscathed.

To dream of a railway wreck in which you are not a participant, you will eventually be interested in some accident because of some relative or friend being hurt, or you will have trouble of a business character.

Disease.

To dream that you are diseased, denotes a slight attack of illness, or of unpleasant dealings with a relative.

For a young woman to dream that she is incurably diseased, denotes that she will be likely to lead a life of single blessedness.

Disgrace.

To be worried in your dream over the disgraceful conduct of children or friends, will bring you unsatisfying hopes, and worries will harass you. To be in disgrace yourself, denotes that you will hold morality at a low rate, and you are in danger of lowering your reputation for uprightness. Enemies are also shadowing you.

Dish.*

To dream of handling dishes, denotes good fortune; but

*See Crockery

if from any cause they should be broken, this signifies that fortune will be short-lived for you.

To see shelves of polished dishes, denotes success in marriage.

To dream of dishes, is prognostic of coming success and gain, and you will be able to fully appreciate your good luck. Soiled dishes, represent dissatisfaction and an unpromising future.

Disinherited.

To dream that you are disinherited, warns you to look well to your business and social standing.

For a young man to dream of losing his inheritance by disobedience, warns him that he will find favor in the eyes of his parents by contracting a suitable marriage. For a woman, this dream is a warning to be careful of her conduct, lest she meet with unfavorable fortune.

Dispute.

To dream of holding disputes over trifles, indicates bad health and unfairness in judging others.

To dream of disputing with learned people, shows that you have some latent ability, but are a little sluggish in developing it.

Distaff.

To dream of a distaff, denotes frugality, with pleasant surroundings. It also signifies that a devotional spirit will be cultivated by you.

Distance.

To dream of being a long way from your residence, denotes that you will make a journey soon in which you may meet many strangers who will be instrumental in changing life from good to bad.

To dream of friends at a distance, denotes slight disappointments.

To dream of distance, signifies travel and a long journey. To see men plowing with oxen at a distance, across broad fields, denotes advancing prosperity and honor. For a man to see strange women in the twilight, at a distance, and throwing kisses to him, foretells that he will enter into an engagement with a new acquaintance, which will result in unhappy exposures.

Ditch.

To dream of falling in a ditch, denotes degradation and personal loss; but if you jump over it, you will live down any suspicion of wrong-doing.

Diving.

To dream of diving in clear water, denotes a favorable termination of some embarrassment. If the water is muddy, you will suffer anxiety at the turn your affairs seem to be taking.

To see others diving, indicates pleasant companions. For lovers to dream of diving, denotes the consummation of happy dreams and passionate love.

Dividend.

To dream of dividends, augments successful speculations or prosperous harvests. To fail in securing hoped-for dividends, proclaims failure in management or love affairs.

Divining Rods.

To see a divining rod in your dreams, foretells ill luck will dissatisfy you with present surroundings.

Divorce.

To dream of being divorced, denotes that you are not satisfied with your companion, and should cultivate a more congenial atmosphere in the home life. It is a dream of warning.

For women to dream of divorce, denotes that a single life may be theirs through the infidelity of lovers.

Docks.

To dream of being on docks, denotes that you are about to make an unpropitious journey. Accidents will threaten you. If you are there, wandering alone, and darkness overtakes you, you will meet with deadly enemies, but if the sun be shining, you will escape threatening dangers.

Doctor.

This is a most auspicious dream, denoting good health and general prosperity, if you meet him socially, for you will not then spend your money for his services. If you be young and engaged to marry him, then this dream warns you of deceit.

To dream of a doctor professionally, signifies discouraging illness and disagreeable differences between members of a family.

To dream that a doctor makes an incision in your flesh, trying to discover blood, but failing in his efforts, denotes that you will be tormented and injured by some evil person, who may try to make you pay out money for his debts. If he finds blood, you will be the loser in some transaction.

Dogs.

To dream of a vicious dog, denotes enemies and unalterable misfortune. To dream that a dog fondles you, indicates great gain and constant friends.

To dream of owning a dog with fine qualities, denotes that you will be possessed of solid wealth.

To dream that a blood-hound is tracking you, you are likely to fall into some temptation, in which there is much danger of your downfall.

To dream of small dogs, indicates that your thoughts and chief pleasures are of a frivolous order.

To dream of dogs biting you, foretells for you a quarrelsome companion either in marriage or business.

Lean, filthy dogs, indicate failure in business, also sickness among children.

To dream of a dog-show, is indicative of many and varied favors from fortune.

To hear the barking of dogs, foretells news of a depressing nature. Difficulties are more than likely to follow. To see dogs on the chase of foxes, and other large game, denotes an unusual briskness in all affairs.

To see fancy pet dogs, signifies a love of show, and that the owner is selfish and narrow. For a young woman, this dream foretells a fop for a sweetheart.

To feel much fright upon seeing a large mastiff, denotes that you will experience inconvenience because of efforts to rise above mediocrity. If a woman dreams this, she will marry a wise and humane man.

To hear the growling and snarling of dogs, indicates that you are at the mercy of designing people, and you will be afflicted with unpleasant home surroundings.

To hear the lonely baying of a dog, foretells a death or a long separation from friends.

To hear dogs growling and fighting, portends that you will be overcome by your enemies, and your life will be filled with depression.

To see dogs and cats seemingly on friendly terms, and suddenly turning on each other, showing their teeth and a general fight ensuing, you will meet with disaster in love and worldly pursuits, unless you succeed in quelling the row.

If you dream of a friendly white dog approaching you, it portends for you a victorious engagement whether in business or love. For a woman, this is an omen of an early marriage.

To dream of a many-headed dog, you are trying to maintain too many branches of business at one time. Success always comes with concentration of energies. A man who wishes to succeed in anything should be warned by this dream.

To dream of a mad dog, your most strenuous efforts will not bring desired results, and fatal disease may be clutching at your vitals. If a mad dog succeeds in biting you, it is a sign that you or some loved one is on the verge of insanity, and a deplorable tragedy may occur.

To dream of traveling alone, with a dog following you, foretells staunch friends and successful undertakings.

To dream of dogs swimming, indicates for you an easy stretch to happiness and fortune.

To dream that a dog kills a cat in your presence, is significant of profitable dealings and some unexpected pleasure.

For a dog to kill a snake in your presence, is an omen of good luck.

Dolphin.

To dream of a dolphin, indicates your liability to come under a new government. It is not a very good dream.

Dome.

To dream that you are in the dome of a building, viewing a strange landscape, signifies a favorable change in your life. You will occupy honorable places among strangers.

To behold a dome from a distance, portends that you will never reach the height of your ambition, and if you are in love, the object of your desires will scorn your attention.

Dominoes.

To dream of playing at dominoes, and lose, you will be affronted by a friend, and much uneasiness for your safety will be entertained by your people, as you will not be discreet in your affairs with women or other matters that engage your attention.

If you are the winner of the game, it foretells that you will be much courted and admired by certain dissolute characters, bringing you selfish pleasures, but much distress to your relatives.

Donkey.

To dream of a donkey braying in your face, denotes that you are about to be publicly insulted by a lewd and unscrupulous person.

To hear the distant braying filling space with melancholy, you will receive wealth and release from unpleasant bonds by the death of some person close to you.

If you see yourself riding on a donkey, you will visit foreign lands and make many explorations into places difficult of passage.

To see others riding donkeys, denotes a meagre inheritance for them and a toiling life.

To dream of seeing many of the old patriarchs traveling on donkeys, shows that the influence of Christians will be thrown against you in your selfish wantonness, causing you to ponder over the rights and duties of man to man.

To drive a donkey, signifies that all your energies and pluck will be brought into play against a desperate effort on the part of enemies to overthrow you. If you are in love, evil women will cause you trouble.

If you are kicked by this little animal, it shows that you are carrying on illicit connections, from which you will suffer much anxiety from fear of betrayal.

If you lead one by a halter, you will be master of every

situation, and lead women into your way of seeing things by flattery.

To see children riding and driving donkeys, signifies health and obedience for them.

To fall or be thrown from one, denotes ill luck and disappointment in secular affairs. Lovers will quarrel and separate.

To see one dead, denotes satiated appetites, resulting from licentious excesses.

To dream of drinking the milk of a donkey, denotes that whimsical desires will be gratified, even to the displacement of important duties.

If you see in your dreams a strange donkey among your stock, or on your premises, you will inherit some valuable effects.

To dream of coming into the possession of a donkey by present, or buying, you will attain to enviable heights in the business or social world, and if single, will contract a congenial marriage.

To dream of a white donkey, denotes an assured and lasting fortune, which will enable you to pursue the pleasures or studies that lie nearest your heart. For a woman, it signals entrance into that society for which she has long entertained the most ardent desire. Woman has in her composition those qualities, docility and stubbornness, which tallies with the same qualities in the donkey; both being supplied from the same storehouse, mother Nature; and consequently, they would naturally maintain an affinity, and the ugliest phase of the donkey in her dreams are nothing but woman's nature being sounded for her warning, or *vice versa* when pleasure is just before her.

Doomsday.

To dream that you are living on, and looking forward

to seeing doomsday, is a warning for you to give substantial and material affairs close attention, or you will find that the artful and scheming friends you are entertaining will have possession of what they desire from you, which is your wealth, and not your sentimentality.

To a young woman, this dream encourages her to throw aside the attention of men above her in station and accept the love of an honest and deserving man near her.

Door.

To dream of entering a door, denotes slander, and enemies from whom you are trying in vain to escape. This is the same of any door, except the door of your childhood home. If it is this door you dream of entering, your days will be filled with plenty and congeniality.

To dream of entering a door at night through the rain, denotes, to women, unpardonable escapades; to a man, it is significant of a drawing on his resources by unwarranted vice, and also foretells assignations.

To see others go through a doorway, denotes unsuccessful attempts to get your affairs into a paying condition. It also means changes to farmers and the political world. To an author, it foretells that the reading public will reprove his way of stating facts by refusing to read his later works.

To dream that you attempt to close a door, and it falls from its hinges, injuring some one, denotes that malignant evil threatens your friend through your unintentionally wrong advice. If you see another attempt to lock a door, and it falls from its hinges, you will have knowledge of some friend's misfortune and be powerless to aid him.

Door Bell.

To dream you hear or ring a door bell, foretells unexpected tidings, or a hasty summons to business, or the bed-side of a sick relative.

Doves.

Dreaming of doves mating and building their nests, indicates peacefulness of the world and joyous homes where children render obedience, and mercy is extended to all.

To hear the lonely, mournful voice of a dove, portends sorrow and disappointment through the death of one to whom you looked for aid. Often it portends the death of a father.

To see a dead dove, is ominous of a separation of husband and wife, either through death or infidelity.

To see white doves, denotes bountiful harvests and the utmost confidence in the loyalty of friends.

To dream of seeing a flock of white doves, denotes peaceful, innocent pleasures, and fortunate developments in the future.

If one brings you a letter, tidings of a pleasant nature from absent friends is intimated, also a lovers' reconciliation is denoted.

If the dove seems exhausted, a note of sadness will pervade the reconciliation, or a sad touch may be given the pleasant tidings by mention of an invalid friend; if of business, a slight drop may follow. If the letter bears the message that you are doomed, it foretells that a desperate illness, either your own or of a relative, may cause you financial misfortune.

Dowry.

To dream that you fail to receive a dowry, signifies penury and a cold world to depend on for a living. If you receive it, your expectations for the day will be fulfilled. The opposite may be expected if the dream is superinduced by the previous action of the waking mind.

Dragon.*

To dream of a dragon, denotes that you allow yourself to be governed by your passions, and that you are likely to place yourself in the power of your enemies through those outbursts of sardonic tendencies. You should be warned by this dream to cultivate self-control.

Drama.

To see a drama, signifies pleasant reunions with distant friends.

To be bored with the performance of a drama, you will be forced to accept an uncongenial companion at some entertainment or secret affair.

To write one, portends that you will be plunged into distress and debt, to be extricated as if by a miracle.

Dram-drinking.

To be given to dram-drinking in your dreams, omens ill-natured rivalry and contention for small possession. To think you have quit dram-drinking, or find that others have done so, shows that you will rise above present estate and rejoice in prosperity.

Draw-knife.

To see or use a draw-knife, portends unfulfilled hopes or desires.

Some fair prospect will loom before you, only to go down in mistake and disappointment.

Dressing.

To think you are having trouble in dressing, while dreaming, means some evil persons will worry and detain you from places of amusement.

---

*See Devil.

If you can't get dressed in time for a train, you will have many annoyances through the carelessness of others. You should depend on your own efforts as far as possible, after these dreams, if you would secure contentment and full success.

Drinking.*

For a woman to dream of hilarious drinking, denotes that she is engaging in affairs which may work to her discredit, though she may now find much pleasure in the same. If she dreams that she fails to drink clear water, though she uses her best efforts to do so, she will fail to enjoy some pleasure that is insinuatingly offered her.

Driving.†

To dream of driving a carriage, signifies unjust criticism of your seeming extravagance. You will be compelled to do things which appear undignified.

To dream of driving a public cab, denotes menial labor, with little chance for advancement. If it is a wagon, you will remain in poverty and unfortunate circumstances for some time. If you are driven in these conveyances by others, you will profit by superior knowledge of the world, and will always find some path through difficulties. If you are a man, you will, in affairs with women, drive your wishes to a speedy consummation. If a woman, you will hold men's hearts at low value after succeeding in getting a hold on them.

Dromedary.

To dream of a dromedary, denotes that you will be the recipient of unexpected beneficence, and will wear your new honors with dignity; you will dispense charity with a

*See Water.
†See Cab or Carriage.

gracious hand. To lovers, this dream foretells congenial dispositions.

Dropsy.

To dream of being afflicted with the dropsy, denotes illness for a time, but from which you will recover with renewed vigor. To see others thus afflicted, denotes that you will hear from the absent shortly, and have tidings of their good health.

Drouth.

This is an evil dream, denoting warring disputes between nations, and much bloodshed therefrom. Shipwrecks and land disasters will occur, and families will quarrel and separate; sickness will work damage also. Your affairs will go awry, as well.

Drought.

To dream of drowning, denotes loss of property and life; but if you are rescued, you will rise from your present position to one of wealth and honor.

To see others drowning, and you go to their relief, signifies that you will aid your friend to high places, and will bring deserved happiness to yourself.

For a young woman to see her sweetheart drowned, denotes her bereavement by death.

Drum.

To hear the muffled beating of a drum, denotes that some absent friend is in distress and calls on you for aid.

To see a drum, foretells amiability of character and a great aversion to quarrels and dissensions. It is an omen of prosperity to the sailor, the farmer and the tradesman alike.

Drunk.

This is an unfavorable dream if you are drunk on heavy liquors, indicating profligacy and loss of employment. You will be disgraced by stooping to forgery or theft.

If drunk on wine, you will be fortunate in trade and love-making, and will scale exalted heights in literary pursuits. This dream is always the bearer of æsthetic experiences.

To see others in a drunken condition, foretells for you, and probably others, unhappy states.

Drunkenness in all forms is unreliable as a good dream. All classes are warned by this dream to shift their thoughts into more healthful channels.

Ducks.

To dream of seeing wild ducks on a clear stream of water, signifies fortunate journeys, perhaps across the sea. White ducks around a farm, indicate thrift and a fine harvest.

To hunt ducks, denotes displacement in employment in the carrying out of plans.

To see them shot, signifies that enemies are meddling with your private affairs.

To see them flying, foretells a brighter future for you. It also denotes marriage, and children in the new home.

Duet.

To dream of hearing a duet played, denotes a peaceful and even existence for lovers. No quarrels, as is customary in this sort of thing. Business people carry on a mild rivalry. To musical people, this denotes competition and wrangling for superiority.

To hear a duet sung, is unpleasant tidings from the

absent; but this will not last, as some new pleasure will displace the unpleasantness.

Dulcimer.

To dream of a dulcimer, denotes that the highest wishes in life will be attained by exalted qualities of mind. To women, this is significant of a life free from those petty jealousies which usually make women unhappy.

Dumb.

To dream of being dumb, indicates your inability to persuade others into your mode of thinking, and using them for your profit by your glibness of tongue. To the dumb, it denotes false friends.

Dun.

To dream that you receive a dun, warns you to look after your affairs and correct all tendency towards neglect of business and love.

Dungeon.

To dream of being in a dungeon, foretells for you struggles with the vital affairs of life but by wise dealing you will disenthrall yourself of obstacles and the designs of enemies. For a woman this is a dark foreboding; by her wilful indiscretion she will lose her position among honorable people.

To see a dungeon lighted up, portends that you are threatened with entanglements of which your better judgment warns you.

Dunghill.

To dream of a dunghill, you will see profits coming in through the most unexpected sources. To the farmer this is a lucky dream, indicating fine seasons and abundant products from soil and stock. For a young woman,

It denotes that she will unknowingly marry a man of great wealth.

Dusk.

This is a dream of sadness; it portends an early decline and unrequited hopes. Dark outlook for trade and pursuits of any nature is prolonged by this dream.

Dust.

To dream of dust covering you, denotes that you will be slightly injured in business by the failure of others. For a young woman, this denotes that she will be set aside by her lover for a newer flame. If you free yourself of the dust by using judicious measures, you will clear up the loss.

Dwarf.

This is a very favorable dream. If the dwarf is well formed and pleasing in appearance, it omens you will never be dwarfed in mind or stature. Health and good constitution will admit of your engaging in many profitable pursuits both of mind and body.

To see your friends dwarfed, denotes their health, and you will have many pleasures through them.

Ugly and hideous dwarfs, always forebodes distressing states.

Dye.

To see the dyeing of cloth or garments in process, your bad or good luck depends on the color. Blues, reds and gold, indicate prosperity; black and white, indicate sorrow in all forms.

Dying.*

To dream of dying, foretells that you are threatened

---

*See Death.

with evil from a source that has contributed to your former advancement and enjoyment.

To see others dying, forebodes general ill luck to you and to your friends.

To dream that you are going to die, denotes that unfortunate inattention to your affairs will depreciate their value. Illness threatens to damage you also.

To see animals in the throes of death, denotes escape from evil influences if the animal be wild or savage.

It is an unlucky dream to see domestic animals dying or in agony.

[As these events of good or ill approach you they naturally assume these forms of agonizing death, to impress you more fully with the joyfulness or the gravity of the situation you are about to enter on awakening to material responsibilities, to aid you in the mastery of self which is essential to meeting all conditions with calmness and determination.]

Dynamite.

To see dynamite in a dream, is a sign of approaching change and the expanding of one's affairs. To be frightened by it, indicates that a secret enemy is at work against you, and if you are not careful of your conduct he will disclose himself at an unexpected and helpless moment.

Dynamo.

To dream of a dynamo, omens successful enterprises if attention is shown to details of business. One out of repair, shows you are nearing enemies who will involve you in trouble.

E.

"And he said, hear now my words, if there be a Prophet among you, I the Lord will make myself known unto him in a vision, and will speak unto him in a dream."—Numbers xii., 6.

Eagles.

To see one soaring above you, denotes lofty ambitions which you will struggle fiercely to realize, nevertheless you will gain your desires.

To see one perched on distant heights, denotes that you will possess fame, wealth and the highest position attainable in your country.

To see young eagles in their eyrie, signifies your association with people of high standing, and that you will profit from wise counsel from them. You will in time come into a rich legacy.

To dream that you kill an eagle, portends that no obstacles whatever would be allowed to stand before you and the utmost heights of your ambition. You will overcome your enemies and be possessed of untold wealth.

Eating the flesh of one, denotes the possession of a powerful will that would not turn aside in ambitious struggles even for death. You will come immediately into rich possessions.

To see a dead eagle killed by others than yourself, signifies high rank and fortune will be wrested from you ruthlessly.

To ride on an eagle's back, denotes that you will make a long voyage into almost unexplored countries in your search for knowledge and wealth which you will eventually gain.

Ears.

To dream of seeing ears, an evil and designing person

is keeping watch over your conversation to work you harm.

Earrings.

To see earrings in dreams, omens good news and interesting work is before you. To see them broken, indicates that gossip of a low order will be directed against you.

Earthquake.

To see or feel the earthquake in your dream, denotes business failure and much distress caused from turmoils and wars between nations.

Earwig.

To dream that you see an earwig or have one in your ear, denotes that you will have unpleasant news affecting your business or family relations.

Eating.*

To dream of eating alone, signifies loss and melancholy spirits. To eat with others, denotes personal gain, cheerful environments and prosperous undertakings.

If your daughter carries away the platter of meat before you are done eating, it foretells that you will have trouble and vexation from those beneath you or dependent upon you. The same would apply to a waiter or waitress.

Ebony.

If you dream of ebony furniture or other articles of ebony, you will have many distressing disputes and quarrels in your home.

Echo.

To dream of an echo, portends that distressful times

---

*See other subjects similar.

are upon you. Your sickness may lose you your employment, and friends will desert you in time of need.

Eclipse.

To dream of the eclipse of the sun, denotes temporary failure in business and other secular affairs, also disturbances in families.

The eclipse of the moon, portends contagious disease or death.

Ecstasy.

To dream of feeling ecstasy, denotes you will enjoy a visit from a long-absent friend. If you experience ecstasy in disturbing dreams you will be subjected to sorrow and disappointment.

Education.

To dream that you are anxious to obtain an education, shows that whatever your circumstances in life may be there will be a keen desire for knowledge on your part, which will place you on a higher plane than your associates. Fortune will also be more lenient to you.

To dream that you are in places of learning, foretells for you many influential friends.

Eel.

To dream of an eel is good if you can maintain your grip on him. Otherwise fortune will be fleeting.

To see an eel in clear water, denotes, for a woman, new but evanescent pleasures.

To see a dead eel, signifies that you will overcome your most maliciously inclined enemies. To lovers, the dream denotes an end to long and hazardous courtship by marriage.

Eggs.

To dream of finding a nest of eggs, denotes wealth of

a substantial character, happiness among the married and many children. This dream signifies many and varied love affairs to women.

To eat eggs, denotes that unusual disturbances threaten you in your home.

To see broken eggs and they are fresh, fortune is ready to shower upon you her richest gifts. A lofty spirit and high regard for justice will make you beloved by the world.

To dream of rotten eggs, denotes loss of property and degradation.

To see a crate of eggs, denotes that you will engage in profitable speculations.

To dream of being spattered with eggs, denotes that you will sport riches of doubtful origin.

To see bird eggs, signifies legacies from distant relations, or gain from an unexpected rise in staple products.

Elbows.

To see elbows in a dream, signifies that arduous labors will devolve upon you, and for which you will receive small reimbursements.

For a young woman, this is a prognostic of favorable opportunities to make a reasonably wealthy marriage. If the elbows are soiled, she will lose a good chance of securing a home by marriage.

Elderberries.

To dream of seeing elderberries on bushes with their foliage, denotes domestic bliss and an agreeable country home with resources for travel and other pleasures.

Elderberries is generally a good dream.

Election.

To dream that you are at an election, foretells you will

214

engage in some controversy which will prove detrimental to your social or financial standing.

Electricity.

To dream of electricity, denotes there will be sudden changes about you, which will not afford you either advancement or pleasure. If you are shocked by it you will face a deplorable danger.

To see live electrical wire, foretells that enemies will disturb your plans, which have given you much anxiety in forming. To dream that you can send a package or yourself out over a wire with the same rapidity that a message can be sent, denotes you will finally overcome obstacles and be able to use your enemies' plans to advance yourself.

Elephant.

To dream of riding an elephant, denotes that you will possess wealth of the most solid character, and honors which you will wear with dignity. You will rule absolutely in all lines of your business affairs and your word will be law in the home.

To see many elephants, denotes tremendous prosperity. One lone elephant, signifies you will live in a small but solid way.

To dream of feeding one, denotes that you will elevate yourself in your community by your kindness to those occupying places below you.

Elevator.

To dream of ascending in an elevator, denotes you will swiftly rise to position and wealth, but if you descend in one your misfortunes will crush and discourage you. If you see one go down and think you are left, you will narrowly escape disappointment in some undertaking. To see one standing, foretells threatened danger.

Elixir of Life.

To dream of the elixir of life, denotes that there will come into your environments new pleasures and new possibilities.

Elopement.

To dream of eloping is unfavorable. To the married, it denotes that you hold places which you are unworthy to fill, and if your ways are not rectified your reputation will be at stake. To the unmarried, it foretells disappointments in love and the unfaithfulness of men.

To dream that your lover has eloped with some one else, denotes his or her unfaithfulness.

To dream of your friend eloping with one whom you do not approve, denotes that you will soon hear of them contracting a disagreeable marriage.

Eloquent.

If you think you are eloquent of speech in your dreams, there will be pleasant news for you concerning one in whose interest you are working.

To fail in impressing others with your eloquence, there will be much disorder in your affairs.

Embalming.

To see embalming in process, foretells altered positions in social life and threatened poverty. To dream that you are looking at yourself embalmed, omens unfortunate friendships for you, which will force you into lower classes than you are accustomed to move in.

Embankment.

To dream that you drive along an embankment, foretells you will be threatened with trouble and unhappiness. If you continue your drive without unpleasant incidents arising, you will succeed in turning these fore-

216

bodings to useful account in your advancement. To ride on horseback along one, denotes you will fearlessly meet and overcome all obstacles in your way to wealth and happiness. To walk along one, you will have a weary struggle for elevation, but will finally reap a successful reward.

Embarrassment.*

Embrace.

To dream of embracing your husband or wife, as the case may be, in a sorrowing or indifferent way, denotes that you will have dissensions and accusations in your family, also that sickness is threatened.

To embrace relatives, signifies their sickness and unhappiness.

For lovers to dream of embracing, foretells quarrels and disagreements arising from infidelity. If these dreams take place under auspicious conditions, the reverse may be expected.

If you embrace a stranger, it signifies that you will have an unwelcome guest.

Embroidery.

If a woman dreams of embroidering, she will be admired for her tact and ability to make the best of everything that comes her way. For a married man to see embroidery, signifies a new member in his household, For a lover, this denotes a wise and economical wife.

Emerald.

To dream of an emerald, you will inherit property concerning which there will be some trouble with others.

For a lover to see an emerald or emeralds on the per-

*See Difficulty.

...or his affianced, warns him that he is about to be discarded for some wealthier suitor.

To dream that you buy an emerald, signifies unfortunate dealings.

Emperor.

To dream of going abroad and meeting the emperor of a nation in your travels, denotes that you will make a long journey, which will bring neither pleasure nor much knowledge.

Employee.

To see one of your employees denotes crosses and disturbances if he assumes a disagreeable or offensive attitude. If he is pleasant and has communications of interest, you will find no cause for evil or embarrassing conditions upon waking.

Employment.

This is not an auspicious dream. It implies depression in business circles and loss of employment to wage earners. It also denotes bodily illness.

To dream of being out of work, denotes that you will have no fear, as you are always sought out for your conscientious fulfilment of contracts, which make you a desired help.

Giving employment to others, indicates loss for yourself. All dreams of this nature may be interpreted as the above.

Empress.

To dream of an empress, denotes that you will be exalted to high honors, but you will let pride make you very unpopular.

To dream of an empress and an emperor is not particularly bad, but brings one no substantial good.

Enchantment.

To dream of being under the spell of enchantment, denotes that if you are not careful you will be exposed to some evil in the form of pleasure. The young should heed the benevolent advice of their elders.

To resist enchantment, foretells that you will be much sought after for your wise counsels and your liberality.

To dream of trying to enchant others, portends that you will fall into evil.

Encyclopedia.

To dream of seeing or searching through encyclopedias, portends that you will secure literary ability to the losing of prosperity and comfort.

Enemy.

To dream that you overcome enemies, denotes that you will surmount all difficulties in business, and enjoy the greatest prosperity.

If you are defamed by your enemies, it denotes that you will be threatened with failures in your work. You will be wise to use the utmost caution in proceeding in affairs of any moment.

To overcome your enemies in any form, signifies your gain. For them to get the better of you is ominous of adverse fortunes. This dream may be literal.

Engagement.

To dream of a business engagement, denotes dulness and worries in trade.

For young people to dream that they are engaged, denotes that they will not be much admired.

To dream of breaking an engagement, denotes a hasty, and an unwise action in some important matter or disappointments may follow.

Engine.

To dream of an engine, denotes you will encounter grave difficulties and journeys, but you will have substantial friends to uphold you.

Disabled engines stand for misfortune and loss of relatives.

Engineer.

To see an engineer, forebodes weary journeys but joyful reunions.

English.

To dream, if you are a foreigner, of meeting English people, denotes that you will have to suffer through the selfish designs of others.

Entertainment.

To dream of an entertainment where there is music and dancing, you will have pleasant tidings of the absent, and enjoy health and prosperity. To the young, this is a dream of many and varied pleasures and the high regard of friends.

Entrails.*

To dream of the human entrails, denotes horrible misery and despair, shutting out all hope of happiness.

To dream of the entrails of a wild beast, signifies the overthrow of your mortal enemy.

To tear the entrails of another, signifies cruel persecutions to further your own interests.

To dream of your own entrails, the deepest despair will overwhelm you.

To dream of the entrails of your own child, denotes that the child's, or your own, dissolution is at hand.

------
*See Intestines.

Envelope.

Envelopes seen in a dream, omens news of a sorrowful cast.

Envy.

To dream that you entertain envy for others, denotes that you will make warm friends by your unselfish deference to the wishes of others.

If you dream of being envied by others, it denotes that you will suffer some inconvenience from friends over-anxious to please you.

Epaulet.

For a man to dream of wearing epaulets, if he is a soldier, denotes his disfavor for a time, but he will finally wear honors.

For a woman to dream that she is introduced to a person wearing epaulets, denotes that she will form unwise attachments, very likely to result in scandal.

Epicure.

To dream of sitting at the table with an epicure, denotes that you will enjoy some fine distinction, but you will be surrounded by people of selfish principles.

To dream that you an epicure yourself, you will cultivate your mind, body and taste to the highest polish.

For a woman to dream of trying to satisfy an epicure, signifies that she will have a distinguished husband, but to her he will be a tyrant.

Epidemic.

To dream of an epidemic, signifies prostration of mental faculties and worry from distasteful tasks. Contagion among relatives or friends is foretold by dreams of this nature.

Ermine.

To dream that you wear this beautiful and costly raiment, denotes exaltation, lofty character and wealth forming a barrier to want and misery.

To see others thus clothed, you will be associated with wealthy people, polished in literature and art.

For a lover to see his sweetheart clothed in ermine, is an omen of purity and faithfulness. If the ermine is soiled, the reverse is indicated.

Errands.

To go on errands in your dreams, means congenial associations and mutual agreement in the home circle. For a young woman to send some person on an errand, denotes she will lose her lover by her indifference to meet his wishes.

Escape.

To dream of escape from injury or accidents, is usually favorable.

If you escape from some place of confinement, it signifies your rise in the world from close application to business.

To escape from any contagion, denotes your good health and prosperity. If you try to escape and fail, you will suffer from the design of enemies, who will slander and defraud you.

Estate.

To dream that you come into the ownership of a vast estate, denotes that you will receive a legacy at some distant day, but quite different to your expectations. For a young woman, this dream portends that her inheritance will be of a disappointing nature. She will have to live quite frugally, as her inheritance will be a poor man and a house full of children.

Europe.

To dream of traveling in Europe, foretells that you will soon go on a long journey, which will avail you in the knowledge you gain of the manners and customs of foreign people. You will also be enabled to forward your financial standing. For a young woman to feel that she is disappointed with the sights of Europe, omens her inability to appreciate chances for her elevation. She will be likely to disappoint her friends or lover.

Eve.

To dream of this ancient character, denotes your hesitancy to accept this ancient story as authentic, and you may encounter opposition in business and social circles because of this doubt.

For a young woman to dream that she impersonates Eve, warns her to be careful. She may be wiser than her ancient relative, but the Evil One still has powerful agents in the disguise of a handsome man. Keep your eye on innocent Eve, young man. That apple tree still bears fruit, and you may be persuaded, unwittingly, to share the wealth of its products.

Evening.

To dream that evening is about you, denotes unrealized hopes, and you will make unfortunate ventures.

To see stars shining out clear, denotes present distress, but brighter fortune is behind your trouble.

For lovers to walk in the evening, denotes separation by the death of one.

Evergreen.

This dream denotes boundless resources of wealth, happiness and learning. It is a free presentiment of prosperity to all classes.

223

Exchange.

Exchange, denotes profitable dealings in all classes of business. For a young woman to dream that she is exchanging sweethearts with her friend, indicates that she will do well to heed this as advice, as she would be happier with another.

Execution.

To dream of seeing an execution, signifies that you will suffer some misfortune from the carelessness of others.

To dream that you are about to be executed, and some miraculous intervention occurs, denotes that you will overthrow enemies and succeed in gaining wealth.

Exile.*

For a woman to dream that she is exiled, denotes that she will have to make a journey which will interfere with some engagement or pleasure.

Explosion.

To dream of explosions, portends that disapproving actions of those connected with you will cause you transient displeasure and loss, and that business will also displease you. To think your face, or the face of others, is blackened or mutilated, signifies you will be accused of indiscretion which will be unjust, though circumstances may convict you.

To see the air filled with smoke and débris, denotes unusual dissatisfaction in business circles and much social antagonism.

To think you are enveloped in the flames, or are up in the air where you have been blown by an explosion, foretells that unworthy friends will infringe on your rights and will abuse your confidence. Young women should

*See Banishment.

be careful of associates of the opposite sex after a dream of this character.

Eye.

To dream of seeing an eye, warns you that watchful enemies are seeking the slightest chance to work injury to your business. This dream indicates to a lover, that a rival will usurp him if he is not careful.

To dream of brown eyes, denotes deceit and perfidy. To see blue eyes, denotes weakness in carrying out any intention. To see gray eyes, denotes a love of flattery for the owner.

To dream of losing an eye, or that the eyes are sore, denotes trouble.

To see a one-eyed man, denotes that you will be threatened with loss and trouble, beside which all others will appear insignificant.

Eyebrows.

Eyebrows, denotes that you will encounter sinister obstacles in your immediate future.

Eyeglass

To dream of seeing or wearing an eyeglass, denotes you will be afflicted with disagreeable friendships, from which you will strive vainly to disengage yourself. For a young woman to see her lover with an eyeglass on, omens disruption of love affairs.

F

"In Gideon the Lord appeared to Solomon in a dream by night."
—1st Kings iii, 5.

Fables.

To dream of reading or telling fables, denotes pleasant tasks and a literary turn of mind. To the young, it signifies romantic attachments.

To hear, or tell, religious fables, denotes that the dreamer will become very devotional.

Face.

This dream is favorable if you see happy and bright faces, but significant of trouble if they are disfigured, ugly, or frowning on you.

To a young person, an ugly face foretells lovers' quarrels; or for a lover to see the face of his sweetheart looking old, denotes separation and the breaking up of happy associations.

To see a strange and weird-looking face, denotes that enemies and misfortunes surround you.

To dream of seeing your own face, denotes unhappiness; and to the married, threats of divorce will be made.

To see your face in a mirror, denotes displeasure with yourself for not being able to carry out plans for self-advancement. You will also lose the esteem of friends.

Faggot.

If you dream of seeing a dense smoke ascending from a pile of faggots, it denotes that enemies are bearing down upon you, but if the faggots are burning brightly, you will escape from all unpleasant complications and enjoy great prosperity.

If you walk on burning faggots, you will be injured by the unwise actions of friends. If you succeed in walking on them without being burned, you will have a miraculous rise in prospects.

To dream of seeing faggots piled up to burn you at the stake, signifies that you are threatened with loss, but if you escape, you will enjoy a long and prosperous life.

Failure.

For a lover, this is sometimes of contrary significance. To dream that he fails in his suit, signifies that he only needs more masterfulness and energy in his daring, as he has already the love and esteem of his sweetheart.

(Contrary dreams are those in which the dreamer suffers fear, and not injury.)

For a young woman to dream that her life is going to be a failure, denotes that she is not applying her opportunities to good advantage.

For a business man to dream that he has made a failure, forebodes loss and bad management, which should be corrected, or failure threatens to materialize in earnest.

Fainting.

To dream of fainting, signifies illness in your family and unpleasant news of the absent.

If a young woman dreams of fainting, it denotes that she will fall into ill health and experience disappointment from her careless way of living.

Fair.

To dream of being at a fair, denotes that you will have a pleasant and profitable business and a congenial companion.

For a young woman, this dream signifies a jovial and even-tempered man for a life partner.

Fairy.

To dream of a fairy, is a favorable omen to all classes.

as it is always a scene with a beautiful face portrayed as a happy child, or woman.

Faithless.

To dream that your friends are faithless, denotes that they will hold you in worthy esteem. For a lover to dream that his sweetheart is faithless, signifies a happy marriage.

Fakir.

To dream of an Indian fakir, denotes uncommon activity and phenomenal changes in your life. Such dreams may sometimes be of gloomy import.

Falcon.

To dream of a falcon, denotes that your prosperity will make you an object of envy and malice. For a young woman, this dream denotes that she will be calumniated by a rival.

Fall.

To dream that you sustain a fall, and are much frightened, denotes that you will undergo some great struggle, but will eventually rise to honor and wealth; but if you are injured in the fall, you will encounter hardships and loss of friends.

Fame.

To dream of being famous, denotes disappointed aspirations. To dream of famous people, portends your rise from obscurity to places of honor.

Famine.

To dream of a famine, foretells that your business will be unremunerative and sickness will prove a scourge. This dream is generally bad.

If you see your enemies perishing by famine, you will be successful in competition. If dreams of famine should break in wild confusion over slumbers, tearing up all heads in anguish, filling every soul with care, hauling down Hope's banners, somber with omens of misfortune and despair, your waking grief more poignant still must grow ere you quench ambition and envy overthrow.

Famish.

To dream that you are famishing, foretells that you are meeting disheartening failure in some enterprise which you considered a promising success. To see others famishing, brings sorrow to others as well as to yourself.

Family.

To dream of one's family as harmonious and happy, is significant of health and easy circumstances; but if there is sickness or contentions, it forebodes gloom and disappointment.

Fan.

To see a fan in your dreams, denotes pleasant news and surprises are awaiting you in the near future. For a young woman to dream of fanning herself, or that some one is fanning her, gives promise of a new and pleasing acquaintances; if she loses an old fan, she will find that a warm friend is becoming interested in other women.

Farewell.

To dream of bidding farewell, is not very favorable, as you are likely to hear unpleasant news of absent friends.

For a young woman to bid her lover farewell, portends his indifference to her. If she feels no sadness in this farewell, she will soon find others to comfort her.

Farm*

To dream that you are living on a farm, denotes that you will be fortunate in all undertakings.

---

*See Estate.

To dream that you are buying a farm, denotes abundant crops to the farmer, a profitable deal of some kind to the business man, and a safe voyage to travelers and sailors.

If you are visiting a farm, it signifies pleasant associations.

Fat.*

To dream that you are getting fat, denotes that you are about to make a fortunate change in your life.

To see others fat, signifies prosperity.

Fates.

To dream of the fates, unnecessary disagreements and unhappiness is foretold. For a young woman to dream of juggling with fate, denotes she will daringly interpose herself between devoted friends or lovers.

Father.

To dream of your father, signifies that you are about to be involved in a difficulty, and you will need wise counsel if you extricate yourself therefrom.

If he is dead, it denotes that your business is pulling heavily, and you will have to use caution in conducting it.

For a young woman to dream of her dead father, portends that her lover will, or is, playing her false.

Father-in-law.

To dream of your father-in-law, denotes contentions with friends or relatives. To see him well and cheerful, foretells pleasant family relations.

Fatigue.

To feel fatigued in a dream, foretells ill health or op-

---

*See Corpulent.

pression in business. For a young woman to see others fatigued, indicates discouraging progress in health.

Favor.

To dream that you ask favors of anyone, denotes that you will enjoy abundance, and that you will not especially need anything.

To grant favors, means a loss.

Fawn.*

To dream of seeing a fawn, denotes that you will have true and upright friends.

To the young, it indicates faithfulness in love.

To dream that a person fawns on you, or cajoles you, is a warning that enemies are about you in the guise of interested friends.

Fears.

To dream that you feel fear from any cause, denotes that your future engagements will not prove so successful as was expected.

For a young woman, this dream forebodes disappointment and unfortunate love.

Feast.

To dream of a feast, foretells that pleasant surprises are being planned for you. To see disorder or misconduct at a feast, foretells quarrels or unhappiness through the negligence or sickness of some person.

To arrive late at a feast, denotes that vexing affairs will occupy you.

Feather.

To dream of seeing feathers falling around you, denotes that your burdens in life will be light and easily borne.

---

* See Deer.

To see eagle feathers, denotes that your aspirations will be realized.

To see chicken feathers, denotes small annoyances. To dream of buying or selling geese or duck feathers, denotes thrift and fortune.

To dream of black feathers, denotes disappointments and unhappy amours.

For a woman to dream of seeing ostrich and other ornamental feathers, denotes that she will advance in society, but her ways of gaining favor will not bear imitating.

February.

To dream of February, denotes continued ill health and gloom, generally. If you happen to see a bright sunshiny day in this month, you will be unexpectedly and happily surprised with some good fortune.

Feeble.

To dream of being feeble, denotes unhealthy occupation and mental worry. Seek to make a change for yourself after this dream.

Feet.

To dream of seeing your own feet, is omnious of despair. You will be overcome by the will and temper of another. To see others' feet, denotes that you will maintain your rights in a pleasant, but determined way, and win for yourself a place above the common walks of life.

To dream that you wash your feet, denotes that you will let others take advantage of you.

To dream that your feet are hurting you, portends troubles of a humiliating character, as they usually are family quarrels.

To see your feet swollen and red, you will make a sudden change in your business by separating from your family. This is an evil dream, as it usually foretells scandal and sensation.

Fence.

To dream of climbing to the top of a fence, denotes that success will crown your efforts.

To fall from a fence, signifies that you will undertake a project for which you are incapable, and you will see your efforts come to naught.

To be seated on a fence with others, and have it fall under you, denotes an accident in which some person will be badly injured.

To dream that you climb through a fence, signifies that you will use means not altogether legitimate to reach your desires.

To throw the fence down and walk into the other side, indicates that you will, by enterprise and energy, overcome the stubbornest barriers between you and success.

To see stock jumping a fence, if into your enclosure, you will receive aid from unexpected sources; if out of your lot, loss in trade and other affairs may follow.

To dream of building a fence, denotes that you are, by economy and industry, laying a foundation for future wealth. For a young woman, this dream denotes success in love affairs; or the reverse, if she dreams of the fence falling, or that she falls from it.

Ferns.

To see ferns in dreams, foretells that pleasant hours will break up gloomy forebodings. To see them withered, indicates that much and varied illness in your family connections will cause you grave unrest.

Ferry.

To wait at a ferry for a boat and see the waters swift

and muddy, you will be baffled in your highest wishes and designs by unforeseen circumstances.

To cross a ferry while the water is calm and clear, you will be very lucky in carrying out your plans, and fortune will crown you.

Festival

To dream of being at a festival, denotes indifference to the cold realities of life, and a love for those pleasures that make one old before his time. You will never want, but will be largely dependent on others.

Fever.*

To dream that you are stricken with this malady, signifies that you are worrying over trifling affairs while the best of life is slipping past you, and you should pull yourself into shape and engage in profitable work.

To dream of seeing some of your family sick with fever, denotes temporary illness for some of them.

Fiddle.†

To dream of a fiddle, foretells harmony in the home and many joyful occasions abroad.

Field.‡

To dream of dead corn or stubble fields, indicates to the dreamer dreary prospects for the future.

To see green fields, or ripe with corn or grain, denotes great abundance and happiness to all classes.

To see newly plowed fields, denotes early rise in wealth and fortunate advancement to places of honor.

To see fields freshly harrowed and ready for planting, denotes that you are soon to benefit by your endeavor and long struggles for success.

---

*See Illness.　　　†See Violin.
‡See Cornfields and Wheat.

Fiend.

To dream that you encounter a fiend, forbodes reckless living and loose morals. For a woman, this dream signifies a blackened reputation.

To dream of a fiend, warns you of attacks to be made on you by false friends. If you overcome one, you will be able to intercept the evil designs of enemies.

Fife.

To dream of hearing a fife, denotes that there will be an unexpected call on you to defend your honor, or that of some person near to you.

To dream that you play one yourself, indicates that whatever else may be said of you, your reputation will remain intact. If a woman has this dream, she will have a soldier husband.

Fight.

To dream that you engage in a fight, denotes that you will have unpleasant encounters with your business opponents, and law suits threaten you.

To see fighting, denotes that you are squandering your time and money. For women, this dream is a warning against slander and gossip.

For a young woman to see her lover fighting, is a sign of his unworthiness.

To dream that you are defeated in a fight, signifies that you will lose your right to property.

To whip your assailant, denotes that you will, by courage and perseverance, win honor and wealth in spite of opposition.

To dream that you see two men fighting with pistols, denotes many worries and perplexities, while no real loss is involved in the dream, yet but small profit is predicted and some unpleasantness is denoted.

To dream that you are on your way home and thugs attack you with razors, you will be disappointed in your business, you will be much vexed with servants, and home associations will be unpleasant.

To dream that you are fighting negroes, you will be annoyed by them or by some one of low character.

Figs.

Figs, signifies a malarious condition of the system, if you are eating them, but usually favorable to health and profit if you see them growing.

For a young woman to see figs growing, signifies that she will soon wed a wealthy and prominent man.

Figure.

To dream of figures, indicates great mental distress and wrong. You will be the loser in a big deal if not careful of your actions and conversation.

Filbert nut.

This is a favorable dream, denoting a peaceful and harmonious domestic life and profitable business ventures.

To dream of eating them, signifies to the young, delightful associations and many true friends.

File.

To dream that you see a file, signifies that you will transact some business which will prove unsatisfactory in the extreme.

To see files, to store away bills and other important papers, foretells animated discussions over subjects which bear relation to significant affairs, and which will cause you much unrest and disquiet. Unfavorable predictions for the future are also implied in this dream.

Fingers.

To dream of seeing your fingers soiled or scratched, with the blood exuding, denotes much trouble and suffering. You will despair of making your way through life.

To see beautiful hands, with white fingers, denotes that your love will be requited and that you will become renowned for your benevolence.

To dream that your fingers are cut clean off, you will lose wealth and a legacy by the intervention of enemies.

Finger-nails.

To dream of soiled finger-nails, forbodes disgrace in your family by the wild escapades of the young.

To see well-kept nails, indicates scholarly tastes and some literary attainments; also, thrift.

Fire.

Fire is favorable to the dreamer if he does not get burned. It brings continued prosperity to seamen and voyagers, as well as to those on land.

To dream of seeing your home burning, denotes a loving companion, obedient children, and careful servants.

For a business man to dream that his store is burning, and he is looking on, foretells a great rush in business and profitable results.

To dream that he is fighting fire and does not get burned, denotes that he will be much worked and worried as to the conduct of his business. To see the ruins of his store after a fire, forebodes ill luck. He will be almost ready to give up the effort of amassing a handsome fortune and a brilliant business record as useless, but some unforeseen good fortune will bear him up again.

If you dream of kindling a fire, you may expect many pleasant surprises. You will have distant friends to visit.

To see a large conflagration, denotes to sailors a profitable and safe voyage. To men of literary affairs, advancement and honors; to business people, unlimited success.

Firebrand.

To dream of a firebrand, denotes favorable fortune, if you are not burned or distressed by it.

Fire Brigade.

To dream of a fire brigade, denotes disagreement over small matters.

Fire-engine.

To see a fire-engine, denotes worry under extraordinary circumstances, but which will result in good fortune. To see one broken down, foretells accident or serious loss. For a young woman to ride on one, denotes she will engage in some unladylike and obnoxious affair.

Fireman.

To see a fireman in your dreams, signifies the constancy of your friends. For a young woman to see a fireman crippled, or meet with an accident otherwise, implies grave danger is threatening a close friend.

Fireworks.

To see fireworks, indicates enjoyment and good health. For a young woman, this dream signifies entertainments and pleasant visiting to distant places.

Firmament.*

To dream of the firmament filled with stars, denotes many crosses and almost superhuman efforts ere you

*See Illumination.

reach the pinnacle of your ambition. Beware of the snare of enemies in your work.

To see the firmament illuminated and filled with the heavenly hosts, denotes great spiritual research, but a final pulling back on Nature for sustenance and consolation. You will often be disappointed in fortune also.

To see people you know in the firmament, signifies that they are about to commit some unwise act through you, and others must be the innocent sufferers. Great disasters usually follow this dream.

Fish.

To dream that you see fish in clear-water streams, denotes that you will be favored by the rich and powerful.

Dead fish, signifies the loss of wealth and power through some dire calamity.

For a young woman to dream of seeing fish, portends that she will have a handsome and talented lover.

To dream of catching a catfish, denotes that you will be embarrassed by evil designs of enemies, but your luck and presence of mind will tide you safely over the trouble.

To wade in water, catching fish, denotes that you will possess wealth acquired by your own ability and enterprise.

To dream of fishing, denotes energy and economy; but if you do not succeed in catching any, your efforts to obtain honors and wealth will be futile.

Eating fish, denotes warm and lasting attachments.

Fisherman.

To dream of a fisherman, denotes you are nearing times of greater prosperity than you have yet known.

Fishhooks.

To dream of fishhooks, denotes that you have opportunities to make for yourself a fortune and an honorable name if you rightly apply them.

Fish Market.

To visit a fish market in your dream, brings competence and pleasure.

To see decayed fish, foretells distress will come in the guise of happiness.

Fish-net.

To dream of a fish-net, portends numerous small pleasures and gains. A torn one, represents vexatious disappointments.

Fish-pond.

To dream of a fish-pond, denotes illness through dissipation, if muddy. To see one clear and well stocked with fish, portends profitable enterprises and extensive pleasures. To see one empty, proclaims the near approach of deadly enemies.

For a young woman to fall into a clear pond, omens decided good fortune and reciprocal love. If muddy, the opposite is foretold.

Fits.

To dream of having fits, denotes that you will fall a prey to ill health and will lose employment.

To see others in this plight, denotes that you will have much unpleasantness in your circle, caused by quarrels from those under you.

Flag.

To dream of your national flag, portends victory if at war, and if at peace, prosperity.

For a woman to dream of a flag, denotes that she will be ensnared by a soldier.

To dream of foreign flags, denotes ruptures and breach of confidence between nations and friends.

To dream of being signaled by a flag, denotes that you should be careful of your health and name, as both are threatened.

Flame.*

To dream of fighting flames, foretells that you will have to put forth your best efforts and energy if you are successful in amassing wealth.

Flax.

To see flax in a dream, prosperous enterprises are denoted.

Flax Spinning.

Flax spinning, foretells you will be given to industrious and thrifty habits.

Fleas.

To dream of fleas, indicates that you will be provoked to anger and retaliation by the evil machinations of those close to you.

For a woman to dream that fleas bite her, foretells that she will be slandered by pretended friends. To see fleas on her lover, denotes inconstancy.

Fleet.

To see a large fleet moving rapidly in your dreams, denotes a hasty change in the business world. Where dulness oppressed, brisk workings of commercial wheels will go forward and some rumors of foreign wars will be heard.

Flies.

To dream of flies, denotes sickness and contagious maladies. Also that enemies surround you. To a young

---

*See Fire.

woman this dream is significant of unhappiness. If she kills or exterminates flies, she will reinstate herself in the love of her intended by her ingenuity.

Flight.

To dream of flight, signifies disgrace and unpleasant news of the absent.

For a young woman to dream of flight, indicates that she has not kept her character above reproach, and her lover will throw her aside.

To see anything fleeing from you, denotes that you will be victorious in any contention.

Floating.

To dream of floating, denotes that you will victoriously overcome obstacles which are seemingly overwhelming you. If the water is muddy your victories will not be gratifying.

Floods.*

To dream of floods destroying vast areas of country and bearing you on with its muddy débris, denotes sickness, loss in business, and the most unhappy and unsettled situation in the marriage state.

Flour.

To dream of flour, denotes a frugal but happy life. For a young woman to dream that she sees flour on herself, denotes that she will be ruled by her husband, and that her life will be full of pleasant cares.

To dream of dealing in flour, denotes hazardous speculations.

Flower.†

To dream of seeing flowers blooming in gardens, sig-

---

* See Water.   † See Bouquet.

nifies pleasure and gain, if bright-hued and fresh; white denotes sadness. Withered and dead flowers, signify disappointments and gloomy situations.

For a young woman to receive a bouquet of mixed flowers, foretells that she will have many admirers.

To see flowers blooming in barren soil without vestage of foliage, foretells you will have some grievous experience, but your energy and cheerfulness will enable you to climb through these to prominence and happiness.

> "Held in slumber's soft embrace,
> She enters realms of flowery grace,
> Where tender love and fond caress,
> Bids her awake to happiness."

Flute.

To dream of hearing notes from a flute, signifies a pleasant meeting with friends from a distance, and profitable engagements.

For a young woman to dream of playing a flute, denotes that she will fall in love because of her lover's engaging manners.

Flux.

To dream of having flux, or thinking that you are thus afflicted, denotes desperate or fatal illness will overtake you or some member of your family. To see others thsu afflicted, implies disappointment in carrying out some enterprise through the neglect of others. Inharmonious states will vex you.

Flying.

To dream of flying high through a space, denotes marital calamities.

To fly low, almost to the ground, indicates sickness and uneasy states from which the dreamer will recover.

To fly over muddy water, warns you to keep close with your private affairs, as enemies are watching to enthrall you.

To fly over broken places, signifies ill luck and gloomy surroundings. If you notice green trees and vegetation below you in flying, you will suffer temporary embarrassment, but will have a flood of prosperity upon you.

To dream of seeing the sun while flying, signifies useless worries, as your affairs will succeed despite your fears of evil.

To dream of flying through the firmament passing the moon and other planets, foretells famine, wars, and troubles of all kinds.

To dream that you fly with black wings, portends bitter disappointments. To fall while flying, signifies your downfall. If you wake while falling, you will succeed in reinstating yourself.

For a young man to dream that he is flying with white wings above green foliage, foretells advancement in business, and he will also be successful in love. If he dreams this often it is a sign of increasing prosperity and the fulfilment of desires. If the trees appear barren or dead, there will be obstacles to combat in obtaining desires. He will get along, but his work will bring small results.

For a woman to dream of flying from one city to another, and alighting on church spires, foretells she will have much to contend against in the way of false persuasions and declarations of love. She will be threatened with a disastrous season of ill health, and the death of some one near to her may follow.

For a young woman to dream that she is shot at while flying, denotes enemies will endeavor to restrain her advancement into higher spheres of usefulness and prosperity.

Flying Machine.

To dream of seeing a flying machine, foretells that you will make satisfactory progress in your future speculations. To see one failing to work, foretells gloomy returns for much disturbing and worrisome planning.

Fly-paper.

To dream of fly-paper, signifies ill health and disrupted friendships.

Fly-trap.

To see a fly-trap in a dream, is signal of malicious designing against you. To see one full of flies, denotes that small embarrassments will ward off greater ones.

Foal.

To dream of a foal, indicates new undertakings in which you will be rather fortunate.

Fog.

To dream of traveling through a dense fog, denotes much trouble and business worries. To emerge from it, foretells a weary journey, but profitable.

For a young woman to dream of being in a fog, denotes that she will be mixed up in a salacious scandal, but if she gets out of the fog she will prove her innocence and regain her social standing.

Foot-log.*

To dream of crossing a clear stream of water on a foot-log, denotes pleasant employment and profit. If the water is thick and muddy, it indicates loss and temporary disturbance. For a woman this dream indicates

*See Bridge.

245

either a quarrelsome husband, or one of mild temper and regular habits, as the water is muddy or clear.

To fall from a foot-log into clear water, signifies short widowhood terminating in an agreeable marriage. If the water is not clear, gloomy prospects.

Forest.

To dream that you find yourself in a dense forest, denotes loss in trade, unhappy home influences and quarrels among families. If you are cold and feel hungry, you will be forced to make a long journey to settle some unpleasant affair.

To see a forest of stately trees in foliage, denotes prosperity and pleasures. To literary people, this dream foretells fame and much appreciation from the public. A young lady relates the following dream and its fulfilment: "I was in a strange forest of what appeared to be cocoanut trees, with red and yellow berries growing on them. The ground was covered with blasted leaves, and I could hear them crackle under my feet as I wandered about lost. The next afternoon I received a telegram announcing the death of a dear cousin."

Forehead.

To dream of a fine and smooth forehead, denotes that you will be thought well of for your judgment and fair dealings.

An ugly forehead, denotes displeasure in your private affairs.

To pass your hand over the forehead of your child, indicates sincere praises from friends, because of some talent and goodness displayed by your children.

For a young woman to dream of kissing the forehead of her lover, signifies that he will be displeased with her for gaining notice by indiscreet conduct.

Fork.

To dream of a fork, denotes that enemies are working for your displacement. For a woman, this dream denotes unhappy domestic relations, and separation for lovers.

Form.

To see anything ill formed, denotes disappointment. To have a beautiful form, denotes favorable conditions to health and business.

Forsaking.*

For a young woman to dream of forsaking her home or friend, denotes that she will have troubles in love, as her estimate of her lover will decrease with acquaintance and association.

Fort.

To dream of defending a fort, signifies your honor and possessions will be attacked, and you will have great worry over the matter.

To dream that you attack a fort and take it, denotes victory over your worst enemy, and fortunate engagements.

Fortress.

To dream that you are confined in a fortress, denotes that enemies will succeed in placing you in an undesirable situation.

To put others in a fortress, denotes your ability to rule in business or over women.

Fortune-telling.

To dream of telling, or having your fortune told, in-

---

*See Abandoned and Lover.

dicates that you are deliberating over some vexed affair, and you should use much caution in giving consent to its consummation. For a young woman, this portends a choice between two rivals. She will be worried to find out the standing of one in business and social circles. To dream that she is engaged to a fortune-teller, denotes that she has gone through the forest and picked the proverbial stick. She should be self-reliant, or poverty will attend her marriage.

Fountain.

To dream that you see a clear fountain sparkling in the sunlight, denotes vast possessions, ecstatic delights and many pleasant journeys.

A clouded fountain, denotes the insincerity of associates and unhappy engagements and love affairs.

A dry and broken fountain, indicates death and cessation of pleasures.

For a young woman to see a sparkling fountain in the moonlight, signifies ill-advised pleasure which may result in a desertion.

Fowl.*

To dream of seeing fowls, denotes temporary worry or illness. For a woman to dream of fowls, indicates a short illness or disagreement with her friends.

Fox.

To dream of chasing a fox, denotes that you are engaging in doubtful speculations and risky love affairs.

If you see a fox slyly coming into your yard, beware of envious friendships; your reputation is being slyly assailed.

To kill a fox, denotes that you will win in every engagement.

*See Chickens.

Fraud.

To dream that you are defrauding a person, denotes that you will deceive your employer for gain, indulge in degrading pleasures, and fall into disrepute.

If you are defrauded, it signifies the useless attempt of enemies to defame you and cause you loss.

To accuse some one of defrauding you, you will be offered a place of high honor.

Freckles.

For a woman to dream that her face is freckled, denotes that many displeasing incidents will insinuate themselves into her happiness. If she sees them in a mirror, she will be in danger of losing her lover to a rival.

Friend.

To dream of friends being well and happy, denotes pleasant tidings of them, or you will soon see them or some of their relatives.

To see your friend troubled and haggard, sickness or distress is upon them.

To see your friends dark-colored, denotes unusual sickness or trouble to you or to them. To see them take the form of animals, signifies that enemies will separate you from your closest relations.

To see your friend who dresses in somber colors in flaming red, foretells that unpleasant things will transpire, causing you anxiety if not loss, and that friends will be implicated.

To dream you see a friend standing like a statue on a hill, denotes you will advance beyond present pursuits, but will retain former impressions of justice and knowledge, seeking these through every change. If the figure below be low, you will ignore your friends of former days in your future advancement. If it is on a plane or level with you, you will fail in your ambition to reach other spheres. If you seem to be going from it, you will force yourself to seek a change in spite of friendly ties or self-admonition.

To dream you see a friend with a white cloth tied over his face, denotes that you will be injured by some person who will endeavor to keep up friendly relations with you.

To dream that you are shaking hands with a person who has wronged you, and he is taking his departure and looks sad, foretells you will have differences with a close friend and alienation will perhaps follow. You are most assuredly nearing loss of some character.

Frightened.*

To dream that you are frightened at anything, denotes temporary and fleeting worries.

Frogs.

To dream of catching frogs, denotes carelessness in watching after your health, which may cause no little distress among those of your family.

To see frogs in the grass, denotes that you will have a pleasant and even-tempered friend as your confidant and counselor.

To see a bullfrog, denotes, for a woman, marriage with a wealthy widower, but there will be children with him to be cared for.

To see frogs in low marshy places, foretells trouble, but you will overcome it by the kindness of others.

To dream of eating frogs, signifies fleeting joys and very little gain from associating with some people.

To hear frogs, portends that you will go on a visit to friends, but it will in the end prove fruitless of good.

* See Affrighted.

Frost.

To dream of seeing frost on a dark gloomy morning, signifies exile to a strange country, but your wanderings will end in peace.

To see frost on a small sunlit landscape, signifies gilded pleasures from which you will be glad to turn later in life, and by your exemplary conduct will succeed in making your circle forget past escapades.

To dream that you see a friend in a frost, denotes a love affair in which your rival will be worsted. For a young woman, this dream signifies the absence of her lover and danger of his affections waning. This dream is bad for all classes in business and love.

Fruit.

To dream of seeing fruit ripening among its foliage, usually foretells to the dreamer a prosperous future. Green fruit signifies disappointed efforts or hasty action.

For a young woman to dream of eating green fruit, indicates her degradation and loss of inheritance. Eating fruit is unfavorable usually.

To buy or sell fruit, denotes much business, but not very remunerative.

To see or eat ripe fruit, signifies uncertain fortune and pleasure.

Fruit Seller.

To dream of a fruit seller, denotes you will endeavor to recover your loss too rapidly and will engage in unfortunate speculations.

Funeral.

To see a funeral, denotes an unhappy marriage and sickly offspring.

To dream of the funeral of a stranger, denotes unexpected worries. To see the funeral of your child, may denote the health of your family, but very grave disappointments may follow from a friendly source.

To attend a funeral in black, foretells an early widowhood. To dream of the funeral of any relative, denotes nervous troubles and family worries.

Furnace.

To dream of a furnace, foretells good luck if it is running. If out of repair, you will have trouble with children or hired help. To fall into one, portends some enemy will overpower you in a business struggle.

Furs.

To dream of dealing in furs, denotes prosperity and an interest in many concerns.

To be dressed in fur, signifies your safety from want and poverty.

To see fine fur, denotes honor and riches. For a young woman to dream that she is wearing costly furs, denotes that she will marry a wise man.

Future.

To dream of the future, is a prognostic of careful reckoning and avoiding of detrimental extravagance.

G.

"They answered again and said, 'Let the King tell his servants the dream and we will show the interpretation of it.'"—Dan. ii, 7.

Gaiter.

To dream of gaiters, foretells pleasant amusements and rivalries.

Gale.

To dream of being caught in a gale, signifies business losses and troubles for working people.

Gallows.

To dream of seeing a friend on the gallows of execution, foretells that desperate emergencies must be met with decision, or a great calamity will befall you.

To dream that you are on a gallows, denotes that you will suffer from the maliciousness of false friends.

For a young woman to dream that she sees her lover executed by this means, denotes that she will marry an unscrupulous and designing man.

If you rescue any one from the gallows, it portends desirable acquisitions.

To dream that you hang an enemy, denotes victory in all spheres.

Gambling-house.

To dream that you are gambling and win, signifies low associations and pleasure at the expense of others. If you lose, it foretells that your disgraceful conduct will be the undoing of one near to you.

Game.

To dream of game, either shooting or killing or by other means, denotes fortunate undertakings; but selfish motions; if you fail to take game on a hunt, it denotes bad management and loss.

Gangrene.

To dream that you see any one afflicted with gangrene, foretells the death of a parent or near relative.

Gaol.*

If you dream of being confined in a gaol, you will be prevented from carrying forward some profitable work by the intervention of envious people; but if you escape from the gaol, you will enjoy a season of favorable business.

Garbage.

To see heaps of garbage in your dreams, indicates thoughts of social scandal and unfavorable business of every character. For females this dream is ominous of disparagement and desertion by lovers.

Garden.

To see a garden in your dreams, filled with evergreen and flowers, denotes great peace of mind and comfort.

To see vegetables, denotes misery or loss of fortune and calumny. To females, this dream foretells that they will be famous, or exceedingly happy in domestic circles.

To dream of walking with one's lover through a garden where flowering shrubs and plants abound, indicates unalloyed happiness and independent means.

Garlic.

To dream of passing through a garlic patch, denotes a rise from penury to prominence and wealth. To a young woman, this denotes that she will marry from a sense of business, and love will not be considered.

To eat garlic in your dreams, denotes that you will take a sensible view of life and leave its ideals to take care of themselves.

Garret.

To dream of climbing to a garret, denotes your inclination to run after theories while leaving the cold realities

---

*See Jail.

of life to others less able to bear them than yourself. To the poor, this dream is an omen of easier circumstances. To a woman, it denotes that her vanity and sefishness should be curbed.

Garter.

For a lover to find his lady's garter, foretells that he will lose caste with her. He will find rivals.

For a woman to dream that she loses her garter, signifies that her lover will be jealous and suspicious of a handsomer person.

For a married man to dream of a garter, foretells that his wife will hear of his clandestine attachments, and he will have a stormy scene.

For a woman to dream that she is admiring beautiful jeweled garters on her limbs, denotes that she will be betrayed in her private movements, and her reputation will hang in the balance of public opinion. If she dreams that her lover fastens them on her, she will hold his affections and faith through all adverse criticisms.

Gas.

To dream of gas, denotes you will entertain harmful opinions of others, which will cause you to deal with them unjustly, and you will suffer consequent remorse. To think you are asphyxiated, denotes you will have trouble which you will needlessly incur through your own wastefulness and negligence. To try to blow gas out, signifies you will entertain enemies unconsciously, who will destroy you if you are not wary.

To extinguish gas, denotes you will ruthlessly destroy your own happiness. To light it, you will easily find a way out of oppressive ill fortune.

Gas Lamps.

To see a gas lamp, denotes progress and pleasant surroundings. To see one explode, or out of order otherwise, foretells you are threatened with unseasonable distress.

Gasoline.

To dream of gasoline, denotes you have a competency coming to you through a struggling source.

Gate.

To dream of seeing or passing through a gate, foretells that alarming tidings will reach you soon of the absent. Business affairs will not be encouraging.

To see a closed gate, inability to overcome present difficulties is predicted. To lock one, denotes successful enterprises and well chosen friends. A broken one, signifies failure and discordant surroundings. To be troubled to get through one, or open it, denotes your most engrossing labors will fail to be remunerative or satisfactory. To swing on one, foretells you will engage in idle and dissolute pleasures.

Gauze.

To dream of being dressed in gauze, denotes uncertain fortune. For a lover to see his sweetheart clothed in filmy material, suggests his ability to influence her for good.

Gavel.

To dream of a gavel, denotes you will be burdened with some unprofitable yet not unpleasant pursuit. To use one, denotes that officiousness will be shown by you toward your friends.

Geese.

To dream that you are annoyed by the quacking of geese, denotes a death in your family. To see them swimming, denotes that your fortune is gradually increasing.

To see them in grassy places, denotes assured success. If you see them dead, you will suffer loss and displeasure.

For a lover, geese denotes the worthiness of his affianced.

If you are picking them, you will come into an estate. To eat them, denotes that your possessions are disputed.

Gems.*

To dream of gems, foretells a happy fate both in love and business affairs.

Genealogical Tree.

To dream of your genealogical tree, denotes you will be much burdened with family cares, or will find pleasure in other domains than your own. To see others studying it, foretells that you will be forced to yield your rights to others. If any of the branches are missing, you will ignore some of your friends because of their straightened circumstances.

Geography.†

To dream of studying geography, denotes that you will travel much and visit places of renown.

Ghost.‡

To dream of the ghost of either one of your parents, denotes that you are exposed to danger, and you should be careful in forming partnerships with strangers.

To see the ghost of a dead friend, foretells that you will make a long journey with an unpleasant companion, and suffer disappointments.

For a ghost to speak to you, you will be decoyed into the hands of enemies. For a woman, this is a prognostication of widowhood and deception.

---

*See Jewelry.   †See Atlas.   ‡See Death, Dead.

To see an angel or a ghost appear in the sky, denotes the loss of kindred and misfortunes.

To see a female ghost on your right in the sky and a male on your left, both of pleasing countenance, signifies a quick rise from obscurity to fame, but the honor and position will be filled only for a short space, as death will be a visitor and will bear you off.

To see a female ghost in long, clinging robes floating calmly through the sky, indicates that you will make progression in scientific studies and acquire wealth almost miraculously, but there will be an under note of sadness in your life.

To dream that you see the ghost of a living relative or friend, denotes that you are in danger of some friend's malice, and you are warned to carefully keep your affairs under personal supervision. If the ghost appears to be haggard, it may be the intimation of the early death of that friend.

Giant.

To dream of a giant appearing suddenly before you, denotes that there will be a great struggle between you and your opponents. If the giant succeeds in stopping your journey, you will be overcome by your enemy. If he runs from you, prosperity and good health will be yours.

Gift.

To dream that you receive gifts from any one, denotes that you will not be behind in your payments, and be unusually fortunate in speculations or love matters.

To send a gift, signifies displeasure will be shown you, and ill luck will surround your efforts.

For a young woman to dream that her lover sends her rich and beautiful gifts, denotes that she will make a wealthy and congenial marriage.

Gig.*

To run a gig in your dream, you will have to forego a pleasant journey to entertain unwelcome visitors. Sickness also threatens you.

Girdle.

To dream of wearing a girdle, and it presses you, denotes that you will be influenced by designing people.

To see others wearing velvet, or jeweled girdles, foretells that you will strive for wealth more than honor.

For a woman to receive one, signifies that honors will be conferred upon her.

Girls.

To dream of seeing a well, bright-looking girl, foretells pleasing prospects and domestic joys. If she is thin and pale, it denotes that you will have an invalid in your family, and much unpleasantness.

For a man to dream that he is a girl, he will be weak-minded, or become an actor and play female parts.

Glass.

To dream that you are looking through glass, denotes that bitter disappointments will cloud your brightest hopes.

To see your image in a mirror, foretells unfaithfulness and neglect in marriage, and fruitless speculations.

To see another face with your own in a mirror, indicates that you are leading a double life. You will deceive your friends.

To break a mirror, portends an early and accidental death.

To break glass dishes, or windows, foretells the unfavorable termination to enterprises.

*See Cart.

259

To receive cut glass, denotes that you will be admired for your brilliancy and talent.

To make presents of cut glass ornaments, signifies that you will fail in your undertakings.

For a woman to see her lover in a mirror, denotes that she will have cause to institute a breach of promise suit.

For a married woman to see her husband in a mirror, is a warning that she will have cause to feel anxiety for her happiness and honor.

To look clearly through a glass window, you will have employment, but will have to work subordinately. If the glass is clouded, you will be unfortunately situated.

If a woman sees men, other than husband or lover, in a looking glass, she will be discovered in some indiscreet affair which will be humiliating to her and a source of worry to her relations.

For a man to dream of seeing strange women in a mirror, he will ruin his health and business by foolish attachments.

Glass-blower.

To dream that you see glass-blowers at their work, denotes you will contemplate change in your business, which will appear for the better, but you will make it at a loss to yourself.

Glass House.

To see a glass house, foretells you are likely to be injured by listening to flattery. For a young woman to dream that she is living in a glass house, her coming trouble and threatened loss of reputation is emphasized.

Gleaning.

To see gleaners at work at harvest time, denotes prosperous business, and, to the farmer, a bountiful yield of crops. If you are working with the gleaners, you will come into an estate, after some trouble in establishing rights. For a woman, this dream foretells marriage with a stranger.

Gloomy.*

To be surrounded by many gloomy situations in your dream, warns you of rapidly approaching unpleasantness and loss.

Gloves.

To dream of wearing new gloves, denotes that you will be cautious and economical in your dealings with others, but not mercenary. You will have law suits, or business troubles, but will settle them satisfactorily to yourself.

If you wear old or ragged gloves, you will be betrayed and suffer loss.

If you dream that you lose your gloves, you will be deserted and earn your own means of livelihood.

To find a pair of gloves, denotes a marriage or new love affair.

For a man to fasten a lady's glove, he has, or will have, a woman on his hands who threatens him with exposure.

If you pull your glove off, you will meet with poor success in business or love.

Goat.

To dream of goats wandering around a farm, is significant of seasonable weather and a fine yield of crops. To see them otherwise, denotes cautious dealings and a steady increase of wealth.

If a billy goat butts you, beware that enemies do not get possession of your secrets or business plans.

For a woman to dream of riding a billy goat, denotes that she will be held in disrepute because of her coarse and ill-bred conduct.

---

*See Despair.

If a woman dreams that she drinks goat's milk, she will marry for money and will not be disappointed.

Goblet.

If you dream that you drink water from a silver goblet, you will meet unfavorable business results in the near future.

To see goblets of ancient design, you will receive favors and benefits from strangers.

For a woman to give a man a glass goblet full of water, denotes illicit pleasures.

God.

If you dream of seeing God, you will be domineered over by a tyrannical woman masquerading under the cloak of Christianity. No good accrues from this dream.

If God speaks to you, beware that you do not fall into condemnation. Business of all sorts will take an unfavorable turn. It is the forerunner of the weakening of health and may mean early dissolution.

If you dream of worshiping God, you will have cause to repent of an error of your own making. Look well to observing the ten commandments after this dream.

To dream that God confers distinct favors upon you, you will become the favorite of a cautious and prominent person who will use his position to advance yours.

To dream that God sends his spirit upon you, great changes in your beliefs will take place. Views concerning dogmatic Christianity should broaden after this dream, or you may be severely chastised for some indiscreet action which has brought shame upon you. God speaks oftener to those who transgress than those who do not. It is the genius of spiritual law or economy to reinstate the prodigal child by signs and visions. Elijah, Jonah, David, and Paul were brought to the altar of repentence through the vigilant energy of the hidden forces within.

Goggles.

To dream of goggles, is a warning of disreputable companions who will wheedle you into lending your money foolishly.

For a young woman to dream of goggles, means that she will listen to persuasion which will mar her fortune.

Gold.

If you handle gold in your dream, you will be unusually successful in all enterprises. For a woman to dream that she receives presents of gold, either money or ornaments, she will marry a wealthy but mercenary man.

To find gold, indicates that your superior abilities will place you easily ahead in the race for honors and wealth.

If you lose gold, you will miss the grandest opportunity of your life through negligence.

To dream of finding a gold vein, denotes that some uneasy honor will be thrust upon you.

If you dream that you contemplate working a gold mine, you will endeavor to usurp the rights of others, and should beware of domestic scandals.

Goldfish.

To dream of goldfish, is a prognostic of many successful and pleasant adventures. For a young woman, this dream is indicative of a wealthy union with a pleasing man. If the fish are sick or dead, heavy disappointments will fall upon her.

Gold Leaves.

To dream of gold leaves, signifies a flattering future is before you.

Golf.

To be playing golf or watching the game, denotes that pleasant and successive wishing will be indulged in by you. To see any unpleasantness connected with golf, you will be humiliated by some thoughtless person.

Gong.

To hear the sound of a gong while dreaming, denotes false alarm of illness, or loss will vex you excessively.

Gooseberries.

To dream of gathering gooseberries, is a sign of happiness after trouble, and a favorable indication of brighter prospects in one's business affairs.

If you are eating green gooseberries, you will make a mistake in your course to pleasure, and be precipitated into the vertex of sensationalism. Bad results are sure to follow the tasting of green gooseberries.

To see gooseberries in a dream, foretells you will escape some dreaded work. For a young woman to eat them, foretells she will be slightly disappointed in her expectations.

Gossip.

To dream of being interested in common gossip, you will undergo some humiliating trouble caused by overconfidence in transient friendships.

If you are the object of gossip, you may expect some pleasurable surprise.

Gout.

If you dream of having the gout, you will be sure to be exasperated beyond endurance by the silly conduct of some relative, and suffer small financial loss through the same person.

Gown.*

If you dream that you are in your nightgown, you will be afflicted with a slight illness. If you see others thus

---

*See Clothes.

clad, you will have unpleasant news of absent friends. Business will receive a back set.

If a lover sees his sweetheart in her night gown, he will be superseded.

Grain.

Grain is a most fortunate dream, betokening wealth and happiness. For a young woman, it is a dream of fortune. She will meet wealthy and adoring companions.

Grammar.

To dream that you are studying grammar, denotes you are soon to make a wise choice in momentous opportunities.

Gramophone.

To dream of hearing the gramophone, foretells the advent of some new and pleasing comrade who will lend himself willingly to advance your enjoyment. If it is broken, some fateful occurrence will thwart and defeat delights that you hold in anticipation.

Grandparents.

To dream of meeting your grandparents and conversing with them, you will meet with difficulties that will be hard to surmount, but by following good advice you will overcome many barriers.

Grapes.

To eat grapes in your dream, you will be hardened with many cares; but if you only see them hanging in profuseness among the leaves, you will soon attain to eminent positions and will be able to impart happiness to others. For a young woman, this dream is one of bright promise. She will have her most ardent wish gratified.

To dream of riding on horseback and passing muscadine bushes and gathering and eating some of its fruit, denotes profitable employment and the realization of great desires. If there arises in your mind a question of the poisonous quality of the fruit you are eating, there will come doubts and fears of success, but they will gradually cease to worry you.

Grass.

This is a very propitious dream indeed. It gives promise of a happy and well advanced life to the tradesman, rapid accumulation of wealth, fame to literary and artistic people, and a safe voyage through the turbulent sea of love is promised to all lovers.

To see a rugged mountain beyond the green expanse of grass, is momentous of remote trouble.

If in passing through green grass, you pass withered places, it denotes your sickness or embarrassments in business.

To be a perfect dream, the grass must be clear of obstruction or blemishes. If you dream of withered grass, the reverse is predicted.

Grasshopper.

To dream of seeing grasshoppers on green vegetables, denotes that enemies threaten your best interests. If on withered grasses, ill health. Disappointing business will be experienced.

If you see grasshoppers between you and the sun, it denotes that you will have a vexatious problem in your immediate business life to settle, but using caution it will adjust itself in your favor. To call peoples' attention to the grasshoppers, shows that you are not discreet in dispatching your private business.

Grave.

To dream that you see a newly made grave, you will have to suffer for the wrongdoings of others.

If you visit a newly made grave, dangers of a serious nature is hanging over you. Grave is an unfortunate dream. Ill luck in business transactions will follow, also sickness is threatened.

To dream of walking on graves, predicts an early death or an unfortunate marriage.

If you look into an empty grave, it denotes disappointment and loss of friends.

If you see a person in a grave with the earth covering him, except the head, some distressing situation will take hold of that person and loss of property is indicated to the dreamer.

To see your own grave, foretells that enemies are warily seeking to engulf you in disaster, and if you fail to be watchful they will succeed.

To dream of digging a grave, denotes some uneasiness over some undertaking, as enemies will seek to thwart you, but if you finish the grave you will overcome opposition. If the sun is shining, good will come out of seeming embarrassments.

If you return for a corpse, to bury it, and it has disappeared, trouble will come to you from obscure quarters.

For a woman to dream that night overtakes her in a graveyard, and she can find no place to sleep but in an open grave, foreshows she will have much sorrow and disappointment through death or false friends. She may lose in love, and many things seek to work her harm.

To see a graveyard barren, except on top of the graves, signifies much sorrow and despondency for a time, but greater benefits and pleasure await you if you properly shoulder your burden.

To see your own corpse in a grave, foreshadows hopeless and despairing oppression.

Gravel.

To dream of gravel, denotes unfruitful schemes and enterprises.

If you see gravel mixed with dirt, it foretells you will unfortunately speculate and lose good property.

Gravy.

To dream of eating gravy, portends failing health and disappointing business.

Grease.

To dream you are in grease, is significant of travels being enjoyed with disagreeable but polished strangers.

Greek.

To dream of reading Greek, denotes that your ideas will be discussed and finally accepted and put in practical use. To fail to read it, denotes that technical difficulties are in your way.

Greyhound.

A greyhound is a fortunate object to see in your dream. If it is following a young girl, you will be surprised with a legacy from unknown people. If a greyhound is owned by you, it signifies friends where enemies were expected.

Grindstone.

For a person to dream of turning a grindstone, his dream is prophetic of a life of energy and well directed efforts bringing handsome competency.

If you are sharpening tools, you will be blessed with a worthy helpmate.

To deal in grindstones, is significant of small but honest gain.

Groans.

If you hear groans in your dream, decide quickly on your course, for enemies are undermining your business. If you are groaning with fear, you will be pleasantly surprised at the turn for better in your affairs, and you may look for pleasant visiting among friends.

Groceries.

To dream of general groceries, if they are fresh and clean, is a sign of ease and comfort.

Grotto.

To see a grotto in your dreams, is a sign of incomplete and inconstant friendships. Change from comfortable and simple plenty will make showy poverty unbearable.

Guardian.

To dream of a guardian, denotes you will be treated with consideration by your friends. For a young woman to dream that she is being unkindly dealt with by her guardian, foretells that she will have loss and trouble in the future.

Guitar.

To dream that you have a guitar, or is playing one in a dream, signifies a merry gathering and serious love making. For a young woman to think it is unstrung or broken, foretells that disappointments in love are sure to overtake her.

Upon hearing the weird music of a guitar, the dreamer should fortify herself against flattery and soft persuasion, for she is in danger of being tempted by a fascinating evil. If the dreamer be a man, he will be courted, and will be likely to lose his judgment under the wiles of seductive women.

If you play on a guitar, your family affairs will be harmonious.

Gulls.

To dream of gulls, is a prophecy of peaceful dealings with ungenerous persons. Seeing dead gulls, means wide separation for friends.

Gun.

This is a dream of distress. Hearing the sound of a gun, denotes loss of employment, and bad management to proprietors of establishments.

If you shoot a person with a gun, you will fall into dishonor.

If you are shot, you will be annoyed by evil persons, and perhaps suffer an acute illness.

For a woman to dream of shooting, forecasts for her a quarreling and disagreeable reputation connected with sensations. For a married woman, unhappiness through other women.

Gutter.

To dream of a gutter, is a sign of degradation. You will be the cause of unhappiness to others.

To find articles of value in a gutter, your right to certain property will be questioned.

Gymnast.

To dream of a gymnast, denotes you will have misfortune in speculation or trade.

Gypsy.

If you dream of visiting a gypsy camp, you will have an offer of importance and will investigate the standing of the parties to your disadvantage.

For a woman to have a gypsy tell her fortune, is an omen of a speedy and unwise marriage. If she is already married, she will be unduly jealous of her husband.

For a man to hold any conversation with a gypsy, he will be likely to lose valuable property.

To dream of trading with a gypsy, you will lose money in speculation. This dream denotes that material pleasures are the biggest items in your life.

H.

"And being warned of God in a dream that they should not return to Herod, they departed into their own country another way."—Matthew ii, 12.

Haggard.

To see a haggard face in your dreams, denotes misfortune and defeat in love matters.

To see your own face haggard and distressed, denotes trouble over female affairs, which may render you unable to meet business engagements in a healthy manner.

Hail.

If you dream of being in a hail storm, you will meet poor success in any undertaking.

If you watch hail-stones fall through sunshine and rain, you will be harassed by cares for a time, but fortune will soon smile upon you. For a young woman, this dream indicates love after many slights.

To hear hail beating the house, indicates distressing situations.

Hair.

If a woman dreams that she has beautiful hair and combs it, she will be careless in her personal affairs, and will lose advancement by neglecting mental application.

For a man to dream that he is thinning his hair, foreshadows that he will become poor by his generosity, and suffer illness through mental worry.

To see your hair turning gray, foretells death and contagion in the family of some relative or some friend.

To see yourself covered with hair, omens indulgence in vices to such an extent as will debar you from the society of refined people. If a woman, she will resolve herself into a world of her own, claiming the right to act for her own pleasure regardless of moral codes.

If a man dreams that he has black, curling hair, he will deceive people through his pleasing address. He will very likely deceive the women who trust him. If a woman's hair seems black and curly, she will be threatened with seduction.

If you dream of seeing a woman with golden hair, you will prove a fearless lover and be woman's true friend.

To dream that your sweetheart has red hair, you will be denounced by the woman you love for unfaithfulness. Red hair usually suggests changes.

If you see brown hair, you will be unfortunate in choosing a career.

If you see well kept and neatly combed hair, your fortune will improve.

To dream you cut your hair close to the scalp, denotes that you will be generous to lavishness towards a friend Frugality will be the fruits growing out therefrom.

To see the hair growing out soft and luxuriant, signifies happiness and luxury.

For a woman to compare a white hair with a black one, which she takes from her head, foretells that she will be likely to hesitate between two offers of seeming fortune, and unless she uses great care, will choose the one that will afford her loss or distress instead of pleasant fortune.

To see tangled and unkempt hair, life will be a veritable burden, business will fall off, and the marriage yoke will be troublesome to carry.

If a woman is unsuccessful in combing her hair, she will lose a worthy man's name by needless show of temper and disdain.

For a young woman to dream of women with gray hair, denotes that they will come into her life as rivals in the affection of a male relative, or displace the love of her affianced.

To dream of having your hair cut, denotes serious disappointments.

For a woman to dream that her hair is falling out, and baldness is apparent, she will have to earn her own livelihood, as fortune has passed her by.

For man or woman to dream that they have hair of snowy whiteness, denotes that they will enjoy a pleasing and fortunate journey through life.

For a man to caress the hair of a woman, shows he will enjoy the love and confidence of some worthy woman who will trust him despite the world's condemnation.

To see flowers in your hair, foretells troubles approaching which, when they come, will give you less fear than when viewed from a distance.

For a woman to dream that her hair turns to white flowers, augurs that troubles of a various nature will confront her, and she does well if she strengthens her soul with patience, and endeavors to bear her trials with fortitude.

To dream that a lock of your hair turns gray and falls out, is a sign of trouble and disappointment in your affairs. Sickness will cast gloom over bright expectations.

To see one's hair turn perfectly white in one night, and the face seemingly young, foretells sudden calamity and deep grief. For a young woman to have this dream, signifies that she will lose her lover by a sudden sickness or accident. She will likely come to grief from some indiscretion on her part. She should be careful of her associates.

Hair-dresser.

Should you visit a hair-dresser in your dreams, you will be connected with a sensation caused by the indiscretion of a good looking woman. To a woman, this dream means a family disturbance and well merited censures.

For a woman to dream of having her hair colored, she will narrowly escape the scorn of society, as enemies will seek to blight her reputation. To have her hair dressed, denotes that she will run after frivolous things, and use any means to bend people to her wishes.

Hairy Hands.

To dream that your hands are covered with hair like that of a beast, signifies you will intrigue against innocent people, and will find that you have alert enemies who are working to forestall your designs.

Halter.

To dream that you put a halter on a young horse, shows that you will manage a very prosperous and clean business. Love matters will shape themselves to suit you.

To see other things haltered, denotes that fortune will be withheld from you for a while. You will win it, but with much toil.

Ham.

To dream of seeing hams, signifies you are in danger of being treacherously used. To cut large slices of ham, denotes that all opposition will be successfully met by you. To dress a ham, signifies you will be leniently treated by others.

To dream of dealing in hams, prosperity will come to you. Also good health is foreboded.

To eat ham, you will lose something of great value. To smell ham cooking, you will be benefited by the enterprises of others.

Hammer.

To dream of seeing a hammer, denotes you will have some discouraging obstacles to overcome in order to establish firmly your fortune.

Hand.*

If you see beautiful hands in your dream, you will enjoy great distinction, and rise rapidly in your calling; but ugly and malformed hands point to disappointments and poverty. To see blood on them, denotes estrangement and unjust censure from members of your family.

If you have an injured hand, some person will succeed to what you are striving most to obtain.

To see a detached hand, indicates a solitary life, that is, people will fail to understand your views and feelings. To burn your hands, you will overreach the bounds of reason in your struggles for wealth and fame, and lose thereby.

To see your hands covered with hair, denotes that you will not become a solid and leading factor in your circle.

To see your hands enlarged, denotes a quick advancement in your affairs. To see them smaller, the reverse is predicted.

To see your hands soiled, denotes that you will be envious and unjust to others.

*See Fingers.

To wash your hands, you will participate in some joyous festivity.

For a woman to admire her own hands, is proof that she will win and hold the sincere regard of the man she prizes above all others.

To admire the hands of others, she will be subjected to the whims of a jealous man. To have a man hold her hands, she will be enticed into illicit engagements. If she lets others kiss her hands, she will have gossips busy with her reputation. To handle fire without burning her hands, she will rise to high rank and commanding positions.

To dream that your hands are tied, denotes that you will be involved in difficulties. In loosening them, you will force others to submit to your dictations.

Handbills.

To dream of distributing handbills over the country, is a sign of contentions and possible lawsuits.

If you dream of printing handbills, you will hear unfavorable news.

Handcuffs.

To find yourself handcuffed, you will be annoyed and vexed by enemies. To see others thus, you will subdue those oppressing you and rise above your associates.

To see handcuffs, you will be menaced with sickness and danger.

To dream of handcuffs, denotes formidable enemies are surrounding you with objectionable conditions. To break them, is a sign that you will escape toils planned by enemies.

Handkerchiefs.

To dream of handkerchiefs, denotes flirtations and contingent affairs.

To lose one, omens a broken engagement through no fault of yours.

To see torn ones, foretells that lovers' quarrels will reach such straits that reconciliation will be improbable if not impossible.

To see them soiled, foretells that you will be corrupted by indiscriminate associations.

To see pure white ones in large lots, foretells that you will resist the insistent flattery of unscrupulous and evil-minded persons, and thus gain entrance into high relations with love and matrimony.

To see them colored, denotes that while your engagements may not be strictly moral, you will manage them with such ingenuity that they will elude opprobrium.

If you see silk handkerchiefs, it denotes that your pleasing and magnetic personality will shed its radiating cheerfulness upon others, making for yourself a fortunate existence.

For a young woman to wave adieu or a recognition with her handkerchief, or see others doing this, denotes that she will soon make a questionable pleasure trip, or she may knowingly run the gauntlet of disgrace to secure some fancied pleasure.

Handsome.

To see yourself handsome-looking in your dreams, you will prove yourself an ingenious flatterer.

To see others appearing handsome, denotes that you will enjoy the confidence of fast people.

Handwriting.

To dream that you see and recognize your own handwriting, foretells that malicious enemies will use your expressed opinion to foil you in advancing to some competed position.

Hanging.*

To see a large concourse of people gathering at a hanging, denotes that many enemies will club together to try to demolish your position in their midst.

Hare.†

If you see a hare escaping from you in a dream, you will lose something valuable in a mysterious way. If you capture one, you will be the victor in a contest.

If you make pets of them, you will have an orderly but unintelligent companion.

A dead hare, betokens death to some friend. Existence will be a prosy affair.

To see hares chased by dogs, denotes trouble and contentions among your friends, and you will concern yourself to bring about friendly relations.

If you dream that you shoot a hare, you will be forced to use violent measures to maintain your rightful possessions.

Harem.

To dream that you maintain a harem, denotes that you are wasting your best energies on low pleasures. Life holds fair promises, if your desires are rightly directed.

If a woman dreams that she is an inmate of a harem, she will seek pleasure where pleasure is unlawful, as her desires will be toward married men as a rule. If she dreams that she is a favorite of a harem, she will be preferred before others in material pleasures, but the distinction will be fleeting.

Harlequin.

To dream of a harlequin cheating you, you will find

---

*See Execution.   †See Rabbit.

uphill work to identify certain claims that promise profit to you. If you dream of a harlequin, trouble will beset you.

To be dressed as a harlequin, denotes passionate error and unwise attacks on strength and purse. Designing women will lure you to paths of sin.

Harlot.

To dream of being in the company of a harlot, denotes ill-chosen pleasures and trouble in your social circles, and business will suffer depression. If you marry one, life will be threatened by an enemy.

Harness.

To dream of possessing bright new harness, you will soon prepare for a pleasant journey.

Harp.

To hear the sad sweet strains of a harp, denotes the sad ending to what seems a pleasing and profitable enterprise.

To see a broken harp, betokens illness, or broken troth between lovers.

To play a harp yourself, signifies that your nature is too trusting, and you should be more careful in placing your confidence as well as love matters.

Harvest.

To dream of harvest time, is a forerunner of prosperity and pleasure. If the harvest yields are abundant, the indications are good for country and state, as political machinery will grind to advance all conditions.

A poor harvest is a sign of small profits.

Hash.

To dream you are eating hash, many sorrows and vexations are foretold.

You will probably be troubled with various little jealousies and contentions over mere trifles, and your health will be menaced through worry.

For a woman to dream that she cooks hash, denotes that she will be jealous of her husband, and children will be a stumbling block to her wantonness.

Hassock.

To dream of a hassock, forebodes the yielding of your power and fortune to another. If a woman dreams of a hassock, she should cultivate spirit and independence.

Hat.

To dream of losing your hat, you may expect unsatisfactory business and failure of persons to keep important engagements.

For a man to dream that he wears a new hat, predicts change of place and business, which will be very much to his advantage. For a woman to dream that she wears a fine new hat, denotes the attainment of wealth, and she will be the object of much admiration.

For the wind to blow your hat off, denotes sudden changes in affairs, and somewhat for the worse.

Hatchet.

A hatchet seen in a dream, denotes that wanton wastefulness will expose you to the evil designs of envious persons. If it is rusty or broken, you will have grief over wayward people.

Hate.

To dream that you hate a person, denotes that if you

are not careful you will do the party an inadvertent injury or a spiteful action will bring business loss and worry.

If you are hated for unjust causes, you will find sincere and obliging friends, and your associations will be most pleasant. Otherwise, the dream forebodes ill.

Hawk.

To dream of a hawk, foretells you will be cheated in some way by intriguing persons. To shoot one, foretells you will. surmount obstacles after many struggles. For a young woman to frighten hawks away from her chickens, signifies she will obtain her most extravagant desires through diligent attention to her affairs.

It also denotes that enemies are near you, and they are ready to take advantage of your slightest mistakes. If you succeed in scaring it away before your fowls are injured, you will be lucky in your business.

To see a dead hawk, signifies that your enemies will be vanquished.

To dream of shooting at a hawk, you will have a contest with enemies, and will probably win.

Hay.

If you dream of mowing hay, you will find much good in life, and if a farmer your crops will yield abundantly.

To see fields of newly cut hay, is a sign of unusual prosperity.

If you are hauling and putting hay into barns, your fortune is assured, and you will realize great profit from some enterprise.

To see loads of hay passing through the street, you will meet influential strangers who will add much to your pleasure.

To feed hay to stock, indicates that you will offer aid

to some one who will return the favor with love and advancement to higher states.

Head.

To see a person's head in your dream, and it is well-shaped and prominent, you will meet persons of power and vast influence who will lend you aid in enterprises of importance.

If you dream of your own head, you are threatened with nervous or brain trouble.

To see a head severed from its trunk, and bloody, you will meet sickening disappointments, and the overthrow of your dearest hopes and anticipations.

To see yourself with two or more heads, foretells phenomenal and rapid rise in life, but the probabilities are that the rise will not be stable.

To dream that your head aches, denotes that you will be oppressed with worry.

To dream of a swollen head, you will have more good than bad in your life.

To dream of a child's head, there will be much pleasure in store for you and signal financial success.

To dream of the head of a beast, denotes that the nature of your desires will run on a low plane, and only material pleasures will concern you.

To wash your head, you will be sought after by prominent people for your judgment and good counsel.

Headgear.

To dream of seeing rich headgear, you will become famous and successful. To see old and worn headgear, you will have to yield up your possessions to others.

Hearse.

To dream of a hearse, denotes uncongenial relations

in the home, and failure to carry on business in a satisfactory manner. It also betokens the death of one near to you, or sickness and sorrow.

If a hearse crosses your path, you will have a bitter enemy to overcome.

Heart.

To dream of your heart paining and suffocating you, there will be trouble in your business. Some mistake of your own will bring loss if not corrected.

Seeing your heart, foretells sickness and failure of energy.

To see the heart of an animal, you will overcome enemies and merit the respect of all.

To eat the heart of a chicken, denotes strange desires will cause you to carry out very difficult projects for your advancement.

Heat.

To dream that you are oppressed by heat, denotes failure to carry out designs on account of some friend betraying you. Heat is not a very favorable dream.

Heather Bells.

To dream of heather bells, foretells that joyous occasions will pass you in happy succession.

Heaven.

If you ascend to heaven in a dream, you will fail to enjoy the distinction you have labored to gain, and joy will end in sadness.

If young persons dream of climbing to heaven on a ladder, they will rise from a low estate to one of unusual prominence, but will fail to find contentment or much pleasure.

To dream of being in heaven and meeting Christ and

friends, you will meet with many losses, but will reconcile yourself to them through your true understanding of human nature.

To dream of the Heavenly City, denotes a contented and spiritual nature, and trouble will do you small harm.

Hedges.

To dream of hedges of evergreens, denotes joy and profit.

Bare hedges, foretells distress and unwise dealings.

If a young woman dreams of walking beside a green hedge with her lover, it foretells that her marriage will soon be consummated.

If you dream of being entangled in a thorny hedge, you will be hampered in your business by unruly partners or persons working under you. To lovers, this dream is significant of quarrels and jealousies.

Heir.

To dream that you fall heir to property or valuables, denotes that you are in danger of losing what you already possess. and warns you of coming responsibilities. Pleasant surprises may also follow this dream.

Hell.

If you dream of being in hell, you will fall into temptations, which will almost wreck you financially and morally.

To see your friends in hell, denotes distress and burdensome cares. You will hear of the misfortune of some friend.

To dream of crying in hell, denotes the powerlessness of friends to extricate you from the snares of enemies.

Helmet.

To dream of seeing a helmet, denotes threatened misery and loss will be avoided by wise action.

Hemp.

To dream of hemp, denotes you will be successful in all undertakings, especially large engagements. For a young woman to dream that some accident befalls her through cultivating hemp, foretells the fatal quarrel and separation from her friend.

Hemp Seed.

To see hemp seed in dreams, denotes the near approach of a deep and continued friendship. To the business man, is shown favorable opportunity for money-making.

Hen.*

To dream of hens, denotes pleasant family reunions with added members.

Herbs.

To dream of herbs, denotes that you will have vexatious cares, though some pleasures will ensue.

To dream of poisonous herbs, warns you of enemies.

Balm and other useful herbs, denotes satisfaction in business and warm friendships.

Hermit.

To dream of a hermit, denotes sadness and loneliness caused by the unfaithfulness of friends.

If you are a hermit yourself, you will pursue researches into intricate subjects, and will take great interest in the discussions of the hour.

---

*See Chickens.

To find yourself in the abode of a hermit, denotes unselfishness toward enemies and friends alike.

Herring.

To dream of seeing herring, indicates a tight squeeze to escape financial embarrassment, but you will have success later.

Hide.

To dream of the hide of an animal, denotes profit and permanent employment.

Hidden.

To dream that you have hidden away any object, denotes embarrassment in your circumstances.

To find hidden things, you will enjoy unexpected pleasures.

For a young woman to dream of hiding objects, she will be the object of much adverse gossip, but will finally prove her conduct orderly.

Hieroglyphs.

Hieroglyphs seen in a dream, foretells that wavering judgment in some vital matter may cause you great distress and money loss. To be able to read them, your success in overcoming some evil is foretold.

High School.

To dream of a high school, foretells ascension to more elevated positions in love, as well as social and business affairs. For a young woman to be suspended from a high school, foretells she will have troubles in social circles.

High Tide.

To dream of high tide is indicative of favorable progression in your affairs.

Hills.*

To dream of climbing hills is good if the top is reached, but if you fall back, you will have much envy and contrariness to fight against.

Hips.

To dream that you admire well-formed hips, denotes that you will be upbraided by your wife.

For a woman to admire her hips, shows she will be disappointed in love matters.

To notice fat hips on animals, foretells ease and pleasure.

For a woman to dream that her hips are too narrow, omens sickness and disappointments. If too fat, she is in danger of losing her reputation.

Hissing.

To dream of hissing persons, is an omen that you will be displeased beyond endurance at the discourteous treatment shown you while among newly made acquaintances. If they hiss you, you will be threatened with the loss of a friend.

History.

To dream that you are reading history, indicates a long and pleasant recreation.

Hives.

To dream that your child is affected with hives, denotes that it will enjoy good health and be docile.

To see strange children thus affected, you will be unduly frightened over the condition of some favorite.

Hoe.

To dream of seeing a hoe, denotes that you will have

---

* See Ascend and Descend.

no time for idle pleasures, as there will be others depending upon your work for subsistence.

To dream of using a hoe, you will enjoy freedom from poverty by directing your energy into safe channels.

For a woman to dream of hoeing, she will be independent of others, as she will be self-supporting. For lovers, this dream is a sign of faithfulness.

To dream of a foe striking at you with a hoe, your interests will be threatened by enemies, but with caution you will keep aloof from real danger.

Hogs.

To dream of seeing fat, strong-looking hogs, foretells brisk changes in business and safe dealings. Lean hogs predict vexatious affairs and trouble with servants and children.

To see a sow and litter of pigs, denotes abundant crops to the farmer, and advance in the affairs of others.

To hear hogs squealing, denotes unpleasant news from absent friends, and foretells disappointment by death, or failure to realize the amounts you expected in deals of importance.

To dream of feeding your own hogs, denotes an increase in your personal belongings.

To dream that you are dealing in hogs, you will accumulate considerable property, but you will have much rough work to perform.

Holiday.

To dream of a holiday, foretells interesting strangers will soon partake of your hospitality. For a young woman to dream that she is displeased with a holiday, denotes she will be fearful of her own attractions in winning a friend back from a rival.

Holy Communion.

To dream that you are taking part in the Holy Communion, warns you that you will resign your independent opinions to gain some frivolous desire.

If you dream that there is neither bread nor wine for the supper, you will find that you have suffered your ideas to be proselytized in vain, as you are no nearer your goal.

If you are refused the right of communion and feel worthy, there is hope for your obtaining some prominent position which has appeared extremely doubtful, as your opponents are popular and powerful. If you feel unworthy, you will meet with much discomfort.

To dream that you are in a body of Baptists who are taking communion, denotes that you will find that your friends are growing uncongenial, and you will look to strangers for harmony.

Home.*

To dream of visiting your old home, you will have good news to rejoice over.

To see your old home in a dilapidated state, warns you of the sickness or death of a relative. For a young woman this is a dream of sorrow. She will lose a dear friend.

To go home and find everything cheery and comfortable, denotes harmony in the present home life and satisfactory results in business.

Hominy.

To dream of hominy, denotes pleasant love-making will furnish you interesting recreation from absorbing study and planning for future progression.

---

*See Abode.

Homesick.

To dream of being homesick, foretells you will lose fortunate opportunities to enjoy travels of interest and pleasant visits.

Homicide.*

To dream that you commit homicide, foretells that you will suffer great anguish and humiliation through the indifference of others, and your gloomy surroundings will cause perplexing worry to those close to you.

To dream that a friend commits suicide, you will have trouble in deciding a very important question.

Honey.

To dream that you see honey, you will be possessed of considerable wealth.

To see strained honey, denotes wealth and ease, but there will be an undercurrent in your life of unlawful gratification of material desires.

To dream of eating honey, foretells that you will attain wealth and love. To lovers, this indicates a swift rush into marital joys.

Honeysuckle.

To see or gather, honeysuckles, denotes that you will be contentedly prosperous and your marriage will be a singularly happy one.

Hood.

For a young woman to dream that she is wearing a hood, is a sign she will attempt to allure some man from rectitude and bounden duty.

Hook.

To dream of a hook, foretells unhappy obligations will be assumed by you.

*See Kill.

Hoop.

To dream of a hoop, foretells you will form influential friendships. Many will seek counsel of you. To jump through, or see others jumping through hoops, denotes you will have discouraging outlooks, but you will overcome them with decisive victory.

Hops.

To dream of hops, denotes thrift, energy and the power to grasp and master almost any business proposition. Hops is a favorable dream to all classes, lovers and tradesmen.

Horn.

To dream that you hear the sound of a horn, foretells hasty news of a joyful character.

To see a broken horn, denotes death or accident.

To see children playing with horns, denotes congeniality in the home.

For a woman to dream of blowing a horn, foretells that she is more anxious for marriage than her lover.

Hornet.

To dream of a hornet, signals disruption to lifelong friendship, and loss of money.

For a young woman to dream that one stings her, or she is in a nest of them, foretells that many envious women will seek to disparage her before her admirers.

Horoscope.

To dream of having your horoscope drawn by an astrologist, foretells unexpected changes in affairs and a long journey; associations with a stranger will probably happen.

If the dreamer has the stars pointed out to him, as his

fate is being read, he will find disappointments where fortune and pleasure seem to await him.

Horse.

If you dream of seeing or riding a white horse, the indications are favorable for prosperity and pleasurable commingling with congenial friends and fair women. If the white horse is soiled and lean, your confidence will be betrayed by a jealous friend or a woman. If the horse is black, you will be successful in your fortune, but you will practice deception, and will be guilty of assignations. To a woman, this dream denotes that her husband is unfaithful.

To dream of dark horses, signifies prosperous conditions, but a large amount of discontent. Fleeting pleasures usually follow this dream.

To see yourself riding a fine bay horse, denotes a rise in fortune and gratification of passion. For a woman, it foretells a yielding to importunate advances. She will enjoy material things.

To ride or see passing horses, denotes ease and comfort.

To ride a runaway horse, your interests will be injured by the folly of a friend or employer.

To see a horse running away with others, denotes that you will hear of the illness of friends.

To see fine stallions, is a sign of success and high living, and undue passion will master you.

To see brood mares, denotes congeniality and absence of jealousy between the married and sweethearts.

To ride a horse to ford a stream, you will soon experience some good fortune and will enjoy rich pleasures. If the stream is unsettled or murky, anticipated joys will be somewhat disappointing.

To swim on a horse's back through a clear and beautiful stream of water, your conception of passionate bliss will be swiftly realized. To a business man, this dream portends great gain.

To see a wounded horse, foretells the trouble of friends.

To dream of a dead horse, signifies disappointments of various kinds.

To dream of riding a horse that bucks, denotes that your desires will be difficult of consummation. To dream that he throws you, you will have a strong rival, and your business will suffer slightly through competition.

To dream that a horse kicks you, you will be repulsed by one you love. Your fortune will be embarrassed by ill health.

To dream of catching a horse to bridle and saddle, or harness it, you will see a great improvement in business of all kinds, and people of all callings will prosper. If you fail to catch it, fortune will play you false.

To see spotted horses, foretells that various enterprises will bring you profit.

To dream of having a horse shod, your success is assured. For a woman, this dream omens a good and faithful husband.

To dream that you shoe a horse, denotes that you will endeavor to and perhaps make doubtful property your own.

To dream of race horses, denotes that you will be surfeited with fast living, but to the farmer this dream denotes prosperity.

To dream that you ride a horse in a race, you will be prosperous and enjoy life.

To dream of killing a horse, you will injure your friends through selfishness.

To mount a horse bareback, you will gain wealth and ease by hard struggles.

To ride bareback in company with men, you will have honest people to aid you, and your success will be merited. If in company with women, your desires will be loose, and your prosperity will not be so abundant as might be if women did not fill your heart.

To curry a horse, your business interests will not be neglected for frivolous pleasures.

To dream of trimming a horse's mane, or tail, denotes that you will be a good financier or farmer. Literary people will be painstaking in their work and others will look after their interest with. solicitude.

To dream of horses, you will amass wealth and enjoy life to its fullest extent.

To see horses pulling vehicles, denotes wealth with some incumbrance, and love will find obstacles.

If you are riding up a hill and the horse falls but you gain the top, you will win fortune, though you will have to struggle against enemies and jealousy. If both the horse and you get to the top, your rise will be phenomenal, but substantial.

For a young girl to dream that she rides a black horse, denotes that she should be dealt with by wise authority. Some wishes will be gratified at an unexpected time. Black in horses, signifies postponements in anticipations.

To see a horse with a tender foot, denotes that some unexpected unpleasantness will insinuate itself into your otherwise propitious state.

If you attempt to fit a broken shoe which is too small for the horse's foot, you will be charged with making fraudulent deals with unsuspecting parties.

To ride a horse down hill, your affairs will undoubtedly disappoint you. For a young woman to dream that a friend rides behind her on a horse, denotes that she will be foremost in the favors of many prominent and successful men. If she was frightened, she is likely to stir up jealous sensations. If after she alights from the horse it turns into a pig, she will carelessly pass by honorable offers of marriage, preferring freedom until her chances of a desirable marriage are lost. If afterward she sees the pig sliding gracefully along the telegraph wire, she will by intriguing advance her position.

For a young woman to dream that she is riding a white horse up and down hill, often looking back and seeing some one on a black horse, pursuing her, denotes she will have a mixed season of success and sorow, but through it all a relentless enemy is working to overshadow her with gloom and disappointment.

To see a horse in human flesh, descending on a hammock through the air, and as it nears your house is metamorphosed into a man, and he approaches your door and throws something at you which seems to be rubber but turns into great bees, denotes miscarriage of hopes and useless endeavors to regain lost valuables. To see animals in human flesh, signifies great advancement to the dreamer, and new friends will be made by modest wearing of well-earned honors. If the human flesh appears diseased or freckled, the miscarriage of well-laid plans is denoted.

Horseshoe.

To dream of a horseshoe, indicates advance in business and lucky engagements for women.

To see them broken, ill fortune and sickness is portrayed.

To find a horseshoe hanging on the fence, denotes that your interests will advance beyond your most sanguine expectations.

To pick one up in the road, you will receive profit from a source you know not of.

Horseradish.

To dream of horseradish, foretells pleasant associations with intellectual and congenial people. Fortune is also expressed in this dream. For a woman, it indicates a rise above her present station.

To eat horseradish, you will be the object of pleasant raillery.

Horse-trader.

To dream of a horse-trader, signifies great profit from perilous ventures.

To dream that you are trading horses, and the trader cheats you, you will lose in trade or love. If you get a better horse than the one you traded, you will better yourself in fortune.

Hospital.

If you dream that you are a patient in a hospital, you will have a contagious disease in your community, and will narrowly escape affliction. If you visit patients there, you will hear distressing news of the absent.

Hotel.

To dream of living in a hotel, denotes ease and profit.

To visit women in a hotel, your life will be rather on a dissolute order.

To dream of seeing a fine hotel, indicates wealth and travel.

If you dream that you are the proprietor of a hotel, you will earn all the fortune you will ever possess.

To work in a hotel, you could find a more remunerative employment than what you have.

To dream of hunting a hotel, you will be baffled in your search for wealth and happiness.

Hounds.*

To dream of hounds on a hunt, denotes coming delights and pleasant changes. For a woman to dream of hounds, she will love a man below her in station. To dream that hounds are following her, she will have many admirers, but there will be no real love felt for her.

House.†

To dream of building a house, you will make wise changes in your present affairs.

To dream that you own an elegant house, denotes that you will soon leave your home for a better, and fortune will be kind to you.

Old and dilapidated houses, denote failure in business or any effort, and declining health.

Housekeeper.

To dream that you are a housekeeper, denotes you will have labors which will occupy your time, and make pleasure an ennobling thing. To employ one, signifies comparative comfort will be possible for your obtaining.

Hugging.

If you dream of hugging, you will be disappointed in love affairs and in business.

For a woman to dream of hugging a man, she will accept advances of a doubtful character from men.

For a married woman to hug others than her husband, she will endanger her honor in accepting attentions from others in her husband's absence.

Humidity.‡

To dream that you are overcome with humidity, fore-

---

*See Dogs.   †See Building.   ‡See Air.

tells that you will combat enemies fiercely, but their superior force will submerge you in overwhelming defeat.

Hunchback.

To dream of a hunchback, denotes unexpected reverses in your prospects.

Hunger.

To dream that you are hungry, is an unfortunate omen. You will not find comfort and satisfaction in your home, and to lovers it means an unhappy marriage.

Hunting.*

If you dream of hunting, you will struggle for the unattainable.

If you dream that you hunt game and find it, you will overcome obstacles and gain your desires.

Hurt.

If you hurt a person in your dreams, you will do ugly work, revenging and injuring.

If you are hurt, you will have enemies who will overcome you.

Hurricane.

To hear the roar and see a hurricane heading towards you with its frightful force, you will undergo torture and suspense, striving to avert failure and ruin in your affairs.

If you are in a house which is being blown to pieces by a hurricane, and you struggle in the awful gloom to extricate some one from the falling timbers, your life will suffer a change. You will move and remove to distant places, and still find no improvement in domestic or business affairs.

If you dream of looking on débris and havoc wrought

* See Gain.

by a hurricane, you will come close to trouble, which will be averted by the turn in the affairs of others.

To see dead and wounded caused by a hurricane, you will be much distressed over the troubles of others.

Husband.

To dream that your husband is leaving you, and you do not understand why, there will be bitterness between you, but an unexpected reconciliation will ensue. If he mistreats and upbraids you for unfaithfulness, you will hold his regard and confidence, but other worries will ensue and you are warned to be more discreet in receiving attention from men.

If you see him dead, disappointment and sorrow will envelop you.

To see him pale and careworn, sickness will tax you heavily, as some of the family will linger in bed for a time.

To see him gay and handsome, your home will be filled with happiness and bright prospects will be yours. If he is sick, you will be mistreated by him and he will be unfaithful.

To dream that he is in love with another woman, he will soon tire of his present surroundings and seek pleasure elsewhere.

To be in love with another woman's husband in your dreams, denotes that you are not happily married, or that you are not happy unmarried, but the chances for happiness are doubtful.

For an unmarried woman to dream that she has a husband, denotes that she is wanting in the graces which men most admire.

To see your husband depart from you, and as he recedes from you he grows larger, inharmonious surroundings will prevent immediate congeniality. If disagreeable conclusions are avoided, harmony will be reinstated.

For a woman to dream she sees her husband in a compromising position with an unsuspected party, denotes she will have trouble through the indiscretion of friends. If she dreams that he is killed while with another woman, and a scandal ensues, she will be in danger of separating from her husband or losing property. Unfavorable conditions follow this dream, though the evil is often exaggerated.

Hut.

To dream of a hut, denotes indifferent success.

To dream that you are sleeping in a hut, denotes ill health and dissatisfaction.

To see a hut in a green pasture, denotes prosperity, but fluctuating happiness.

Hyacinth.

To dream that you see, or gather, hyacinths, you are about to undergo a painful separation from a friend, which will ultimately result in good for you.

Hydrophobia.

To dream that you are afflicted with hydrophobia, denotes enemies and change of business.

To see others thus afflicted, your work will be interrupted by death or ungrateful dependence.

To dream that an animal with the rabies bites you, you will be betrayed by your dearest friend, and much scandal will be brought to light.

Hyena.

If you see a hyena in your dreams, you will meet much disappointment and much ill luck in your undertakings, and your companions will be very uncongenial. If lovers have this dream, they will often be involved in quarrels.

If one attacks you, your reputation will be set upon by busybodies.

Hymns.*

To dream of hearing hymns sung, denotes contentment in the home and average prospects in business affairs.

Hypocrite.

To dream that anyone has acted the hypocrite with you, you will be turned over to your enemies by false friends.

To dream that you are a hypocrite, denotes that you will prove yourself a deceiver and be false to friends.

Hyssop.

To dream of hyssop, denotes you will have grave charges preferred against you; and, if a woman, your reputation will be endangered.

———

I.

"And it shall come to pass in the last days, sayeth God, I will pour out my spirit upon all flesh; and your sons and your daughters shall see visions, and your old men shall dream dreams."—Acts ii, 17.

Ice.

To dream of ice, betokens much distress, and evil-minded persons will seek to injure you in your best work.

To see ice floating in a stream of clear water, denotes that your happiness will be interrupted by ill-tempered and jealous friends.

To dream that you walk on ice, you risk much solid comfort and respect for evanescent joys.

For a young woman to walk on ice, is a warning that only a thin veil hides her from shame.

———

* See Singing.

To see icicles on the eaves of houses, denotes misery and want of comfort. Ill health is foreboded.

To see icicles on the fence, denotes suffering bodily and mentally.

To see them on trees, despondent hopes will grow gloomier.

To see them on evergreens, a bright future will be overcast with the shadow of doubtful honors.

To dream that you make ice, you will make a failure of your life through egotism and selfishness.

Eating ice, foretells sickness. If you drink ice-water, you will bring ill health from dissipation.

Bathing in ice-water, anticipated pleasures will be interrupted with an unforeseen event.

Ice Cream.

To dream that you are eating ice cream, foretells you will have happy success in affairs already undertaken. To see children eating it, denotes prosperity and happiness will attend you most favorably.

For a young woman to upset her ice cream in the presence of her lover or friend, denotes she will be flirted with because of her unkindness to others. To see sour ice cream, denotes some unexpected trouble will interfere with your pleasures. If it is melted, your anticipated pleasure will reach stagnation before it is realized.

Icicles.*

To see icicles falling from trees, denotes that some distinctive misfortune, or trouble, will soon vanish.

Ideal.

For a young woman to dream of meeting her ideal, foretells a season of uninterrupted pleasure and content-

---

*See Ice.

ment. For a bachelor to dream of meeting his ideal, denotes he will soon experience a favorable change in his affairs.

Idiot.

Idiots in a dream, foretells disagreements and losses.

To dream that you are an idiot, you will feel humiliated and downcast over the miscarriage of plans.

To see idiotic children, denotes affliction and unhappy changes in life.

Idle.

If you dream of being idle, you will fail to accomplish your designs.

To see your friends in idleness, you will hear of some trouble affecting them.

For a young woman to dream that she is leading an idle existence, she will fall into bad habits, and is likely to marry a shiftless man.

Idols.

Should you dream of worshiping idols, you will make slow progress to wealth or fame, as you will let petty things tyrannize over you.

To break idols, signifies a strong mastery over self, and no work will deter you in your upward rise to positions of honor.

To see others worshiping idols, great differences will rise up between you and warm friends.

To dream that you are denouncing idolatry, great distinction is in store for you through your understanding of the natural inclinations of the human mind.

Illness.*

For a woman to dream of her own illness, foretells that

_____
* See Sickness.

some unforeseen event will throw her into a frenzy of despair by causing her to miss some anticipated visit or entertainment.

Illumination.

If you see strange and weird illuminations in your dreams, you will meet with disappointments and failures on every hand.

Illuminated faces, indicate unsettled business, both private and official.

To see the heavens illuminated, with the moon in all her weirdness, unnatural stars and a red sun, or a golden one, you may look for distress in its worst form. Death, family troubles, and national upheavals will occur.

To see children in the lighted heavens, warns you to control your feelings, as irrevocable wrong may be done in a frenzy of feeling arising over seeming neglect by your dear ones.

To see illuminated human figures or animals in the heavens, denotes failure and trouble; dark clouds overshadow fortune. To see them fall to the earth and men shoot them with guns, many troubles and obstacles will go to nought before your energy and determination to rise.

To see illuminated snakes, or any other creeping thing, enemies will surround you, and use hellish means to overthrow you.

Image.

If you dream that you see images, you will have poor success in business or love.

To set up an image in your home, portends that you will be weak minded and easily led astray. Women should be careful of their reputation after a dream of this kind. If the images are ugly, you will have trouble in your home.

Imitation.

To dream of imitations, means that persons are working to deceive you. For a young woman to dream some one is imitating her lover or herself, foretells she will be imposed upon, and will suffer for the faults of others.

Implements.

To dream of implements, denotes unsatisfactory means of accomplishing some work. If the implements are broken, you will be threatened with death or serious illness of relatives or friends, or failure n business.

Imps.

To see imps in your dream, signifies trouble from what seems a passing pleasure.

To dream that you are an imp, denotes that folly and vice will bring you to poverty.

Inauguration.

To dream of inauguration, denotes you will rise to higher position than you have yet enjoyed. For a young woman to be disappointed in attending an inauguration, predicts she will fail to obtain her wishes.

Incantation.

To dream you are using incantations, signifies unpleasantness between husband and wife, or sweethearts. To hear others repeating them, implies dissembling among your friends.

Incest.

To dream of incestuous practices, denotes you will fall from honorable places, and will also suffer loss in business.

Incoherent.

To dream of incoherency, usually denotes extreme nervousness and excitement through the oppression of changing events.

Income.

To dream of coming into the possession of your income, denotes that you may deceive some one and cause trouble to your family and friends.

To dream that some of your family inherits an income, predicts success for you.

For a woman to dream of losing her income, signifies disappointments in life.

To dream that your income is insufficient to support you, denotes trouble to relatives or friends.

To dream of a portion of your income remaining, signifies that you will be very successful for a short time, but you may expect more than you receive.

Increase.

To dream of an increase in your family, may denote failure in some of your plans, and success to another.

To dream of an increase in your business, signifies that you will overcome existing troubles.

Independent.

To dream that you are very independent, denotes that you have a rival who may do you an injustice.

To dream that you gain an independence of wealth, you may not be so succcessful at that time as you expect, but good results are promised.

India Rubber.

To dream of India rubber, denotes unfavorable changes

in your affairs. If you stretch it, you will try to establish a greater business than you can support.

Indifference.

To dream of indifference, signifies pleasant companions for a very short time.

For a young woman to dream that her sweetheart is indifferent to her, signifies that he may not prove his affections in the most appropriate way. To dream that she is indifferent to him, means that she will prove untrue to him.

Indigo.

To see indigo in a dream, denotes you will deceive friendly persons in order to cheat them out of their belongings. To see indigo water, foretells you will be involved in an ugly love affair.

Indigestion.

To dream of indigestion, indicates unhealthy and gloomy surroundings.

Indistinct.

If in your dreams you see objects indistinctly, it portends unfaithfulness in friendships, and uncertain dealings.

Indulgence.

For a woman to dream of indulgence, denotes that she will not escape unfavorable comment on her conduct.

Industry.

To dream that you are industrious, denotes that you will be unusually active in planning and working out ideas to further your interests, and that you will be successful in your undertakings.

For a lover to dream of being industriously at work, shows he will succeed in business, and that his companion will advance his position.

To see others busy, is favorable to the dreamer.

Infants.

To dream of seeing a newly born infant, denotes pleasant surprises are nearing you. For a young woman to dream she has an infant, foretells she will be accused of indulgence in immoral pastime. To see an infant swimming, portends a fortunate escape from some entanglement.

Infirmary.*

To dream that you leave an infirmary, denotes your escape from wily enemies who will cause you much worry.

Infirmities.

To dream of infirmities, denotes misfortune in love and business; enemies are not to be misunderstood, and sickness may follow.

To dream that you see others infirm, denotes that you may have various troubles and disappointments in business.

Influence.

If you dream of seeking rank or advancement through the influence of others, your desires will fail to materialize; but if you are in an influential position, your prospects will assume a bright form.

To see friends in high positions, your companions will be congenial, and you will be free from vexations.

*See Hospital.

308

Inheritance.*

To dream that you receive an inheritance, foretells that you will be successful in easily obtaining your desires.

Injury.†

To dream of an injury being done you, signifies that an unfortunate occurrence will soon grieve and vex you.

Ink.

To see ink spilled over one's clothing, many small and spiteful meannesses will be wrought you through envy.

If a young woman sees ink, she will be slandered by a rival.

To dream that you have ink on your fingers, you will be jealous and seek to injure some one unless you exercise your better nature. If it is red ink, you will be involved in a serious trouble.

To dream that you make ink, you will engage in a low and debasing business, and you will fall into disreputable associations.

To see bottles of ink in your dreams, indicates enemies and unsuccessful interests.

Ink-stand.

Empty ink-stands denote that you will narrowly escape public denunciation for some supposed injustice.

To see them filled with ink, if you are not cautious, enemies will succeed in calumniation.

Inn.

To dream of an inn, denotes prosperity and pleasures, if the inn is commodious and well furnished.

* See Estate.   †See Hurt.

To be at a dilapidated and ill kept inn, denotes poor success, or mournful tasks, or unhappy journeys.

Inquest.

To dream of an inquest, foretells you will be unfortunate in your friendships.

Inquisition.

To dream of an inquisition, bespeaks for you an endless round of trouble and great disappointment.

If you are brought before an inquisition on a charge of wilfulness, you will be unable to defend yourself from malicious slander.

Insane.

To dream of being insane, forebodes disastrous results to some newly undertaken work, or ill health may work sad changes in your prospects.

To see others insane, denotes disagreeable contact with suffering and appeals from the poverty-stricken. The utmost care should be taken of the health after this dream.

Inscription.

To dream you see an inscription, foretells you will shortly receive unpleasant communications. If you are reading them on tombs, you will be distressed by sickness of a grave nature. To write one, you will lose a valued friend.

Insolvent.

If you dream that you are insolvent, you will not have to resort to this means to square yourself with the world, as your energy and pride will enable you to transact business in a fair way. But other worries may sorely afflict you.

To dream that others are insolvent, you will meet with

honest men in your dealings, but by their frankness they may harm you. For a young woman, it means her sweetheart will be honest and thrifty, but vexatious discords may arise in her affairs.

Intemperance.

To dream of being intemperate in the use of your intellectual forces, you will seek after foolish knowledge, fail to benefit yourself, and give pain and displeasure to your friends.

If you are intemperate in love, or other passions, you will reap disease or loss of fortune and esteem. For a young woman to thus dream, she will lose a lover and incur the displeasure of close friends.

Intercede.

To intercede for some one in your dreams, shows you will secure aid when you desire it most.

Intermarry.

To dream of intermarrying, denotes quarrels and contentions which will precipitate you into trouble and loss.

Interpreter.

To dream of an interpreter, denotes you will undertake affairs which will fail in profit.

Intestine.

To dream of seeing intestines, signifies you are about to be visited by a grave calamity, which will remove some friend. To see your own intestines, denotes grave situations are closing around you; sickness of a nature to affect you in your daily communications with others threatens you. Probable loss, with much displeasure, is also denoted. If you think you lay them upon something, which turns out to be a radiator, and they begin to grow hot and make you very uncomfortable, and you ask others to assist you, and they refuse, it foretells unexpected calamity, which will probably come in the form of a desperate illness or a misfortune for which you will be censured by those formerly your friends. You may have trouble in extricating yourself from an unpromising predicament.

Intoxication.*

To dream of intoxication, denotes that you are cultivating your desires for illicit pleasures.

Inundation.†

To dream of seeing cities or country submerged in dark, seething waters, denotes great misfortune and loss of life through some dreadful calamity.

To see human beings swept away in an inundation, portends bereavements and despair, making life gloomy and unprofitable.

To see a large area inundated with clear water, denotes profit and ease after seemingly hopeless struggles with fortune.

Invalid.

To dream of invalids, is a sign of displeasing companions interfering with your interest. To think you are one, portends you are threatened with displeasing circumstances.

Invective.

To dream of using invectives, warns you of passionate outbursts of anger, which may estrange you from close companions.

To hear others using them, enemies are closing you in to apparent wrong and deceits.

---

*See Drunk.   †See Food.

Inventor.

To dream of an inventor, foretells you will soon achieve some unique work which will add honor to your name. To dream that you are inventing something, or feel interested in some invention, denotes you will aspire to fortune and will be successful in your designs.

Invite.

To dream that you invite persons to visit you, denotes that some unpleasant event is near, and will cause worry and excitement in your otherwise pleasant surroundings.

If you are invited to make a visit, you will receive sad news.

For a woman to dream that she is invited to attend a party, she will have pleasant anticipations, but ill luck will mar them.

Iron.

To dream of iron, is a harsh omen of distress.

To feel an iron weight bearing you down, signifies mental perplexities and material losses.

To strike with iron, denotes selfishness and cruelty to those dependent upon you.

To dream that you manufacture iron, denotes that you will use unjust means to accumulate wealth.

To sell iron, you will have doubtful success, and your friends will not be of noble character.

To see old, rusty iron, signifies poverty and disappointment.

To dream that the price of iron goes down, you will realize that fortune is a very unsafe factor in your life.

If iron advances, you will see a gleam of hope in a dark prospectus.

To see red-hot iron in your dreams, denotes failure for you by misapplied energy.

Ironing.

To dream of ironing, denotes domestic comforts and orderly business.

If a woman dreams that she burns her hands while ironing, it foretells she will have illness or jealousy to disturb her peace. If she scorches the clothes, she will have a rival who will cause her much displeasure and suspicions. If the irons seem too cold, she will lack affection in her home.

Island.

To dream that you are on an island in a clear stream, signifies pleasant journeys and fortunate enterprises. To a woman, this omens a happy marriage.

A barren island, indicates forfeiture of happiness and money through intemperance.

To see an island, denotes comfort and easy circumstances after much striving and worrying to meet honorable obligations.

To see people on an island, denotes a struggle to raise yourself higher in prominent circles.

Itch.

To see persons with the itch, and you endeavor to escape contact, you will stand in fear of distressing results when your endeavors will bring pleasant success.

If you dream you have the itch yourself, you will be harshly used, and will defend yourself by incriminating others. For a young woman to have this dream, omens she will fall into dissolute companionship.

To dream that you itch, denotes unpleasant avocations.

Ivory.

To dream of ivory, is favorable to the fortune of the dreamer.

To see huge pieces of ivory being carried, denotes financial success and pleasures unalloyed.

Ivy.

To dream of seeing ivy growing on trees or houses, predicts excellent health and increase of fortune. Innumerable joys will succeed this dream. To a young woman, it augurs many prized distinctions. If she sees ivy clinging to the wall in the moonlight, she will have clandestine meetings with young men.

Withered ivy, denotes broken engagements and sadness.

J.

"Then thou scarest me with dreams, and terrifiest me through visions."—Job vii, 14.

Jackdaw.

To see a jackdaw, denotes ill health and quarrels. To catch one, you will outwit enemies.

To kill one, you will come into possession of disputed property.

Jail.*

To see others in jail, you will be urged to grant privileges to persons whom you believe to be unworthy

To see children in jail, denotes worries and loss through negligence of underlings.

For a young woman to dream that her lover is in jail, she will be disappointed in his character, as he will prove a deceiver.

*See Gaol.

Jailer.

To see a jailer, denotes that treachery will embarrass your interests and evil women will enthrall you.

To see a mob attempting to break open a jail, is a forerunner of evil, and desperate measures will be used to extort money and bounties from you.

Jam.

To dream of eating jam, if pure, denotes pleasant surprises and journeys.

To dream of making jam, foretells to a woman a happy home and appreciative friends.

Janitor.

To dream of a janitor, denotes bad management and disobedient children. Unworthy servants will annoy you.

To look for a janitor and fail to find him, petty annoyances will disturb your otherwise placid existence. If you find him, you will have pleasant associations with strangers, and your affairs will have no hindrances.

January.

To dream of this month, denotes you will be afflicted with unloved companions or children.

Jar.

To dream of empty jars, denotes impoverishment and distress.

To see them full, you will be successful.

If you buy jars, your success will be precarious and your burden will be heavy.

To see broken jars, distressing sickness or deep disappointment awaits you.

Jasper.

To dream of seeing jasper, is a happy omen, bringing

success and love. For a young woman to lose a jasper, is a sign of disagreement with her lover.

Jaundice.

To dream that you have the jaundice, denotes prosperity after temporary embarrassments.

To see others with jaundice, you will be worried with unpleasant companions and discouraging prospects.

Javelin.

To dream of defending yourself with a javelin, your most private affairs will be searched into to establish claims of dishonesty, and you will prove your innocence after much wrangling.

If you are pierced by a javelin, enemies will succeed in giving you trouble.

To see others carrying javelins, your interests are threatened.

Jaws.

To dream of seeing heavy, misshapen jaws, denotes disagreements, and ill feeling will be shown between friends.

If you dream that you are in the jaws of a wild beast, enemies will work injury to your affairs and happiness. This is a vexatious and perplexing dream.

If your own jaws ache with pain, you will be exposed to climatic changes, and malaria may cause you loss in health and finances.

Jay-bird.

To dream of a jay-bird, foretells pleasant visits from friends and interesting gossips.

To catch a jay-bird, denotes pleasant, though unfruitful, tasks.

To see a dead jay-bird, denotes domestic unhappiness and many vicissitudes.

Jealousy.

To dream that you are jealous of your wife, denotes the influence of enemies and narrow-minded persons. If jealous of your sweetheart, you will seek to displace a rival.

If a woman dreams that she is jealous of her husband, she will find many shocking incidents to vex and make her happiness a travesty.

If a young woman is jealous of her lover, she will find that he is more favorably impressed with the charms of some other woman than herself.

If men and women are jealous over common affairs, they will meet many unpleasant worries in the discharge of every-day business.

Jelly.

To dream of eating jelly, many pleasant interruptions will take place.

For a woman to dream of making jelly, signifies she will enjoy pleasant reunions with friends.

Jasmine.

To dream of *Jasmine*, denotes you are approximating some exquisite pleasure, but which will be fleeting.

Jester.

To dream of a jester, foretells you will ignore important things in looking after silly affairs.

Jew.

To dream of being in company with a Jew, signifies untiring ambition and a strong longing for wealth and high position, which will not be realized to a large extent.

To have transactions with a Jew, you will prosper legally in important affairs.

For a young woman to dream of a Jew, omens that she will mistake flattery for truth, and find that she is a companion for pleasure.

For a man to dream of a Jewess, denotes that his desires run parallel with material comfort.

For a Gentile to dream of Jews, signifies worldly cares and great gain from dealing with them.

To argue with them, your reputation may be endangered in business.

Jewelry.

To dream of broken jewelry, denotes keen disappointment in attaining one's highest desires.

If the jewelry be cankered, trusted friends will fail you, and business cares will be on you.

Jewels.

To dream of jewels, denotes much pleasure and riches.

To wear them, brings rank and satisfied ambitions.

To see others wearing them, distinguished places will be held by you, or by some friend.

To dream of jeweled garments, betokens rare good fortune to the dreamer. Inheritance or speculation will raise him to high positions.

If you inherit jewelry, your prosperity will be unusual, but not entirely satisfactory.

To dream of giving jewelry away, warns you that some vital estate is threatening you.

For a young woman to dream that she receives jewelry, indicates much pleasure and a desirable marriage. To dream that she loses jewels, she will meet people who will flatter and deceive her.

319

To find jewels, denotes rapid and brilliant advancement in affairs of interest. To give jewels away, you will unconsciously work detriment to yourself.

To buy them, proves that you will be very successful in momentous affairs, especially those pertaining to the heart.

Jew's-harp.

To dream of a Jew's-harp, foretells you will experience a slight improvement in your affairs. To play one, is a sign that you will fall in love with a stranger.

Jig.

To dance a jig, denotes cheerful occupations and light pleasures.

To see negroes dancing a jig, foolish worries will offset pleasure.

To see your sweetheart dancing a jig, your companion will be possessed with a merry and hopeful disposition.

To see ballet girls dancing a jig, you will engage in undignified amusements and follow low desires.

Jockey.

To dream of a jockey, omens you will appreciate a gift from an unexpected source. For a young woman to dream that she associates with a jockey, or has one for a lover, indicates she will win a husband out of her station. To see one thrown from a horse, signifies you will be called on for aid by strangers.

Jolly.

To dream that you feel jolly and are enjoying the merriment of companions, you will realize pleasure from the good behavior of children and have satisfying results in business. If there comes the least rift in the merriment, worry will intermingle with the success of the future.

Journey.

To dream that you go on a journey, signifies profit or a disappointment, as the travels are pleasing and successful or as accidents and disagreeable events take active part in your journeying.

To see your friends start cheerfully on a journey, signifies delightful change and more harmonious companions than you have heretofore known. If you see them depart looking sad, it may be many moons before you see them again. Power and loss are implied.

To make a long-distance journey in a much shorter time than you expected, denotes you will accomplish some work in a surprisingly short time, which will be satisfactory in the way of reimbursement.

Journeyman.

To dream of a journeyman, denotes you are soon to lose money by useless travels. For a woman, this dream brings pleasant trips, though unexpected ones.

Joy.

To dream that you feel joy over any event, denotes harmony among friends.

Jubilee.

To dream of a jubilee, denotes many pleasureable enterprises in which you will be a participant. For a young woman, this is a favorable dream, pointing to matrimony and increase of temporal blessings.

To dream of a religious jubilee, denotes close but comfortable environments.

Judge.

To dream of coming before a judge, signifies that disputes will be settled by legal proceedings. Business or divorce cases may assume gigantic proportions. To have the case decided in your favor, denotes a successful termination to the suit; if decided against you, then you are the aggressor and you should seek to right injustice.

Judgment Day.

To dream of the judgment day, foretells that you will accomplish some well-planned work, if you appear resigned and hopeful of escaping punishment. Otherwise, your work will prove a failure.

For a young woman to appear before the judgment bar and hear the verdict of " Guilty," denotes that she will cause much distress among her friends by her selfish and unbecoming conduct. If she sees the dead rising, and all the earth solemnly and fearfully awaiting the end, there will be much struggling for her, and her friends will refuse her aid. It is also a forerunner of unpleasant gossip, and scandal is threatened. Business may assume hopeless aspects.

Jug.

If you dream of jugs well filled with transparent liquids, your welfare is being considered by more than yourself. Many true friends will unite to please and profit you. If the jugs are empty, your conduct will estrange you from friends and station.

Broken jugs, indicate sickness and failures in employment.

If you drink wine from a jug, you will enjoy robust health and find pleasure in all circles. Optimistic views will possess you.

To take an unpleasant drink from a jug, disappointment and disgust will follow pleasant anticipations.

July.

To dream of this month, denotes you will be depressed

with gloomy outlooks, but, as suddenly, your spirits will rebound to unimagined pleasure and good fortune.

Jumping.

If you dream of jumping over any object, you will succeed in every endeavor; but if you jump and fall back, disagreeable affairs will render life almost intolerable.

To jump down from a wall, denotes reckless speculations and disappointment in love.

Jumping-jack.

To dream of a jumping-jack, denotes that idleness and trivial pastimes will occupy your thoughts to the exclusion of serious and sustaining plans.

June.

To dream of June, foretells unusual gains in all undertakings.

For a woman to think that vegetation is decaying, or that a drouth is devastating the land, she will have sorrow and loss which will be lasting in its effects.

Juniper.

To dream of seeing a juniper tree, portends happiness and wealth out of sorrow and depressed conditions. For a young woman, this dreams omens a bright future after disappointing love affairs. To the sick, this is an augury of speedy recovery.

To eat, or gather, the berries of a juniper tree, foretells trouble and sickness.

Jury.

To dream that you are on the jury, denotes dissatisfaction with your employments, and you will seek to materially change your position.

If you are cleared from a charge by the jury, your business will be successful and affairs will move your way, but if you should be condemned, enemies will overpower you and harass you beyond endurance.

Justice.

To dream that you demand justice from a person, denotes that you are threatened with embarrassments through the false statements of people who are eager for your downfall.

If some one demands the same of you, you will find that your conduct and reputation are being assailed, and it will be extremely doubtful if you refute the charges satisfactorily.

K.

"In thoughts from the vision of the night, when deep sleep falleth on men, fear came upon me, and trembling, which made all my bones to shake."—Job iv, 13-14.

Kaleidoscope.

Kaleidosçopes working before you in a dream, portend swift changes with little of favorable promise in them.

Kangaroo.

To see a kangaroo in your dreams, you will outwit a wily enemy who seeks to place you in an unfavorable position before the public and the person you are striving to win.

If a kangaroo attacks you, your reputation will be in jeopardy.

If you kill one, you will succeed in spite of enemies and obstacles.

To see a kangaroo's hide, denotes that you are in a fair way to success.

Katydids (Grasshoppers).

To dream of hearing katydids, is a prognostic of misfortune and unusual dependence on others. If any sick person ask you what they are, foretells there will be surprising events in your present and future.

For a woman to see them, signifies she will have a quarrelsome husband or lover.

Keg.

To dream of a keg, denotes you will have a struggle to throw off oppression. Broken ones, indicate separation from family or friends.

Kettle.

To see kettles in your dream, denotes great and laborious work before you.

To see a kettle of boiling water, your struggles will soon end and a change will come to you.

To see a broken kettle, denotes failure after a mighty effort to work out a path to success.

For a young woman to dream of handling dark kettles, foretells disappointment in love and marriage; but a light-colored kettle brings to her absolute freedom from care, and her husband will be handsome and worthy.

Key.

To dream of keys, denotes unexpected changes.

If the keys are lost, unpleasant adventures will affect you.

To find keys, brings domestic peace and brisk turns to business.

Broken keys, portends separation either through death or jealousy.

For a young woman to dream of losing the key to any personal ornament, denotes she will have quarrels with her lover, and will suffer much disquiet therefrom. If she dreams of unlocking a door with a key, she will have a new lover and have over-confidence in him. If she locks a door with a key, she will be successful in selecting a husband. If she gives the key away, she will fail to use judgment in conversation and darken her own reputation.

Keyhole.

To dream that you spy upon others through a keyhole, you will damage some person by disclosing confidence. If you catch others peeping through a keyhole, you will have false friends delving into your private matters to advance themselves over you.

To dream that you cannot find the keyhole, you will unconsciously injure a friend.

Kid.

To dream of a kid, denotes you will not be over-scrupulous in your morals or pleasures. You will be likely to bring grief to some loving heart.

Kidneys.

To dream about your kidneys, foretells you are threatened with a serious illness, or there will be trouble in marriage relations for you.

If they act too freely, you will be a party to some racy intrigue. If they refuse to perform their work, there will be a sensation, and to your detriment. If you eat kidney-stew, some officious person will cause you disgust in some secret lover affair.

Killing.

To dream of killing a defenseless man, prognosticates sorrow and failure in affairs.

If you kill one in defense, or kill a ferocious beast, it denotes victory and a rise in position.

King.

To dream of a king, you are struggling with your might, and ambition is your master.

To dream that you are crowned king, you will rise above your comrades and co-workers.

If you are censured by a king, you will be reproved for a neglected duty.

For a young woman to be in the presence of a king, she will marry a man whom she will fear. To receive favors from a king, she will rise to exalted positions and be congenially wedded.

Kiss.

To dream that you see children kissing, denotes happy reunions in families and satisfactory work.

To dream that you kiss your mother, you will be very successful in your enterprises, and be honored and beloved by your friends.

To kiss a brother or sister, denotes much pleasure and good in your association.

To kiss your sweetheart in the dark, denotes dangers and immoral engagements.

To kiss her in the light, signifies honorable intentions occupy your mind always in connection with women.

To kiss a strange woman, denotes loose morals and perverted integrity.

To dream of kissing illicitly, denotes dangerous pasttimes. The indulgence of a low passion may bring a tragedy into well-thought-of homes.

To see your rival kiss your sweetheart, you are in danger of losing her esteem.

For married people to kiss each other, denotes that harmony is prized in the home life.

To dream of kissing a person on the neck, denotes passionate inclinations and weak mastery of self.

If you dream of kissing an enemy, you will make advance towards reconciliation with an angry friend.

For a young woman to dream that some person sees her kiss her lover, indicates that spiteful envy is entertained for her by a false friend. For her to see her lover kiss another, she will be disappointed in her hopes of marriage.

Kitchen.

To dream of a kitchen, denotes you will be forced to meet emergencies which will depress your spirits. For a woman to dream that her kitchen is clean and orderly, foretells she will become the mistress of interesting fortunes.

Kite.

To dream of flying a kite, denotes a great show of wealth, or business, but with little true soundness to it all.

To see the kite thrown upon the ground, foretells disappointment and failure.

To dream of making a kite, you will speculate largely on small means and seek to win the one you love by misrepresentations.

To see children flying kites, denotes pleasant and light occupation. If the kite ascends beyond the vision high hopes and aspirations will resolve themselves into disappointments and loss.

Kitten.*

For a woman to dream of a beautiful fat, white kitten, omens artful deception will be practised upon her, which will almost ensnare her to destruction, but her good sense and judgment will prevail in warding off unfortunate

*See Cats.

complications. If the kittens are soiled, or colored and lean, she will be victimized into glaring indiscretions.

To dream of kittens, denotes abominable small troubles and vexations will pursue and work you loss, unless you kill the kitten, and then you will overcome these worries.

To see snakes kill kittens, you have enemies who in seeking to injure you will work harm to themselves.

Knapsack.

To see a knapsack while dreaming, denotes you will find your greatest pleasure away from the associations of friends. For a woman to see an old dilapidated one means poverty and disagreeableness for her.

Knee.

To dream that your knees are too large, denotes sudden ill luck for you. If they are stiff and pain you, swift and fearful calamity awaits you.

For a woman to dream that she has well-formed and smooth knees, predicts she will have many admirers, but none to woo her in wedlock.

If they are soiled, sickness from dissipation is portended. If they are unshapely, unhappy changes in her fortune will displace ardent hopes.

To dream of knees is an unfortunate omen.

Knife.

To dream of a knife is bad for the dreamer, as it portends separation and quarrels, and losses in affairs of a business character.

To see rusty knives, means dissatisfaction, and complaints of those in the home, and separation of lovers.

Sharp knives and highly polished, denotes worry. Foes are ever surrounding you.

Broken knives, denotes defeat whatever the pursuit, whether in love or business.

To dream that you are wounded with a knife, foretells domestic troubles, in which disobedient children will figure largely. To the unmarried, it denotes that disgrace may follow.

To dream that you stab another with a knife, denotes baseness of character, and you should strive to cultivate a higher sense of right.

Knife Grinder.

To dream of a knife grinder, foretells unwarrantable liberties will be taken with your possessions. For a woman, this omens unhappy unions and much drudgery.

Knitting.

For a woman to dream of knitting, denotes that she will possess a quiet and peaceful home, where a loving companion and dutiful children delight to give pleasure.

For a man to be in a kniting-mill, indicates thrift and a solid rise in prospects.

For a young woman to dream of knitting, is an omen of a hasty but propitious marriage.

For a young woman to dream that she works in a knitting-mill, denotes that she will have a worthy and loyal lover. To see the mill in which she works dilapidated, she will meet with reverses in fortune and love.

Knocker.

To dream of using a knocker, foretells you will be forced to ask aid and counsel of others.

Knocking.

To hear knocking in your dreams, denotes that tidings of a grave nature will soon be received by you. If you are awakened by the knocking, the news will affect you the more seriously.

Knots.

To dream of seeing knots, denotes much worry over the most trifling affairs. If your sweetheart notices another, you will immediately find cause to censure him.

To tie a knot, signifies an independent nature, and you will refuse to be nagged by ill-disposed lover or friend.

Krishna.

To see Krishna in your dreams, denotes that your greatest joy will be in pursuit of occult knowledge, and you will school yourself to the taunts of friends, and cultivate a philosophical bearing toward life and sorrow.

L.

"And he dreamed yet another dream, and told it to his brethren, and said, 'Behold, I have dreamed a dream more; and, behold, the sun and the moon and the eleven stars made obeisance to me.'" —Gen. xxxvii, 9.

Label.

To dream of a label, foretells you will let an enemy see the inside of your private affairs, and will suffer from the negligence.

Labor.

To dream that you watch domestic animals laboring under heavy burdens, denotes that you will be prosperous, but unjust to your servants, or those employed by you.

To see men toiling, signifies profitable work, and robust health. To labor yourself, denotes favorable outlook for any new enterprise, and bountiful crops if the dreamer is interested in farming.

Laboratory.

To dream of being in a laboratory, denotes great energies wasted in unfruitful enterprises when you might succeed in some more practical business.

If you think yourself an alchemist, and try to discover a process to turn other things into gold, you will entertain far-reaching and interesting projects, but you will fail to reach the apex of your ambition. Wealth will prove a myth, and the woman you love will hold a false position towards you.

Labyrinth.

If you dream of a labyrinth, you will find yourself entangled in intricate and perplexing business conditions, and your wife will make the home environment intolerable; children and sweethearts will prove ill-tempered and unattractive.

If you are in a labyrinth of night or darkness, it foretells passing, but agonizing sickness and trouble.

A labyrinth of green vines and timbers, denotes unexpected happiness from what was seemingly a cause for loss and despair.

In a network, or labyrinth of railroads, assures you of long and tedious journeys. Interesting people will be met, but no financial success will aid you on these journeys.

Lace.

See to it, if you are a lover, that your sweetheart wears lace, as this dream brings fidelity in love and a rise in position.

If a woman dreams of lace, she will be happy in the realization of her most ambitious desires, and lovers will bow to her edict. No questioning or imperiousness on their part.

If you buy lace, you will conduct an expensive establishment, but wealth will be a solid friend.

If you sell laces, your desires will outrun your resources.

For a young girl to dream of making lace, forecasts that she will win a handsome, wealthy husband. If she dreams of garnishing her wedding garments with lace, she will be favored with lovers who will bow to her charms, but the wedding will be far removed from her.

Ladder.*

To dream of a ladder being raised for you to ascend to some height, your energetic and nervy qualifications will raise you into prominence in business affairs.

To ascend a ladder, means prosperity and unstinted happiness.

To fall from one, denotes despondency and unsuccessful transactions to the tradesman, and blasted crops to the farmer.

To see a broken ladder, betokens failure in every instance.

To descend a ladder, is disappointment in business, and unrequited desires.

To escape from captivity, or confinement, by means of a ladder, you will be successful, though many perilous paths may intervene.

To grow dizzy as you ascend a ladder, denotes that you will not wear new honors serenely. You are likely to become haughty and domineering in your newly acquired position.

Ladle.

To see a ladle in your dreams, denotes you will be for-

*See Hill, Ascend, or Fall.

tunate in the selection of a companion. Children will prove sources of happiness.

If the ladle is broken or uncleanly, you will have a grievous loss.

Lagoon.

To dream of a lagoon, denotes that you will be drawn into a whirlpool of doubt and confusion through misapplication of your intelligence.

Lake.

For a young woman to dream that she is alone on a turbulent and muddy lake, foretells many vicissitudes are approaching her, and she will regret former extravagances, and disregard of virtuous teaching.

If the water gets into the boat, but by intense struggling she reaches the boat-house safely, it denotes she will be under wrong persuasion, but will eventually overcome it, and rise to honor and distinction.

It may predict the illness of some one near her.

If she sees a young couple in the same position as herself, who succeed in rescuing themselves, she will find that some friend has committed indiscretions, but will succeed in reinstating himself in her favor.

To dream of sailing on a clear and smooth lake, with happy and congenial companions, you will have much happiness, and wealth will meet your demands.

A muddy lake, surrounded with bleak rocks and bare trees, denotes unhappy terminations to business and affection.

A muddy lake, surrounded by green trees, portends that the moral in your nature will fortify itself against passionate desires, and overcoming the same will direct your energy into a safe and remunerative channel. If the lake be clear and surrounded by barrenness, a profitable existence will be marred by immoral and passionate dissipation.

To see yourself reflected in a clear lake, denotes coming joys and many ardent friends.

To see foliaged trees reflected in the lake, you will enjoy to a satiety Love's draught of passion and happiness.

To see slimy and uncanny inhabitants of the lake rise up and menace you, denotes failure and ill health from squandering time, energy and health on illicit pleasures. You will drain the utmost drop of happiness, and drink deeply of Remorse's bitter concoction.

Lamb.*

To dream of lambs frolicing in green pastures, betokens chaste friendships and joys. Bounteous and profitable crops to the farmers, and increase of possessions for others.

To see a dead lamb, signifies sadness and desolation.

Blood showing on the white fleece of a lamb, denotes that innocent ones will suffer from betrayal through the wrong doing of others.

A lost lamb, denotes that wayward people will be under your influence, and you should be careful of your conduct.

To see lamb skins, denotes comfort and pleasure usurped from others.

To slaughter a lamb for domestic uses, prosperity will be gained through the sacrifice of pleasure and contentment.

To eat lamb chops, denotes illness, and much anxiety over the welfare of children.

To see lambs taking nourishment from their mothers,

*See Sheep.

denotes happiness through pleasant and intelligent home companions, and many lovable and beautiful children.

To dream that dogs, or wolves devour lambs, innocent people will suffer at the hands of insinuating and designing villains.

To hear the bleating of lambs, your generosity will be appealed to.

To see them in a winter storm, or rain, denotes disappointment in expected enjoyment and betterment of fortune.

To own lambs in your dreams, signifies that your environments will be pleasant and profitable.

If you carry lambs in your arms, you will be encumbered with happy cares upon which you will lavish a wealth of devotion, and no expense will be regretted in responding to appeals from the objects of your affection.

To shear lambs, shows that you will be cold and mercenary. You will be honest, but inhumane.

For a woman to dream that she is peeling the skin from a lamb, and while doing so, she discovers that it is her child, denotes that she will cause others sorrow which will also rebound to her grief and loss.

> "Fair prototype of innocence,
>   Sleep upon thy emerald bed,
> No coming evil vents
>   A shade above thy head."

Lame.*

For a woman to dream of seeing any one lame, foretells that her pleasures and hopes will be unfruitful and disappointing.

Lament.

To dream that you bitterly lament the loss of friends,

* See Cripple.

or property, signifies great struggles and much distress, from which will spring causes for joy and personal gain.

To lament the loss of relatives, denotes sickness or disappointments, which will bring you into closer harmony with companions, and will result in brighter prospects for the future.

Lamp.

To see lamps filled with oil, denotes the demonstration of business activity, from which you will receive gratifying results.

Empty lamps, represent depression and despondency.

To see lighted lamps burning with a clear flame, indicates merited rise in fortune and domestic bliss. If they give out a dull, misty radiance, you will have jealousy and envy, coupled with suspicion, to combat, in which you will be much pleased to find the right person to attack.

To drop a lighted lamp, your plans and hopes will abruptly turn into failure.

If it explodes, former friends will unite with enemies in damaging your interests.

Broken lamps, indicate the death of relatives or friends.

To light a lamp, denotes that you will soon make a change in your affairs, which will lead to profit.

To carry a lamp, portends that you will be independent and self-sustaining, preferring your own convictions above others. If the light fails, you will meet with unfortunate conclusions, and perhaps the death of friends or relatives.

If you are much affrighted, and throw a bewildering light from your window, enemies will ensnare you with professions of friendship and interest in your achievements.

To ignite your apparel from a lamp, you will sustain

humiliation from sources from which you expected encouragement and sympathy, and your business will not be fraught with much good.

Lamp-post.

To see a lamp-post in your dreams, some stranger will prove your staunchiest friend in time of pressing need.

To fall against a lamp-post, you will have deception to overcome, or enemies will ensnare you.

To see a lamp-post across your path, you will have much adversity in your life.

Lance.

To dream of a lance, denotes formidable enemies and injurious experiments.

To be wounded by a lance, error of judgment will cause you annoyance.

To break a lance, denotes seeming impossibilities will be overcome and your desires will be fulfilled.

Land.*

To dream of land, when it appears fertile, omens good; but if sterile and rocky, failure and dispondency is prognosticated.

To see land from the ocean, denotes that vast avenues of prosperity and happiness will disclose themselves to you.

Landau.

To dream that you ride in a landau, with your friend or sweetheart, denotes that incidents of a light, but pleasant character will pass in rapid succession through your life.

If the vehicle is overturned, then pleasure will abruptly turn into woe.

---

*See Fields and Earth.

Lantern.

To dream of seeing a lantern going before you in the darkness, signifies unexpected affluence. If the lantern is suddenly lost to view, then your success will take an unfavorable turn.

To carry a lantern in your dreams, denotes that your benevolence will win you many friends. If it goes out, you fail to gain the prominence you wish. If you stumble and break it, you will seek to aid others, and in so doing lose your own station, or be disappointed in some undertaking.

To clean a lantern, signifies great possibilities are open to you.

To lose a lantern, means business depression, and disquiet in the home.

If you buy a lantern, it signifies fortunate deals.

For a young woman to dream that she lights her lover's lantern, foretells for her a worthy man, and a comfortable home. If she blows it out, by her own imprudence she will lose a chance of getting married.

Lap.

To dream of sitting on some person's lap, denotes pleasant security from vexing engagements. If a young woman dreams that she is holding a person on her lap, she will be exposed to unfavorable criticism.

To see a serpent in her lap, foretells she is threatened with humiliation at the hands of enemies. If she sees a cat in her lap, she will be endangered by a seductive enemy.

Lap-dog.

To dream of a lap-dog, foretells you will be succored by friends in some approaching dilemma. If it be thin and ill-looking, there will be distressing occurrences to detract from your prospects.

Lap-robe.

To dream of a lap-robe, indicates suspicious engagements will place you under the surveillance of enemies or friends.

To lose one, your actions will be condemned by enemies to injure your affairs.

Lard.

To dream of lard, signifies a rise in fortune will soon gratify you. For a woman to find her hand in melted lard, foretells her disappointment in attempting to rise in social circles.

Lark.

To see larks flying, denotes high aims and purposes through the attainment of which you will throw off selfishness and cultivate kindly graces of mind.

To hear them singing as they fly, you will be very happy in a new change of abode, and business will flourish.

To see them fall to the earth and singing as they fall, despairing gloom will overtake you in pleasure's bewildering delights.

A wounded or dead lark, portends sadness or death.

To kill a lark, portends injury to innocence through wantonness.

If they fly around and light on you, Fortune will turn her promising countenance towards you.

To catch them in traps, you will win honor and love easily.

To see them eating, denotes a plentiful harvest.

Latch.

To dream of a latch, denotes you will meet urgent

appeals for aid, to which you will respond unkindly. To see a broken latch, foretells disagreements with your dearest friend. Sickness is also foretold in this dream.

Latin.

To dream of studying this language, denotes victory and distinction in your efforts to sustain your opinion on subjects of grave interest to the public welfare.

Laudanum.

To dream that you take laudanum, signifies weakness of your own; and that you will have a tendency to be unduly influenced by others. You should cultivate determination.

To prevent others from taking this drug, indicates that you will be the means of conveying great joy and good to people.

To see your lover taking laudanum through disappointment, signifies unhappy affairs and the loss of a friend.

To give it, slight ailments will attack some member of your domestic circle.

Laughing.

To dream that you laugh and feel cheerful, means success in your undertakings, and bright companions socially.

Laughing immoderately at some weird object, denotes disappointment and lack of harmony in your surroundings.

To hear the happy laughter of children, means joy and health to the dreamer.

To laugh at the discomfiture of others, denotes that you will wilfully injure your friends to gratify your own selfish desires.

To hear mocking laughter, denotes illness and disappointing affairs.

Laundry.

To dream of laundering clothes, denotes struggles, but a final victory in winning fortune. If the clothes are done satisfactorily, then your endeavors will bring complete happiness. If they come out the reverse, your fortune will fail to procure pleasure.

To see pretty girls at this work, you will seek pleasure out of your rank.

If a laundryman calls at your house, you are in danger of sickness, or of losing something very valuable.

To see laundry wagons, portends rivalry and contention.

Laurel.

Dreaming of the laurel, brings success and fame. You will acquire new possessions in love. Enterprises will be laden with gain.

For a young woman to wreath laurel about her lover's head, denotes that she will have a faithful man, and one of fame to woo her.

Law and Lawsuits.*

To dream of engaging in a lawsuit, warns you of enemies who are poisoning public opinion against you. If you know that the suit is dishonest on your part, you will seek to dispossess true owners for your own advancement.

If a young man is studying law, he will make rapid rise in any chosen profession.

For a woman to dream that she engages in a law suit, means she will be calumniated, and find enemies among friends.

Lawns.

To dream of walking upon well-kept lawns, denotes occasions for joy and great prosperity.

---

*See Judge and Jury.

To join a merry party upon a lawn, denotes many secular amusements, and business engagements will be successfully carried on.

For a young woman to wait upon a green lawn for the coming of a friend or lover, denotes that her most ardent wishes concerning wealth and marriage will be gratified. If the grass be dead and the lawn marshy, quarrels and separation may be expected.

To see serpents crawling in the grass before you, betrayal and cruel insinuations will fill you with despair.

Lawyer.*

For a young woman to dream that she is connected in any way with a lawyer, foretells that she will unwittingly commit indiscretions, which will subject her to unfavorable and mortifying criticism.

Lazy.

To dream of feeling lazy, or acting so, denotes you will make a mistake in the formation of enterprises, and will suffer keen disappointment.

For a young woman to think her lover is lazy, foretells she will have bad luck in securing admiration. Her actions will discourage men who mean marriage.

Lead.

To dream of lead. foretells poor success in any engagement.

A lead mine, indicates that your friends will look with suspicion on your money making. Your sweetheart will surprise you with her deceit and ill temper.

To dream of lead ore, foretells distress and accidents. Business will assume a gloomy cast.

To hunt for lead, denotes discontentment, and a constant changing of employment.

---

*See Attorney.

To melt lead, foretells that by impatience you will bring failure upon yourself and others.

Leaking.

To dream of seeing a leak in anything, is usually significant of loss and vexations.

Leaping.*

For a young woman to dream of leaping over an obstruction, denotes that she will gain her desires after much struggling and opposition.

Learning.

To dream of learning, denotes that you will take great interest in acquiring knowledge, and if you are economical of your time, you will advance far into the literary world.

To enter halls, or places of learning, denotes rise from obscurity, and finance will be a congenial adherent.

To see learned men, foretells that your companions will be interesting and prominent.

For a woman to dream that she is associated in any way with learned people, she will be ambitious and excel in her endeavors to rise into prominence.

Leather.

To dream of leather, denotes successful business and favorable engagements with women. You will go into lucky speculations if you dream that you are dressed in leather.

Ornaments of leather, denotes faithfulness in love and to the home.

Piles of leather, denotes fortune and happiness.

To deal in leather, signifies no change in the disposition

---

*See Jumping.

of your engagements is necessary for successful accumulation of wealth.

Leaves.

To dream of leaves, denotes happiness and wonderful improvement in your business.

Withered leaves, indicate false hopes and gloomy forebodings will harass your spirit into a whirlpool of despondency and loss.

If a young woman dreams of withered leaves, she will be left lonely on the road to conjugality. Death is sometimes implied.

If the leaves are green and fresh, she will come into a legacy and marry a wealthy and prepossessing husband.

Ledger.

To dream of keeping a ledger, you will have perplexities and disappointing conditions to combat.

To dream that you make wrong entries on your ledger, you will have small disputes and a slight loss will befall you.

To put a ledger into a safe, you will be able to protect your rights under adverse circumstances.

To get your ledger misplaced, your interests will go awry through neglect of duty.

To dream that your ledger gets destroyed by fire, you will suffer through the carelessness of friends.

To dream that you have a woman to keep your ledger, you will lose money trying to combine pleasure with business.

For a young woman to dream of ledgers, denotes she will have a solid business man to make her a proposal of marriage.

To dream that your ledger has worthless accounts, denotes bad management and losses; but if the accounts are good, then your business will assume improved conditions.

Leeches.

To dream of leeches, foretells that enemies will run over your interests.

If they are applied to you for medicinal purposes, you will have a serious illness in your family (if you escape yourself).

To see them applied to others, denotes sickness or trouble to friends.

If they should bite you, there is danger for you in unexpected places, and you should heed well this warning.

Leeward.

To dream of sailing leeward, denotes to the sailor a prosperous and merry voyage. To others, a pleasant journey.

Legerdemain.

To dream of practising legerdemain, or seeing others doing so, signifies you will be placed in a position where your energy and power of planning will be called into strenuous play to extricate yourself.

Legislature.

To dream that you are a member of a legislature, foretells you will be vain of your possessions and will treat members of your family unkindly. You will have no real advancement.

Legs.

If you dream of admiring well-shaped feminine legs, you will lose your judgment, and act very silly over some fair charmer.

To see misshapen legs, denotes unprofitable occupations and ill-tempered comrades.

A wounded leg, foretells losses and agonizing attacks of malaria.

To dream that you have a wooden leg, denotes that you will bemean yourself in a false way to your friends.

If ulcers are on your legs, it signifies a drain on your income to aid others.

To dream that you have three, or more, legs, indicates that more enterprises are planned in your imagination than will ever benefit you.

If you can't use your legs, it portends poverty.

To have a leg amputated, you will lose valued friends, and the home influence will render life unbearable.

For a young woman to admire her own legs, denotes vanity, and she will be repulsed by the man she admires. If she has hairy legs, she will dominate her husband.

If your own legs are clean and well shaped, it denotes a happy future and devoted friends.

Lemonade.

If you drink lemonade in a dream, you will concur with others in signifying some entertainment as a niggardly device to raise funds for the personal enjoyment of others at your expense.

Lemons.

To dream of seeing lemons on their native trees among rich foliage, denotes jealousy toward some beloved object, but demonstrations will convince you of the absurdity of the charge.

To eat lemons, foretells humiliation and disappointments.

Green lemons, denotes sickness and contagion.

To see shriveled lemons, denotes divorce, if married, and separation, to lovers.

Lending.

To dream that you are lending money, foretells difficulties in meeting payments of debts and unpleasant influence in private.

To lend other articles, denotes impoverishment through generosity.

To refuse to lend things, you will be awake to your interests and keep the respect of friends.

For others to offer to lend you articles, or money, denotes prosperity and close friendships.

Lentil.

If you dream of lentils, it denotes quarrels and unhealthy surroundings. For a young woman, this dream portends dissatisfaction with her lover, but parental advice will cause her to accept the inevitable.

Leopard.

To dream of a leopard attacking you, denotes that while the future seemingly promises fair, success holds many difficulties through misplaced confidence.

To kill one, intimates victory in your affairs.

To see one caged, denotes that enemies will surround but fail to injure you.

To see leopards in their native place trying to escape from you, denotes that you will be embarrassed in business or love, but by persistent efforts you will overcome difficulties.

To dream of a leopard's skin, denotes that your interests will be endangered by a dishonest person who will win your esteem.

Leprosy.

To dream that you are infected with this dread disease,

foretells sickness, by which you will lose money and incur the displeasure of others.

If you see others afflicted thus, you will meet discouraging prospects and love will turn into indifference.

Letter.

To dream that you see a registered letter, foretells that some money matters will disrupt long-established relations.

For a young woman to dream that she receives such a letter, intimates that she will be offered a competency, but it will not be on strictly legal, or moral grounds; others may play towards her a dishonorable part.

To the lover, this bears heavy presentments of disagreeable mating. His sweetheart will covet other gifts than his own.

To dream of an anonymous letter, denotes that you will receive injury from an unsuspected source.

To write one, foretells that you will be jealous of a rival, whom you admit to be your superior.

To dream of getting letters bearing unpleasant news, denotes difficulties or illness. If the news is of a joyous character, you will have many things to be thankful for. If the letter is affectionate, but is written on green, or colored, paper, you will be slighted in love and business. Despondency will envelop you. Blue ink, denotes constancy and affection, also bright fortune.

Red colors in a letter, imply estrangements through suspicion and jealousy, but this may be overcome by wise maneuvering of the suspected party.

If a young woman dreams that she receives a letter from her lover and places it near her heart, she will be worried very much by a good-looking rival. Truthfulness is often rewarded with jealousy.

If you fail to read the letter, you will lose something either in a business or social way.

Letters nearly always bring worry.

To have your letter intercepted, rival enemies are working to defame you.

To dream of trying to conceal a letter from your sweetheart or wife, intimates that you are interested in unworthy occupations.

To dream of a letter with a black border, signifies distress and the death of some relative.

To receive a letter written on black paper with white ink, denotes that gloom and disappointment will assail you, and friendly interposition will render small relief. If the letter passes between husband and wife, it means separation under sensational charges. If lovers, look for quarrels and threats of suicide. To business people, it denotes enviousness and covetousness.

To dream that you write a letter, denotes that you will be hasty in condemning some one on suspicion, and regrets will follow.

A torn letter, indicates that hopeless mistakes may ruin your reputation.

To receive a letter by hand, denotes that you are acting ungenerously towards your companions or sweetheart, and you also are not upright in your dealings.

To dream often of receiving a letter from a friend, foretells his arrival, or you will hear from him by letter or otherwise.

Letter-carrier.

If you dream of a letter-carrier coming with your letters, you will soon receive news of an unwelcome and an unpleasant character.

To hear his whistle, denotes the unexpected arrival of a visitor.

If he passes without your mail, disappointment and sadness will befall you.

If you give him letters to mail, you will suffer injury through envy or jealousy.

To converse with a letter-carrier, you will implicate yourself in some scandalous proceedings.

Letter-file.

To see a letter-file in your dreams, is significant of important news, which will cause you an irksome journey. For a woman, this dream implies distressful news and unfaithful friends.

Lettuce.

To see lettuce growing green and thrifty, denotes that you will enjoy some greatly desired good, after an unimportant embarrassment.

If you eat lettuce, illness will separate you from your lover or companion, or perhaps it may be petty jealousy.

For a woman to dream of sowing lettuce, portends she will be the cause of her own early sickness or death.

To gather it, denotes your superabundant sensitiveness, and that your jealous disposition will cause you unmitigated distress and pain.

To buy lettuce, denotes that you will court your own downfall.

Liar.

To dream of thinking people are liars, foretells you will lose faith in some scheme which you had urgently put forward. For some one to call you a liar, means you will have vexations through deceitful persons.

For a woman to think her sweetheart a liar, warns her that her unbecoming conduct is likely to lose her a valued friend.

351

Library.

To dream that you are in a library, denotes that you will grow discontented with your environments and associations and seek companionship in study and the exploration of ancient customs.

To find yourself in a library for other purpose than study, foretells that your conduct will deceive your friends, and where you would have them believe that you had literary aspirations, you will find illicit assignations.

Lice.

A dream of lice contains much waking worry and distress. It often implies offensive ailments.

Lice on stock, foretells famine and loss.

To have lice on your body, denotes that you will conduct yourself unpleasantly with your acquaintances.

To dream of catching lice, foretells sickness, and that you will cultivate morbidity.

License.

To dream of a license, is an omen of disputes and loss. Married women will exasperate your cheerfulness. For a woman to see a marriage license, foretells that she will soon enter unpleasant bonds, which will humiliate her pride.

Life-boat.

To dream of being in a life-boat, denotes escape from threatened evil.

To see a life-boat sinking, friends will contribute to your distress.

To be lost in a life-boat, you will be overcome with trouble, in which your friends will be included to some extent. If you are saved, you will escape a great calamity.

Life-insurance Man.

To see life-insurance men in a dream, means that you are soon to meet a stranger who will contribute to your business interests, and change in your home life is foreshadowed, as interests will be mutual.

If they appear distorted or unnatural, the dream is more unfortunate than good.

Light.

If you dream of light, success will attend you. To dream of weird light, or if the light goes out, you will be disagreeably surprised by some undertaking resulting in nothing.

To see a dim light, indicates partial success.

Lighthouse.

If you see a lighthouse through a storm, difficulties and grief will assail you, but they will disperse before prosperity and happiness.

To see a lighthouse from a placid sea, denotes calm joys and congenial friends.

Lightning.

Lightning in your dreams, foreshadows happiness and prosperity of short duration.

If the lightning strikes some object near you, and you feel the shock, you will be damaged by the good fortune of a friend, or you may be worried by gossipers and scandalmongers.

To see livid lightning parting black clouds, sorrow and difficulties will follow close on to fortune.

If it strikes you, unexpected sorrows will overwhelm you in business or love.

To see the lightning above your head, heralds the advent of joy and gain.

To see lightning in the south, fortune will hide herself from you for awhile.

If in the southwest, luck will come your way. In the west, your prospects will be brighter than formally. In the north, obstacles will have to be removed before your prospects will brighten up. If in the east, you will easily win favors and fortune. Lightning from dark and ominous-looking clouds, is always a forerunner of threats, of loss and of disappointments. Business men should stay close to business, and women near their husbands or mothers; children and the sick should be looked after closely.

Lightning-rod.

To see a lightning-rod, denotes that threatened destruction to some cherished work will confront you. To see one change into a serpent, foretells enemies will succeed in their schemes against you. If the lightning strikes one, there will be an accident or sudden news to give you sorrow.

If you are having one put up, it is a warning to beware how you begin a new enterprise, as you will likely be overtaken by disappointment.

To have them taken down, you will change your plans and thereby further your interests. To see many lightning rods, indicates a variety of misfortunes.

Lily.

To dream of a lily, denotes much chastisement through illness and death. To see lilies growing with their rich foliage, denotes early marriage to the young and subsequent separation through death.

To see little children among the flowers, indicates sickness and fragile constitutions to these little ones.

For a young woman to dream of admiring, or gathering,

lilies, denotes much sadness coupled with joy, as the one she loves will have great physical suffering, if not an early dissolution. If she sees them withered, sorrow is even nearer than she could have suspected.

To dream that you breathe the fragrance of lilies, denotes that sorrow will purify and enhance your mental qualities.

Lime.

To dream of lime, foretells that disaster will prostrate you for a time, but you will revive to greater and richer prosperity than before.

Lime-kiln.

To dream of a lime-kiln, foretells the immediate future holds no favor for speculations in love or business

Limes,

To dream of eating limes, foretells continued sickness and adverse straits.

Limp.*

To dream that you limp in your walk, denotes that a small worry will unexpectedly confront you, detracting much from your enjoyment.

To see others limping, signifies that you will be naturally offended at the conduct of a friend. Small failures attend this dream.

Linen.

To see linen in your dream, augurs prosperity and enjoyment.

If a person appears to you dressed in linen garments, you will shortly be the recipient of joyful tidings in the nature of an inheritance.

*See Cripple and Lamed.

If you are apparelled in clean, fine linen, your fortune and fullest enjoyment in life is assured. If it be soiled, sorrow and ill luck will be met with occasionally, mingled with the good in your life.

Linseed Oil.

To see linseed oil in your dreams, denotes your impetuous extravagance will be checked by the kindly interference of a friend.

Lion.

To dream of a lion, signifies that a great force is driving you.

If you subdue the lion, you will be victorious in any engagement.

If it overpowers you, then you will be open to the successful attacks of enemies.

To see caged lions, denotes that your success depends upon your ability to cope with opposition.

To see a man controlling a lion in its cage, or out denotes success in business and great mental power. You will be favorably regarded by women.

To see young lions, denotes new enterprises, which will bring success if properly attended.

For a young woman to dream of young lions, denotes new and fascinating lovers.

For a woman to dream that she sees Daniel in the lions' den, signifies that by her intellectual qualifications and personal magnetism she will win fortune and lovers to her highest desire.

To hear the roar of a lion, signifies unexpected advancement and preferment with women.

To see a lion's head over you, showing his teeth by snarls, you are threatened with defeat in your upward rise to power.

To see a lion's skin, denotes a rise to fortune and happiness.

To ride one, denotes courage and persistency in surmounting difficulties.

To dream you are defending your children from a lion with a pen-knife, foretells enemies will threaten to overpower you, and will well nigh succeed if you allow any artfulness to persuade you for a moment from duty and business obligations.

Lips.

To dream of thick, unsightly lips, signifies disagreeable encounters, hasty decision, and ill temper in the marriage relation.

Full, sweet, cherry lips, indicates harmony and affluence. To a lover, it augurs reciprocation in love, and fidelity.

Thin lips, signifies mastery of the most intricate subjects.

Sore, or swollen lips, denotes privations and unhealthful desires.

Liquor.

To dream of buying liquor, denotes selfish usurpation of property upon which you have no legal claim. If you sell it, you will be criticised for niggardly benevolence.

To drink some, you will come into doubtful possession of wealth, but your generosity will draw around you convivial friends, and women will seek to entrance and hold you.

To see liquor in barrels, denotes prosperity, but unfavorable tendency toward making home pleasant.

If in bottles, fortune will appear in a very tangible form.

For a woman to dream of handling, or drinking liquor, foretells for her a happy Bohemian kind of existence. She will be good natured but shallow minded. To treat others,

357

she will be generous to rivals, and the indifference of lovers or husband will not seriously offset her pleasures or contentment.

Liver.

To dream of a disordered liver, denotes a querulous person will be your mate, and fault-finding will occupy her time, and disquiet will fill your hours.

To dream of eating liver, indicates that some deceitful person has installed himself in the affection of your sweetheart.

Lizard.

To dream of lizards, foretells attacks upon you by enemies.

If you kill a lizard, you will regain your lost reputation or fortune; but if it should escape, you will meet vexations and crosses in love and business.

For a woman to dream that a lizard crawls up her skirt, or scratches her, she will have much misfortune and sorrow. Her husband will be a victim to invalidism and she will be left a widow, and little sustenance will be eked out by her own labors.

Load.

To dream that you carry a load, signifies a long existence filled with labors of love and charity.

To fall under a load, denotes your inability to attain comforts that are necessary to those looking to you for subsistence.

To see others thus engaged, denotes trials for them in which you will be interested.

Loadstone.

To dream of a loadstone, denotes you will make favorable opportunities for your own advancement in a material way. For a young woman to think a loadstone is attracting her, is an omen of happy changes in her family.

Loaves.

To dream of loaves of bread, denotes frugality. If they be of cake, the dreamer has cause to rejoice over his good fortune, as love and wealth will wait obsequiously upon you.

Broken loaves, bring discontent and bickerings between those who love.

To see loaves multiply phenomenally, prognosticates great success. Lovers will be happy in their chosen ones.

Lobster.

To dream of seeing lobsters, denotes great favors, and riches will endow you.

If you eat them, you will sustain contamination by associating too freely with pleasure-seeking people.

If the lobsters are made into a salad, success will not change your generous nature, but you will enjoy to the fullest your ideas of pleasure.

To order a lobster, you will hold prominent positions and command many subordinates.

Lock.

To dream of a lock, denotes bewilderment. If the lock works at your command, or efforts, you will discover that some person is working you injury. If you are in love, you will find means to aid you in overcoming a rival; you will also make a prosperous journey.

If the lock resists your efforts, you will be derided and scorned in love and perilous voyages will bring to you no benefit.

To put a lock upon your fiancée's neck and arm, foretells that you are distrustful of her fidelity, but future episodes will disabuse your mind of doubt.

Locket.

If a young woman dreams that her lover places a locket around her neck, she will be the recipient of many beautiful offerings, and will soon be wedded, and lovely children will crown her life. If she should lose a locket, death will throw sadness into her life.

If a lover dreams that his sweetheart returns his locket, he will confront disappointing issues. The woman he loves will worry him and conduct herself in a displeasing way toward him.

If a woman dreams that she breaks a locket, she will have a changeable and unstable husband, who will dislike constancy in any form, be it business or affection.

Lockjaw.

To dream that you have lockjaw, signifies there is trouble ahead for you, as some person is going to betray your confidence. For a woman to see others with lockjaw, foretells her friends will unconsciously detract from her happiness by assigning her unpleasant tasks. If stock have it, you will lose a friend.

Locomotive.

To dream of a locomotive running with great speed, denotes a rapid rise in fortune, and foreign travel. If it is disabled, then many vexations will interfere with business affairs, and anticipated journeys will be laid aside through the want of means.

To see one completely demolished, signifies great distress and loss of property.

To hear one coming, denotes news of a foreign nature.

Business will assume changes that will mean success to all classes.

To hear it whistle, you will be pleased and surprised at the appearance of a friend who has been absent, or an unexpected offer, which means preferment to you.

Locust.

To dream of locusts, foretells discrepancies will be found in your business, for which you will worry and suffer. For a woman, this dream foretells she will bestow her affections upon ungenerous people.

Lodger.

For a woman to dream that she has lodgers, foretells she will be burdened with unpleasant secrets. If one goes away without paying his bills, she will have unexpected trouble with men. For one to pay his bill, omens favor and accumulation of money.

Looking-glass.*

For a woman to dream of a looking-glass, denotes that she is soon to be confronted with shocking deceitfulness and discrepancies, which may result in tragic scenes or separations.

Loom.

To dream of standing by and seeing a loom operated by a stranger, denotes much vexation and useless irritation from the talkativeness of those about you. Some disappointment with happy expectations are coupled with this dream.

To see good-looking women attending the loom, denotes unqualified success to those in love. It predicts congenial pursuits to the married. It denotes you are drawing closer together in taste.

---

*See Mirror.

For a woman to dream of weaving on an oldtime loom, signifies that she will have a thrifty husband and beautiful children will fill her life with happy solicitations.

To see an idle loom, denotes a sulky and stubborn person, who will cause you much anxious care.

Lord's Prayer.

To dream of repeating the Lord's Prayer, foretells that you are threatened with secret foes and will need the alliance and the support of friends to tide you over difficulties.

To hear others repeat it, denotes the danger of some friend.

Lottery.

To dream of a lottery, and that you are taking great interest in the drawing, you will engage in some worthless enterprise, which will cause you to make an unpropitious journey. If you hold the lucky number, you will gain in a speculation which will perplex and give you much anxiety.

To see others winning in a lottery, denotes convivialities and amusements, bringing many friends together.

If you lose in a lottery, you will be the victim of designing persons. Gloomy depressions in your affairs will result.

For a young woman to dream of a lottery in any way, denotes that her careless way of doing things will bring her disappointment, and a husband who will not be altogether reliable or constant.

To dream of a lottery, denotes you will have unfavorable friendships in business. Your love affairs will produce temporary pleasure.

Louse.*

To dream of a louse, foretells that you will have uneasy feelings regarding your health, and an enemy will give you exasperating vexation.

Love.

To dream of loving any object, denotes satisfaction with your present environments.

To dream that the love of others fills you with happy forebodings, successful affairs will give you contentment and freedom from the anxious cares of life. If you find that your love fails, or is not reciprocated, you will become despondent over some conflicting question arising in your mind as to whether it is best to change your mode of living or to marry and trust fortune for the future advancement of your state.

For a husband or wife to dream that their companion is loving, foretells great happiness around the hearthstone, and bright children will contribute to the sunshine of the home.

To dream of the love of parents, foretells uprightness in character and a continual progress toward fortune and elevation.

The love of animals, indicates contentment with what you possess, though you may not think so. For a time, fortune will crown you.

Lovely.

Dreaming of lovely things, brings favor to all persons connected with you.

For a lover to dream that his sweetheart is lovely of person and character, foretells for him a speedy and favorable marriage.

---

*See Lice.

If through the vista of dreams you see your own fair loveliness, fate bids you, with a gleaming light, awake to happiness.

Lozenges.

To dream of lozenges, foretells success in small matters. For a woman to eat or throw them away, foretells her life will be harassed by little spites from the envious.

Lucky.

To dream of being lucky, is highly favorable to the dreamer. Fulfilment of wishes may be expected and pleasant duties will devolve upon you.

To the despondent, this dream forebodes an uplifting and a renewal of prosperity.

Luggage.

To dream of luggage, denotes unpleasant cares. You will be encumbered with people who will prove distasteful to you.

If you are carrying your own luggage, you will be so full of your own distresses that you will be blinded to the sorrows of others.

To lose your luggage, denotes some unfortunate speculation or family dissensions. To the unmarried, it foretells broken engagements.

Lumber.

To dream of lumber, denotes many difficult tasks and but little remuneration or pleasure.

To see piles of lumber burning, indicates profit from an unexpected source.

To dream of sawing lumber, denotes unwise transactions and unhappiness.

Lute.

To dream of playing on one, is auspicious of joyful news from absent friends.

Pleasant occupations follow the dreaming of hearing the music of a lute.

Luxury.

To dream that you are surrounded by luxury, indicates much wealth, but dissipation and love of self will reduce your income.

For a poor woman to dream that she enjoys much luxury, denotes an early change in her circumstances.

Lying.

To dream that you are lying to escape punishment, denotes that you will act dishonorably towards some innocent person.

Lying to protect a friend from undeserved chastisement, denotes that you will have many unjust criticisms passed upon your conduct, but you will rise above them and enjoy prominence.

To hear others lying, denotes that they are seeking to entrap you.

Lynx.

To dream of seeing a lynx, enemies are undermining your business and disrupting your home affairs. For a woman, this dream indicates that she has a wary woman rivaling her in the affections of her lover. If she kills the lynx, she will overcome her rival.

Lyre.

To dream of listening to the music of a lyre, foretells chaste pleasures and congenial companionship. Business will run smoothly.

For a young woman to dream of playing on one, denotes that she will enjoy the undivided affection of a worthy man.

M.

"And they dreamed a dream both of them, each man his dream in one night, each man according to his interpretation of his dream, the butler and the baker of the King of Egypt, which were bound in the prison."—Gen. xl., 5.

Macadamize.

To dream that you see or travel on a macadamized road, is significant of pleasant journeys, from which you will derive much benefit. For young people, this dream foretells noble aspirations.

Macaroni.

To dream of eating macaroni, denotes small losses. To see it in large quantities, denotes that you will save money by the strictest economy. For a young woman, this dream means that a stranger will enter her life.

Machinery.

To dream of machinery, denotes you will undertake some project which will give great anxiety, but which will finally result in good for you.

To see old machinery, foretells enemies will overcome in your strivings to build up your fortune. To become entangled in machinery, foretells loss in your business, and much unhappiness will follow.

Loss from bad deals generally follows this dream.

Mad Dog.*

To dream of seeing a mad dog, denotes that enemies will make scurrilous attacks upon you and your friends, but if you succeed in killing the dog, you will overcome adverse opinions and prosper greatly in a financial way.

---

*See Dog.

Madness.

To dream of being mad, shows trouble ahead for the dreamer. Sickness, by which you will lose property, is threatened.

To see others suffering under this malady, denotes inconstancy of friends and gloomy ending of bright expectations.

For a young woman to dream of madness, foretells disappointment in marriage and wealth.

Madstone.

To see a madstone applied to a wound from the fangs of some mad animal, denotes that you will endeavour, to the limits of your energy, to shield self from the machinations of enemies, which will soon envelop you with the pall of dishonorable defeat.

Magic.

To dream of accomplishing any design by magic, indicates pleasant surprises.

To see others practising this art, denotes profitable changes to all who have this dream.

To dream of seeing a magician, denotes much interesting travel to those concerned in the advancement of higher education, and profitable returns to the mercenary.

Magic here should not be confounded with sorcery or spiritism. If the reader so interprets, he may expect the opposite to what is here forecast to follow. True magic is the study of the higher truths of Nature.

Magistrate.*

To dream of a magistrate, foretells that you will be harassed with threats of law suits and losses in your business.

---

*See Judge and Jury.

Magnet.

To dream of a magnet, denotes that evil influences will draw you from the path of honor. A woman is probably luring you to ruin. To a woman, this dream foretells that protection and wealth will be showered upon her.

Magnifying-glass.

To look through a magnifying-glass in your dreams, means failure to accomplish your work in a satisfactory manner. For a woman to think she owns one, foretells she will encourage the attention of persons who will ignore her later.

Magpie.

To dream of a magpie, denotes much dissatisfaction and quarrels. The dreamer should guard well his conduct and speech after this dream.

Malice.

To dream of entertaining malice for any person, denotes that you will stand low in the opinion of friends because of a disagreeable temper. Seek to control your passion.

If you dream of persons maliciously using you, an enemy in friendly garb is working you harm.

Mallet.

To dream of a mallet, denotes you will meet unkind treatment from friends on account of your ill health. Disorder in the home is indicated.

Malt.

To dream of malt, betokens a pleasant existence and riches that will advance your station.

To dream of taking malted drinks, denotes that you will interest yourself in some dangerous affair, but will reap much benefit therefrom.

Man.

To dream of a man, if handsome, well formed and supple, denotes that you will enjoy life vastly and come into rich possessions. If he is misshapen and sour-visaged, you will meet disappointments and many perplexities will involve you.

For a woman to dream of a handsome man, she is likely to have distinction offered her. If he is ugly, she will experience trouble through some one whom she considers a friend.

Manners.

To dream of seeing ugly-mannered persons, denotes failure to carry out undertakings through the disagreeableness of a person connected with the affair.

If you meet people with affable manners, you will be pleasantly surprised by affairs of moment with you taking a favorable turn.

Man-of-war.

To dream of a man-of-war, denotes long journeys and separation from country and friends, dissension in political affairs is portended.

If she is crippled, foreign elements will work damage to home interests.

If she is sailing upon rough seas, trouble with foreign powers may endanger private affairs.

Personal affairs may also go awry.

Mansion.

To dream that you are in a mansion where there is a haunted chamber, denotes sudden misfortune in the midst of contentment.

To dream of being in a mansion, indicates for you wealthy possessions.

369

To see a mansion from distant points, foretells future advancement.

Manslaughter.*

For a woman to dream that she sees, or is in any way connected with, manslaughter, denotes that she will be desperately scared lest her name be coupled with some scandalous sensation.

Mantilla.

To dream of seeing a mantilla, denotes an unwise enterprise which will bring you into unfavorable notice.

Manufactory.†

To dream of a large manufactory, denotes unusual activity in business circles.

Manure.

To dream of seeing manure, is a favorable omen. Much good will follow the dream. Farmers especially will feel a rise in fortune.

Manuscript.

To dream of manuscript in an unfinished state, forebodes disappointment. If finished and clearly written, great hopes will be realized.

If you are at work on manuscript, you will have many fears for some cherished hope, but if you keep the blurs out of your work you will succeed in your undertakings. If it is rejected by the publishers, you will be hopeless for a time, but eventually your most sanguine desires will become a reality.

If you lose it, you will be subjected to disappointment.

If you see it burn, some work of your own will bring you profit and much elevation.

---

*See Murder.   †See Factory.

Map.

To dream of a map, or studying one, denotes a change will be contemplated in your business. Some disappointing things will occur, but much profit also will follow the change.

To dream of looking for one, denotes that a sudden discontent with your surroundings will inspire you with new energy, and thus you will rise into better conditions. For a young woman, this dream denotes that she will rise into higher spheres by sheer ambition.

Marble.

To dream of a marble quarry, denotes that you life will be a financial success, but that your social surroundings will be devoid of affection.

To dream of polishing marble, you will come into a pleasing inheritance.

To see it broken, you will fall into disfavor among your associates by defying all moral codes.

March.

To dream of marching to the strains of music, indicates that you are ambitious to become a soldier or a public official, but you should consider all things well before making final decision.

For women to dream of seeing men marching, foretells their inclination for men in public positions. They should be careful of their reputations, should they be thrown much with men.

To dream of the month of March, portends disappointing returns in business, and some woman will be suspicious of your honesty.

Mare.*

To dream of seeing mares in pastures, denotes success

*See Horse.

371

in business and congenial companions. If the pasture is barren, it foretells poverty, but warm friends. For a young woman, this omens a happy marriage and beautiful children.

Marigold.

To dream of seeing marigolds, denotes contentment with frugality should be your aim.

Mariner.

To dream that you are a mariner, denotes a long journey to distant countries, and much pleasure will be connected with the trip.

If you see your vessel sailing without you, much personal discomfort will be wrought you by rivals.

Market.

To dream that you are in a market, denotes thrift and much activity in all occupations.

To see an empty market, indicates depression and gloom.

To see decayed vegetables or meat, denotes losses in business.

For a young woman, a market foretells pleasant changes.

Marmalade.

To dream of eating marmalade, denotes sickness and much dissatisfaction.

For a young woman to dream of making it, denotes unhappy domestic associations.

Marmot.

To dream of seeing a marmot, denotes that sly enemies are approaching you in the shape of fair women.

For a young woman to dream of a marmot, foretells that temptation will beset her in the future.

Marriage.*

For a woman to dream that she marries an old, decrepit man, wrinkled face and gray headed, denotes she will have a vast amount of trouble and sickness to encounter. If, while the ceremony is in progress, her lover passes, wearing black and looking at her in a reproachful way, she will be driven to desperation by the coldness and lack of sympathy of a friend.

To dream of seeing a marriage, denotes high enjoyment, if the wedding guests attend in pleasing colors and are happy; if they are dressed in black or other somber hues, there will be mourning and sorrow in store for the dreamer.

If you dream of contracting a marriage, you will have unpleasant news from the absent.

If you are an attendant at a wedding, you will experience much pleasure from the thoughtfulness of loved ones, and business affairs will be unusually promising.

To dream of any unfortunate occurrence in connection with a marriage, foretells distress, sickness, or death in your family.

For a young woman to dream that she is a bride, and unhappy or indifferent, foretells disappointments in love, and probably her own sickness. She should be careful of her conduct, as enemies are near her.

Mars.

To dream of Mars, denotes that your life will be made miserable and hardly worth living by the cruel treatment of friends. Enemies will endeavor to ruin you.

If you feel yourself drawn up toward the planet, you

---

*See Bride.

will develop keen judgment and advance beyond your friends in learning and wealth.

Marsh.

To dream of walking through marshy places, denotes illness resulting from overwork and worry. You will suffer much displeasure from the unwise conduct of a near relative.

Martyr.

To dream of martyrs, denotes that false friends, domestic unhappiness and losses in affairs which concern you most.

To dream that you are a martyr, signifies the separation from friends, and enemies will slander you.

Mask.

To dream that you are wearing a mask, denotes temporary trouble, as your conduct towards some dear one will be misinterpreted, and your endeavors to aid that one will be misunderstood, but you will profit by the temporary estrangements.

To see others masking, denotes that you will combat falsehood and envy.

To see a mask in your dreams, denotes some person will be unfaithful to you, and your affairs will suffer also. For a young woman to dream that she wears a mask, foretells she will endeavor to impose upon some friendly person.

If she unmasks, or sees others doing so, she will fail to gain the admiration sought for. She should demean herself modestly after this dream.

Mason.

To dream that you see a mason plying his trade, denotes

a rise in your circumstances and a more congenial social atmosphere will surround you.

If you dream of seeing a band of the order of masons in full regalia, it denotes that you will have others beside yourself to protect and keep from the evils of life.

Masquerade.

To dream of attending a masquerade, denotes that you will indulge in foolish and harmful pleasures to the neglect of business and domestic duties.

For a young woman to dream that she participates in a masquerade, denotes that she will be deceived.

Mast.

To dream of seeing the masts of ships, denotes long and pleasant voyages, the making of many new friends, and the gaining of new possessions.

To see the masts of wrecked ships, denotes sudden changes in your circumstances which will necessitate giving over anticipated pleasures.

If a sailor dreams of a mast, he will soon sail on an eventful trip.

Master.

To dream that you have a master, is a sign of incompetency on your part to command others, and you will do better work under the leadership of some strong-willed person.

If you are a master, and command many people under you, you will excel in judgment in the fine points of life, and will hold high positions and possess much wealth.

Mat.

Keep away from mats in your dreams, as they will usher you into sorrow and perplexities.

Match.

To dream of matches, denotes prosperity and change when least expected.

To strike a match in the dark, unexpected news and fortune is foreboded.

Matting.

To dream of matting, foretells pleasant prospects and cheerful news from the absent. If it is old or torn, you will have vexing things come before you.

Mattress.

To dream of a mattress, denotes that new duties and responsibilities will shortly be assumed.

To sleep on a new mattress, signifies contentment with present surroundings.

To dream of a mattress factory, denotes that you will be connected in business with thrifty partners and will soon amass wealth.

Mausoleum.

To dream of a mausoleum, indicates the sickness, death, or trouble of some prominent friend.

To find yourself inside a mausoleum, foretells your own illness.

May.

To dream of the month of May, denotes prosperous times, and pleasure for the young.

To dream that nature appears freakish, denotes sudden sorrow and disappointment clouding pleasure.

May Bugs.

To dream of May bugs, denotes an ill-tempered companion where a congenial one was expected.

Meadow.

To dream of meadows, predicts happy reunions under bright promises of future prosperity.

Meals.*

To dream of meals, denotes that you will let trifling matters interfere with momentous affairs and business engagements.

Measles.

To dream that you have measles, denotes much worry, and anxious care will interfere with your business affairs.

To dream that others have this disease, denotes that you will be troubled over the condition of others.

Meat.†

For a woman to dream of raw meat, denotes that she will meet with much discouragement in accomplishing her aims. If she sees cooked meat, it denotes that others will obtain the object for which she will strive.

Mechanic.

To dream of a mechanic, denotes change in your dwelling place and a more active business. Advancement in wages usually follows after seeing mechanics at work on machinery.

Medal.

To dream of medals, denotes honors gained by application and industry.

To lose a medal, denotes misfortune through the unfaithfulness of others.

Medicine.

To dream of medicine, if pleasant to the taste, a trouble will come to you, but in a short time it will work for your

*See Eating.   †See Beef.

377

good; but if you take disgusting medicine, you will suffer a protracted illness or some deep sorrow or loss will overcome you.

To give medicine to others, denotes that you will work to injure some one who trusted you.

Melancholy.

To dream that you feel melancholy over any event, is a sign of disappointment in what was thought to be favorable undertakings.

To dream that you see others melancholy, denotes unpleasant interruption in affairs. To lovers, it brings separation.

Melon.

To dream of melons, denotes ill health and unfortunate ventures in business.

To eat them, signifies that hasty action will cause you anxiety.

To see them growing on green vines, denotes that present troubles will result in good fortune for you.

Memorandum.

To dream that you make memoranda, denotes that you will engage in an unprofitable business, and much worry will result for you.

To see others making a memorandum, signifies that some person will worry you with appeals for aid.

To lose your memorandum, you will experience a slight loss in trade.

To find a memorandum, you will assume new duties that will cause much pleasure to others.

Memorial.

To dream of a memorial, signifies there will be occasion

for you to show patient kindness, as trouble and sickness threatens your relatives.

Menagerie.

To dream of visiting a menagerie, denotes various troubles.

Mendicant.

For a woman to dream of mendicants, she will meet with disagreeable interferences in her plans for betterment and enjoyment.

Mending.

To dream of mending soiled garments, denotes that you will undertake to right a wrong at an inopportune moment; but if the garment be clean, you will be successful in adding to your fortune.

For a young woman to dream of mending, foretells that she will be a systematic help to her husband.

Mercury.

To dream of mercury, is significant of unhappy changes through the constant oppression of enemies. For a woman to be suffering from mercurial poison, foretells she will be deserted by and separated from her family.

Merry.

To dream being merry, or in merry company, denotes that pleasant events will engage you for a time, and affairs will assume profitable shapes.

Meshes.

To dream of being entangled in the meshes of a net, or other like constructions, denotes that enemies will oppress you in time of seeming prosperity. To a young woman, this dream foretells that her environments will bring her into evil and consequent abandonment. If she succeeds in disengaging herself from the meshes, she will narrowly escape slander.

Message.

To dream of receiving a message, denotes that changes will take place in your affairs.

To dream of sending a message, denotes that you will be placed in unpleasant situations.

Metamorphose.

To dream of seeing anything metamorphose, denotes that sudden changes will take place in your life, for good or bad, as the metamorphose was pleasant or frightful.

Mice.

To dream of mice, foretells domestic troubles and the insincerity of friends. Business affairs will assume a discouraging tone.

To kill mice, denotes that you will conquer your enemies.

To let them escape you, is significant of doubtful struggles.

For a young woman to dream of mice, warns her of secret enemies, and that deception is being practised upon her. If she should see a mouse in her clothing, it is a sign of scandal in which she will figure.

Microscope.

To dream of a microscope, denotes you will experience failure or small returns in your enterprises.

Midwife.

To see a midwife in your dreams, signifies unfortunate sickness with a narrow escape from death.

For a young woman to dream of such a person, foretells that distress and calumny will attend her.

Mile-post.

To dream you see or pass a mile-post, foretells that you will be assailed by doubtful fears in business or love. To see one down, portends accidents are threatening to give disorder to your affairs.

Milk.*

To dream of drinking milk, denotes abundant harvest to the farmer and pleasure in the home; for a traveler, it foretells a fortunate voyage. This is a very propitious dream for women.

To see milk in large quantities, signifies riches and health.

To dream of dealing in milk commercially, denotes great increase in fortune.

To give milk away, shows that you will be too benevolent for the good of your own fortune.

To spill milk, denotes that you will experience a slight loss and suffer temporary unhappiness at the hands of friends.

To dream of impure milk, denotes that you will be tormented with petty troubles.

To dream of sour milk, denotes that you will be disturbed over the distress of friends.

To dream of trying unsuccessfully to drink milk, signifies that you will be in danger of losing something of value or the friendship of a highly esteemed person.

To dream of hot milk, foretells a struggle, but the final winning of riches and desires.

To dream of bathing in milk, denotes pleasures and companionships of congenial friends.

---

*See Buttermilk.

Milking.

To dream of milking, and it flows in great streams from the udder, while the cow is restless and threatening, signifies you will see great opportunities withheld from you, but which will result in final favor for you.

Mill.*

To dream of a mill, indicates thrift and fortunate undertakings.

To see a dilapidated mill, denotes sickness and ill fortune.

Mill-dam.

To dream that you see clear water pouring over a mill-dam, foretells pleasant enterprises, either of a business or social nature. If the water is muddy or impure, you will meet with losses, and troubles will arise where pleasure was anticipated.

If the dam is dry, your business will assume shrunken proportions.

Miller.

To see a miller in your dreams, signifies your surroundings will grow more hopeful. For a woman to dream of a miller failing in an attempt to start his mill, foretells she will be disappointed in her lover's wealth, as she will think him in comfortable circumstances.

Mine.†

To dream of being in a mine, denotes failure in affairs. To own a mine, denotes future wealth.

Mineral.

To dream of minerals, denotes your present unpromis-

---

*See Cotton Mill, etc.   † See Coal Mine.

ing outlook will grow directly brighter. To walk over mineral land, signifies distress, from which you will escape and be bettered in your surroundings.

Mineral Water.

To dream of drinking mineral water, foretells fortune will favor your efforts, and you will enjoy your opportunities to satisfy your cravings for certain pleasures.

Mining.

To see mining in your dreams, denotes that an enemy is seeking your ruin by bringing up past immoralities in your life. You will be likely to make unpleasant journeys, if you stand near the mine.

If you dream of hunting for mines, you will engage in worthless pursuits.

Minister.*

To dream of seeing a minister, denotes unfortunate changes and unpleasant journeys.

To hear a minister exhort, foretells that some designing person will influence you to evil.

To dream that you are a minister, denotes that you will usurp another's rights.

Minuet.

To dream of seeing the minuet danced, signifies a pleasant existence with congenial companions.

To dance it yourself, good fortune and domestic joys are foretold.

Minx.

To dream of a minx, denotes you will have sly enemies to overcome.

If you kill one, you will win your desires. For a young woman to dream that she is partial to minx furs, she will

---

*See Preacher and Priest.

find protection and love in some person who will be inordinately jealous.

Mire.

To dream of going through mire, indicates that your dearest wishes and plans will receive a temporary check by the intervention of unusual changes in your surroundings.

Mirror.*

To dream of seeing yourself in a mirror, denotes that you will meet many discouraging issues, and sickness will cause you distress and loss in fortune.

To see a broken mirror, foretells the sudden or violent death of some one related to you.

To see others in a mirror, denotes that others will act unfairly towards you to promote their own interests.

To see animals in a mirror, denotes disappointment and loss in fortune.

For a young woman to break a mirror, foretells unfortunate friendships and an unhappy marriage. To see her lover in a mirror looking pale and careworn, denotes death or a broken engagement. If he seems happy, a slight estrangement will arise, but it will be of short duration.

Miser.

To dream of a miser, foretells you will be unfortunate in finding true happiness owing to selfishness, and love will disappoint you sorely.

For a woman to dream that she is befriended by a miser, foretells she will gain love and wealth by her intelligence and tactful conduct.

To dream that you are miserly, denotes that you will be obnoxious to others by your conceited bearing.

*See Glass.

To dream that any of your friends are misers, foretells that you will be distressed by the importunities of others.

Mist.

To dream that you are enveloped in a mist, denotes uncertain fortunes and domestic unhappiness. If the mist clears away, your troubles will be of short duration.

To see others in a mist, you will profit by the misfortune of others.

Mistletoe.

To dream of mistletoe, foretells happiness and great rejoicing.

To the young, it omens many pleasant pastimes.

If seen with unpromising signs, disappointment will displace pleasure or fortune.

Mocking-bird.

To see or hear a mocking-bird, signifies you will be invited to go on a pleasant visit to friends, and your affairs will move along smoothly and prosperously. For a woman to see a wounded or dead one, her disagreement with a friend or lover is signified.

Models.

To dream of a model, foretells your social affairs will deplete your purse, and quarrels and regrets will follow. For a young woman to dream that she is a model or seeking to be one, foretells she will be entangled in a love affair which will give her trouble through the selfishness of a friend.

Molasses.

To dream of molasses, is a sign that some one is going to extend you pleasant hospitality, and, through its acceptance, you will meet agreeable and fortunate surprises.

To eat it, foretells that you will be discouraged and disappointed in love. To have it smeared on your clothing, denotes you will have disagreeable offers of marriage, and probably losses in business.

Moles.

To dream of moles, indicates secret enemies.

To dream of catching a mole, you will overcome any opposition and rise to prominence.

To see moles, or such blemishes, on the person, indicates illness and quarrels.

Money.

To dream of finding money, denotes small worries, but much happiness. Changes will follow.

To pay out money, denotes misfortune.

To receive gold, great prosperity and unalloyed pleasures.

To lose money, you will experience unhappy hours in the home and affairs will appear gloomy.

To count your money and find a deficit, you will be worried in making payments.

To dream that you steal money, denotes that you are in danger and should guard your actions.

To save money, augurs wealth and comfort.

To dream that you swallow money, portends that you are likely to become mercenary.

To look upon a quantity of money, denotes that prosperity and happiness are within your reach.

To dream you find a roll of currency, and a young woman claims it, foretells you will lose in some enterprise by the interference of some female friend. The dreamer will find that he is spending his money unwisely and is living beyond his means. It is a dream of caution.

Beware lest the innocent fancies of your brain make a place for your money before payday.

Monk.

To dream of seeing a monk, foretells dissensions in the family and unpleasant journeyings. To a young woman, this dream signifies that gossip and deceit will be used against her.

To dream that you are a monk, denotes personal loss and illness.

Monkey.

To dream of a monkey, denotes that deceitful people will flatter you to advance their own interests.

To see a dead monkey, signifies that your worst enemies will soon be removed.

If a young woman dreams of a monkey, she should insist on an early marriage, as her lover will suspect unfaithfulness.

For a woman to dream of feeding a monkey, denotes that she will be betrayed by a flatterer.

Monster.

To dream of being pursued by a monster, denotes that sorrow and misfortune hold prominent places in your immediate future.

To slay a monster, denotes that you will successfully cope with enemies and rise to eminent positions.

Moon.

To dream of seeing the moon with the aspect of the heavens remaining normal, prognosticates success in love and business affairs.

A weird and uncanny moon, denotes unpropitious love-making, domestic infelicities and disappointing enterprises of a business character.

The moon in eclipse, denotes that contagion will ravage your community.

387

To see the new moon, denotes an increase in wealth and congenial partners in marriage.

For a young woman to dream that she appeals to the moon to know her fate, denotes that she will soon be rewarded with marriage to the one of her choice. If she sees two moons, she will lose her lover by being mercenary. If she sees the moon grow dim, she will let the supreme happiness of her life slip for want of womanly tact.

To see a blood red moon, indicates war and strife, and she will see her lover march away in defence of his country.

Morgue.

To dream that you visit a morgue searching for some one, denotes that you will be shocked by news of the death of a relative or friend.

To see many corpses there, much sorrow and trouble will come under your notice.

Morning.

To see the morning dawn clear in your dreams, prognosticates a near approach of fortune and pleasure.

A cloudy morning, portends weighty affairs will overwhelm you.

Morocco.

To see morocco in your dreams, foretells that you will receive substantial aid from unexpected sources. Your love will be rewarded by faithfulness.

Mortgage.

To dream that you give a mortgage on your property, denotes that you are threatened with financial upheavals, which will throw you into embarrassing positions.

To take, or hold one, against others, is ominous of adequate wealth to liquidate your obligations.

To find yourself reading or examining mortgages, denotes great possibilities before you of love or gain.

To lose a mortgage, if it cannot be found again, implies loss and worry.

Morose.

If you find yourself morose in dreams, you will awake to find the world, as far as you are concerned, going fearfully wrong.

To see others morose, portends unpleasant occupations and unpleasant companions.

Mortification.

To dream that you feel mortified over any deed committed by yourself, is a sign that you will be placed in an unenviable position before those to whom you most wish to appear honorable and just. Financial conditions will fall low.

To see mortified flesh, denotes disastrous enterprises and disappointment in love.

Moses.

To dream that you see Moses, means personal gain and a connubial alliance which will be a source of sweet congratulation to yourself.

Mosquito.

To see mosquitoes in your dreams, you will strive in vain to remain impregnable to the sly attacks of secret enemies. Your patience and fortune will both suffer from these designing persons.

If you kill mosquitoes, you will eventually overcome obstacles and enjoy fortune and domestic bliss.

Moss.

To dream of moss, denotes that you will fill dependent

positions, unless the moss grows in rich soil, when you will be favored with honors.

Moth.

To see a moth in a dream, small worries will lash you into hurried contracts, which will prove unsatisfactory. Quarrels of a domestic nature are prognosticated.

Mother.

To see your mother in dreams as she appears in the home, signifies pleasing results from any enterprise.

To hold her in conversation, you will soon have good news from interests you are anxious over.

For a woman to dream of mother, signifies pleasant duties and connubial bliss.

To see one's mother emaciated or dead, foretells sadness caused by death or dishonor.

To hear your mother call you, denotes that you are derelict in your duties, and that you are pursuing the wrong course in business.

To hear her cry as if in pain, omens her illness, or some affliction is menacing you.

Mother-in-law.

To dream of your mother-in-law, denotes there will be pleasant reconciliations for you after some serious disagreement. For a woman to dispute with her mother-in-law, she will find that quarrelsome and unfeeling people will give her annoyance.

Mountain.

For a young woman to dream of crossing a mountain in company with her cousin and dead brother, who was smiling, denotes she will have a distinctive change in her life for the better, but there are warnings against allurements and deceitfulness of friends. If she becomes exhausted and refuses to go further, she will be slightly disappointed in not gaining quite so exalted a position as was hoped for by her.

If you ascend a mountain in your dreams, and the way is pleasant and verdant, you will rise swiftly to wealth and prominence. If the mountain is rugged, and you fail to reach the top, you may expect reverses in your life, and should strive to overcome all weakness in your nature. To awaken when you are at a dangerous point in ascending, denotes that you will find affairs taking a flattering turn when they appear gloomy.

Mourning.

To dream that you wear mourning, omens ill luck and unhappiness.

If others wear it, there will be disturbing influences among your friends causing you unexpected dissatisfaction and loss. To lovers, this dream foretells misunderstanding and probable separation.

Mouse.*

For a woman to dream of a mouse, denotes that she will have an enemy who will annoy her by artfulness and treachery.

Mouse-trap.

To see a mouse-trap in dreams, signifies your need to be careful of character, as wary persons have designs upon you.

To see it full of mice, you will likely fall into the hands of enemies.

To set a trap, you will artfully devise means to overcome your opponents.

Mud.

To dream that you walk in mud, denotes that you will

---

*See Mice.

have cause to lose confidence in friendships, and there will be losses and disturbances in family circles.

To see others walking in mud, ugly rumors will reach you of some friend or employee. To the farmer, this dream is significant of short crops and unsatisfactory gains from stock.

To see mud on your clothing, your reputation is being assailed. To scrape it off, signifies that you will escape the calumny of enemies.

Muff.

To dream of wearing a muff, denotes that you will be well provided for against the vicissitudes of fortune.

For a lover to see his sweetheart wearing a muff, denotes that a worthier man will usurp his place in her affections.

Mulberries.

To see mulberries in your dreams, denotes that sickness will prevent you from obtaining your desires, and you will be called upon often to relieve suffering.

To eat them, signifies bitter disappointments.

Mule.

If you dream that your are riding on a mule, it denotes that you are engaging in pursuits which will cause you the greatest anxiety, but if you reach your destination without interruption, you will be recompensed with substantial results.

For a young woman to dream of a white mule, shows she will marry a wealthy foreigner, or one who, while wealthy, will not be congenial in tastes. If she dreams of mules running loose, she will have beaux and admirers, but no offers of marriage.

To be kicked by a mule, foretells disappointment in love and marriage.

To see one dead, portends broken engagements and social decline.

Murder.*

To see murder committed in your dreams, foretells much sorrow arising from the misdeeds of others. Affair will assume dulness. Violent deaths will come under your notice.

If you commit murder, it signifies that you are engaging in some dishonorable adventure, which will leave a stigma upon your name.

To dream that you are murdered, foretells that enemies are secretly working to overthrow you.

Muscle.

To dream of seeing your muscle well developed, you will have strange encounters with enemies, but you will succeed in surmounting their evil works, and gain fortune.

If they are shrunken, your inability to succeed in your affairs is portended. For a woman, this dream is prophetic of toil and hardships.

Museum.

To dream of a museum, denotes you will pass through many and varied scenes in striving for what appears your rightful position. You will acquire useful knowledge,

---

*See Killing and kindred words.

which will stand you in better light than if you had pursued the usual course to learning. If the museum is distasteful, you will have many causes for vexation.

Music.

To dream of hearing harmonious music, omens pleasure and prosperity.

Discordant music foretells troubles with unruly children, and unhappiness in the household.

Musical Instruments.

To see musical instruments, denotes anticipated pleasures.

If they are broken, the pleasure will be marred by uncongenial companionship. For a young woman, this dream foretells for her the power to make her life what she will.

Mushroom.

To see mushrooms in your dreams, denotes unhealthy desires, and unwise haste in amassing wealth, as it may vanish in law suits and vain pleasures.

To eat them, signifies humiliation and disgraceful love.

For a young woman to dream of them, foretells her defiance of propriety in her pursuit of foolish pleasures.

Musk.

To dream of musk, foretells unexpected occasions of joy, and lovers will agree and cease to be unfaithful.

Mussels.

To dream of water mussels, denotes small fortune, but contentment and domestic enjoyment.

Mustache.

To dream that you have a mustache, denotes that your

egotism and effrontery will cause you a poor inheritance in worldy goods, and you will betray women to their sorrow.

If a woman dreams of admiring a mustache, her virtue is in danger, and she should be mindful of her conduct.

If a man dreams that he has his mustache shaved, he will try to turn from evil companions and pleasures, and seek to reinstate himself in former positions of honor.

Mustard.

To see mustard growing, and green, foretells success and joy to the farmer, and to the seafaring it prognosticates wealth.

To eat mustard seed and feel the burning in your mouth, denotes that you will repent bitterly some hasty action, which has caused you to suffer.

To dream of eating green mustard cooked, indicates the lavish waste of fortune, and mental strain.

For a young woman to eat newly grown mustard, foretells that she will sacrifice wealth for personal desires.

Mute.

To converse with a mute in your dreams, foretells that unusual crosses in your life will fit you for higher positions, which will be tendered you.

To dream that you are a mute, portends calamities and unjust persecution.

Myrrh.

To see myrrh in a dream, signifies your investments will give satisfaction. For a young woman to dream of myrrh, brings a pleasing surprise to her in the way of a new and wealthy acquaintance.

Myrtle.

To see myrtle in foliage and bloom in your dream,

denotes that your desires will be gratified, and pleasures will possess you.

For a young woman to dream of wearing a sprig of myrtle, foretells to her an early marriage with a well-to-do and intelligent man.

To see it withered, denotes that she will miss happiness through careless conduct.

Mystery.

To find yourself bewildered by some mysterious event, denotes that strangers will harass you with their troubles and claim your aid. It warns you also of neglected duties, for which you feel much aversion. Business will wind you into unpleasant complications.

To find yourself studying the mysteries of creation, denotes that a change will take place in your life, throwing you into a higher atmosphere of research and learning, and thus advancing you nearer the attainment of true pleasure and fortune.

N.

"And he slept and dreamed the second time; and, behold, seven ears of corn came up upon one stalk, rank and good."—Gen. xli., 5.

Nails.

To see nails in your dreams, indicates much toil and small recompense.

To deal in nails, shows that you will engage in honorable work, even if it be lowly.

To see rusty or broken nails, indicates sickness and failure in business.

Naked.

To dream that you are naked, foretells scandal and unwise engagements.

To see others naked, foretells that you will be tempted by designing persons to leave the path of duty. Sickness will be no small factor against your success.

To dream that you suddenly discover your nudity, and are trying to conceal it, denotes that you have sought illicit pleasure contrary to your noblest instincts and are desirous of abandoning those desires.

For a young woman to dream that she admires her nudity, foretells that she will win, but not hold honest men's regard. She will win fortune by her charms. If she thinks herself ill-formed, her reputation will be sullied by scandal. If she dreams of swimming in clear water naked, she will enjoy illicit loves, but nature will revenge herself by sickness, or loss of charms. If she sees naked men swimming in clear water, she will have many admirers. If the water is muddy, a jealous admirer will cause ill-natured gossip about her.

Napkin.

To dream of a napkin, foretells convivial entertainments in which you will figure prominently. For a woman to dream of soiled napkins, foretells that humiliating affairs will thrust themselves upon her.

Navy.*

To dream of the navy, denotes victorious struggles with unsightly obstacles, and the promise of voyages and tours of recreation. If in your dream you seem frightened or disconcerted, you will have strange obstacles to overcome before you reach fortune. A dilapidated navy is an indication of unfortunate friendships in business or love.

Nearsighted.

To dream that you are nearsighted, signifies embarrass-

* See Gunboat.

ing failure and unexpected visits from unwelcome persons. For a young woman, this dream foretells unexpected rivalry.

To dream that your sweetheart is nearsighted, denotes that she will disappoint you.

Neck.

To dream that you see your own neck, foretells that vexatious family relations will interfere with your business.

To admire the neck of another, signifies your worldly mindedness will cause broken domestic ties.

For a woman to dream that her neck is thick, foretells that she will become querulous and something of a shrew if she fails to control her temper.

Necklace

For a woman to dream of receiving a necklace, omens for her a loving husband and a beautiful home.

To lose a necklace, she will early feel the heavy hand of bereavement.

Necromancer.*

To dream of a necromancer and his arts, denotes that you are threatened with strange acquaintances who will influence you for evil.

Need.

To dream that you are in need, denotes that you will speculate unwisely and distressing news of absent friends will oppress you.

To see others in need, foretells that unfortunate affairs will affect yourself with others.

Needle.

To use a needle in your dream, is a warning of ap-

---

* See Hypnotist.

proaching affliction, in which you will suffer keenly the loss of sympathy, which is rightfully yours.

To dream of threading a needle, denotes that you will be burdened with the care of others than your own household.

To look for a needle, foretells useless worries.

To find a needle, foretells that you will have friends who will appreciate you.

To break one, signifies loneliness and poverty.

Neighbor.

To see your neighbors in your dreams, denotes many profitable hours will be lost in useless strife and gossip. If they appear sad, or angry, it foretells dissensions and quarrels.

Nephew.

To dream of your nephew, denotes you are soon to come into a pleasing competency, if he is handsome and well looking; otherwise, there will be disappointment and discomfort for you.

Nest.*

To dream of seeing birds' nests, denotes that you will be interested in an enterprise which will be prosperous. For a young woman, this dream foretells change of abode.

To see an empty nest, indicates sorrow through the absence of a friend.

---

*See Birds' Nest.

Hens' nests, foretells that you will be interested in domesticities, and children will be cheerful and obedient.

To dream of a nest filled with broken or bad eggs, portends disappointments and failure.

Nets.

To dream of ensnaring anything with a net, denotes that you will be unscrupulous in your dealings and deportment with others.

To dream of an old or torn net, denotes that your property has mortgages, or attachments, which will cause you trouble.

Nettles.

If in your dreams you walk among nettles without being stung, you will be prosperous.

To be stung by them, you will be discontented with yourself and make others unhappy.

For a young woman to dream of passing through nettles, foretells that she will be offered marriage by different men, and her decision will fill her with anxious foreboding.

To dream of nettles, is portentous of stringent circumstances and disobedience from children or servants.

News.

To hear good news in a dream, denotes that you will be fortunate in affairs, and have harmonious companions; but if the news be bad, contrary conditions will exist.

Newspaper.

To dream of newspapers, denotes that frauds will be detected in your dealings, and your reputation will likewise be affected.

To print a newspaper, you will have opportunities of making foreign journeys and friends.

Trying, but failing to read a newspaper, denotes that you will fail in some uncertain enterprise.

Newspaper Reporter.

If in your dreams you unwillingly see them, you will be annoyed with small talk, and perhaps quarrels of a low character.

If you are a newspaper reporter in your dreams, there will be a varied course of travel offered you, though you may experience unpleasant situations, yet there will be some honor and gain attached.

New Year.

To dream of the new year, signifies prosperity and connubial anticipations. If you contemplate the new year in weariness, engagement will be entered into inauspiciously.

Niece.

For a woman to dream of her niece, foretells she will have unexpected trials and much useless worry in the near future.

Night.*

If you are surrounded by night in your dreams, you may expect unusual oppression and hardships in business. If the night seems to be vanishing, conditions which hitherto seemed unfavorable will now grow bright, and affairs will assume prosperous phases.

Nightmare.

To dream of being attacked with this hideous sensation, denotes wrangling and failure in business. For a young woman, this is a dream prophetic of disappointment and unmerited slights. It may also warn the dreamer to be careful of her health, and food.

Nightingale.

To dream that you are listening to the harmonious notes of the nightingale, foretells a pleasing existence, and prosperous and healthy surroundings. This is a most favorable dream to lovers, and parents.

To see nightingales silent, foretells slight misunderstandings among friends.

Ninepins.

To dream that you play ninepins, denotes that you are foolishly wasting your energy and opportunities. You should be careful in the selection of companions. All phases of this dream are bad.

*See Darkness.

Nobility.

To dream of associating with the nobility, denotes that your aspirations are not of the right nature, as you prefer show and pleasures to the higher development of the mind.

For a young woman to dream of the nobility, foretells that she will choose a lover for his outward appearance, instead of wisely accepting the man of merit for her protector.

Noise.

If you hear a strange noise in your dream, unfavorable news is presaged. If the noise awakes you, there will be a sudden change in your affairs.

Noodles.

To dream of noodles, denotes an abnormal appetite and desires. There is little good in this dream.

Nose.

To see your own nose, indicates force of character, and consciousness of your ability to accomplish whatever enterprise you may choose to undertake.

If your nose looks smaller than natural, there will be failure in your affairs. Hair growing on your nose, indicates extraordinary undertakings, and that they will be carried through by sheer force of character, or will.

A bleeding nose, is prophetic of disaster, whatever the calling of the dreamer may be.

Notary.

To dream of a notary, is a prediction of unsatisfied desires, and probable lawsuits. For a woman to associate with a notary, foretells she will rashly risk her reputation, in gratification of foolish pleasure.

November.

To dream of November, augers a season of indifferent success in all affairs.

Numbness.

To dream that you feel a numbness creeping over you, in your dreams, is a sign of illness, and disquieting conditions.

Numbers.*

To dream of numbers, denotes that unsettled conditions in business will cause you uneasiness and dissatisfaction.

Nuns.

For a religiously inclined man to dream of nuns, foretells that material joys will interfere with his spirituality. He should be wise in the control of self.

For a woman to dream of nuns, foretells her widowhood, or her separation from her lover. If she dreams that she is a nun, it portends her discontentment with present environments.

*See Figures.

404

To see a dead nun, signifies despair over the unfaithfulness of loved ones, and impoverished fortune.

For one to dream that she discards the robes of her order, foretells that longing for worldly pleasures will unfit her for her chosen duties.

Nuptial.*

For a woman to dream of her nuptials, she will soon enter upon new engagements, which will afford her distinction, pleasure, and harmony.

Nurse.

To dream that a nurse is retained in your home, foretells distressing illness, or unlucky visiting among friends.

To see a nurse leaving your house, omens good health in the family.

For a young woman to dream that she is a nurse, denotes that she will gain the esteem of people, through her self-sacrifice. If she parts from a patient, she will yield to the persuasion of deceit.

Nursing.

For a woman to dream of nursing her baby, denotes pleasant employment.

For a young woman to dream of nursing a baby, foretells that she will occupy positions of honor and trust.

For a man to dream of seeing his wife nurse their baby, denotes harmony in his pursuits.

Nuts.

To dream of gathering nuts, augurs successful enterprises, and much favor in love.

To eat them, prosperity will aid you in grasping any desired pleasure.

---

*See Marriage.

For a woman to dream of nuts, foretells that her fortune will be on blissful heights.

Nutmegs.

To dream of nutmegs, is a sign of prosperity, and pleasant journeyings.

Nymph.

To see nymphs bathing in clear water, denotes that passionate desires will find an ecstatic realization. Convivial entertainments will enchant you.

To see them out of their sphere, denotes disappointment with the world.

For a young woman to see them bathing, denotes that she will have great favor and pleasure, but they will not rest strictly within the moral code. To dream that she impersonates a nymph, is a sign that she is using her attractions for selfish purposes, and thus the undoing of men.

O.

"And it shall come to pass afterward, that I will pour out my spirit upon all flesh; and your sons and your daughters shall prophesy, your old men shall dream dreams, your young men shall see visions."—Joel ii., 28.

Oak.

To dream of seeing a forest of oaks, signifies great prosperity in all conditions of life.

To see an oak full of acorns, denotes increase and promotion.

If blasted oak, it denotes sudden and shocking surprises.

For sweethearts to dream of oaks, denotes that they will soon begin life together under favorable circumstances.

Oar.

To dream of handling oars, portends disappointments for you, inasmuch as you will sacrifice your own pleasure for the comfort of others.

To lose an oar, denotes vain efforts to carry out designs satisfactorily.

A broken oar represents interruption in some anticipated pleasure.

Oath.

Whenever you take an oath in your dreams, prepare for dissension and altercations on waking.

Oatmeal.

To dream of eating oatmeal, signifies the enjoyment of worthily earned fortune.

For a young woman to dream of preparing it for the table, denotes that she will soon preside over the destiny of others.

Oats.

To dream that oats hold the vision, portends a variety of good things. The farmer will especially advance in fortune and domestic harmony.

To see decayed oats, foretells that sorrow will displace bright hopes.

Obedience.

To dream that you render obedience to another, foretells for you a common place, a pleasant but uneventful period of life.

If others are obedient to you, it shows that you will command fortune and high esteem.

Obelisk.

An obelisk looming up stately and cold in your dreams is the forerunner of melancholy tidings.

407

For lovers to stand at the base of an obelisk, denotes fatal disagreements.

Obituary.

To dream of writing an obituary, denotes that unpleasant and discordant duties will devolve upon you.

If you read one, news of a distracting nature will soon reach you.

Obligation.

To dream of obligating yourself in any incident, denotes that you will be fretted and worried by the thoughtless complaints of others.

If others obligate themselves to you, it portends that you will win the regard of acquaintances and friends.

Observatory.

To dream of viewing the heavens and beautiful landscapes from an observatory, denotes your swift elevation to prominent positions and places of trust. For a young woman this dream signals the realization of the highest earthly joys. If the heavens are clouded, your highest aims will miss materialization.

Occultist.

To dream that you listen to the teachings of an occultist, denotes that you will strive to elevate others to a higher plane of justice and forbearance. If you accept his views, you will find honest delight by keeping your mind and person above material frivolities and pleasures.

Ocean.

To dream of the ocean when it is calm is propitious. The sailor will have a pleasant and profitable voyage. The business man will enjoy a season of remuneration, and the young man will revel in his sweetheart's charms.

To be far out on the ocean, and hear the waves lash the ship, forebodes disaster in business life, and quarrels and stormy periods in the household.

To be on shore and see the waves of the ocean foaming against each other, foretells your narrow escape from injury and the designs of enemies.

To dream of seeing the ocean so shallow as to allow wading, or a view of the bottom, signifies prosperity and pleasure with a commingling of sorrow and hardships.

To sail on the ocean when it is calm, is always propitious.

October.

To imagine you are in October is ominous of gratifying success in your undertakings. You will also make new acquaintances which will ripen into lasting friendships.

Oculist.

To dream of consulting an oculist, denotes that you will be dissatisfied with your progress in life, and will use artificial means of advancement.

Odd-Fellow.

To dream of this order, signifies that you will have sincere friends, and misfortune will touch you but lightly.

To join this order, foretells that you will win distinction and conjugal bliss.

Odor.

To dream of inhaling sweet odors, is a sign of a beautiful woman ministering to your daily life, and successful financiering.

To smell disgusting odors, foretells unpleasant disagreements and unreliable servants.

Offense.

To dream of being offended, denotes that errors will be detected in your conduct, which will cause you inward rage while attempting to justify yourself.

To give offense, predicts for you many struggles before reaching your aims.

For a young woman to give, or take offense, signifies that she will regret hasty conclusions, and disobedience to parents or guardian.

Offering.

To bring or make an offering, foretells that you will be cringing and hypocritical unless you cultivate higher views of duty.

Office.

For a person to dream that he holds office, denotes that his aspirations will sometimes make him undertake dangerous paths, but his boldness will be rewarded with success. If he fails by any means to secure a desired office he will suffer keen disappointment in his affairs.

To dream that you are turned out of office, signifies loss of valuables.

Offspring.

To dream of your own offspring, denotes cheerfulness and the merry voices of neighbors and children.

To see the offspring of domestic animals, denotes increase in prosperity.

Oil.

To dream of anointing with oil, foretells events in which you will be the particular moving power.

Quantities of oil, prognosticates excesses in pleasurable enterprises.

For a man to dream that he deals in oil, denotes unsuccessful love making, as he will expect unusual concessions.

For a woman to dream that she is anointed with oil, shows that she will be open to indiscreet advances.

Oilcloth.

To dream of oilcloth is a warning that you will meet coldness and treachery.

To deal in it, denotes uncertain speculations.

Ointment.

To dream of ointment, denotes that you will form friendships which will prove beneficial and pleasing to you.

For a young woman to dream that she makes ointment, denotes that she will be able to command her own affairs whether they be of a private or public character.

Old Man, or Woman.*

To dream of seeing an old man, or woman, denotes that unhappy cares will oppress you, if they appear otherwise than serene.

Olives.

Gathering olives with a merry band of friends, foretells favorable results in business, and delightful surprises.

If you take them from bottles, it foretells conviviality

To break a bottle of olives, indicates disappointments on the eve of pleasure.

To eat them, signifies contentment and faithful friends.

Omelet.

To see omelet being served in your dream, warns you

---

*See Faces, Men, and Women.

of flattery and deceit, which is about to be used against you.

To eat it, shows that you will be imposed upon by some one seemingly worthy of your confidence.

Omnibus.*

To dream that you are being drawn through the streets in an omnibus, foretells misunderstandings with friends, and unwise promises will be made by you.

One-Eyed.

To see one-eyed creatures in your dreams, is portentous of an over-whelming intimation of secret intriguing against your fortune and happiness.

Onions.

Seeing quantities of onions in your dreams, represents the amount of spite and envy that you will meet, by being successful.

If you eat them, you will overcome all opposition.

If you see them growing, there will be just enough of rivalry in your affairs, to make things interesting.

Cooked onions, denote placidity and small gains in business.

To dream that you are cutting onions and feel the escaping juice in your eyes, denotes that you will be defeated by your rivals.

Opera.

To dream of attending an opera, denotes that you will be entertained by congenial friends, and find that your immediate affairs will be favorable.

Opium.

To dream of opium, signifies strangers will obstruct

*See Carriage.

your chances of improving your fortune, by sly and seductive means.

Opulence.*

For a young woman to dream that she lives in fairy like opulence, denotes that she will be deceived, and will live for a time in luxurious ease and splendor, to find later that she is mated with shame and poverty. When young women dream that they are enjoying solid and real wealth and comforts, they will always wake to find some real pleasure, but when abnormal or fairy-like dreams of luxury and joy seem to encompass them, their waking moments will be filled with disappointments; as the dreams are warnings, superinduced by their practicality being supplanted by their excitable imagination and lazy desires, which should be overcome with energy, and the replacing of practicality on her base. No young woman should fill her mind with idle day dreams, but energetically strive to carry forward noble ideals and thoughts, and promising and helpful dreams will come to her while she restores physical energies in sleep.

Oranges.

Seeing a number of orange trees in a healthy condition, bearing ripe fruit, is a sign of health and prosperous surroundings.

To eat oranges is signally bad. Sickness of friends or relatives will be a source of worry to you. Dissatisfaction will pervade the atmosphere in business circles. If they are fine and well-flavored, there will be a slight abatement of ill luck. A young woman is likely to lose her lover, if she dreams of eating oranges. If she dreams of seeing a fine one pitched up high, she will be discreet in choosing a husband from many lovers.

---

*See Wealth.

To slip on an orange peel, foretells the death of a relative.

To buy oranges at your wife's solicitation, and she eats them, denotes that unpleasant complications will resolve themselves into profit.

Orang-utang.

To dream of an orang-utang, denotes that some person is falsely using your influence to further selfish schemes. For a young woman, it portends an unfaithful lover.

Orator.

Being under the spell of an orator's eloquence, denotes that you will heed the voice of flattery to your own detriment, as you will be persuaded into offering aid to unworthy people.

If a young woman falls in love with an orator, it is proof that in her loves she will be affected by outward show.

Orchard.

Dreaming of passing through leaving and blossoming orchards with your sweetheart, omens a delightful consummation of a long courtship. If the orchard is filled with ripening fruit, it denotes recompense for faithful service to those under masters, and full fruition of designs for the leaders of enterprises. Happy homes, with loyal husbands and obedient children, for wives.

If you are in an orchard and see hogs eating the fallen fruit, it is a sign that you will lose property in trying to claim what are not really your own belongings.

To gather the ripe fruit, is a happy omen of plenty to all classes.

Orchards infested with blight, denotes a miserable existence, amid joy and wealth.

To be caught in brambles, while passing through an

orchard, warns you of a jealous rival, or, if married, a private but large row with your partner.

If you dream of seeing a barren orchard, opportunities to rise to higher stations in life will be ignored.

If you see one robbed of its verdure by seeming winter, it denotes that you have been careless of the future in the enjoyment of the present.

To see a storm-swept orchard, brings an unwelcome guest, or duties.

Orchestra.

Belonging to an orchestra and playing, foretells pleasant entertainments, and your sweetheart will be faithful and cultivated.

To hear the music of an orchestra, denotes that the knowledge of humanity will at all times prove you to be a much-liked person, and favors will fall unstintedly upon you.

Organ.

To hear the pealing forth of an organ in grand anthems, signifies lasting friendships and well-grounded fortune.

To see an organ in a church, denotes despairing separation of families, and death, perhaps, for some of them.

If you dream of rendering harmonious music on an organ, you will be fortunate in the way to worldly comfort, and much social distinction will be given you.

To hear doleful singing and organ accompaniment. denotes you are nearing a wearisome task, and probable loss of friends or position.

Organist.

To see an organist in your dreams, denotes a friend will cause you much inconvenience from hasty action. For a young woman to dream that she is an organist, foretells she will be so exacting in her love that she will be threatened with desertion.

Ornament.

If you wear ornaments in dreams, you will have a flattering honor conferred upon you.

If you receive them, you will be fortunate in undertakings.

Giving them away, denotes recklessness and lavish extravagance.

Losing an ornament, brings the loss either of a lover, or a good situation.

Orphan.

Condoling with orphans in a dream, means that the unhappy cares of others will touch your sympathies and cause you to sacrifice much personal enjoyment.

If the orphans be related to you, new duties will come into your life, causing estrangement from friends and from some person held above mere friendly liking.

Ostrich.

To dream of an ostrich, denotes that you will secretly amass wealth, but at the same time maintain degrading intrigues with women.

To catch one, your resources will enable you to enjoy travel and extensive knowledge.

Otter.

To see otters diving and sporting in limpid streams is certain to bring the dreamer waking happiness and good fortune. You will find ideal enjoyment in an early marriage, if you are single; wives may expect unusual tenderness from their spouses after this dream.

Ottoman.*

Dreams in which you find yourself luxuriously reposing upon an ottoman, discussing the intricacies of love with your sweetheart, foretells that envious rivals will seek to defame you in the eyes of your affianced, and a hasty marriage will be advised.

Ouija.

To dream of working on an ouija board, foretells the miscarriage of plans and unlucky partnerships.

To fail to work, one is ominous of complications, caused by substituting pleasure for business.

If it writes fluently, you may expect fortunate results from some well-planned enterprise.

If a thief steals it, you will meet with trials and vexations past endurance. To recover it, foretells that grievances will meet a favorable adjustment.

Oven.

For a woman to dream that her baking oven is red hot, denotes that she will be loved by her own family and friends, for her sweet and unselfish nature. If she is baking, temporary disappointments await her. If the oven is broken, she will undergo many vexations from children and servants.

Overcoat.

To dream of an overcoat, denotes you will suffer from contrariness, exhibited by others. To borrow one, foretells you will be unfortunate through mistakes made by strangers. If you see or are wearing a handsome new overcoat, you will be exceedingly fortunate in realizing your wishes.

---

*See Couch.

Over-alls.

For a woman to dream that she sees a man wearing over-alls, she will be deceived as to the real character of her lover. If a wife, she will be deceived in her husband's frequent absence, and the real cause will create suspicions of his fidelity.

Owl.

To hear the solemn, unearthly sound of the muffled voice of the owl, warns dreamers that death creeps closely in the wake of health and joy. Precaution should be taken that life is not ruthlessly exposed to his unyielding grasp. Bad tidings of the absent will surely follow this dream.

To see a dead owl, denotes a narrow escape from desperate illness or death.

To see an owl, foretells that you will be secretly maligned and be in danger from enemies.

Ox.*

To see a well-fed ox, signifies that you will become a leading person in your community, and receive much adulation from women.

To see fat oxen in green pastures, signifies fortune, and your rise to positions beyond your expectations. If they are lean, your fortune will dwindle, and your friends will fall away from you.

If you see oxen well-matched and yoked, it betokens a happy and wealthy marriage, or that you are already joined to your true mate.

To see a dead ox, is a sign of bereavement.

If they are drinking from a clear pond, or stream, you will possess some long-desired estate, perhaps it will be in the form of a lovely and devoted woman. If a woman she will win the embraces of her lover.

*See Cattle.

Oysters.

If you dream that you eat oysters, it denotes that you will lose all sense of propriety and morality in your pursuit of low pleasures, and the indulgence of an insatiate thirst for gaining.

To deal in oysters, denotes that you will not be over-modest in your mode of winning a sweetheart, or a fortune.

To see them, denotes easy circumstances, and many children are promised you.

Oyster Shells.

To see oyster shells in your dreams, denotes that you will be frustrated in your attempt to secure the fortune of another.

P.

"And the King said unto them, I have dreamed a dream, and my spirit was troubled to know the dream."—Dan. ii., 3.

Pacify.

To endeavor to pacify suffering ones, denotes that you will be loved for your sweetness of disposition. To a young woman, this dream is one of promise of a devoted husband or friends.

Pacifying the anger of others, denotes that you will labor for the advancement of others.

If a lover dreams of soothing the jealous suspicions of his sweetheart, he will find that his love will be unfortunately placed.

Packet.

To dream of seeing a packet coming in, foretells that some pleasant recreation is in store for you.

To see one going out, you will experience slight losses and disappointments.

Page.

To see a page, denotes that you will contract a hasty union with one unsuited to you. You will fail to control your romantic impulses.

If a young woman dreams she acts as a page, it denotes that she is likely to participate in some foolish escapade.

Pagoda.

To see a pagoda in your dreams, denotes that you will soon go on a long desired journey.

If a young woman finds herself in a pagoda with her sweetheart, many unforeseen events will transpire before her union is legalized. An empty one, warns her of separation from her lover.

Pail.

To dream of full pails of milk, is a sign of fair prospects and pleasant associations.

An empty pail is a sign of famine, or bad crops.

For a young woman to be carrying a pail, denotes household employment.

Pain.

To dream that you are in pain, will make sure of your own unhappiness. This dream foretells useless regrets over some trivial transaction.

To see others in pain, warns you that you are making mistakes in your life.

Paint and Painting.

To see newly painted houses in dreams, foretells that you will succeed with some devised plan.

To have paint on your clothing, you will be made unhappy by the thoughtless criticisms of others.

To dream that you use the brush yourself, denotes that you will be well pleased with your present occupation.

To dream of seeing beautiful paintings, denotes that friends will assume false positions towards you, and you will find that pleasure is illusive.

For a young woman to dream of painting a picture, she will be deceived in her lover, as he will transfer his love to another.

Palace.*

Wandering through a palace and noting its grandeur, signifies that your prospects are growing brighter and you will assume new dignity.

To see and hear fine ladies and men dancing and conversing, denotes that you will engage in profitable and pleasing associations.

For a young woman of moderate means to dream that she is a participant in the entertainment, and of equal social standing with others, is a sign of her advancement through marriage, or the generosity of relatives.

This is often a very deceitful and misleading dream to the young woman of humble circumstances; as it is generally induced in such cases by the unhealthy day dreams of her idle, empty brain. She should strive after this dream, to live by honest work, and restrain deceitful ambition by observing the fireside counsels of mother, and friends.

Palisade.

To dream of the palisades, denotes that you will alter well-formed plans to please strangers, and by so doing, you will impair your own interests.

Pall.

To dream that you see a pall, denotes that you will have sorrow and misfortune.

*See Opulence.

If you raise the pall from a corpse, you will doubtless soon mourn the death of one whom you love.

Pall-bearer.

To dream of a pall-bearer, indicates some enemy will provoke your ill feeling, by constant attacks on your integrity. If you see a pall-bearer, you will antagonize worthy institutions, and make yourself obnoxious to friends.

Pallet.

To dream of a pallet, denotes that you will suffer temporary uneasiness over your love affairs. For a young woman, it is a sign of a jealous rival.

Palmistry.

For a young woman to dream of palmistry, foretells she will be the object of suspicion.

If she has her palms read, she will have many friends of the opposite sex, but her own sex will condemn her. If she reads others' hands, she will gain distinction by her intelligent bearing. If a minister's hand, she will need friends, even in her elevation.

Palm Tree.

Palm trees seen in your dreams, are messages of hopeful situations and happiness of a high order.

For a young woman to pass down an avenue of palms, omens a cheerful home and a faithful husband. If the palms are withered, some unexpected sorrowful event will disturb her serenity.

Palsy.

To dream that you are afflicted with palsy, denotes that you are making unstable contracts.

To see your friend so afflicted, there will be uncertainty

as to his faithfulness and sickness, too, may enter your home.

For lovers to dream that their sweethearts have palsy, signifies that dissatisfaction over some question will mar their happiness.

Pancake.

To dream of eating pancakes, denotes that you will have excellent success in all enterprises undertaken at this time.

To cook them, denotes that you will be economical and thrifty in your home.

Pane of Glass.

To dream that you handle a pane of glass, denotes that you are dealing in uncertainties. If you break it, your failure will be accentuated.

To talk to a person through a pane of glass, denotes that there are obstacles in your immediate future, and they will cause you no slight inconvenience.

Panorama.

To dream of a panorama, denotes that you will change your occupation or residence. You should curb your inclinations for change of scene and friends.

Panther.

To see a panther and experience fright, denotes that contracts in love or business may be canceled unexpectedly, owing to adverse influences working against your honor. But killing, or over-powering it, you will experience joy and be successful in your undertakings. Your surroundings will take on fair prospects.

If one menaces you by its presence, you will have disappointments in business. Other people will likely recede from their promises to you.

If you hear the voice of a panther, and experience terror or fright, you will have unfavorable news, coming in the way of reducing profit or gain, and you may have social discord; no fright forebodes less evil.

A panther, like the cat, seen in a dream, portends evil to the dreamer, unless he kills it.

Pantomime.

To dream of seeing pantomimes, denotes that your friends will deceive you. If you participate in them, you will have cause of offense. Affairs will not prove satisfactory.

Paper or parchment.

If you have occasion in your dreams to refer to, or handle, any paper or parchment, you will be threatened with losses. They are likely to be in the nature of a lawsuit. For a young woman, it means that she will be angry with her lover and that she fears the opinion of acquaintances. Beware, if you are married, of disagreements in the precincts of the home.

Parables.

To dream of parables, denotes that you will be undecided as to the best course to pursue in dissenting to some business complication. To the lover, or young woman, this is a prophecy of misunderstandings and disloyalty.

Paradise.

To dream that you are in Paradise, means loyal friends, who are willing to aid you. This dream holds out bright hopes to sailors or those about to make a long voyage. To mothers, this means fair and obedient children. If you are sick and unfortunate, you will have a speedy recovery and your fortune will ripen. To lovers, it is the promise of wealth and faithfulness.

To dream that you start to Paradise and find yourself bewildered and lost, you will undertake enterprises which look exceedingly feasible and full of fortunate returns, but which will prove disappointing and vexatious.

Paralysis.

Paralysis is a bad dream, denoting financial reverses and disappointment in literary attainment. To lovers, it portends a cessation of affections.

Parasol.*

To dream of a parasol, denotes, for married people, illicit enjoyments.

If a young woman has this dream, she will engage in many flirtations, some of which will cause her interesting disturbances, lest her lover find out her inclinations.

Parcel.

To dream of a parcel being delivered to you, denotes that you will be pleasantly surprised by the return of some absent one, or be cared for in a worldly way.

If you carry a parcel, you will have some unpleasant task to perform.

To let a parcel fall on the way as you go to deliver it, you will see some deal fail to go through.

Pardon.†

To dream that you are endeavoring to gain pardon for an offense which you never committed, denotes that you will be troubled, and seemingly with cause, over your affairs, but it will finally appear that it was for your advancement. If offense was committed, you will realize embarrassment in affairs.

*See Umbrella.   †See kindred words.

To receive pardon, you will prosper after a series of misfortunes.

Parents.*

To see your parents looking cheerful while dreaming, denotes harmony and pleasant associates.

If they appear to you after they are dead, it is a warning of approaching trouble, and you should be particular of your dealings.

To see them while they are living, and they seem to be in your home and happy, denotes pleasant changes for you. To a young woman, this usually brings marriage and prosperity. If pale and attired in black, grave disappointments will harass you.

To dream of seeing your parents looking robust and contented, denotes you are under fortunate environments; your business and love interests will flourish. If they appear indisposed or sad, you will find life's favors passing you by without recognition.

Park.

To dream of walking through a well-kept park, denotes enjoyable leisure. If you walk with your lover, you will be comfortably and happily married. Ill-kept parks, devoid of green grasses and foliage, is ominous of unexpected reverses.

Parrot.

Parrots chattering in your dreams, signifies frivolous employments and idle gossip among your friends.

To see them in repose, denotes a peaceful intermission of family broils.

For a young woman to dream that she owns a parrot, denotes that her lover will believe her to be quarrelsome.

---

* See Father and Mother.

To teach a parrot, you will have trouble in your private affairs.

A dead parrot, foretells the loss of social friends.

Parsley.

To dream of parsley, denotes hard-earned success, usually the surroundings of the dreamer are healthful and lively.

To eat parsley, is a sign of good health, but the care of a large family will be your portion.

Parsnips.

To see or eat parsnips, is a favorable omen of successful business or trade, but love will take on unfavorable and gloomy aspects.

Parting.

To dream of parting with friends and companions, denotes that many little vexations will come into your daily life.

If you part with enemies, it is a sign of success in love and business.

Partner.

To dream of seeing your business partner with a basket of crockery on his back, and, letting it fall, gets it mixed with other crockery, denotes your business will sustain a loss through the indiscriminate dealings of your partner. If you reprimand him for it, you will, to some extent, recover the loss.

Partnership.

To dream of forming a partnership with a man, denotes uncertain and fluctuating money affairs. If your partner be a woman, you will engage in some enterprise which you will endeavor to keep hidden from friends.

To dissolve an unpleasant partnership, denotes that

things will arrange themselves agreeable to your desires; but if the partnership was pleasant, there will be disquieting news and disagreeable turns in your affairs.

Partridge.

Partridges seen in your dreams, denotes that conditions will be good in your immediate future for the accumulation of property.

To ensnare them, signifies that you will be fortunate in expectations.

To kill them, foretells that you will be successful, but much of your wealth will be given to others.

To eat them, signifies the enjoyment of deserved honors.

To see them flying, denotes that a promising future is before you.

Party.

To dream of an unknown party of men assaulting you for your money or valuables, denotes that you will have enemies banded together against you. If you escape uninjured, you will overcome any opposition, either in business or love.

To dream of attending a party of any kind for pleasure, you will find that life has much good, unless the party is an inharmonious one.

Passenger.

To dream that you see passengers coming in with their luggage, denotes improvement in your surroundings. If they are leaving you will lose an opportunity of gaining some desired property. If you are one of the passengers leaving home, you will be dissatisfied with your present living and will seek to change it.

Passing Bell.

To hear a passing bell, unexpected intelligence of the sorrow or illness of the absent.

To ring one yourself, denotes ill health and reverses.

Password.

To dream of a password, foretells you will have influential aid in some slight trouble soon to attack you. For a woman to dream that she has given away the password, signifies she will endanger her own standing through seeking frivolous or illicit desires.

Pasteboard.

To dream of pasteboard, denotes that unfaithful friends will deceive you concerning important matters. To cut pasteboard, you will throw aside difficulties in your struggle to reach eminent positions.

Pastry.*

To dream of pastry, denotes that you will be deceived by some artful person.

To eat it, implies heartfelt friendships.

If a young woman dreams that she is cooking it, she will fail to deceive others as to her real intentions.

Patch.

To dream that you have patches upon your clothing, denotes that you will show no false pride in the discharge of obligations.

To see others wearing patches, denotes want and misery are near.

If a young woman discovers a patch on her new dress, it indicates that she will find trouble facing her when she imagines her happiest moments are approaching near. If she tries to hide the patches, she will endeavor to keep some ugly trait in her character from her lover. If she

---

*See Pies.

is patching, she will assume duties for which she has no liking.

For a woman to do family patching, denotes close and loving bonds in the family, but a scarcity of means is portended.

Patent.

To dream of securing a patent, denotes that you will be careful and painstaking with any task you set about to accomplish. If you fail in securing your patent, you will suffer failure for the reason that you are engaging in enterprises for which you have no ability.

If you buy one, you will have occasion to make a tiresome and fruitless journey.

To see one, you will suffer unpleasantness from illness.

Patent Medicine.

To dream that you resort to patent medicine in your search for health, denotes that you will use desperate measures in advancing your fortune, but you will succeed, to the disappointment of the envious.

To see or manufacture patent medicines, you will rise from obscurity to positions above your highest imaginings.

Path.

To dream that you are walking in a narrow and rough path, stumbling over rocks and other obstructions, denotes that you will have a rough encounter with adversity, and feverish excitement will weigh heavily upon you.

To dream that you are trying to find your path, foretells that you will fail to accomplish some work that you have striven to push to desired ends.

To walk through a pathway bordered with green grass and flowers, denotes your freedom from oppressing loves.

Paunch.

To see a large paunch, denotes wealth and the total absence of refinement.

To see a shriveled paunch, foretells illness and reverses.

Pauper.*

To dream that you are a pauper, implies unpleasant happenings for you.

To see paupers, denotes that there will be a call upon your generosity.

Pawn-shop.

If in your dreams you enter a pawn-shop, you will find disappointments and losses in your waking moments.

To pawn articles, you will have unpleasant scenes with your wife or sweetheart, and perhaps disappointments in business.

For a woman to go to a pawn-shop, denotes that she is guilty of indiscretions, and she is likely to regret the loss of a friend.

To redeem an article, denotes that you will regain lost positions.

To dream that you see a pawn-shop, denotes you are negligent of your trust and are in danger of sacrificing your honorable name in some salacious affair.

Peaches.†

Dreaming of seeing or eating peaches, implies the sickness of children, disappointing returns in business, and failure to make anticipated visits of pleasure; but if you see them on trees with foliage, you will secure some desired position or thing after much striving and risking of health and money.

---

*See Beggars and kindred words.   † See Orchard.

To see dried peaches, denotes that enemies will steal from you.

For a young woman to dream of gathering luscious peaches from well-filled trees, she will, by her personal charms and qualifications, win a husband rich in worldly goods and wise in travel. If the peaches prove to be green and knotty, she will meet with unkindness from relatives and ill health will steal away her attractions.

Peacock.

For persons dreaming of peacocks, there lies below the brilliant and flashing ebb and flow of the stream of pleasure and riches, the slums of sorrow and failure, which threaten to mix with its clearness at the least disturbing influence.

For a woman to dream that she owns peacocks, denotes that she will be deceived in her estimate of man's honor.

To hear their harsh voices while looking upon their proudly spread plumage, denotes that some beautiful and well-appearing person will work you discomfort and uneasiness of mind.

Pearls.

To dream of pearls, is a forerunner of good business and trade and affairs of social nature.

If a young woman dreams that her lover sends her gifts of pearls, she will indeed be most fortunate, as there will be occasions of festivity and pleasure for her, besides a loving and faithful affianced devoid of the jealous inclinations so ruinous to the peace of lovers. If she loses or breaks her pearls, she will suffer indescribable sadness and sorrow through bereavement or misunderstandings. To find herself admiring them, she will covet and strive for love or possessions with a pureness of purpose.

Pears.

To dream of eating pears, denotes poor success and debilitating health.

To admire the golden fruit upon graceful trees, denotes that fortune will wear a more promising aspect than formerly.

To dream of gathering them, denotes pleasant surprises will follow quickly upon disappointment.

To preserve them, denotes that you will take reverses philosophically.

Baking them, denotes insipid love and friendships.

Peas.

Dreaming of eating peas, augurs robust health and the accumulation of wealth. Much activity is indicated for farmers and their women folks.

To see them growing, denotes fortunate enterprises.

To plant them, denotes that your hopes are well grounded and they will be realized.

To gather them, signifies that your plans will culminate in good and you will enjoy the fruits of your labors.

To dream of canned peas, denotes that your brightest hopes will be enthralled in uncertainties for a short season, but they will finally be released by fortune.

To see dried peas, denotes that you are overtaxing your health.

To eat dried peas, foretells that you will, after much success, suffer a slight decrease in pleasure or wealth.

Pebbles.

For a young woman to dream of a pebble-strewn walk, she will be vexed with many rivals and find that there are others with charms that attract besides her own. She who dreams of pebbles is selfish and should cultivate leniency towards others' faults.

Pecans.

To dream of eating this appetizing nut, you will see one of your dearest plans come to full fruition, and seeming failure prove a prosperous source of gain.

To see them growing among leaves, signifies a long, peaceful existence. Failure in love or business will follow in proportion as the pecan is decayed.

If they are difficult to crack and the fruit is small, you will succeed after much trouble and expense, but returns will be meagre.

Pelican.

To dream of a pelican, denotes a mingling of disappointments with successes.

To catch one, you will be able to overcome disappointing influences.

To kill one, denotes that you will cruelly set aside the rights of others.

To see them flying, you are threatened with changes, which will impress you with ideas of uncertainty as to good.

Pen.

To dream of a pen, foretells you are unfortunately being led into serious complications by your love of adventure. If the pen refuses to write, you will be charged with a serious breach of morality.

Penalties.

To dream that you have penalties imposed upon you, foretells that you will have duties that will rile you and find you rebellious.

To pay a penalty, denotes sickness and financial loss. To escape the payment, you will be victor in some contest.

Pencil.

To dream of pencils, denotes favorable occupations. For a young woman to write with one, foretells she will be fortunate in marriage, if she does not rub out words; in that case, she will be disappointed in her lover.

Penitentiary.

To dream of a penitentiary, denotes you will have engagements which will, unfortunately, result in your loss. To be an inmate of one, foretells discontent in the home and failing business. To escape from one, you will overcome difficult obstacles.

Penny.

To dream of pennies, denotes unsatisfactory pursuits. Business will suffer, and lovers and friends will complain of the smallness of affection.

To lose them, signifies small deference and failures.

To find them, denotes that prospects will advance to your improvement.

To count pennies, foretells that you will be business-like and economical.

Pension.

To dream of drawing a pension, foretells that you will be aided in your labors by friends.

To fail in your application for a pension, denotes that you will lose in an undertaking and suffer the loss of friendships.

People.*

Pepper.

To dream of pepper burning your tongue, foretells that you will suffer from your acquaintances through your love of gossip.

---

*See Crowd.

435

To see red pepper growing, foretells for you a thrifty and an independent partner in the marriage state.

To see piles of red pepper pods, signifies that you will aggressively maintain your rights.

To grind black pepper, denotes that you will be victimized by the wiles of ingenious men or women. To see it in stands on the table, omens sharp reproaches or quarrels.

For a young woman to put it on her food, foretells that she will be deceived by her friends.

Peppermint.

To dream of peppermint, denotes pleasant entertainments and interesting affairs.

To see it growing, denotes that you will participate in some pleasure in which there will be a dash of romance.

To enjoy drinks in which there is an effusion of peppermint, denotes that you will enjoy assignations with some attractive and fascinating person. To a young woman, this dream warns her against seductive pleasures.

Perfume.

To dream of inhaling perfume, is an augury of happy incidents.

For you to perfume your garments and person, denotes that you will seek and obtain adulation.

Being oppressed by it to intoxication, denotes that excesses in joy will impair your mental qualities.

To spill perfume, denotes that you will lose something which affords you pleasure.

To break a bottle of perfume, foretells that your most cherished wishes and desires will end disastrously, even while they promise a happy culmination.

To dream that you are distilling perfume, denotes that

your employments and associations will be of the pleasantest character.

For a young woman to dream of perfuming her bath, foretells ecstatic happenings. If she receives it as a gift from a man, she will experience fascinating, but dangerous pleasures.

Perspiration.

To dream that you are in a perspiration, foretells that you will come out of some difficulty, which has caused much gossip, with new honors.

Pest.

To dream of being worried over a pest of any nature, foretells that disturbing elements will prevail in your immediate future.

To see others thus worried, denotes that you will be annoyed by some displeasing development.

Petticoat.

To dream of seeing new petticoats, denotes that pride in your belongings will make you an object of raillery among your acquaintances.

To see them soiled or torn, portends that your reputation will be in great danger.

If a young woman dream that she wears silken, or clean, petticoats, it denotes that she will have a doting, but manly husband. If she suddenly perceives that she has left off her petticoat in dressing, it portends much ill luck and disappointment. To see her petticoat falling from its place while she is at some gathering, or while walking, she will have trouble in retaining her lover, and other disappointments may follow.

Pewter.*

To dream of pewter, foretells straitened circumstances.

*See Dishes.

Phantom.*

To dream that a phantom pursues you, foretells strange and disquieting experiences.

To see a phantom fleeing from you, foretells that trouble will assume smaller proportions.

Pheasant.

Dreaming of pheasants, omens good fellowship among your friends.

To eat one, signifies that the jealousy of your wife will cause you to forego friendly intercourse with your friends.

To shoot them, denotes that you will fail to sacrifice one selfish pleasure for the comfort of friends.

Phosphorus.

To dream of seeing phosphorus, is indicative of evanescent joys.

For a young woman, it foretells a brilliant but brief success with admirers.

Photography.

If you see photographs in your dreams, it is a sign of approaching deception.

If you receive the photograph of your lover, you are warned that he is not giving you his undivided loyalty, while he tries to so impress you.

For married people to dream of the possession of other persons' photographs, foretells unwelcome disclosures of one's conduct.

To dream that you are having your own photograph made, foretells that you will unwarily cause yourself and others' trouble.

Physician.

For a young woman to dream of a physician, denotes

* See Ghost.

that she is sacrificing her beauty in engaging in frivolous pastimes. If she is sick and thus dreams, she will have sickness or worry, but will soon overcome them, unless the physician appears very anxious, and then her trials may increase, ending in loss and sorrow.

Piano.

To dream of seeing a piano, denotes some joyful occasion.

To hear sweet and voluptuous harmony from a piano, signals success and health. If discordant music is being played, you will have many exasperating matters to consider. Sad and plaintive music, foretells sorrowful tidings.

To find your piano broken and out of tune, portends dissatisfaction with your own accomplishments and disappointment in the failure of your friends or children to win honors.

To see an old-fashioned piano, denotes that you have, in trying moments, neglected the advices and opportunities of the past, and are warned not to do so again.

For a young woman to dream that she is executing difficult, but entrancing music, she will succeed in winning an indifferent friend to be a most devoted and loyal lover.

Pickaxe.

To dream of a pickaxe, denotes a relentless enemy is working to overthrow you socially. A broken one, implies disaster to all your interests.

Pickles.

To dream of pickles, denotes that you will follow worthless pursuits if you fail to call energy and judgment to your aid.

For a young woman to dream of eating pickles, foretells an unambitious career.

To dream of pickles, denotes vexation in love, but final triumph.

For a young woman to dream that she is eating them, or is hungry for them, foretells she will find many rivals, and will be overcome unless she is careful of her private affairs. Impure pickles, indicate disappointing engagements and love quarrels.

Pickpocket.

To dream of a pickpocket, foretells some enemy will succeed in harassing and causing you loss. For a young woman to have her pocket picked, denotes she will be the object of some person's envy and spite, and may lose the regard of a friend through these evil machinations, unless she keeps her own counsel. If she picks others' pockets, she will incur the displeasure of a companion by her coarse behavior.

Picnic.*

To dream of attending a picnic, foreshadows success and real enjoyment.

Dreams of picnics, bring undivided happiness to the young.

Storms, or any interfering elements at a picnic, implies the temporary displacement of assured profit and pleasure in love or business.

Pictures.†

Pictures appearing before you in dreams, prognosticate deception and the ill will of contemporaries.

To make a picture, denotes that you will engage in some unremunerative enterprise.

To destroy pictures, means that you will be pardoned for using strenuous means to establish your rights.

---

* See Kindred Words.   † See Painting and Photographs.

To buy them, foretells worthless speculation.

To dream of seeing your likeness in a living tree, appearing and disappearing, denotes that you will be prosperous and seemingly contented, but there will be disappointments in reaching out for companionship and reciprocal understanding of ideas and plans.

To dream of being surrounded with the best efforts of the old and modern masters, denotes that you will have insatiable longings and desires for higher attainments, compared to which present success will seem poverty-stricken and miserable.

Pier.

To stand upon a pier in your dream, denotes that you will be brave in your battle for recognition in prosperity's realm, and that you will be admitted to the highest posts of honor.

If you strive to reach a pier and fail, you will lose the distinction you most coveted.

Pies.*

To dream of eating pies, you will do well to watch your enemies, as they are planning to injure you.

For a young woman to dream of making pies, denotes that she will flirt with men for pastime. She should accept this warning.

Pig.†

To dream of a fat, healthy pig, denotes reasonable success in affairs. If they are wallowing in mire, you will have hurtful associates, and your engagements will be subject to reproach. This dream will bring to a young woman a jealous and greedy companion though the chances are that he will be wealthy.

---

*See Pastry.   † See Hog.

Pigeon.

To dream of seeing pigeons and hearing them cooing above their cotes, denotes domestic peace and pleasure-giving children. For a young woman, this dream indicates an early and comfortable union.

To see them being used in a shooting match, and, if you participate, it denotes that cruelty in your nature will show in your dealings, and you are warned of low and debasing pleasures.

To see them flying, denotes freedom from misunderstanding, and perhaps news from the absent.

Pilgrim.

To dream of pilgrims, denotes that you will go on an extended journey, leaving home and its dearest objects in the mistaken idea that it must be thus for their good.

To dream that you are a pilgrim, portends struggles with poverty and unsympathetic companions.

For a young woman to dream that a pilgrim approaches her, she will fall an easy dupe to deceit. If he leaves her, she will awaken to her weakness of character and strive to strengthen independent thought.

Pill.

To dream that you take pills, denotes that you will have responsibilities to look after, but they will bring you no little comfort and enjoyment.

To give them to others, signifies that you will be criticised for your disagreeableness.

Pillow.

To dream of a pillow, denotes luxury and comfort.

For a young woman to dream that she makes a pillow, she will have encouraging prospects of a pleasant future.

Pimple.

To dream of your flesh being full of pimples, denotes worry over trifles.

To see others with pimples on them, signifies that you will be troubled with illness and complaints from others.

For a woman to dream that her beauty is marred by pimples, her conduct in home or social circles will be criticised by friends and acquaintances. You may have small annoyances to follow this dream.

Pincers.

To dream of feeling pincers on your flesh, denotes that you will be burdened with exasperating cares. Any dream of pincers, signifies unfortunate incidents.

Pineapple.

To dream of pineapples, is exceedingly propitious. Success will follow in the near future, if you gather pineapples or eat them.

To dream that you prick your fingers while preparing a pineapple for the table, you will experience considerable vexation over matters which will finally bring pleasure and success.

Pine Tree.

To see a pine tree in a dream, foretells unvarying success in any undertaking. Dead pine, for a woman, represents bereavement and cares.

Pins.

To dream of pins, augurs differences and quarrels in families.

To a young woman, they warn her of unladylike conduct towards her lover.

To dream of swallowing a pin, denotes that accidents will force you into perilous conditions.

To lose one, implies a petty loss or disagreement.

To see a bent or rusty pin, signifies that you will lose esteem because of your careless ways.

To stick one into your flesh, denotes that some person will irritate you.

Pipe.

Pipes seen in dreams, are representatives of peace and comfort after many struggles.

Sewer, gas, and such like pipes, denotes unusual thought and prosperity in your community.

Old and broken pipe, signifies ill health and stagnation of business.

To dream that you smoke a pipe, denotes that you will enjoy the visit of an old friend, and peaceful settlements of differences will also take place.

Pirate.

To dream of pirates, denotes that you will be exposed to the evil designs of false friends.

To dream that you are a pirate, denotes that you will fall beneath the society of friends and former equals.

For a young woman to dream that her lover is a pirate, is a sign of his unworthiness and deceitfulness. If she is captured by pirates, she will be induced to leave her home under false pretenses.

Pistol.

Seeing a pistol in your dream, denotes bad fortune, generally.

If you own one, you will cultivate a low, designing character.

If you hear the report of one, you will be made aware of some scheme to ruin your interests.

To dream of shooting off your pistol, signifies that you

will bear some innocent person envy, and you will go far to revenge the imagined wrong.

Pit.

If you are looking into a deep pit in your dream, you will run silly risks in business ventures and will draw uneasiness about your wooing.

To fall into a pit denotes calamity and deep sorrow. To wake as you begin to feel yourself falling into the pit, brings you out of distress in fairly good shape.

To dream that you are descending into one, signifies that you will knowingly risk health and fortune for greater success.

Pitcher.

To dream of a pitcher, denotes that you will be of a generous and congenial disposition. Success will attend your efforts.

A broken pitcher, denotes loss of friends.

Pitchfork.

Pitchforks in dreams, denotes struggles for betterment of fortune and great laboring, either physically or mentally.

To dream that you are attacked by some person using a pitchfork, implies that you will have personal enemies who would not scruple to harm you.

Plague.

To dream of a plague raging, denotes disappointing returns in business, and your wife or lover will lead you a wretched existence.

If you are afflicted with the plague, you will keep your business out of embarrassment with the greatest maneuvering. If you are trying to escape it, some trouble, which looks impenetrable, is pursuing you.

Plain.*

For a young woman to dream of crossing a plain, denotes that she will be fortunately situated, if the grasses are green and luxuriant; if they are arid, or the grass is dead, she will have much discomfort and loneliness.

Plane.

To dream that you use a plane, denotes that your liberality and successful efforts will be highly commended.

To see carpenters using their planes, denotes that you will progress smoothly in your undertakings.

To dream of seeing planes, denotes congeniality and even success.

A love of the real, and not the false, is portended by this dream.

Planet.

To dream of a planet, foretells an uncomfortable journey and depressing work.

Plank.

For a young woman to dream that she is walking across muddy water on a rotten plank, denotes that she will feel keenly the indifference shown her by one she loves, or other troubles may arise; or her defence of honor may be in danger of collapse.

Walking a good, sound plank, is a good omen, but a person will have to be unusually careful in conduct after such a dream.

Plaster.

To dream of seeing walls plainly plastered, denotes that success will come, but it will not be stable.

To have plaster fall upon you, denotes unmitigated disasters and disclosure.

*See Prairie.

To see plasterers at work, denotes that you will have a sufficient competency to live above penury.

Plate.*

For a woman to dream of plates, denotes that she will practise economy and win a worthy husband. If already married, she will retain her husband's love and respect by the wise ordering of his household.

Play.†

For a young woman to dream that she attends a play, foretells that she will be courted by a genial friend, and will marry to further her prospects and pleasure seeking. If there is trouble in getting to and from the play, or discordant and hideous scenes, she will be confronted with many displeasing surprises.

Pleasure.‡

To dream of pleasure, denotes gain and personal enjoyment.

Plow.

To dream of a plow, signifies unusual success, and affairs will reach a pleasing culmination.

To see persons plowing, denotes activity and advancement in knowledge and fortune.

For a young woman to see her lover plowing, indicates that she will have a noble and wealthy husband. Her joys will be deep and lasting.

To plow yourself, denotes rapid increase in property and joys.

Plums.

Plums, if they are green, unless seen on trees, are signs of personal and relative discomfort.

---

*See Dishes.   †See Theater.   ‡See Joy.

To see them ripe, denotes joyous occasions, which, however, will be of short duration.

To eat them, denotes that you will engage in flirtations and other evanescent pleasures.

To gather them, you will obtain your desires, but they will not prove so solid as you had imagined.

If you find yourself gathering them up from the ground, and find rotten ones among the good, you will be forced to admit that your expectations are unrealized, and that there is no life filled with pleasure alone.

Pocket.

To dream of your pocket, is a sign of evil demonstrations against you.

Pocketbook.

To find a pocketbook filled with bills and money in your dreams, you will be quite lucky, gaining in nearly every instance your desire. If empty, you will be disappointed in some big hope.

If you lose your pocketbook, you will unfortunately disagree with your best friend, and thereby lose much comfort and real gain.

Poinard.*

To dream of some one stabbing you with a poinard, denotes that secret enemies will cause you uneasiness of mind.

If you attack any person with one of these weapons, you will unfortunately suspect your friends of unfaithfulness.

Dreaming of poinards, omens evil.

Poison.

To feel that you are poisoned in a dream, denotes that some painful influence will immediately reach you.

---

*See Dagger.

If you seek to use poison on others, you will be guilty of base thoughts, or the world will go wrong for you.

For a young woman to dream that she endeavors to rid herself of a rival in this way, she will be likely to have a deal of trouble in securing a lover.

To throw the poison away, denotes that by sheer force you will overcome unsatisfactory conditions.

To handle poison, or see others with it, signifies that unpleasantness will surround you.

To dream that your relatives or children are poisoned, you will receive injury from unsuspected sources.

If an enemy or rival is poisoned, you will overcome obstacles.

To recover from the effects of poison, indicates that you will succeed after worry.

To take strychnine or other poisonous medicine under the advice of a physician, denotes that you will undertake some affair fraught with danger.

Poker.

To dream of seeing a red hot poker, or fighting with one, signifies that you will meet trouble with combative energy.

To play at poker, warns you against evil company; and young women, especially, will lose their moral distinctiveness if they find themselves engaged in this game.

Polar Bear.*

Polar bears in dreams, are prognostic of deceit, as misfortune will approach you in a seeming fair aspect. Your bitterest enemies will wear the garb of friendship. Rivals will try to supersede you.

To see the skin of one, denotes that you will successfully overcome any opposition.

---

*See Bear.

Pole-cat.

To dream of a pole-cat, signifies salacious scandals.

To inhale the odor of a pole-cat on your clothes, or otherwise smell one, you will find that your conduct will be considered rude, and your affairs will prove unsatisfactory.

To kill one, denotes that you will overcome formidable obstacles.

Police.

If the police are trying to arrest you for some crime of which you are innocent, it foretells that you will successfully outstrip rivalry.

If the arrest is just, you will have a season of unfortunate incidents.

To see police on parole, indicates alarming fluctuations in affairs.

Polishing.

To dream of polishing any article, high attainments will place you in enviable positions.

Politician.

To dream of a politician, denotes displeasing companionships, and incidences where you will lose time and means.

If you engage in political wrangling, it portends that misunderstandings and ill feeling will be shown you by friends.

For a young woman to dream of taking interest in politics, warns her against designing duplicity.

Polka.*

To dream of dancing the polka, denotes pleasant occupations.

---

*See Dancing.

Pomegranate.

Pomegranates, when dreamed of, denotes that you will wisely use your talents for the enrichment of the mind rather than seeking those pleasures which destroy morality and health.

If your sweetheart gives you one, you will be lured by artful wiles to the verge of distraction by woman's charms, but inner forces will hold you safe from thralldom.

To eat one, signifies that you will yield yourself a captive to the personal charms of another.

Pond.*

To see a pond in your dream, denotes that events will bring no emotion, and fortune will retain a placid outlook.

If the pond is muddy, you will have domestic quarrels.

Pony.

To see ponies in your dreams, signifies moderate speculations will be rewarded with success.

Poor.†

To dream that you, or any of your friends, appear to be poor, is significant of worry and losses.

Poor-house.

To see a poor-house in your dream, denotes you have unfaithful friends, who will care for you only as they can use your money and belongings.

Pope.

Any dream in which you see the Pope, without speaking to him, warns you of servitude. You will bow to the will of some master, even to that of women.

---

*See Water Puddle and kindred words.   †See Pauper.

To speak to the Pope, denotes that certain high honors are in store for you. To see the Pope looking sad or displeased, warns you against vice or sorrow of some kind.

Poplars.

To dream of seeing poplars, is an omen of good, if they are in leaf or bloom.

For a young woman to stand by her lover beneath the blossoms and leaves of a tulip poplar, she will realize her most extravagant hopes.

Her lover will be handsome and polished. Wealth and friends will be hers. If they are leafless and withered, she will meet with disappointments.

Poppies.

Poppies seen in dreams, represents a season of seductive pleasures and flattering business, but they all occupy unstable foundations.

If you inhale the odor of one, you will be the victim of artful persuasions and flattery.

(The mesmeric influence of the poppy inducts one into strange atmospheres, leaving materiality behind while the subjective self explores these realms as in natural sleep; yet these dreams do not bear truthful warnings to the material man. Being, in a manner, enforced.)

Porcelain.

To dream of porcelain, signifies you will have favorable opportunities of progressing in your affairs. To see it broken or soiled, denotes mistakes will be made which will cause grave offense.

Porch.

To dream of a porch, denotes that you will engage in

new undertakings, and the future will be full of uncertainties.

If a young woman dreams that she is with her lover on a porch, implies her doubts of some one's intentions.

To dream that you build a porch, you will assume new duties.

Porcupine.

To see a porcupine in your dreams, denotes that you will disapprove any new enterprise and repel new friendships with coldness.

For a young woman to dream of a porcupine, portends that she will fear her lover.

To see a dead one, signifies your abolishment of ill feelings and possessions.

Pork.*

If you eat pork in your dreams, you will encounter real trouble, but if you only see pork, you will come out of a conflict victoriously.

Porpoise.

To see a porpoise in your dreams, denotes enemies are thrusting your interest aside, through your own inability to keep people interested in you.

Porter.

Seeing a porter in a dream, denotes decided bad luck and eventful happenings.

To imagine yourself a porter, denotes humble circumstances.

To hire one, you will be able to enjoy whatever success comes to you.

To discharge one, signifies that disagreeable charges will be preferred against you.

---

*See Bacon.

Portfolio.

To dream of a portfolio, denotes that your employment will not be to your liking, and you will seek a change in your location.

Portrait.*

To dream of gazing upon the portrait of some beautiful person, denotes that, while you enjoy pleasure, you can but feel the disquieting and treacherousness of such joys. Your general affairs will suffer loss after dreaming of portraits.

Postage.

To dream of postage stamps, denotes system and remuneration in business.

If you try to use cancelled stamps, you will fall into disrepute.

To receive stamps, signifies a rapid rise to distinction.

To see torn stamps, denotes that there are obstacles in your way.

Postman.†

To dream of a postman, denotes that hasty news will more frequently be of a distressing nature than otherwise.

Post-office.

To dream of a post-office, is a sign of unpleasant tidings, and ill luck generally.

Pot.

To dream of a pot, foretells that unimportant events will work you vexation. For a young woman to see a boiling pot, omens busy employment of pleasant and social duties. To see a broken or rusty one, implies that keen disappointment will be experienced by you.

---

*See Pictures, Photographs, and Paintings.
† See Letter Carrier.

Potatoes.

Dreaming of potatoes, brings incidents often of good.

To dream of digging them, denotes success.

To dream of eating them, you will enjoy substantial gain.

To cook them, congenial employment.

Planting them, brings realization of desires.

To see them rotting, denotes vanished pleasure and a darkening future.

Potter.

To dream of a potter, denotes constant employment, with satisfactory results. For a young woman to see a potter, foretells she will enjoy pleasant engagements.

Potter's Field.

To see a potter's field in your dreams, denotes you will have poverty and misery to distress you. For a young woman to walk through a potter's field with her lover, she will give up the one she loves in the hope of mercenary gain.

Poultry.

To see dressed poultry in a dream, foretells extravagant habits will reduce your security in money matters. For a young woman to dream that she is chasing live poultry, foretells she will devote valuable time to frivolous pleasure.

Powder.

To see powder in your dreams, denotes unscrupulous people are dealing with you. You may detect them through watchfulness.

Prairie.

To dream of a prairie, denotes that you will enjoy ease, and even luxury and unobstructed progress.

An undulating prairie, covered with growing grasses and flowers, signifies joyous happenings.

A barren prairie, represents loss and sadness through the absence of friends.

To be lost on one, is a sign of sadness and ill luck.

Prayer.

To dream of saying prayers, or seeing others doing so, foretells you will be threatened with failure, which will take strenuous efforts to avert.

Preacher.

To dream of a preacher, denotes that your ways are not above reproach, and your affairs will not move evenly.

To dream that you are a preacher, foretells for you losses in business, and distasteful amusements will jar upon you.

To hear preaching, implies that you will undergo misfortune.

To argue with a preacher, you will lose in some contest.

To see one walk away from you, denotes that your affairs will move with new energy. If he looks sorrowful, reproaches will fall heavily upon you.

To see a long-haired preacher, denotes that you are shortly to have disputes with overbearing and egotistical people.

Precipice.*

To dream of standing over a yawning precipice, portends the threatenings of misfortunes and calamities.

To fall over a precipice, denotes that you will be engulfed in disaster.

Pregnancy.

For a woman to dream that she is pregnant, denotes

*See Abyss and Pit.

456

she will be unhappy with her husband, and her children will be unattractive.

For a virgin, this dream omens scandal and adversity. If a woman is really pregnant and has this dream, it prognosticates a safe delivery and swift recovery of strength.

Present.*

To receive presents in your dreams, denotes that you will be unusually fortunate.

Priest.†

A priest is an augury of ill, if seen in dreams.

If he is in the pulpit, it denotes sickness and trouble for the dreamer.

If a woman dreams that she is in love with a priest, it warns her of deceptions and an unscrupulous lover. If the priest makes love to her, she will be reproached for her love of gaiety and practical joking.

To confess to a priest, denotes that you will be subjected to humiliation and sorrow.

These dreams imply that you have done, or will do, something which will bring discomfort to yourself or relatives. The priest or preacher is your spiritual adviser, and any dream of his professional presence is a warning against your own imperfections. Seen in social circles, unless they rise before you as spectres, the same rules will apply as to other friends.

Primrose.

To dream of this little flower starring the grass at your feet, is an omen of joys laden with comfort and peace.

Printer.

To see a printer in your dreams, is a warning of pov-

---

*See Gifts.   †See Preacher.

erty, if you neglect to practice economy and cultivate energy. For a woman to dream that her lover or associate is a printer, foretells she will fail to please her parents in the selection of a close friend.

Printing Office.

To be in a printing office in dreams, denotes that slander and contumely will threaten you.

To run a printing office is indicative of hard luck.

For a young woman to dream that her sweetheart is connected with a printing office, denotes that she will have a lover who is unable to lavish money or time upon her, and she will not be sensible enough to see why he is so stingy.

Prison.*

To dream of a prison, is the forerunner of misfortune in every instance, if it encircles your friends, or yourself.

To see any one dismissed from prison, denotes that you will finally overcome misfortune.

Privacy.

To dream that your privacy suffers intrusion, foretells you will have overbearing people to worry you. For a woman, this dream warns her to look carefully after private affairs. If she intrudes on the privacy of her husband or lover, she will disabuse some one's confidence, if not careful of her conversation.

Prize Fight.

To see a prize fight in your dreams, denotes your affairs will give you trouble in controlling them.

Prize Fighter.

For a young woman to see a prize fighter, foretells she

---

*See Jail.

will have pleasure in fast society, and will give her friends much concern about her reputation.

Procession.

To dream of a procession, denotes that alarming fears will possess you relative to the fulfilment of expectations. If it be a funeral procession, sorrow is fast approaching, and will throw a shadow around pleasures.

To see or participate in a torch-light procession, denotes that you will engage in gaieties which will detract from your real merit.

Profanity.

To dream of profanity, denotes that you will cultivate those traits which render you coarse and unfeeling toward your fellow man.

To dream that others use profanity, is a sign that you will be injured in some way, and probably insulted also.

Profits.*

To dream of profits, brings success in your immediate future.

Promenade.

To dream of promenading, foretells that you will engage in energetic and profitable pursuits.

To see others promenading, signifies that you will have rivals in your pursuits.

Property.†

To dream that you own vast property, denotes that you will be successful in affairs, and gain friendships.

Prostitute.‡

To dream that you are in the company of a prostitute,

---

*See Gain.   †See Wealth.   ‡See Harlot.

denotes that you will incur the righteous scorn of friends for some ill-mannered conduct.

For a young woman to dream of a prostitute, foretells that she will deceive her lover as to her purity or candor. This dream to a married woman brings suspicion of her husband and consequent quarrels.

Publican.

To dream of a publican, denotes that you will have your sympathies aroused by some one in a desperate condition, and you will diminish your own gain for his advancement. To a young woman, this dream brings a worthy lover; but because of his homeliness she will trample on his feelings unnecessarily.

Publisher.

To dream of a publisher, foretells long journeys and aspirations to the literary craft.

If a woman dreams that her husband is a publisher, she will be jealous of more than one woman of his acquaintance, and spicy scenes will ensue.

For a publisher to reject your manuscript, denotes that you will suffer disappointment at the miscarriage of cherished designs. If he accepts it, you will rejoice in the full fruition of your hopes. If he loses it, you will suffer evil at the hands of strangers.

Puddings.

To dream of puddings, denotes small returns from large investments, if you only see it.

To eat it, is proof that your affairs will be disappointing.

For a young woman to cook, or otherwise prepare a pudding, denotes that her lover will be sensual and worldly minded, and if she marries him, she will see her love and fortune vanish.

Puddle.

To find yourself stepping into puddles of clear water in a dream, denotes a vexation, but some redeeming good in the future. If the water be muddy, unpleasantness will go a few rounds with you.

To wet your feet by stepping into puddles, foretells that your pleasure will work you harm afterwards.

Pulpit.

To dream of a pulpit, denotes sorrow and vexation.

To dream that you are in a pulpit, foretells sickness, and unsatisfactory results in business or trades of any character.

Pulse.

To dream of your pulse, is warning to look after your affairs and health with close care, as both are taking on debilitating conditions.

To dream of feeling the pulse of another, signifies that you are committing depredations in Pleasure's domain.

Pump.

To see a pump in a dream, denotes that energy and faithfulness to business will produce desired riches, good health also is usually betokened by this dream.

To see a broken pump, signifies that the means of advancing in life will be absorbed by family cares. To the married and the unmarried, it intimates blasted energies.

If you work a pump, your life will be filled with pleasure and profitable undertakings.

Punch.

To dream of drinking the concoction called punch, denotes that you will prefer selfish pleasures to honorable distinction and morality .

To dream that you are punching any person with a club or fist, denotes quarrels and recriminations.

Pup.*

To dream of pups, denotes that you will entertain the innocent and hapless, and thereby enjoy pleasure. The dream also shows that friendships will grow stronger, and fortune will increase if the pups are healthful and well formed, and *vice versa* if they are lean and filthy.

Purchases.

To dream of purchases usually augurs profit and advancement with pleasure.

Purse.†

To dream of your purse being filled with diamonds and new bills, denotes for you associations where "Good Cheer" is the watchword, and harmony and tender loves will make earth a beautiful place.

Putty.

To dream of working in putty, denotes that hazardous chances will be taken with fortune.

If you put in a window-pane with putty, you will seek fortune with poor results.

Pyramid.

To dream of pyramids, denotes that many changes will come to you.

If you scale them, you will journey along before you find the gratification of desires. For the young woman, it prognosticates a husband who is in no sense congenial.

To dream that you are studying the mystery of the

---

*See Dogs and Hound Pups. † See Pocket-book.

ancient pyramids, denotes that you will develop a love for the mysteries of nature, and you will become learned and polished.

* * *

Q.

"And he dreamed, and behold a ladder set up on the earth, and the top of it reached to heaven; and behold, the angels of God ascending and descending on it."—Gen. xxviii., 12.

Quack Doctor.

To see a quack doctor in your dreams, denotes you will be alarmed over some illness and its improper treatment.

Quack Medicine.

To dream you take quack medicine, shows that you are growing morbid under some trouble, and should overcome it by industrious application to duty. To read the advertisement of it, foretells unhappy companions will wrong and distress you.

Quadrille.*

To dream of dancing a quadrille, foretells that some pleasant engagement will occupy your time.

Quagmire.

To dream of being in a quagmire, implies your inability to meet obligations. To see others thus situated, denotes that the failures of others will be felt by you. Illness is sometimes indicated by this dream.

Quail.

To see quails in your dream, is a very favorable omen, if they are alive; if dead, you will undergo serious ill luck.

*See Dancing.

To shoot quail, foretells that ill feelings will be shown by you to your best friends.

To eat them, signifies extravagance in your personal living.

Quaker.

To dream of a Quaker, denotes that you will have faithful friends and fair business. If you are one, you will deport yourself honorably toward an enemy.

For a young woman to attend a Quaker meeting, portends that she will by her modest manners win a faithful husband who will provide well for her household.

Quarantine.

To dream of being in quarantine, denotes that you will be placed in a disagreeable position by the malicious intriguing of enemies.

Quarrel.

Quarrels in dreams, portends unhappiness, and fierce altercations. To a young woman, it is the signal of fatal unpleasantries, and to a married woman it brings separation or continuous disagreements.

To hear others quarreling, denotes unsatisfactory business and disappointing trade.

Quarry.

To dream of being in a quarry and seeing the workmen busy, denotes that you will advance by hard labor.

An idle quarry, signifies failure, disappointment, and often death.

Quartette.

To dream of a quartette, and you are playing or singing, denotes favorable affairs, jolly companions, and good times.

To see or hear a quartette, foretells that you will aspire to something beyond you.

Quay.

To dream of a quay, denotes that you will contemplate making a long tour in the near future.

To see vessels while standing on the quay, denotes the fruition of wishes and designs.

Queen.*

To dream of a queen, foretells succesful ventures. If she looks old or haggard, there will be disappointments connected with your pleasures.

Question.

To question the merits of a thing in your dreams, denotes that you will suspect some one whom you love of unfaithfulness, and you will fear for your speculations.

To ask a question, foretells that you will earnestly strive for truth and be successful.

If you are questioned, you will be unfairly dealt with.

Quicksand.

To find yourself in quicksand while dreaming, you will meet with loss and deceit.

If you are unable to overcome it, you will be involved in overwhelming misfortunes.

For a young woman to be rescued by her lover from quicksand, she will possess a worthy and faithful husband, who will still remain her lover.

Quills.

To dream of quills, denotes to the literary inclined a season of success.

*See Empress.

465

To dream of them as ornaments, signifies a rushing trade, and some remuneration.

For a young woman to be putting a quill on her hat, denotes that she will attempt many conquests, and her success will depend upon her charms.

Quilts.

To dream of quilts, foretells pleasant and comfortable circumstances. For a young woman, this dream foretells that her practical and wise business-like ways will advance her into the favorable esteem of a man who will seek her for a wife.

If the quilts are clean, but having holes in them, she will win a husband who appreciates her worth, but he will not be the one most desired by her for a companion. If the quilts are soiled, she will bear evidence of carelessness in her dress and manners, and thus fail to secure a very upright husband.

Quinine.

To dream of quinine, denotes you will soon be possessed of great happiness, though your prospects for much wealth may be meager. To take some foretells improvement in health and energy. You will also make new friends, who will lend you commercial aid.

Quinsy.

To dream of being afflicted with this disease, denotes discouraging employments.

To see others with it, sickness will cause you much anxiety.

Quoits.

To play at quoits in dreams, foretells low engagements and loss of good employment. To lose, portends of distressing conditions.

R.

"And the angel of God spake unto me in a dream, saying 'Jacob:'. And I said, 'Here I am.'"—Gen. xxxi., 11.

Rabbit.*

To dream of rabbits, foretells favorable turns in conditions, and you will be more pleased with your gains than formerly.

To see white rabbits, denotes faithfulness in love, to the married or single.

To see rabbits frolicing about, denotes that children will contribute to your joys.

Raccoon.

To dream of a raccoon, denotes you are being deceived by the friendly appearance of enemies.

Race.

To dream that you are in a race, foretells that others will aspire to the things you are working to possess, but if you win in the race, you will overcome your competitors.

Rack.

To dream of a rack, denotes the uncertainty of the outcome of some engagement which gives you much anxious thought.

Racket.

To dream of a racket, denotes that you will be foiled in some anticipated pleasure. For a young woman, this dream is ominous of disappointment in not being able to participate in some amusement that has engaged her attention.

-----

*See Hare.

Radish.

To dream of seeing a bed of radishes growing, is an omen of good luck. Your friends will be unusually kind, and your business will prosper.

If you eat them, you will suffer slightly through the thoughtlessness of some one near to you.

To see radishes, or plant them, denotes that your anticipations will be happily realized.

Raffle.

If you dream of raffling any article, you will fall a victim to speculation.

If you are at a church raffle, you will soon find that disappointment is clouding your future. For a young woman, this dream means empty expectations.

Raft.

To dream of a raft, denotes that you will go into new locations to engage in enterprises, which will prove successful.

To dream of floating on a raft, denotes uncertain journeys. If you reach your destination, you will surely come into good fortune.

If a raft breaks, or any such mishap befalls it, yourself or some friend will suffer from an accident, or sickness will bear unfortunate results.

Rage.

To be in a rage and scolding and tearing up things generally, while dreaming, signifies quarrels, and injury to your friends.

To see others in a rage, is a sign of unfavorable conditions for business, and unhappiness in social life.

For a young woman to see her lover in a rage, denotes

that there will be some discordant note in their love, and misunderstandings will naturally occur.

Railing.

To dream of seeing railings, denotes that some person is trying to obstruct your pathway in love or business.

To dream of holding on to a railing, foretells that some desperate chance will be taken by you to obtain some object upon which you have set your heart. It may be of love, or of a more material form.

Railroad.

If you dream cf a railroad, you will find that your business will need close attention, as enemies are trying to usurp you.

For a young woman to dream of railroads, she will make a journey to visit friends, and will enjoy some distinction.

To see an obstruction on these roads, indicates foul play in your affairs.

To walk the cross ties of a railroad, signifies a time of worry and laborious work.

To walk the rails, you may expect to obtain much happiness from your skilful manipulation of affairs.

To see a road inundated with clear water, foretells that pleasure will wipe out misfortune for a time, but it will rise, phœnix like, again.

Rain.

To be out in a clear shower of rain, denotes that pleasure will be enjoyed with the zest of youth, and prosperity will come to you.

If the rain descends from murky clouds, you will feel alarmed over the graveness of your undertakings.

To see and hear rain approaching, and you escape being wet, you will succeed in your plans, and your designs will mature rapidly.

To be sitting in the house and see through the window a downpour of rain, denotes that you will possess fortune, and passionate love will be requited.

To hear the patter of rain on the roof, denotes a realization of domestic bliss and joy. Fortune will come in a small way.

To dream that your house is leaking during a rain, if the water is clear, foretells that illicit pleasure will come to you rather unexpectedly; but if filthy or muddy, you may expect the reverse, and also exposure.

To find yourself regretting some duty unperformed while listening to the rain, denotes that you will seek pleasure at the expense of another's sense of propriety and justice.

To see it rain on others, foretells that you will exclude friends from your confidence.

For a young woman to dream of getting her clothes wet and soiled while out in a rain, denotes that she will entertain some person indiscreetly, and will suffer the suspicions of friends for the unwise yielding to foolish enjoyments.

To see it raining on farm stock, foretells disappointment in business, and unpleasantness in social circles.

Stormy rains are always unfortunate.

Rainbow.

To see a rainbow in a dream, is prognostic of unusual happenings. Affairs will assume a more promising countenance, and crops will give promise of a plentiful yield.

For lovers to see the rainbow, is an omen of much happiness from their union.

To see the rainbow hanging low over green trees, signifies unconditional success in any undertaking.

Raisins.

To dream of eating raisins, implies that discouragements will darken your hopes when they seem about to be realized.

Rake.

To dream of using a rake, portends that some work which you have left to others will never be accomplished unless you superintend it yourself.

To see a broken rake, denotes that sickness, or some accident will bring failure to your plans.

To see others raking, foretells that you will rejoice in the fortunate condition of others.

Ram.*

To dream that a ram pursues you, foretells that some misfortune threatens you.

To see one quietly grazing denotes that you will have powerful friends, who will use their best efforts for your good.

Ramble.

To dream that you are rambling through the country, denotes that you will be oppressed with sadness, and the separation from friends, but your worldly surroundings will be all that one could desire. For a young woman, this dream promises a comfortable home, but early bereavement.

Ramrod.

To dream of a ramrod, denotes unfortunate adventures. You will have cause for grief. For a young woman

*See Sheep and Lamb.

to see one bent or broken, foretells that a dear friend or lover will fail her.

Ransom.

To dream that a ransom is made for you, you will find that you are deceived and worked for money on all sides. For a young woman, this is prognostic of evil, unless some one pays the ransom and relieves her.

Rape.

To dream that rape has been committed among your acquaintances, denotes that you will be shocked at the distress of some of your friends.

For a young woman to dream that she has been the victim of rape, foretells that she will have troubles, which will wound her pride, and her lover will be estranged.

Rapids.

To imagine that you are being carried over rapids in a dream, denotes that you will suffer appalling loss from the neglect of duty and the courting of seductive pleasures.

Raspberry.

To see raspberries in a dream, foretells you are in danger of entanglements which will prove interesting before you escape from them.

For a woman to eat them, means distress over circumstantial evidence in some occurrence causing gossip.

Rat.*

To dream of rats, denotes that you will be deceived, and injured by your neighbors. Quarrels with your companions is also foreboded.

To catch rats, means you will scorn the baseness of others, and worthily outstrip your enemies.

To kill one, denotes your victory in any contest.

---

*See Mice.

Rat-trap.*

To dream of falling into a rat-trap, denotes that you will be victimized and robbed of some valuable object.

To see an empty one, foretells the absence of slander or competition.

A broken one, denotes that you will be rid of unpleasant associations.

To set one, you will be made aware of the designs of enemies, but the warning will enable you to outwit them.

Rattan Cane.

To dream of a rattan cane, foretells that you will depend largely upon the judgment of others, and you should cultivate independence in planning and executing your own affairs.

Rattle.

To dream of seeing a baby play with its rattle, omens peaceful contentment in the home, and enterprises will be honorable and full of gain. To a young woman, it augurs an early marriage and tender cares of her own.

To give a baby a rattle, denotes unfortunate investments.

Raven.†

To dream of a raven, denotes reverse in fortune and inharmonious surroundings. For a young woman, it is implied that her lover will betray her.

Razor.

To dream of a razor, portends disagreements and contentions over troubles.

To cut yourself with one, denotes that you will be unlucky in some deal which you are about to make.

---

*See Mouse-trap.   †See Crow.

Fighting with a razor, foretells disappointing business, and that some one will keep you harassed almost beyond endurance.

A broken or rusty one, brings unavoidable distress.

Reading.

To be engaged in reading in your dreams, denotes that you will excel in some work, which appears difficult.

To see others reading, denotes that your friends will be kind, and are well disposed.

To give a reading, or to discuss reading, you will cultivate your literary ability.

Indistinct, or incoherent reading, implies worries and disappointments.

Reapers.*

To dream of seeing reapers busy at work at their task, denotes prosperity and contentment. If they appear to be going through dried stubble, there will be a lack of good crops, and business will consequently fall off.

To see idle ones, denotes that some discouraging event will come in the midst of prosperity .

To see a broken reaping machine, signifies loss of employment, or disappointment in trades.

Reception.†

To dream of attending a reception, denotes that you will have pleasant engagements. Confusion at a reception will work you disquietude.

Refrigerator.

To see a refrigerator in your dreams, portends that your selfishness will offend and injure some one who endeavors to gain an honest livelihood.

To put ice in one, brings the dreamer into disfavor.

---

*See Mowing.   † See Entertainment.

Register.

To dream that some one registers your name at a hotel for you, denotes you will undertake some work which will be finished by others.

If you register under an assumed name, you will engage in some guilty enterprise which will give you much uneasiness of mind.

Reindeer.

To dream of a reindeer, signifies faithful discharge of duties, and remaining staunch to friends in their adversity.

To drive them, foretells that you will have hours of bitter anguish, but friends will attend you.

Religion.

If you dream of discussing religion and feel religiously inclined, you will find much to mar the calmness of your life, and business will turn a disagreeable front to you.

If a young woman imagines that she is over religious, she will disgust her lover with her efforts to act ingenuous innocence and goodness.

If she is irreligious and not a transgressor, it foretells that she will have that independent frankness and kind consideration for others, which wins for women profound respect, and love from the opposite sex as well as her own; but if she is a transgressor in the eyes of religion, she will find that there are moral laws, which, if disregarded, will place her outside the pale of honest recognition. She should look well after her conduct. If she weeps over religion, she will be disappointed in the desires of her heart. If she is defiant, but innocent of offence, she will shoulder burdens bravely, and stand firm against deceitful admonitions.

If you are self-reproached in the midst of a religious excitement, you will find that you will be almost induced to give up your own personality to please some one whom you hold in reverent esteem.

To see religion declining in power, denotes that your life will be more in harmony with creation than formerly. Your prejudices will not be so aggressive.

To dream that a minister in a social way tells you that he has given up his work, foretells that you will be the recipient of unexpected tidings of a favorable nature, but if in a professional and warning way, it foretells that you will be overtaken in your deceitful intriguing, or other disappointments will follow.

(These dreams are sometimes fulfilled literally in actual life. When this is so, they may have no symbolical meaning. Religion is thrown around men to protect them from vice, so when they propose secretly in their minds to ignore its teachings, they are likely to see a minister or some place of church worship in a dream as a warning against their contemplated action. If they live pure and correct lives as indicated by the church, they will see little of the solemnity of the church or preachers.)

Rent.

To dream that you rent a house, is a sign that you will enter into new contracts, which will prove profitable.

To fail to rent out property, denotes that there will be much inactivity in business.

To pay rent, signifies that your financial interest will be satisfactory.

If you can't pay your rent, it is unlucky for you, as you will see a falling off in trade, and social pleasures will be of little benefit.

Reprieve.

To be under sentence in a dream and receive a reprieve, foretells that you will overcome some difficulty which is causing you anxiety.

For a young woman to dream that her lover has been reprieved, denotes that she will soon hear of some good luck befalling him, which will be of vital interest to her.

Reptile.

If a reptile attacks you in a dream, there will be trouble of a serious nature ahead for you. If you succeed in killing it, you will finally overcome obstacles.

To see a dead reptile come to life, denotes that disputes and disagreements, which were thought to be settled, will be renewed and pushed with bitter animosity.

To handle them without harm to yourself, foretells that you will be oppressed by the ill humor and bitterness of friends, but you will succeed in restoring pleasant relations.

For a young woman to see various kinds of reptiles, she will have many conflicting troubles. Her lover will develop fancies for others. If she is bitten by any of them, she will be superseded by a rival.

Rescue.

To dream of being rescued from any danger, denotes that you will be threatened with misfortune, and will escape with a slight loss.

To rescue others, foretells that you will be esteemed for your good deeds.

Resign.

To dream that you resign any position, signifies that you will unfortunately embark in new enterprises.

To hear of others resigning, denotes that you will have unpleaasant tidings.

Resurrection.

To dream that you are resurrected from the dead, you

will have some great vexation, but will eventually gain your desires. To see others resurrected, denotes unfortunate troubles will be lightened by the thoughtfulness of friends.

Resuscitate.

To dream that you are being resuscitated, denotes that you will have heavy losses, but will eventually regain more than you lose, and happiness will attend you.

To resuscitate another, you will form new friendships, which will give you prominence and pleasure.

Revelation.

To dream of a revelation, if it be of a pleasant nature, you may expect a bright outlook, either in business or love; but if the revelation be gloomy you will have many discouraging features to overcome.

Revenge.

To dream of taking revenge, is a sign of a weak and uncharitable nature, which if not properly governed, will bring you troubles and loss of friends.

If others revenge themselves on you, there will be much to fear from enemies.

Revival.*

To dream you attend a religious revival, foretells family disturbances and unprofitable engagements.

If you take a part in it, you will incur the displeasure of friends by your contrary ways.

Revolver.†

For a young woman to dream that she sees her sweetheart with a revolver, denotes that she will have a serious disagreement with some friend, and probably separation from her lover.

---

*See Religion.   †See Pistol, Firearms, etc.

Rheumatism.

To feel rheumatism attacking you in a dream, foretells unexpected delay in the accomplishment of plans.

To see others so afflicted brings disappointments.

Rhinestones.

To dream of rhinestones, denotes pleasures and favors of short duration. For a young woman to dream that a rhinestone proves to be a diamond, foretells she will be surprised to find that some insignificant act on her part will result in good fortune.

Rhinoceros.

To dream that you see a rhinoceros, foretells you will have a great loss threatening you, and that you will have secret troubles. To kill one, shows that you will bravely overcome obstacles.

Rhubarb.

To dream of rhubarb growing, denotes that pleasant entertainments will occupy your time for a while.

To cook it, foretells spirited arguments in which you will lose a friend.

To eat it, denotes dissatisfaction with present employment.

Rib.

To dream of seeing ribs, denotes poverty and misery.

Ribbon.

Seeing ribbons floating from the costume of any person in your dreams, indicates you will have gay and pleasant companions, and practical cares will not trouble you greatly.

For a young woman to dream of decorating herself with ribbons, she will soon have a desirable offer of marriage, but frivolity may cause her to make a mistake. If she sees other girls wearing ribbons, she will encounter rivalry in her endeavors to secure a husband. If she buys them, she will have a pleasant and easy place in life. If she feels angry or displeased about them, she will find that some other woman is dividing her honors and pleasures with her in her social realm.

Rice.

Rice is good to see in dreams, as it foretells success and warm friendships. Prosperity to all trades is promised, and the farmer will be blessed with a bounteous harvest.

To eat it, signifies happiness and domestic comfort.

To see it mixed with dirt or otherwise impure, denotes sickness and separation from friends.

For a young woman to dream of cooking it, shows she will soon assume new duties, which will make her happier, and she will enjoy wealth.

Riches.*

To dream that you are possessed of riches, denotes that you will rise to high places by your constant exertion and attention to your affairs.

Riddles.

To dream that you are trying to solve riddles, denotes you will engage in some enterprise which will try your patience and employ your money.

The import of riddles is confusion and dissatisfaction.

Ride.

To dream of riding is unlucky for business or pleasure. Sickness often follows this dream.

---

*See Wealth.

480

If you ride slowly, you will have unsatisfactory results in your undertakings.

Swift riding sometimes means prosperity under hazardous conditions.

Riding School.

To attend a riding school, foretells some friend will act falsely by you, but you will throw off the vexing influence occasioned by it.

Ring.

To dream of wearing rings, denotes new enterprises in which you will be successful.

A broken ring, foretells quarrels and unhappiness in the married state, and separation to lovers.

For a young woman to receive a ring, denotes that worries over her lover's conduct will cease, as he will devote himself to her pleasures and future interest.

To see others with rings, denotes increasing prosperity and many new friends.

Ringworms.

To dream of having ringworms appear on you, you will have a slight illness, and some exasperating difficulty in the near future.

To see them on others, beggars and appeals for charity will beset you.

Riot.

To dream of riots, foretells disappointing affairs.

To see a friend killed in a riot, you will have bad luck in all undertakings, and the death, or some serious illness, of some person will cause you distress.

Rising.

To dream of rising to high positions, denotes that study and advancement will bring you desired wealth.

If you find yourself rising high into the air, you will come into unexpected riches and pleasures, but you are warned to be careful of your engagements, or you may incur displeasing prominence.

Rival.

To dream you have a rival, is a sign that you will be slow in asserting your rights, and will lose favor with people of prominence.

For a young woman, this dream is a warning to cherish the love she already holds, as she might unfortunately make a mistake in seeking other bonds.

If you find that a rival has outwitted you, it signifies that you will be negligent in your business, and that you love personal ease to your detriment.

If you imagine that you are the successful rival, it is good for your advancement, and you will find congeniality in your choice of a companion.

River.

If you see a clear, smooth, flowing river in your dream, you will soon succeed to the enjoyment of delightful pleasures, and prosperity will bear flattering promises.

If the waters are muddy or tumultuous, there will be disagreeable and jealous contentions in your life.

If you are water-bound by the overflowing of a river, there will be temporary embarrassments in your business, or you will suffer uneasiness lest some private escapade will reach public notice and cause your reputation harsh criticisms.

If while sailing upon a clear river you see corpses in the bottom, you will find that trouble and gloom will follow swiftly upon present pleasures and fortune.

To see empty rivers, denotes sickness and unusual ill-luck.

Road.

Traveling over a rough, unknown road in a dream, signifies new undertakings, which will bring little else than grief and loss of time.

If the road is bordered with trees and flowers, there will be some pleasant and unexpected fortune for you. If friends accompany you, you will be successful in building an ideal home, with happy children and faithful wife, or husband.

To lose the road, foretells that you will make a mistake in deciding some question of trade, and suffer loss in consequence.

Roast.

To see or eat roast in a dream, is an omen of domestic infelicity and secret treachery.

Rocket.

To see a rocket ascending in your dream, foretells sudden and unexpected elevation, successful wooing, and faithful keeping of the marriage vows.

To see them falling, unhappy unions may be expected.

Rocking-chair.

Rocking-chairs seen in dreams, bring friendly intercourse and contentment with any environment.

To see a mother, wife, or sweetheart in a rocking-chair, is ominous of the sweetest joys that earth affords.

To see vacant rocking-chairs, forebodes bereavement or estrangement. The dreamer will surely merit misfortune in some form.

Rocks.*

To dream of rocks, denotes that you will meet reverses, and that there will be discord and general unhappiness.

---

*See Stones.

To climb a steep rock, foretells immediate struggles and disappointing surroundings.

Rogue.

To see or think yourself a rogue, foretells you are about to commit some indiscretion which will give your friends uneasiness of mind. You are likely to suffer from a passing malady.

For a woman to think her husband or lover is a rogue, foretells she will be painfully distressed over neglect shown her by a friend.

Rogue's Gallery.

To dream that you are in a rogue's gallery, foretells you will be associated with people who will fail to appreciate you. To see your own picture, you will be overawed by a tormenting enemy.

Roman Candle.*

To see Roman candles while dreaming, is a sign of speedy attainment of coveted pleasures and positions.

To imagine that you have a loaded candle and find it empty, denotes that you will be disappointed with the possession of some object which you have long striven to obtain.

Roof.

To find yourself on a roof in a dream, denotes unbounded success. To become frightened and think you are falling, signifies that, while you may advance, you will have no firm hold on your position.

To see a roof falling in, you will be threatened with a sudden calamity.

To repair, or build a roof, you will rapidly increase your fortune.

*See Rocket.

To sleep on one, proclaims your security against enemies and false companions. Your health will be robust.

Roof Corner.

To see a person dressed in mourning sitting on a roof corner, foretells there will be unexpected and dismal failures in your business.

Affairs will appear unfavorable in love.

Rooks.

To dream of rooks, denotes that while your friends are true, they will not afford you the pleasure and contentment for which you long, as your thoughts and tastes will outstrip their humble conception of life.

A dead rook, denotes sickness or death in your immediate future.

Rooster.*

To dream of a rooster, foretells that you will be very successful and rise to prominence, but you will allow yourself to become conceited over your fortunate rise.

To see roosters fighting, foretells altercations and rivals.

Roots.

To dream of seeing roots of plants or trees, denotes misfortune, as both business and health will go into decline.

To use them as medicine, warns you of approaching illness or sorrow.

Ropes.

Ropes in dreams, signify perplexities and complications in affairs, and uncertain love making.

If you climb one, you will overcome enemies who are working to injure you.

------

*See Chickens.

To decend a rope, brings disappointment to your most sanguine moments.

If you are tied with them, you are likely to yield to love contrary to your judgment.

To break them, signifies your ability to overcome enmity and competition.

To tie ropes, or horses, denotes that you will have power to control others as you may wish.

To walk a rope, signifies that you will engage in some hazardous speculation, but will surprisingly succeed. To see others walking a rope, you will benefit by the fortunate ventures of others.

To jump a rope, foretells that you will startle your associates with a thrilling escapade bordering upon the sensational.

To jump rope with children, shows that you are selfish and overbearing; failing to see that children owe very little duty to inhuman parents. To catch a rope with the foot, denotes that under cheerful conditions you will be benevolent and tender in your administrations.

To dream that you let a rope down from an upper window to people below, thinking the proprietors would be adverse to receiving them into the hotel, denotes that you will engage in some affair which will not look exactly proper to your friends, but the same will afford you pleasure and interest. For a young woman, this dream is indicative of pleasures which do not bear the stamp of propriety.

Rosebush.

To see a rosebush in foliage but no blossoms, denotes prosperous circumstances are enclosing you. To see a dead rosebush, foretells misfortune and sickness for you or relatives.

Rosemary.

Rosemary, if seen in dreams, denotes that sadness and

indifference will cause unhappiness in homes where there is every appearance of prosperity.

Roses.

To dream of seeing roses blooming and fragrant, denotes that some joyful occasion is nearing, and you will possess the faithful love of your sweetheart.

For a young woman to dream of gathering roses, shows she will soon have an offer of marriage, which will be much to her liking.

Withered roses, signify the absence of loved ones.

White roses, if seen without sunshine or dew, denotes serious if not fatal illness.

To inhale their fragrance, brings unalloyed pleasure.

For a young woman to dream of banks of roses, and that she is gathering and tying them into bouquets, signifies that she will be made very happy by the offering of some person whom she regards very highly.

Rosette.

To wear or see rosettes on others while in dreams, is significant of frivolous waste of time; though you will experience the thrills of pleasure, they will bring disappointments.

Rouge.

To dream of using rouge, denotes that you will practice deceit to obtain your wishes.

To see others with it on their faces, warns you that you are being artfully used to further the designs of some deceitful persons.

If you see it on your hands, or clothing, you will be detected in some scheme.

If it comes off of your face, you will be humiliated before some rival, and lose your lover by assuming unnatural manners.

Roundabout.

To dream of seeing a roundabout, denotes that you will struggle unsuccessfully to advance in fortune or love.

Rowboat.

To dream that you are in a rowboat with others, denotes that you will derive much pleasure from the companionship of gay and worldly persons. If the boat is capsized, you will suffer financial losses by engaging in seductive enterprises.

If you find yourself defeated in a rowing race, you will lose favors to your rivals with your sweetheart. If you are the victor, you will easily obtain supremacy with women. Your affairs will move agreeably.

Rubber.

To dream of being clothed in rubber garments, is a sign that you will have honors conferred upon you because of your steady and unchanging stand of purity and morality. If the garments are ragged or torn, you should be cautious in your conduct, as scandal is ready to attack your reputation.

To dream of using "rubber" as a slang term, foretells that you will be easy to please in your choice of pleasure and companions.

If you find that your limbs will stretch like rubber, it is a sign that illness is threatening you, and you are likely to use deceit in your wooing and business.

To dream of rubber goods, denotes that your affairs will be conducted on a secret basis, and your friends will fail to understand your conduct in many instances.

Rubbish.

To dream of rubbish, denotes that you will badly manage your affairs.

Ruby.

To dream of a ruby, foretells you will be lucky in speculations of business or love. For a woman to lose one, is a sign of approaching indifference of her lover.

Rudder.

To dream of a rudder, you will soom make a pleasant journey to foreign lands, and new friendships will be formed.

A broken rudder, augurs disappointment and sickness.

Ruins.

To dream of ruins, signifies broken engagements to lovers, distressing conditions in business, destruction to crops, and failing health.

To dream of ancient ruins, foretells that you will travel extensively, but there will be a note of sadness mixed with the pleasure in the realization of a long-cherished hope. You will feel the absence of some friend.

Rum.*

To dream of drinking rum, foretells that you will have wealth, but will lack moral refinement, as you will lean to gross pleasures.

Running.

To dream of running in company with others, is a sign that you will participate in some festivity, and you will find that your affairs are growing towards fortune. If you stumble or fall, you will lose property and reputation.

Running alone, indicates that you will outstrip your friends in the race for wealth, and you will occupy a higher place in social life.

---

*See other intoxicating drinks.

If you run from danger, you will be threatened with losses, and you will despair of adjusting matters agreeably. To see others thus running, you will be oppressed by the threatened downfall of friends.

To see stock running, warns you to be careful in making new trades or undertaking new tasks.

Rupture.

To dream that you are ruptured, denotes you will have physical disorders or disagreeable contentions. If it be others you see in this condition, you will be in danger of irreconcilable quarrels.

Rust.

To dream of rust on articles, old pieces of tin, or iron, is significant of depression of your surroundings. Sickness, decline in fortune and false friends are filling your sphere.

Rye.

To see rye, is a dream of good, as prosperity envvelopes your future in brightest promises.

To see coffee made of rye, denotes that your pleasures will be tempered with sound judgment, and your affairs will be managed without disagreeable friction.

To see stock entering rye fields, denotes that you will be prosperous.

Rye Bread.

To see or eat rye bread in your dreams, foretells you will have a cheerful and well-appointed home.

S.

"And it came to pass at the end of the two full years, that Pharaoh dreamed; and behold, he stood by the river."—Gen. xli., I.

Saddle.

To dream of saddles, foretells news of a pleasant nature, also unannounced visitors. You are also, probably, to take a trip which will prove advantageous.

Safe.

To dream of seeing a safe, denotes security from discouraging affairs of business and love.

To be trying to unlock a safe, you will be worried over the failure of your plans not reaching quick maturity.

To find a safe empty, denotes trouble.

Saffron.

Saffron seen in a dream warns you that you are entertaining false hopes, as bitter enemies are interfering secretly with your plans for the future.

To drink a tea made from saffron, foretells that you will have quarrels and alienations in your family.

Sage.

To dream of sage, foretells thrift and economy will be practised by your servants or family. For a woman to think she has too much in her viands, omens she will regret useless extravagance in love as well as fortune.

Sailing.*

To dream of sailing on calm waters, foretells easy access to blissful joys, and immunity from poverty and whatever brings misery.

---

*See Ocean and Sea.

491

To sail on a small vessel, denotes that your desires will not excel your power of possessing them.

Sailor.

To dream of sailors, portends long and exciting journeys.

For a young woman to dream of sailors, is ominous of a separation from her lover through a frivolous flirtation. If she dreams that she is a sailor, she will indulge in some unmaidenly escapade, and be in danger of losing a faithful lover.

Salad.

To dream of eating salad, foretells sickness and disagreeable people around you.

For a young woman to dream of making it, is a sign that her lover will be changeable and quarrelsome.

Salmon.

Dreaming of salmon, denotes that much good luck and pleasant duties will employ your time.

For a young woman to eat it, foretells that she will marry a cheerful man, with means to keep her comfortable.

Salt.

Salt is an omen of discordant surroundings when seen in dreams. You will usually find after dreaming of salt that everything goes awry, and quarrels and dissatisfaction show themselves in the family circle.

To salt meat, portends that debts and mortgages will harass you.

For a young woman to eat salt, she will be deserted by her lover for a more beautiful and attractive girl, thus causing her deep chagrin.

Saltpeter.

To dream of saltpeter, denotes change in your living will add loss to some unconquerable grief.

Salve.

To dream of salve, denotes you will prosper under adverse circumstances and convert enemies into friends.

Samples.

To dream of receiving merchandise samples, denotes improvement in your business. For a traveling man to lose his samples, implies he will find himself embarrassed in business affairs, or in trouble through love engagements. For a woman to dream that she is examining samples sent her, denotes she will have chances to vary her amusements.

Sand.

To dream of sand, is indicative of famine and losses.

Sanskrit.

To dream of Sanskrit, denotes that you will estrange yourself from friends in order to investigate hidden subjects, taking up those occupying the minds of cultured and progressive thinkers.

Sapphire.

To dream of sapphire, is ominous of fortunate gain, and to woman, a wise selection in a lover.

Sardines.

To eat sardines in a dream, foretells that distressing events will come unexpectedly upon you.

For a young woman to dream of putting them on the table, denotes that she will be worried with the attentions of a person who is distasteful to her.

Sardonyx.

To dream of sardonyx, signifies gloomy surroundings will be cleared away by your energetic overthrow of poverty. For a woman, this dream denotes an increase in her possessions, unless she loses or throws them away, then it might imply a disregard of opportunities to improve her condition.

Sash.

To dream of wearing a sash, foretells that you will seek to retain the affections of a flirtatious person.

For a young woman to buy one, she will be faithful to her lover, and win esteem by her frank, womanly ways.

Satan.*

To dream of Satan, foretells that you will have some dangerous adventures, and you will be forced to use strategy to keep up honorable appearances.

To dream that you kill him, foretells that you will desert wicked or immoral companions to live upon a higher plane.

If he comes to you under the guise of literature, it should be heeded as a warning against promiscuous friendships, and especialiy flatterers.

If he comes in the shape of wealth or power, you will fail to use your influence for harmony, or the elevation of others.

If he takes the form of music, you are likely to go down before his wiles.

If in the form of a fair woman, you will probably crush every kindly feeling you may have for the caresses of this moral monstrosity.

To feel that you are trying to shield yourself from satan, denotes that you will endeavor to throw off the bondage of selfish pleasure, and seek to give others their best deserts.

Sausage.

To dream of making sausage, denotes that you will be successful in many undertakings.

----

*See Devil.

494

To eat them, you will have a humble, but pleasant home.

Saw.

To dream that you use a hand-saw, indicates an energetic and busy time, and cheerful home life.

To see big saws in machinery, foretells that you will superintend a big enterprise, and the same will yield fair returns. For a woman, this dream denotes that she will be esteemed, and her counsels will be heeded.

To dream of rusty or broken saws, denotes failure and accidents.

To lose a saw, you will engage in affairs which will culminate in disaster.

To hear the buzz of a saw, indicates thrift and prosperity.

To find a rusty saw, denotes that you will probably restore your fortune.

To carry a saw on your back, foretells that you will carry large, but profitable, responsibilities.

Sawdust.

To dream of sawdust, signifies that grievous mistakes will cause you distress and quarreling in your home.

Scabbard.

To dream of a scabbard, denotes some misunderstanding will be amicably settled. If you wonder where your scabbard can be, you will have overpowering difficulties to meet.

Scaffold.

To dream of a scaffold, denotes that you will undergo keen disappointment in failing to secure the object of your affection.

To ascend one, you will be misunderstood and censured

by your friends for some action, which you never committed.

To descend one, you will be guilty of wrong doing, and you will suffer the penalty.

To fall from one, you will be unexpectedly surprised while engaged in deceiving and working injury to others.

Scaldhead (Dandruff).

To see any one with scaldhead (dandruff) in your dreams, there will be uneasiness felt over the sickness or absence of someone near to you.

If you dream that your own head is thus afflicted, you are in danger of personal illness or accidents.

Scalding.

To dream of being scalded, portends that distressing incidents will blot out pleasurable anticipations.

Scales.

To dream of weighing on scales, portends that justice will temper your conduct, and you will see your prosperity widening.

For a young woman to weigh her lover, the indications are that she will find him of solid worth, and faithfulness will balance her love.

Scandal.

To dream that you are an object of scandal, denotes that you are not particular to select good and true companions, but rather enjoy having fast men and women contribute to your pleasure. Trade and business of any character will suffer dulness after this dream.

For a young woman to dream that she discussed a scandal, foretells that she will confer favors, which should be sacred, to some one who will deceive her into believing that he is honorably inclined. Marriage rarely follows swiftly after dreaming of scandal.

Scarcity.

To dream of scarcity, foretells sorrow in the household and failing affairs.

Scarlet Fever.

To dream of scarlet fever, foretells you are in danger of sickness, or in the power of an enemy. To dream a relative dies suddenly with it, foretells you will be overcome by villainous treachery.

Sceptre.

To imagine in your dreams that you wield a sceptre, foretells that you will be chosen by friends to positions of trust, and you will not disappoint their estimate of your ability.

To dream that others wield the sceptre over you, denotes that you will seek employment under the supervision of others, rather than exert your energies to act for yourself.

School.

To dream of attending school, indicates distinction in literary work. If you think you are young and at school as in your youth, you will find that sorrow and reverses will make you sincerely long for the simple trusts and pleasures of days of yore.

To dream of teaching a school, foretells that you will strive for literary attainments, but the bare necessities of life must first be forthcoming.

To visit the schoolhouse of your childhood days, portends that discontent and discouraging incidents overshadows the present.

School Teacher.

To dream of a school teacher, denotes you are likely to enjoy learning and amusements in a quiet way. If you are one, you are likely to reach desired success in literary and other works.

Scissors.

To dream of scissors is an unlucky omen; wives will be jealous and distrustful of their husbands, and sweethearts will quarrel and nag each other into crimination and recrimination. Dulness will overcast business horizons.

To dream that you have your scissors sharpened, denotes that you will work to do that which will be repulsive to your feelings.

To break them, there will be quarrels, and probable separations for you.

To lose them, you will seek to escape from unpleasant tasks.

Scorpion.

To dream of a scorpion, foretells that false friends will improve opportunities to undermine your prosperity. If you fail to kill it, you will suffer loss from an enemy's attack.

Scrap-book.

To dream of a scrap-book, denotes disagreeable acquaintances will shortly be made.

Scratch.

To scratch others in your dream, denotes that you will be ill-tempered and fault-finding in your dealings with others.

If you are scratched, you will be injured by the enmity of some deceitful person.

Scratch Head.

To dream that you scratch your head, denotes strangers will annoy you by their flattering attentions, which you will feel are only shown to win favors from you.

Screech-owl.

To dream that you hear the shrill startling notes of the screech-owl, denotes that you will be shocked with news of the desperate illness, or death of some dear friend.

Screw.

To dream of seeing screws, denotes that tedious tasks must be performed, and peevishness in companions must be combated. It also denotes that you must be economical and painstaking.

Sculptor.

To dream of a sculptor, foretells you will change from your present position to one less lucrative but more distinguished.

For a woman to dream that her husband or lover is a sculptor, foretells she will enjoy favors from men of high position.

Scum.

To dream of scum, signifies disappointment will be experienced by you over social defeats.

Scythe.

To dream of a scythe, foretells accidents or sickness will prevent you from attending to your affairs, or making journeys. An old or broken scythe, implies separation from friends, or failure in some business enterprise.

Sea.*

To dream of hearing the lonely sighing of the sea, foretells that you will be fated to spend a weary and unfruitful life devoid of love and comradeship.

Dreams of the sea, prognosticate unfulfilled anticipations, while pleasures of a material form are enjoyed, there is an inward craving for pleasure that flesh cannot requite.

For a young woman to dream that she glides swiftly over the sea with her lover, there will come to her sweet fruition of maidenly hopes, and joy will stand guard at the door of the consummation of changeless vows.

Sea Foam.

For a woman to dream of sea foam, foretells that indiscriminate and demoralizing pleasures will distract her from the paths of rectitude. If she wears a bridal veil of sea foam, she will engulf herself in material pleasure to the exclusion of true refinement and innate modesty. She will be likely to cause sorrow to some of those dear to her, through their inability to gratify her ambition.

Seal.

To dream that you see seals, denotes that you are striving for a place above your power to maintain.

Dreams of seals usually show that the dreamer has high aspirations and discontent will harass him into struggles to advance his position.

Seamstress.

To see a seamstress in a dream, portends you will be deterred from making pleasant visits by unexpected luck.

Seaport.

To dream of visiting a seaport, denotes that you will

---

*See Ocean.

have opportunities of traveling and acquiring knowledge, but there will be some who will object to your anticipated tours.

Seat.

To think, in a dream, that some one has taken your seat, denotes you will be tormented by people calling on you for aid. To give a woman your seat, implies your yielding to some fair one's artfulness.

Secret Order.

To dream of any secret order, denotes a sensitive and excited organism, and the owner should cultivate practical and unselfish ideas and they may soon have opportunities for honest pleasures, and desired literary distinctions.

There is a vision of selfish and designing friendships for one who joins a secret order.

Young women should heed the counsel of their guardians, lest they fall into discreditable habits after this dream.

If a young woman meets the head of the order, she should oppose with energy and moral rectitude against allurements that are set brilliantly and prominently before those of her sex. For her to think her mother has joined the order, and she is using her best efforts to have her mother repudiate her vows, denotes that she will be full of love for her parents, yet will wring their hearts with anguish by thoughtless disobedience.

To see or hear that the leader is dead, foretells severe strains, and trials will eventually end in comparative good.

Seducer.

For a young woman to dream of being seduced, foretells that she will be easily influenced by showy persons.

For a man to dream that he has seduced a girl, is a warning for him to be on his guard, as there are those who will falsely accuse him. If his sweetheart appears shocked or angry under these proposals, he will find that the woman he loves is above reproach. If she consents, he is being used for her pecuniary pleasures.

Seed.

To dream of seed, foretells increasing prosperity, though present indications appear unfavorable.

Sentry.

To dream of a sentry, denotes that you will have kind protectors, and your life will be smoothly conducted.

Serenade.

To hear a serenade in your dream, you will have pleasant news from absent friends, and your anticipations will not fail you.

If you are one of the serenaders, there are many delightful things in your future.

Serpents.*

To dream of serpents, is indicative of cultivated morbidity and depressed surroundings. There is usually a disappointment after this dream.

Servant.

To dream of a servant, is a sign that you will be fortunate, despite gloomy appearances. Anger is likely to precipitate you into useless worries and quarrels.

To discharge one, foretells regrets and losses.

To quarrel with one in you. dream, indicates that you will, upon waking, have real cause for censuring some one who is derelict in duty.

---

*See Snakes and Reptiles.

To be robbed by one, shows that you have some one near you, who does not respect the laws of ownership.

Sewing.

To dream of sewing on new garments, foretells that domestic peace will crown your wishes.

Shakers.

To dream of seeing members of the sect called Shakers in a dream, denotes that you will change in your business, and feel coldness growing towards your sweetheart.

If you imagine you belong to them, you will unexpectedly renounce all former ties, and seek new pleasures in distant localities.

Shaking Hands.

For a young woman to dream that she shakes hands with some prominent ruler, foretells she will be surrounded with pleasures and distinction from strangers. If she avails herself of the opportunity, she will stand in high favor with friends. If she finds she must reach up to shake hands, she will find rivalry and opposition. If she has on gloves, she will overcome these obstacles.

To shake hands with those beneath you, denotes you will be loved and honored for your kindness and benevolence. If you think you or they have soiled hands, you will find enemies among seeming friends.

For a young woman to dream of shaking hands with a decrepit old man, foretells she will find trouble where amusement was sought.

Shakspeare.

To dream of Shakspeare, denotes that unhappiness and dispondency will work much anxiety to momentous affairs, and love will be stripped of passion's fever.

To read Shakspeare's works, denotes that you will unalterably attach yourself to literary accomplishments.

Shampoo.

To dream of seeing shampooing going on, denotes that you will engage in undignified affairs to please others.

To have your own head shampooed, you will soon make a secret trip, in which you will have much enjoyment, if you succeed in keeping the real purport from your family or friends.

Shanty.

To dream of a shanty, denotes that you will leave home in the quest of health. This also warns you of decreasing prosperity.

Shark.

To dream of sharks, denotes formidable enemies.

To see a shark pursuing and attacking you, denotes that unavoidable reverses will sink you into dispondent foreboding.

To see them sporting in clear water, foretells that while you are basking in the sunshine of women and prosperity, jealousy is secretly, but surely, working you disquiet, and unhappy fortune.

To see a dead one, denotes reconciliation and renewed prosperity.

Shave.

To merely contemplate getting a shave, in your dream, denotes you will plan for the successful development of enterprises, but will fail to generate energy sufficient to succeed.

Shaving.

To dream that you are being shaved, portends that you will let imposters defraud you.

To shave yourself, foretells that you will govern your own business and dictate to your household, notwithstanding that the presence of a shrew may cause you quarrels.

If your face appears smooth, you will enjoy quiet, and your conduct will not be questioned by your companions. If old and rough, there will be many squalls on the matrimonial sea.

If your razor is dull and pulls your face, you will give your friends cause to criticize your private life.

If your beard seems gray, you will be absolutely devoid of any sense of justice to those having claims upon you.

For a woman to see men shaving, foretells that her nature will become sullied by indulgence in gross pleasures.

If she dreams of being shaved, she will assume so much masculinity that men will turn from her in disgust.

Shawl.

To dream of a shawl, denotes that some one will offer you flattery and favor.

To lose your shawl, foretells sorrow and discomfort. A young woman is in danger of being jilted by a good-looking man, after this dream.

Shears.

To see shears in your dream, denotes that you will become miserly and disagreeable in your dealings.

To see them broken, you will lose friends and standing by your eccentric demeanor.

Sheaves.

To dream of sheaves, denotes joyful occasions. Prosperity holds before you a panorama of delightful events, and fields of enterprise and fortunate gain.

Sheep.*

To dream of shearing them, denotes a season of profitable enterprises will shower down upon you.

To see flocks of sheep, there will be much rejoicing among farmers, and other trades will prosper.

To see them looking scraggy and sick, you will be thrown into despair by the miscarriage of some plan, which promised rich returns.

To eat the flesh of sheep, denotes that ill-natured persons will outrage your feelings.

Sheet Iron.

To see sheet iron in your dream, denotes you are unfortunately listening to the admonition of others. To walk on it, signifies distasteful engagements.

Shells.†

To walk among and gather shells in your dream, denotes extravagance. Pleasure will leave you naught but exasperating regrets and memories.

Shelter.

To dream that you are building a shelter, signifies that you will escape the evil designs of enemies.

If you are seeking shelter, you will be guilty of cheating, and will try to justify yourself.

Shelves.‡

To see empty shelves in dreams, indicates losses and consequent gloom.

Full shelves, augurs happy contentment through the fulfillment of hope and exertions.

---

*See Lamb and Ram.   †See Mussels and Oysters.
‡ See Store.

Shepherd.

To see shepherds in your dreams watching their flocks, portends bounteous crops and pleasant relations for the farmer, also much enjoyment and profit for others.

To see them in idleness, foretells sickness and bereavement.

Sheriff.*

To dream of seeing a sheriff, denotes that you will suffer great uneasiness over the uncertain changes which loom up before you.

To imagine that you are elected sheriff or feel interested in the office, denotes that you will participate in some affair which will afford you neither profit nor honor.

To escape arrest, you will be able to further engage in illicit affairs.

Ship.

To dream of ships, foretells honor and unexpected elevation to ranks above your mode of life.

To hear of a shipwreck is ominous of a disastrous turn in affairs. Your female friends will betray you.

To lose your life in one, denotes that you will have an exceeding close call on your life or honor.

To see a ship on her way through a tempestuous storm, foretells that you will be unfortunate in business transactions, and you will be perplexed to find means of hiding some intrigue from the public, as your partner in the affair will threaten you with betrayal.

To see others shipwrecked, you will seek in vain to shelter some friend from disgrace and insolvency.

Shirt.

To dream of putting on your shirt, is a sign that you

*See Bailiff and Police.

will estrange yourself from your sweetheart by your faithless conduct.

To lose your shirt, augurs disgrace in business or love.

A torn shirt, represents misfortune and miserable surroundings.

A soiled shirt, denotes that contagious diseases will confront you.

Shirt-studs.

To dream of shirt-studs, foretells you will struggle to humor your pride, and will usually be successful. If they are diamonds, and the center one is larger than the others, you will enjoy wealth, or have an easy time, surrounded by congenial friends.

Shoemaker.

To see a shoemaker in your dream, warns you that indications are unfavorable to your advancement. For a woman to dream that her husband or lover is a shoemaker, foretells competency will be hers; her wishes will be gratified.

Shoes.

To dream of seeing your shoes ragged and soiled, denotes that you will make enemies by your unfeeling criticisms.

To have them blacked in your dreams, foretells improvement in your affairs, and some important event will cause you satisfaction.

New shoes, augur changes which will prove beneficial If they pinch your feet, you will be uncomfortably exposed to the practical joking of the fun-loving companions of your sex.

To find them untied, denotes losses, quarrels and ill-health.

To lose them, is a sign of desertion and divorces.

To dream that your shoes have been stolen during the

night, but you have two pairs of hose, denotes you will have a loss, but will gain in some other pursuit.

For a young woman to dream that her shoes are admired while on her feet, warns her to be cautious in allowing newly introduced people, and men of any kind, to approach her in a familiar way.

Shooting.*

To dream that you see or hear shooting, signifies unhappiness between married couples and sweethearts because of over-weaning selfishness, also unsatisfactory business and tasks because of negligence.

Shop.†

To dream of a shop, denotes that you will be opposed in every attempt you make for advancement by scheming and jealous friends.

Shot.

To dream that you are shot, and are feeling the sensations of dying, denotes that you are to meet unexpected abuse from the ill feelings of friends, but if you escape death by waking, you will be fully reconciled with them later on.

To dream that a preacher shoots you, signifies that you will be annoyed by some friend advancing views condemnatory to those entertained by yourself.

Shotgun.‡

To dream of a shotgun, foretells domestic troubles and worry with children and servants.

To shoot both barrels of a double-barreled shotgun, foretells that you will meet such exasperating and unfeeling attention in your private and public life that suave

*See Pistol.　　†See Store.　　‡See Pistol, Revolver, etc.

manners giving way under the strain and your righteous wrath will be justifiable.

Shoulder.

To dream of seeing naked shoulders, foretells that happy changes will make you look upon the world in a different light than formerly.

To see your own shoulders appearing thin, denotes that you will depend upon the caprices of others for entertainment and pleasure.

Shovel.

To see a shovel in a dream, signifies laborious but withal pleasant work will be undertaken. A broken or old one, implies frustration of hopes.

Shower.*

To dream that you are in a shower, foretells that you will derive exquisite pleasure in the study of creation and the proper placing of selfish pleasures.

Shrew.

To dream of a shrew, foretells that you will have a task to keep some friend in a cheerful frame of mind, and that you will unfit yourself for the experiences of everyday existence.

Shroud.

To dream of a shroud, denotes sickness and its attendant distress and anxiety, coupled with the machinations of the evil-minded and false friends. Business will threaten decline after this dream.

To see shrouded corpses, denotes a multitude of misfortunes.

To see a shroud removed from a corpse, denotes that quarrels will result in alienation.

*See Rain.

Sickness.

To dream of sickness, is a sign of trouble and real sickness in your family. Discord is sure to find entrance also.

To dream of your own sickness, is a warning to be unusually cautious of your person.

To see any of your family pale and sick, foretells that some event will break unexpectedly upon your harmonious hearthstone. Sickness is usually attendant upon this dream.

Side.

To dream of seeing only the side of any object, denotes that some person is going to treat your honest proposals with indifference.

To dream that your side pains you, there will be vexations in your affairs that will gall your endurance.

To dream that you have a fleshy, healthy side, you will be successful in courtship and business.

Siege.

For a young woman to dream that she is in a siege, and sees cavalry around her, denotes that she will have serious drawbacks to enjoyments, but will surmount them finally, and receive much pleasure and profit from seeming disappointments.

Sieve.

To dream of a sieve, foretells some annoying transaction will soon be made by you, which will probably be to your loss. If the meshes are too small, you will have the chance to reverse a decision unfavorable to yourself. If too large, you will eventually lose what you have recently acquired.

Sigh.

To dream that you are sighing over any trouble or sad

event, denotes that you will have unexpected sadness, but some redeeming brightness in your season of trouble.

To hear the sighing of others, foretells that the misconduct of dear friends will oppress you with a weight of gloom

Silk.

To dream of wearing silk clothes, is a sign of high ambitions being gratified, and friendly relations will be established between those who were estranged.

For a young woman to dream of old silk, denotes that she will have much pride in her ancestors, and will be wooed by a wealthy, but elderly person. If the silk is soiled or torn, she will drag her ancestral pride in the slums of disgrace.

Silkworm.

If you dream of a silkworm, you will engage in a very profitable work, which will also place you in a prominent position.

To see them dead, or cutting through their cocoons, is a sign of reverses and trying times.

Silver.

To dream of silver, is a warning against depending too largely on money for real happiness and contentment.

To find silver money, is indicative of shortcomings in others. Hasty conclusions are too frequently drawn by yourself for your own peace of mind.

To dream of silverware, denotes worries and unsatisfied desires.

Single.

For married persons to dream that they are single, foretells that their union will not be harmonious, and constant despondency will confront them.

Singing.

To hear singing in your dreams, betokens a cheerful spirit and happy companions. You are soon to have promising news from the absent.

If you are singing while everything around you gives promise of happiness, jealousy will insinuate a sense of insincerity into your joyousness. If there are notes of sadness in the song, you will be unpleasantly surprised at the turn your affairs will take.

Ribald songs, signifies gruesome and extravagant waste.

Skate.

To dream that you are skating on ice, foretells that you are in danger of losing employment, or valuable articles. If you break through the ice, you will have unworthy friends to counsel you.

To see others skating, foretells that disagreeable people will connect your name in scandal with some person who admires you.

To see skates, denotes discord among your associates.

To see young people skating on roller skates, foretells that you will enjoy good health, and feel enthusiastic over the pleasures you are able to contribute to others.

Skeleton.

To dream of seeing a skeleton, is prognostic of illness, misunderstanding and injury at the hands of others, especially enemies.

To dream that you are a skeleton, is a sign that you are suffering under useless worry, and should cultivate a milder disposition.

If you imagine that one haunts you, there will soon come to you a shocking accident or death, or the trouble may take the form of financial disaster.

Skull.

To dream of skulls grinning at you, is a sign of domestic quarrels and jars. Business will feel a shrinkage if you handle them.

To see a friend's skull, denotes that you will receive injury from a friend because of your being preferred to him.

To see your own skull denotes that you will be the servant of remorse.

Sky.*

To dream of the sky, signifies distinguished honors and interesting travel with cultured companions, if the sky is clear. Otherwise, it portends blasted expectations, and trouble with women.

To dream of floating in the sky among weird faces and animals, and wondering all the while if you are really awake, or only dreaming, foretells that all trouble, the most excruciating pain, that reach even the dullest sense will be distilled into one drop called jealousy, and will be inserted into your faithful love, and loyalty will suffer dethronement.

To see the sky turn red indicates that public disquiet and rioting may be expected.

Slander.

To dream that you are slandered, is a sign of your untruthful dealings with ignorance.

If you slander any one, you will feel the loss of friends through selfishness.

Slaughter-house.*

To dream of a slaughter-house, denotes that you will be feared more than loved by your sweetheart or mistress.

*See Heaven and Illumination.   †See Butcher.

Your business will divulge a private drain, and there will be unkind insinuations.

Sleep.

To dream of sleeping on clean, fresh beds, denotes peace and favor from those whom you love.

To sleep in unnatural resting places, foretells sickness and broken engagements.

To sleep beside a little child, betokens domestic joys and reciprocated love.

To see others sleeping, you will overcome all opposition in your pursuit for woman's favor.

To dream of sleeping with a repulsive person or object, warns you that your love will wane before that of your sweetheart, and you will suffer for your escapades.

For a young woman to dream of sleeping with her lover or some fascinating object, warns her against yielding herself a willing victim to his charms.

Sleigh.

To see a sleigh in your dreams, foretells you will fail in some love adventure, and incur the displeasure of a friend. To ride in one, foretells injudicious engagements will be entered into by you.

Sliding.

To dream of sliding, portends disappointments in affairs, and sweethearts will break vows.

To slide down a hillside covered with green grass, foretells that you will be deceived into ruin by flattering promises.

Slighted.

To dream of slighting any person or friend, denotes that you will fail to find happiness, as you will cultivate a morose and repellent bearing.

If you are slighted, you will have cause to bemoan your unfortunate position.

Slippers.

To dream of slippers, warns you that you are about to perform an unfortunate alliance or intrigue. You are likely to find favor with a married person which will result in trouble, if not scandal.

To dream that your slippers are much admired, foretells that you will be involved in a flirtation, which will suggest disgrace.

Smallpox.

To see people with smallpox in your dream, denotes unexpected and shocking sickness, and probably contagion. You will meet failure in accomplishing your designs.

Smoke.

To dream of smoke, foretells that you will be perplexed with doubts and fears.

To be overcome with smoke, denotes that dangerous persons are victimizing you with flattery.

Snakes.*

For a woman to dream that a dead snake is biting her, foretells she will suffer from malice of a pretended friend.

To dream of snakes, is a foreboding of evil in its various forms and stages.

To see them wriggling and falling over others, foretells struggles with fortune and remorse.

To kill them, you will feel that you have used every opportunity of advancing your own interests, or respecting that of others. You will enjoy victory over enemies

To walk over them, you will live in constant fear of

_____
*See Serpents and Reptiles.

sickness, and selfish persons will seek to usurp your place in your companion's life.

If they bite you, you will succumb to evil influences, and enemies will injure your business.

To dream that a common spotted snake approaches you from green herbs, and you quickly step aside as it passes you, and after you had forgotten the incident to again see it approaching and growing in dimensions as it nears you, finally taking on the form of an enormous serpent; if you then, after frantic efforts, succeed in escaping its attack, and altogether lose sight of it, it foretells that you will soon imagine you are being disobeyed and slighted, and things will go on from bad to worse. Sickness, uneasiness and unkindness will increase to frightful proportions in your mind; but they will adjust themselves to a normal basis, and by the putting aside of imaginary trouble, and masterfully shouldering duties, you will be contented and repaid.

To dream that a snake coils itself around you and darts its tongue out at you, is a sign that you will be placed in a position where you will be powerless in the hands of enemies, and you will be attacked with sickness.

To handle them, you will use strategy to aid in overthrowing opposition.

To see hairs turn into snakes, foretells that seeming insignificant incidents will make distressing cares for you.

If snakes turn into unnatural shapes, you will have troubles which will be dispelled if treated with indifference, calmness and will power.

To see or step on snakes while wading or bathing, denotes that there will be trouble where unalloyed pleasure was anticipated.

To see them bite others, foretells that some friend will be injured and criticised by you.

To see little snakes, denotes you will entertain persons with friendly hospitality who will secretly defame you and work to overthrow your growing prospects.

To see children playing with them, is a sign that you will be nonplussed to distinguish your friends from your enemies. For a woman to think a child places one on the back of her head, and she hears the snake's hisses, foretells that she will be persuaded to yield up some possession seemingly for her good, but she will find out later that she has been inveigled into an intrigue in which enemies will tantalize her. To see snakes raising up their heads in a path just behind your friend, denotes that you will discover a conspiracy which has been formed to injure your friend and also yourself. To think your friend has them under control, denotes that some powerful agency will be employed in your favor to ward off evil influences.

For a woman to hypnotize a snake, denotes your rights will be assailed, but you will be protected by law and influential friends.

Snail.

Snails crawling in your dream, signifies that unhealthful conditions surround you.

To step on them, denotes that you will come in contact with disagreeable people.

Sneeze.

To dream that you sneeze, denotes that hasty tidings will cause you to change your plans.

To see or hear others sneeze, some people will bore you with visits.

Snouts.

To dream of snouts, foretells dangerous seasons for

you. Enemies are surrounding you, and difficulties will be numerous.

Snow.

To see snow in your dreams, denotes that while you have no real misfortune, there will be the appearance of illness, and unsatisfactory enterprises.

To find yourself in a snow storm, denotes sorrow and disappointment in failure to enjoy some long-expected pleasure. There always follows more or less discouragement after this dream.

If you eat snow, you will fail to realize ideals.

To see dirty snow, foretells that your pride will be humbled, and you will seek reconciliation with some person whom you held in haughty contempt.

To see it melt, your fears will turn into joy.

To see large, white snowflakes falling while looking through a window, foretells that you will have an angry interview with your sweetheart, and the estrangement will be aggravated by financial depression.

To see snow-capped mountains in the distance, warns you that your longings and ambitions will bring no worthy advancement.

To see the sun shining through landscapes of snow, foretells that you will conquer adverse fortune and possess yourself of power.

For a young woman to dream of sleighing, she will find much opposition to her choice of a lover, and her conduct will cause her much ill-favor.

To dream of snowballing, denotes that you will have to struggle with dishonorable issues, and if your judgment is not well grounded, you will suffer defeat.

If snowbound or lost, there will be constant waves of ill luck breaking in upon you.

Snuff.

To dream of snuff, signifies your enemies are seducing the confidence of your friends. For a woman to use it in her dreams, foretells complications which will involve her separation from a favored friend.

Soap.

To dream of soap, foretells that friendships will reveal interesting entertainment. Farmers will have success in their varied affairs.

For a young woman to be making soap, omens a substantial and satisfactory competency will be hers.

Socialist.

To see a socialist in your dreams, your unenvied position among friends and acquaintances is predicted. Your affairs will be neglected for other imaginary duties.

Soda Fountain.

To dream of being at a soda fountain, denotes pleasure and profit after many exasperating experiences.

To treat others to this and other delectable iced drinks, you will be rewarded in your efforts, though the outlook appears full of contradictions. Inharmonious environments, and desired results will be forthcoming.

Son.

To dream of your son, if you have one, as being handsome and dutiful, foretells that he will afford you proud satisfaction, and will aspire to high honors. If he is maimed, or suffering from illness or accident, there is trouble ahead for you.

For a mother to dream that her son has fallen to the bottom of a well, and she hears cries, it is a sign of deep grief, losses and sickness. If she rescues him, threatened danger will pass away unexpectedly.

Soot.

If you see soot in your dreams, it means that you will meet with ill success in your affairs. Lovers will be quarrelsome and hard to please.

Sold.

To dream that you have sold anything, denotes that unfavorable business will worry you.

Soldiers.

To see soldiers marching in your dreams, foretells for you a period of flagrant excesses, but at the same time you will be promoted to elevations above rivals.

To see wounded soldiers, is a sign of the misfortune of others causing you serious complications in your affairs. Your sympathy will outstrip your judgment.

To dream that you are a worthy soldier, you will have literal fulfilment of ideals. Women are in danger of disrepute if they find themselves dreaming of soldiers.

Somnambulist.

To imagine while dreaming that you are a somnambulist, portends that you will unwittingly consent to some agreement of plans which will bring you anxiety or ill fortune.

Sorcerer.

To dream of a sorcerer, foretells your ambitions will undergo strange disappointments and change.

Sores.

To dream of seeing sores, denotes that illness will cause you loss and mental distress.

To dress a sore, foretells that your personal wishes and desires will give place to the pleasure of others.

To dream of an infant having a deep sore so that you can see the bone, denotes that distressing and annoying incidents will detract from your plans, and children will be threatened with contagion.

To dream of sores on yourself, portends early decay of health and impaired mentality. Sickness and unsatisfactory business will follow this dream.

Soul.

To dream of seeing your soul leaving your body, signifies you are in danger of sacrificing yourself to useless designs, which will dwarf your sense of honor and cause you to become mercenary and uncharitable.

For an artist to see his soul in another, foretells he will gain distinction if he applies himself to his work and leaves off sentimental rôles.

To imagine another's soul is in you, denotes you will derive solace and benefit from some stranger who is yet to come into your life.

For a young woman musician to dream that she sees another young woman on the stage clothed in sheer robes, and imagining it is her own soul in the other person, denotes she will be outrivaled in some great undertaking.

To dream that you are discussing the immortality of your soul, denotes you will improve opportunities which will aid you in gaining desired knowledge and pleasure of intercourse with intellectual people.

Soup.

To dream of soup, is a forerunner of good tidings and comfort.

To see others taking soup, foretells that you will have many good chances to marry.

For a young woman to make soup, signifies that she will not be compelled to do menial work in her household, as she will marry a wealthy man.

To drink oyster soup made of sweet milk, there will be quarrels with some bad luck, but reconciliations will follow.

Sovereign.

To dream of a sovereign, denotes increasing prosperity and new friends.

Sowing.

To dream that you are sowing seed, foretells to the farmer fruitful promises, if he sows in new ploughed soil.

To see others sowing, much business activity is portended, which will bring gain to all.

Spade.

To dream of a kind of shovel called spade, denotes that you will have work to complete, which will give you much annoyance in superintending.

If you dream of cards named spades, you will be enticed into follies which will bring you grief and misfortune.

For a gambler to dream that spades are trumps, means that unfortunate deals will deplete his winnings.

Sparrow.

To dream of sparrows, denotes that you will be surrounded with love and comfort, and this will cause you to listen with kindly interest to tales of woe, and your benevolence will gain you popularity.

To see them distressed or wounded, foretells sadness.

Spectacles.

To dream of spectacles, foretells that strangers will cause changes in your affairs. Frauds will be practised on your credulity.

To dream that you see broken spectacles, denotes estrangement caused by fondness for illegal pleasures.

Spice.

To dream of spice, foretells you will probably damage your own reputation in search of pleasure. For a young woman to dream of eating spice, is an omen of deceitful appearances winning her confidence.

Spider.

To dream of a spider, denotes that you will be careful and energetic in your labors, and fortune will be amassed to pleasing proportions.

To see one building its web, foretells that you will be happy and secure in your own home.

To kill one, signifies quarrels with your wife or sweetheart.

If one bites you, you will be the victim of unfaithfulness and will suffer from enemies in your business.

If you dream that you see many spiders hanging in their webs around you, foretells most favorable conditions, fortune, good health and friends.

To dream of a large spider confronting you, signifies that your elevation to fortune will be swift, unless you are in dangerous contact.

To dream that you see a very large spider and a small one coming towards you, denotes that you will be prosperous, and that you will feel for a time that you are immensely successful; but if the large one bites you, enemies will steal away your good fortune. If the little one bites you, you will be harassed with little spites and jealousies. To imagine that you are running from a large spider, denotes you will lose fortune in slighting opportunities. If you kill the spider you will eventually come into fair estate. If it afterwards returns to life and pursues you, you will be oppressed by sickness and wavering fortunes.

For a young woman to dream she sees gold spiders crawling around her, foretells that her fortune and prospect for happiness will improve, and new friends will surround her.

Spider-web.

To see spider-webs, denotes pleasant associations and fortunate ventures.

Spinning.

To dream that you are spinning, means that you will engage in some enterprise, which will be all you could wish.

Spirit or Specter.

To see spirits in a dream, denotes that some unexpected trouble will confront you. If they are white-robed, the health of your nearest friend is threatened, or some business speculation will be disapproving. If they are robed in black, you will meet with treachery and unfaithfulness.

If a spirit speaks, there is some evil near you, which you might avert if you would listen to the counsels of judgment.

To dream that you hear spirits knocking on doors or walls, denotes that trouble will arise unexpectedly.

To see them moving draperies, or moving behind them, is a warning to hold control over your feelings, as you are likely to commit indiscretions. Quarrels are also threatened.

To see the spirit of your friend floating in your room, foretells disappointment and insecurity.

To hear music supposedly coming from spirits, denotes unfavorable changes and sadness in the household.

Spitting.

To dream of spitting, denotes unhappy terminations of

seemingly auspicious undertakings. For some one to spit on you, foretells disagreements and alienation of affections.

Spleen.

To dream of spleen, denotes that you will have a misunderstanding with some party who will injure you.

Splendor.

To dream that you live in splendor, denotes that you will succeed to elevations, and will reside in a different state to the one you now occupy.

To see others thus living, signifies pleasure derived from the interest that friends take in your welfare.

Splinter.

To dream of splinters sticking into your flesh, denotes that you will have many vexations from members of your family or from jealous rivals.

If while you are visiting you stick a splinter in your foot, you will soon make, or receive, a visit which will prove extremely unpleasant. Your affairs will go slightly wrong through your continued neglect.

Sponges.

Sponges seen in a dream, denote that deception is being practised upon you.

To use one in erasing, you will be the victim of folly.

Spools.

To dream of spools of thread, indicates some long and arduous tasks, but which when completed will meet your most sanguine expectations. If they are empty, there will be disappointments for you.

Spoons.

To see, or use, spoons in a dream, denotes favorable

signs of advancement. Domestic affairs will afford contentment.

To think a spoon is lost, denotes that you will be suspicious of wrong doing.

To steal one, is a sign that you will deserve censure for your contemptible meanness in your home.

To dream of broken or soiled spoons, signifies loss and trouble.

Spring.

To dream that spring is advancing, is a sign of fortunate undertakings and cheerful companions.

To see spring appearing unnaturally, is a foreboding of disquiet and losses.

Spur.

To dream of wearing spurs, denotes that you will engage in some unpleasant controversy.

To see others with them on, foretells that enmity is working you trouble.

Spy.

To dream that spies are harassing you, denotes dangerous quarrels and uneasiness.

To dream that you are a spy, denotes that you will make unfortunate ventures.

Spy-glass.

To dream that you are looking through a spy-glass, denotes that changes will soon occur to your disadvantage.

To see a broken or imperfect one, foretells unhappy dissensions and loss of friends.

Squall.

To dream of squalls, foretells disappointing business and unhappiness.

Squinting.

To dream that you see some person with squinting eyes, denotes that you will be annoyed with unpleasant people.

For a man to dream that his sweetheart, or some good-looking girl, squints her eyes at him, foretells that he is threatened with loss by seeking the favors of women. For a young woman to have this dream about men, she will be in danger of losing her fair reputation.

Squirrel.

To dream of seeing squirrels, denotes that pleasant friends will soon visit you. You will see advancement in your business also.

To kill a squirrel, denotes that you will be unfriendly and disliked.

To pet one, signifies family joy.

To see a dog chasing one, foretells disagreements and unpleasantness among friends.

Stable.

To dream of a stable, is a sign of fortune and advantageous surroundings.

To see a stable burning denotes successful changes, or it may be seen in actual life.

Stag.

To see stags in your dream, foretells that you will have honest and true friends, and will enjoy delightful entertainments.

Stage Driver.

To dream of a stage driver, signifies you will go on a strange journey in quest of fortune and happiness.

Stain.

To see stain on your hands, or clothing, while dreaming, foretells that trouble over small matters will assail you.

To see a stain on the garments of others, or on their flesh, foretells that some person will betray you.

Stairs.

To dream of passing up a stairs, foretells good fortune and much happiness.

If you fall down stairs, you will be the object of hatred and envy.

To walk down, you will be unlucky in your affairs, and your lovemaking will be unfavorable.

To see broad, handsome stairs, foretells approaching riches and honors.

To see others going down stairs, denotes that unpleasant conditions will take the place of pleasure.

To sit on stair steps, denotes a gradual rise in fortune and delight.

Stall.

To dream of a stall, denotes impossible results from some enterprise will be expected by you.

Stallion.

To dream of a stallion, foretells prosperous conditions are approaching you, in which you will hold a position which will confer honor upon you.

To dream you ride a fine stallion, denotes you will rise to position and affluence in a phenomenal way; however, your success will warp your morality and sense of justice. To see one with the rabies, foretells that wealthy surroundings will cause you to assume arrogance, which will be distasteful to your friends, and your pleasures will be deceitful.

Stammer.

To dream that you stammer in your conversation, denotes that worry and illness will threaten your enjoyment.

To hear others stammer, foretells that unfriendly persons will delight in annoying you and giving you needless worry.

Standard-bearer.

To dream that you are a standard-bearer, denotes that your occupation will be pleasant, but varied.

To see others acting as standard-bearers, foretells that you will be jealous and envious of some friend.

Stars.

To dream of looking upon clear, shining stars, foretells good health and prosperity. If they are dull or red, there is trouble and misfortune ahead.

To see a shooting or falling star, denotes sadness and grief.

To see stars appearing and vanishing mysteriously, there will be some strange changes and happenings in your near future.

· If you dream that a star falls on you, there will be a bereavement in your family.

To see them rolling around on the earth, is a sign of formidable danger and trying times.

Starving.

To dream of being in a starving condition, portends unfruitful labors and a dearth of friends.

To see others in this condition, omens misery and dissatisfaction with present companions and employment.

Statues.

To see statues in dreams, signifies estrangement from a loved one. Lack of energy will cause you disappointment in realizing wishes.

Stealing.

To dream of stealing, or of seeing others commit this act, foretells bad luck and loss of character.

To be accused of stealing, denotes that you will be misunderstood in some affair, and suffer therefrom, but you will eventually find that this will bring you favor.

To accuse others, denotes that you will treat some person with hasty inconsideration.

Steeple.

To see a steeple rising from a church, is a harbinger of sickness and reverses.

A broken one, points to death in your circle, or friends.

To climb a steeple, foretells that you will have serious difficulties, but will surmount them.

To fall from one, denotes losses in trade and ill health.

Steps.*

To dream that you ascend steps, denotes that fair prospects will relieve former anxiety.

To decend them, you may look for misfortune.

To fall down them, you are threatened with unexpected failure in your affairs.

Step-sister.

To dream of a step-sister, denotes you will have unavoidable care and annoyance upon you.

Stethoscope.

To dream of a stethoscope, foretells calamity to your hopes and enterprises. There will be troubles and recriminations in love.

Sticks.

To dream of sticks, is an unlucky omen.

*See Stairs.

Stillborn.

To dream of a stillborn infant, denotes that some distressing incident will come before your notice.

Stilts.

To dream of walking on stilts, denotes that your fortune is in an insecure condition.

To fall from them, or feel them break beneath you, you will be precipitated into embarrassments by trusting your affairs to the care of others.

Sting.

To feel that any insect stings you in a dream, is a foreboding of evil and unhappiness.

For a young woman to dream that she is stung, is ominous of sorrow and remorse from over-confidence in men.

Stockings.*

To dream of stockings, denotes that you will derive pleasure from dissolute companionship.

For a young woman to see her stockings ragged, or worn, foretells that she will be guilty of unwise, if not immoral conduct. To dream that she puts on fancy stockings, she will be fond of the attention of men, and she should be careful to whom she shows preference. If white ones appear to be on her feet, she is threatened with woeful disappointment or illness.

Stone.†

To see stones in your dreams, foretells numberless perplexities and failures.

To walk among rocks, or stones, omens that an uneven and rough pathway will be yours for at least a while.

---

*See Knitting.   †See Rock.

To make deals in ore-bearing rock lands, you will be successful in business after many lines have been tried. If you fail to profit by the deal, you will have disappointments. If anxiety is greatly felt in closing the trade, you will succeed in buying or selling something that will prove profitable to you.

Small stones or pebbles, implies that little worries and vexations will irritate you.

If you throw a stone, you will have cause to admonish a person.

If you design to throw a pebble or stone at some belligerent person, it denotes that some evil feared by you will pass because of your untiring attention to right principles.

Stone Mason.

To see stone masons at work while dreaming, foretells disappointment.

To dream that you are a stone mason, portends that your labors will be unfruitful. and your companions will be dull and uncongenial.

Storage Battery.

To dream of a storage battery, opportune speculations will return you handsome gains.

Store.

To dream of a store filled with merchandise, foretells prosperity and advancement.

An empty one, denotes failure of efforts and quarrels.

To dream that your store is burning, is a sign of renewed activity in business and pleasure.

If you find yourself in a department store, it foretells that much pleasure will be derived from various sources of profit.

To sell goods in one, your advancement will be accelerated by your energy and the efforts of friends.

To dream that you sell a pair of soiled, gray cotton gloves to a woman, foretells that your opinion of women will place you in hazardous positions. If a woman has this dream, her preference for some one of the male sex will not be appreciated very much by him.

Storm.*

To see and hear a storm approaching, foretells continued sickness, unfavorable business, and separation from friends, which will cause added distress. If the storm passes, your affliction will not be so heavy.

Straw.

If you dream of straw, your life is threatened with emptiness and failure.

To see straw piles burning, is a signal of prosperous times.

To feed straw to stock, foretells that you will make poor provisions for those depending upon you.

Strawberries.

To dream of strawberries, is favorable to advancement and pleasure. You will obtain some long wished-for object.

To eat them, denotes requited love.

To deal in them, denotes abundant harvest and happiness.

Street.

To dream that you are walking in a street, foretells ill luck and worries. You will almost despair of reaching the goal you have set up in your aspirations.

------

*See Hurricane and Rain.

To be in a familiar street in a distant city, and it appears dark, you will make a journey soon, which will not afford the profit or pleasure contemplated. If the street is brilliantly lighted, you will engage in pleasure, which will quickly pass, leaving no comfort.

To pass down a street and feel alarmed lest a thug attack you, denotes that you are venturing upon dangerous ground in advancing your pleasure or business.

Street-poster.

To dream that you are a street-poster, denotes that you will undertake some unpleasant and unprofitable work.

To see street-posters at work, foretells disagreeable news.

Struggling.

To dream of struggling, foretells that you will encounter serious difficulties, but if you gain the victory in your struggle, you will also surmount present obstacles.

Stumble.

If you stumble in a dream while walking or running, you will meet with disfavor, and obstructions will bar your path to success, but you will eventually surmount them, if you do not fall.

Stumps.

To dream of a stump, foretells you are to have reverses and will depart from your usual mode of living. To see fields of stumps, signifies you will be unable to defend yourself from the encroachments of adversity. To dig or pull them up, is a sign that you will extricate yourself from the environment of poverty by throwing off sentiment and pride and meeting the realities of life with a determination to overcome whatever opposition you may meet.

Suckle.*

To see the young taking suckle, denotes contentment and favorable conditions for success is unfolding to you.

Suffocating.†

To dream that you are suffocating, denotes that you will experience deep sorrow and mortification at the conduct of some one you love. You should be careful of your health after this dream.

Sugar.

To dream of sugar, denotes that you will be hard to please in your domestic life, and will entertain jealousy while seeing no cause for aught but satisfaction and secure joys. There may be worries, and your strength and temper taxed after this dream.

To eat sugar in your dreams, you will have unpleasant matters to contend with for a while, but they will result better than expected.

To price sugar, denotes that you are menaced by enemies.

To deal in sugar and see large quantities of it being delivered to you, you will barely escape a serious loss.

To see a cask of sugar burst and the sugar spilling out, foretells a slight loss.

To hear a labourer singing while unloading sugar, some seemingly insignificant affair will bring you great benefit, either in business or social states.

Sugar-tongs.

To dream of sugar-tongs, foretells that disagreeable tidings of wrong-doings will be received by you.

---

*See Nursing.   †See Smoke.

Suicide.

To commit suicide in a dream, foretells that misfortune will hang heavily over you.

To see or hear others committing this deed, foretells that the failure of others will affect your interests.

For a young woman to dream that her lover commits suicide, her disappointment by the faithlessness of her lover is accentuated.

Sulphur.

To dream of sulphur, warns you to use much discretion in your dealings, as you are threatened with foul play.

To see sulphur burning, is ominous of great care attendant upon your wealth.

To eat sulphur, indicates good health and consequent pleasure.

Sun.

To dream of seeing a clear, shining sunrise, foretells joyous events and prosperity, which give delightful promises.

To see the sun at noontide, denotes the maturity of ambitions and signals unbounded satisfaction.

To see the sunset, is prognostic of joys and wealth passing their zenith, and warns you to care for your interests with renewed vigilance.

A sun shining through clouds, denotes that troubles and difficulties are losing hold on you, and prosperity is nearing you.

If the sun appears weird, or in an eclipse, there will be stormy and dangerous times, but these will eventually pass, leaving your business and domestic affairs in better forms than before.

Sunshade.

To dream of seeing young girls carrying sunshades, foretells prosperity and exquisite delights.

A broken one, foretells sickness and death to the young.

Surgeon.

To dream of a surgeon, denotes you are threatened by enemies who are close to you in business. For a young woman, this dream promises a serious illness from which she will experience great inconvenience.

Surgical Instruments.

To see surgical instruments in a dream, foretells dissatisfaction will be felt by you at the indiscreet manner a friend manifests toward you.

Swallow.

To dream of swallows, is a sign of peace and domestic harmony.

To see a wounded or dead one, signifies unavoidable sadness.

Swamp.*

To walk through swampy places in dreams, foretells that you will be the object of adverse circumstances. Your inheritance will be uncertain, and you will undergo keen disappointments in your love matters.

To go through a swamp where you see clear water and green growths, you will take hold on prosperity and singular pleasures, the obtaining of which will be attended with danger and intriguing.

Swan.

To dream of seeing white swans floating upon placid waters, foretells prosperous outlooks and delightful experiences.

To see a black swan, denotes illicit pleasure, if near clear water.

A dead swan, foretells satiety and discontentment.

*See Marsh.

To see them flying, pleasant anticipations will be realized soon.

Swearing.

To dream of swearing, denotes some unpleasant obstructions in business. A lover will have cause to suspect the faithfulness of his affianced after this dream.

To dream that you are swearing before your family, denotes that disagreements will soon be brought about by your unloyal conduct.

Sweeping.

To dream of sweeping, denotes that you will gain favor in the eyes of your husband, and children will find pleasure in the home.

If you think the floors need sweeping, and you from some cause neglect them, there will be distresses and bitter disappointments awaiting you in the approaching days.

To servants, sweeping is a sign of disagreements and suspicion of the intentions of others.

Sweetheart.*

To dream that your sweetheart is affable and of pleasing physique, foretells that you will woo a woman who will prove a joy to your pride and will bring you a good inheritance. If she appears otherwise, you will be discontented with your choice before the marriage vows are consummated. To dream of her as being sick or in distress, denotes that sadness will be intermixed with joy.

If you dream that your sweetheart is a corpse, you will have a long period of doubt and unfavorable fortune.

Sweet Oil.

Sweet oil in dreams, implies considerate treatment will be withheld from you in some unfortunate occurrence.

*See Lover, Hugging, and Kissing.

Sweet Taste.

To dream of any kind of a sweet taste in your mouth, denotes you will be praised for your pleasing conversation and calm demeanor in a time of commotion and distress.

To dream that you are trying to get rid of a sweet taste, foretells that you will oppress and deride your friends, and will incur their displeasure.

Swelling.

To dream that you see yourself swollen, denotes that you will amass fortune, but your egotism will interfere with your enjoyment.

To see others swollen, foretells that advancement will meet with envious obstructions.

Swimming.*

To dream of swimming, is an augury of success if you find no discomfort in the act. If you feel yourself going down, much dissatisfaction will present itself to you.

For a young woman to dream that she is swimming with a girl friend who is an artist in swimming, foretells that she will be loved for her charming disposition, and her little love affairs will be condoned by her friends.

To swim under water, foretells struggles and anxieties.

Swiss Cheese.

To dream of Swiss cheese, foretells that you will come into possession of substantial property, and healthful amusements will be enjoyed.

Switch.

To dream of a switch, foretells changes and misfortune.

A broken switch, foretells disgrace and trouble.

*See Diving and Bathing.

To dream of a railroad switch, denotes that travel will cause you much loss and inconvenience.

To dream of a switch, signifies you will meet discouragements in momentous affairs.

Sword.

To dream that you wear a sword, indicates that you will fill some public position with honor.

To have your sword taken from you, denotes your vanquishment in rivalry.

To see others bearing swords, foretells that altercations will be attended with danger.

A broken sword, foretells despair.

Sybil.

To dream of a sybil, foretells that you will enjoy assignations and other demoralizing pleasures.

Symphony.*

To dream of symphonies, heralds delightful occupations.

Synagogue.†

To dream of a synagogue, foretells that you have enemies powerfully barricading your entrance into fortune's realms. If you climb to the top on the outside, you will overcome oppositions and be successful.

If you read the Hebrew inscription on a synagogue, you will meet disaster, but will eventually rebuild your fortunes with renewed splendor.

Syringe.

To dream of a syringe, denotes that false alarm of the gravity of a relative's condition will reach you. To see a broken one, foretells you are approaching a period of ill health or worry over slight mistakes in business.

---

*See Music.   †See Church.

T.

"And it was so, when Gideon heard the telling of the dream, and the interpretation thereof, that he worshiped, and returned into the host of Israel, and said, 'Arise; for the Lord hath delivered into your hand the host of Midian.' "—Judges VII., 15.

Table.

To dream of setting a table preparatory to a meal, foretells happy unions and prosperous circumstances.

To see empty tables, signifies poverty or disagreements.

To clear away the table, denotes that pleasure will soon assume the form of trouble and indifference.

To eat from a table without a cloth, foretells that you will be possessed of an independent disposition, and the prosperity or conduct of others will give you no concern.

To see a table walking or moving in some mysterious way, foretells that dissatisfaction will soon enter your life, and you will seek relief in change.

To dream of a soiled cloth on a table, denotes disobedience from servants or children, and quarreling will invariably follow pleasure.

To see a broken table, is ominous of decaying fortune.

To see one standing or sitting on a table, foretells that to obtain their desires they will be guilty of indiscretions.

To see or hear table-rapping or writing, denotes that you will undergo change of feelings towards your friends, and your fortune will be threatened. A loss from the depreciation of relatives or friends is indicated.

Tacks.

To dream of tacks, means to you many vexations and quarrels.

For a woman to drive one, foretells she will master unpleasant rivalry.

If she mashes her finger while driving it, she will be distressed over unpleasant tasks.

Tadpole.

To dream of tadpoles, foretells uncertain speculation will bring cause for uneasiness in business. For a young woman to see them in clear water, foretells she will form a relation with a wealthy but immoral man.

Tail.

To dream of seeing only the tail of a beast, unusual annoyance is indicated where pleasures seemed assured.

To cut off the tail of an animal, denotes that you will suffer misfortune by your own carelessness.

To dream that you have the tail of a beast grown on you, denotes that your evil ways will cause you untold distress, and strange events will cause you perplexity.

Tailor.

To dream of a tailor, denotes that worries will arise on account of some journey to be made.

To have a misunderstanding with one, shows that you will be disappointed in the outcome of some scheme.

For one to take your measure, denotes that you will have quarrels and disagreements.

Talisman.

To dream that you wear a talisman, implies you will have pleasant companions and enjoy favors from the rich. For a young woman to dream her lover gives her one, denotes she will obtain her wishes concerning marriage.

Talking.

To dream of talking, denotes that you will soon hear of the sickness of relatives, and there will be worries in your affairs.

To hear others talking loudly, foretells that you will be accused of interfering in the affairs of others. To think they are talking about you, denotes that you are menaced with illness and disfavor.

Tallow.

To dream of tallow, forebodes that your possessions of love and wealth will quickly vanish.

Tambourine.

To dream of a tambourine, signifies you will have enjoyment in some unusual event which will soon take place.

Tank.

To dream of a tank, foretells you will be prosperous and satisfied beyond your expectations. To see a leaking tank, denotes loss in your affairs.

Tannery.

To dream of a tannery, denotes contagion and other illness. Loss in trade is portended.

To dream that you are a tanner, denotes that you will have to engage in work which is not to your taste, but there will be others dependent upon you.

To buy leather from a tannery, foretells that you will be successful in your undertakings, but will not make many friends.

Tape.

To dream of tape, denotes your work will be wearisome and unprofitable. For a woman to buy it, foretells she will find misfortune laying oppression upon her.

Tapestry.

To dream of seeing rich tapestry, foretells that luxurious living will be to your liking. and if the tapestries are not worn or ragged, you will be able to gratify your inclinations.

If a young woman dreams that her rooms are hung with tapestry, she will soon wed some one who is rich and above her in standing.

Tapeworm.

To dream you see a tapeworm, or have one, denotes disagreeable prospects for health or for pleasure.

Tar.

If you see tar in dreams, it warns you against pitfalls and designs of treacherous enemies.

To have tar on your hands or clothing, denotes sickness and grief.

Tarantula.

To see a tarantula in your dream, signifies enemies are about to overwhelm you with loss. To kill one, denotes you will be successful after much ill-luck.

Target.

To dream of a target, foretells you will have some affair demanding your attention from other more pleasant ones. For a young woman to think she is a target, denotes her reputation is in danger through the envy of friendly associates.

Tassels.

To see tassels in a dream, denotes you will reach the height of your desires and ambition. For a young woman to lose them, denotes she will undergo some unpleasant experience.

Tattoo.

To see your body appearing tattooed, foretells that some difficulty will cause you to make a long and tedious absence from your home.

To see tattooes on others, foretells that strange loves will make you an object of jealousy.

To dream you are a tattooist, is a sign that you will estrange yourself from friends because of your fancy for some strange experience.

Taxes.

To dream that you pay your taxes, foretells you will succeed in destroying evil influences rising around you. If others pay them, you will be forced to ask aid of friends. If you are unable to pay them, you will be unfortunate in experiments you are making.

Tea.

To dream that you are brewing tea, foretells that you will be guilty of indiscreet actions, and will feel deeply remorseful.

To see your friends drinking tea, and you with them, denotes that social pleasures will pall on you, and you will seek to change your feelings by serving others in their sorrows.

To see dregs in your tea, warns you of trouble in love, and affairs of a social nature.

To spill tea, is a sign of domestic confusion and grief.

To find your tea chest empty, unfolds much disagreeable gossip and news.

To dream that you are thirsty for tea, denotes that you will be surprised with uninvited guests.

Teacups.

To dream of teacups, foretells that affairs of enjoyment will be attended by you. For a woman to break or see them broken, omens her pleasure and good fortune will be marred by a sudden trouble. To drink wine from one, foretells fortune and pleasure will be combined in the near future.

Teakettle.

To dream you see a teakettle, implies sudden news which will be likely to distress you. For a woman to pour sparkling, cold water from a teakettle, she will have unexpected favor shown her.

Tears.

To dream that you are in tears, denotes that some affliction will soon envelop you.

To see others shedding tears, foretells that your sorrows will affect the happiness of others,

Teasing.

To find yourself teasing any person while dreaming, denotes that you will be loved and sought after because of your cheerful and amiable manners. Your business will be eventually successful.

To dream of being teased, denotes that you will win the love of merry and well-to-do persons.

For a young woman to dream of being teased, foretells that she will form a hasty attachment, but will not be successful in consummating an early marriage.

Teeth.

An ordinary dream of teeth augurs an unpleasant contact with sickness, or disquieting people.

If you dream that your teeth are loose, there will be failures and gloomy tidings.

If the doctor pulls your tooth, you will have desperate illness, if not fatal; it will be lingering.

To have them filled, you will recover lost valuables after much uneasiness.

To clean or wash your teeth, foretells that some great

struggle will be demanded of you in order to preserve your fortune.

To dream that you are having a set of teeth made, denotes that severe crosses will fall upon you, and you will strive to throw them aside.

If you lose your teeth, you will have burdens which will crush your pride and demolish your affairs.

To dream that you have your teeth knocked out, denotes sudden misfortune. Either your business will suffer, or deaths or accidents will come close to you.

To examine your teeth, warns you to be careful of your affairs, as enemies are lurking near you.

If they appear decayed and snaggled, your business or health will suffer from intense strains.

To dream of spitting out teeth, portends personal sickness, or sickness in your immediate family.

Imperfect teeth is one of the worst dreams. It is full of mishaps for the dreamer. A loss of estates, failure of persons to carry out their plans and desires, bad health, depressed conditions of the nervous system for even healthy persons.

For one tooth to fall out, foretells disagreeable news; if two, it denotes unhappy states that the dreamer will be plunged into from no carelessness on his part. If three fall out, sickness and accidents of a very serious nature will follow.

Seeing all the teeth drop out, death and famine usually will prevail. If the teeth are decayed and you pull them out, the same, only yourself, is prominent in the case.

To dream of tartar or any deposit falling off of the teeth and leaving them sound and white, is a sign of temporary indisposition, which will pass, leaving you wiser in regard to conduct, and you will find enjoyment in the discharge of duty .

To admire your teeth for their whiteness and beauty, foretells that pleasant occupations and much happiness will be experienced through the fulfilment of wishes.

To dream that you pull one of your teeth and lose it, and feeling within your mouth with your tongue for the cavity, and failing to find any, and have a doctor for the same, but to no effect, leaving the whole affair enveloped in mystery, denotes that you are about to enter into some engagement which does not exactly please you, and which you decide to ignore, but will later take it up and secretly prosecute it to your own disquieting satisfaction and under the suspicion of friends.

To dream that a dentist cleans your teeth perfectly, and the next morning you find them rusty, foretells you will believe your interest secure concerning some person or position, but you will find that they have succumbed to the blandishments of an artful man or woman.

Telegram.

To dream that you receive a telegram, denotes that you will soon receive tidings of an unpleasant character. Some friend is likely to misrepresent matters which are of much concern to you.

To send a telegram is a sign that you will be estranged from some one holding a place near you, or business will disappoint you.

If you are the operator sending these messages, you will be affected by them only through the interest of others.

To see or be in a telegraph office, foretells unfortunate engagements.

Telephone.

To dream of a telephone, foretells you will meet strangers who will harass and bewilder you in your affairs. For a woman to dream of talking over one, denotes she will have much jealous rivalry, but will overcome all evil influences. If she cannot hear well in conversing over one, she is threatened with evil gossip, and the loss of a lover.

Telescope.

To dream of a telescope, portends unfavorable seasons for love and domestic affairs, and business will be changeable and uncertain.

To look at planets and stars through one, portends for you journeys which will afford you much pleasure, but later cause you much financial loss.

To see a broken telescope, or one not in use, signifies that matters will go out of the ordinary with you, and trouble may be expected.

Tempest.*

To dream of tempests, denotes that you will have a siege of calamitous trouble, and friends will treat you with indifference.

Temptation.

To dream that you are surrounded by temptations, denotes that you will be involved in some trouble with an envious person who is trying to displace you in the confidence of friends. If you resist them, you will be successful in some affair in which you have much opposition.

Tenant.

For a landlord to see his tenant in a dream, denotes he will have business trouble and vexation. To imagine you are a tenant, foretells you will suffer loss in experi-

*See Storms and Cyclones.

ments of a business character. If a tenant pays you money, you will be successful in some engagements.

Tenpins.

If you dream at playing at tenpins, you will doubtless soon engage in some affair which will bring discredit upon your name, and you will lose your money and true friendship.

To see others engaged in this dream, foretells that you will find pleasure in frivolous people and likely lose employment.

For a young woman to play a successful game of tenpins, is an omen of light pleasures, but sorrow will attend her later.

Tent.

To dream of being in a tent, foretells a change in your affairs.

To see a number of tents, denotes journeys with unpleasant companions.

If the tents are torn or otherwise dilapidated, there will be trouble for you.

Terror.

To dream that you feel terror at any object or happening, denotes that disappointments and loss will envelop you.

To see others in terror, means that unhappiness of friends will seriously affect you.

Text.

To dream of hearing a minister reading his text, denotes that quarrels will lead to separation with some friend.

To dream that you are in a dispute about a text, foretells unfortunate adventures for you.

If you try to recall a text, you will meet with unexpected difficulties.

If you are repeating and pondering over one, you will have great obstacles to overcome if you gain your desires.

Thatch.

To dream that you thatch a roof with any quickly, perishable material, denotes that sorrow and discomfort will surround you.

If you find that a roof which you have thatched with straw is leaking, there will be threatenings of danger, but by your rightly directed energy they may be averted.

Thaw.

To dream of seeing ice thawing, foretells that some affair which has caused you much worry will soon give you profit and pleasure.

To see the ground thawing after a long freeze, foretells prosperous circumstances.

Theater.

To dream of being at a theater, denotes that you will have much pleasure in the company of new friends. Your affairs will be satisfactory after this dream. If you are one of the players, your pleasures will be of short duration.

If you attend a vaudeville theater, you are in danger of losing property through silly pleasures. If it is a grand opera, you will succeed in you wishes and aspirations.

If you applaud and laugh at a theater, you will sacrifice duty to the gratification of fancy.

To dream of trying to escape from one during a fire or other excitement, foretells that you will engage in some enterprise, which will be hazardous.

Thermometer.

To dream of looking at a thermometer, denotes unsatisfactory business, and disagreements in the home.

To see a broken one, foreshadows illness. If the mercury seems to be falling, your affairs will assume a distressing shape. If it is rising, you will be able to throw off bad conditions in your business.

Thief.*

To dream of being a thief and that you are pursued by officers, is a sign that you will meet reverses in business, and your social relations will be unpleasant.

If you pursue or capture a thief, you will overcome your enemies.

Thigh.

To dream of seeing your thigh smooth and white, denotes unusual good luck and pleasure.

To see wounded thighs, foretells illness and treachery.

For a young woman to admire her thigh, signifies willingness to engage in adventures, and she should heed this as a warning to be careful of her conduct.

Thimble.

If you use a thimble in your dreams, you will have many others to please besides yourself. If a woman, you will have your own position to make.

To lose one, foretells poverty and trouble. To see an old or broken one, denotes that you are about to act unwisely in some momentous affair.

To receive or buy a new thimble, portends new associations in which you will find contentment.

To dream that you use an open end thimble, but find

*See Stealing.

553

that it is closed, denotes that you will have trouble, but friends will aid you in escaping its disastrous consequences.

Thirst.

To dream of being thirsty, shows that you are aspiring to things beyond your present reach; but if your thirst is quenched with pleasing drinks, you will obtain your wishes.

To see others thirsty and drinking to slake it, you will enjoy many favors at the hands of wealthy people.

Thorns.

To dream of thorns, is an omen of dissatisfaction, and evil will surround every effort to advancement.

If the thorns are hidden beneath green foliage, your prosperity will be interfered with by secret enemies.

Thread.*

To dream of thread, denotes that your fortune lies beyond intricate paths.

To see broken threads, you will suffer loss through the faithlessness of friends.

Threshing.

To dream of threshing grain, denotes great advancement in business and happiness among families. But if there is an abundance of straw and little grain, unsuccessful enterprises will be undertaken.

To break down or have an accident while threshing, you will have some great sorrow in the midst of prosperity.

Throat.

To dream of seeing a well-developed and graceful throat, portends a rise in position.

*See Spools.

If you feel that your throat is sore, you will be deceived in your estimation of a friend, and will have anxiety over the discovery.

Throne.

If you dream of sitting on a throne, you will rapidly rise to favor and fortune.

To descend from one, there is much disappointment for you.

To see others on a throne, you will succeed to wealth through the favor of others.

Thumb.

To dream of seeing a thumb, foretells that you will be the favorite of artful persons and uncertain fortune.

If you are suffering from a sore thumb, you will lose in business, and your companions will prove disagreeable. To dream that you have no thumb, implies destitution and loneliness. If it seems unnaturally small, you will enjoy pleasure for a time. If abnormally large, your success will be rapid and brilliant.

A soiled thumb indicates gratification of loose desires. If the thumb has a very long nail, you are liable to fall into evil through seeking strange pleasures.

Thunder.

To dream of hearing thunder, foretells you will soon be threatened with reverses in your business.

To be in a thunder shower, denotes trouble and grief are close to you.

To hear the terrific peals of thunder, which make the earth quake, portends great loss and disappointment.

Tickle.

To dream of being tickled, denotes insistent worries and illness.

If you tickle others, you will throw away much enjoyment through weakness and folly.

Ticks.

To dream you see ticks crawling on your flesh, is a sign of impoverished circumstances and ill health. Hasty journeys to sick beds may be made.

To mash a tick on you, denotes that you will be annoyed by treacherous enemies.

To sce in your dreams large ticks on stock, enemies are endeavoring to get possession of your property by foul means.

Tiger.

To dream of a tiger advancing towards you, you will be tormented and persecuted by enemies. If it attacks you, failure will bury you in gloom. If you succeed in warding it off, or killing it, you will be extremely successful in all your undertakings.

To see one running away from you, is a sign that you will overcome opposition, and rise to high positions.

To see them in cages, foretells that you will foil your adversaries.

To see rugs of tiger skins, denotes that you are in the way to enjoy luxurious ease and pleasure.

Till.

To dream of seeing money and valuables in a till, foretells coming success. Your love affairs will be exceedingly favorable. An empty one, denotes disappointed expectations.

Timber.*

To see timber in your dreams, is an augury of prosperous times and peaceful surroundings.

---

*See Forest.

If the timber appears dead, there are great disappointments for you.

Tipsy.

To dream that you are tipsy, denotes that you will cultivate a jovial disposition, and the cares of life will make no serious inroads into your conscience.

To see others tipsy, shows that you are careless as to the demeanor of your associates.

Toad.

To dream of toads, signifies unfortunate adventures. If a woman, your good name is threatened with scandal.

To kill a toad, foretells that your judgment will be harshly criticised.

To put your hands on them, you will be instrumental in causing the downfall of a friend.

Tobacco.

To dream of tobacco, denotes success in business affairs, but poor returns in love.

To use it, warns you against enemies and extravagance.

To see it growing, foretells successful enterprises. To see it dry in the leaf, ensures good crops to farmers, and consequent gain to tradesmen.

To smoke tobacco, denotes amiable friendships.

Tocsin.

To dream of hearing a tocsin sounded, augurs a strife from which you will come victorious. For a woman, this is a warning of separation from her husband or lover.

Toddy.

To dream of taking a toddy, foretells interesting events will soon change your plan of living.

Tomatoes.

To dream of eating tomatoes, signals the approach of good health. To see them growing, denotes domestic enjoyment and happiness.

For a young woman to see ripe ones, foretells her happiness in the married state.

Tomb.

To dream of seeing tombs, denotes sadness and disappointments in business.

Dilapidated tombs omens death or desperate illness.

To dream of seeing your own tomb, portends your individual sickness or disappointments.

To read the inscription on tombs, foretells unpleasant duties.

Tongue.

To dream of seeing your own tongue, denotes that you will be looked upon with disfavor by your acquaintances.

To see the tongue of another, foretells that scandal will villify you.

To dream that your tongue is affected in any way, denotes that your carelessness in talking will get you into trouble

Toothless.

To dream that you are toothless, denotes your inability to advance your interests, and ill health will cast gloom over your prospects.

To see others toothless, foretells that enemies are trying in vain to calumniate you.

Tooth-picks.

To dream of tooth-picks, foretells that small anxieties,

and spites will harass you unnecessarily if you give them your attention.

If you use one, you will be a party to a friend's injury.

Topaz.

To see topaz in a dream, signifies Fortune will be liberal in her favors, and you will have very pleasing companions. For a woman to lose topaz ornaments, foretells she will be injured by jealous friends who court her position. To receive one from another beside a relative, foretells an interesting love affair will occupy her attention.

Tops.

To dream of a top, denotes that you will be involved in frivolous difficulties.

To see one spinning, foretells that you will waste your means in childish pleasures.

To see a top, foretells indiscriminate friendships will involve you in difficulty.

Torch.*

To dream of seeing torches, foretells pleasant amusement and favorable business.

To carry a torch, denotes success in love making or intricate affairs. For one to go out, denotes failure and distress.

Tornado.†

If you dream that you are in a tornado, you will be filled with disappointment and perplexity over the miscarriage of studied plans for swift attainment of fortune.

Torrent.

To dream that you are looking upon a rushing torrent, denotes that you will have unusual trouble and anxiety.

---

*See Lantern and Lamp.   †See Hurricane.

Torture.

To dream of being tortured, denotes that you will undergo disappointment and grief through the machination of false friends.

If you are torturing others, you will fail to carry out well-laid plans for increasing your fortune.

If you are trying to alleviate the torture of others, you will succeed after a struggle in business and love.

Tourist.

To dream that you are a tourist, denotes that you will engage in some pleasurable affair which will take you away from your usual residence.

To see tourists, indicates brisk but unsettled business and anxiety in love.

Tower.*

To dream of seeing a tower, denotes that you will aspire to high elevations. If you climb one, you will succeed in your wishes, but if the tower crumbles as you descend, you will be disappointed in your hopes.

Toys.

To see toys in dreams, foretells family joys, if whole and new, but if broken, death will rend your heart with sorrow.

To see children at play with toys, marriage of a happy nature is indicated.

To give away toys in your dreams, foretells you will be ignored in a social way by your acquaintances.

Trade.

To dream of trading, denotes fair success in your enterprise. If you fail, trouble and annoyances will overtake you.

* See Ladder.

Tragedy.

To dream of a tragedy, foretells misunderstandings and grievous disappointments.

To dream that you are implicated in a tragedy, portends that a calamity will plunge you into sorrow and peril.

Train.

To see a train of cars moving in your dreams, you will soon have cause to make a journey.

To be on a train and it appears to move smoothly along, though there is no track, denotes that you will be much worried over some affair which will eventually prove a source of profit to you.

To see freight trains in your dreams, is an omen of changes which will tend to your elevation.

To find yourself, in a dream, on top of a sleeping car, denotes you will make a journey with an unpleasant companion, with whom you will spend money and time that could be used in a more profitable and congenial way, and whom you will seek to avoid.

Traitor.

To see a traitor in your dream, foretells you will have enemies working to despoil you. If some one calls you one, or if you imagine yourself one, there will be unfavorable prospects of pleasure for you.

Transfiguration.

To dream of the transfiguration, foretells that your faith in man's own nearness to God will raise you above trifling opinions, and elevate you to a worthy position, in which capacity you will be able to promote the well being of the ignorant and persecuted.

To see yourself transfigured, you will stand high in the esteem of honest and prominent men.

Trap.

To dream of setting a trap, denotes that you will use intrigue to carry out your designs.

If you are caught in a trap, you will be outwitted by your opponents.

If you catch game in a trap, you will flourish in whatever vocation you may choose.

To see an empty trap, there will be misfortune in the immediate future.

An old or broken trap, denotes failure in business, and sickness in your family may follow.

Traveling.*

To dream of traveling, signifies profit and pleasure combined. To dream of traveling through rough unknown places, portends dangerous enemies, and perhaps sickness. Over bare or rocky steeps, signifies apparent gain, but loss and disappointment will swiftly follow. If the hills or mountains are fertile and green, you will be eminently prosperous and happy.

To dream you travel alone in a car, denotes you may possibly make an eventful journey, and affairs will be worrying. To travel in a crowded car, foretells fortunate adventures, and new and entertaining companions.

Tray.

To see trays in your dream, denotes your wealth will be foolishly wasted, and surprises of unpleasant nature will shock you. If the trays seem to be filled with valuables, surprises will come in the shape of good fortune.

*See Journey.

Treasures.

To dream that you find treasures, denotes that you will be greatly aided in your pursuit of fortune by some unexpected generosity.

If you lose treasures, bad luck in business and the inconstancy of friends is foretold.

Trees.*

To dream of trees in new foliage, foretells a happy consummation of hopes and desires. Dead trees signal sorrow and loss.

To climb a tree is a sign of swift elevation and preferment.

To cut one down, or pull it up by the roots, denotes that you will waste your energies and wealth foolishly.

To see green trees newly felled, portends unhappiness coming unexpectedly upon scenes of enjoyment, or prosperity.

Trenches.†

To see trenches in dreams, warns you of distant treachery. You will sustain loss if not careful in undertaking new enterprises, or associating with strangers.

To see filled trenches, denotes many anxieties are gathering around you.

Triangle.

To dream of a triangle, foretells separation from friends, and love affairs will terminate in disagreements.

Tripe.

To see tripe in a dream, means sickness and danger.

To eat tripe, denotes that you will be disappointed in some serious matter.

---

*See Forest.   †See Ditch.

Triplets.

To dream of seeing triplets, foretells success in affairs where failure was feared.

For a man to dream that his wife has them, signifies a pleasant termination to some affair which has been long in dispute.

To hear newly-born triplets crying, signifies disagreements which will be hastily reconciled to your pleasure.

For a young woman to dream that she has triplets, denotes that she will suffer loss and disappointment in love, but will succeed to wealth.

Trophy.

To see trophies in a dream, signifies some pleasure or fortune will come to you through the endeavors of mere acquaintances. For a woman to give away a trophy, implies doubtful pleasures and fortune.

Trousers.

To dream of trousers, foretells that you will be tempted to dishonorable deeds.

If you put them on wrong side out, you will find that a fascination is fastening its hold upon you.

Trout.

To dream of seeing trout, is significant of growing prosperity. To eat some, denotes that you will be happily conditioned.

To catch one with a hook, foretells assured pleasure and competence. If it falls back into the water, you will have a short season of happiness.

To catch them with a seine, is a sign of unparalleled prosperity.

To see them in muddy water shows that your success in love will bring you to grief and disappointments.

Trowel.

To dream of a trowel, denotes you will experience reaction in unfavorable business, and will vanquish poverty. To see one rusty or broken, unavoidable ill luck is fast approaching you.

Trumpet.

To dream of a trumpet, denotes that something of unusual interest is about to befall you.

To blow a trumpet, signifies that you will gain your wishes.

Trunk.

To dream of trunks, foretells journeys and ill luck. To pack your trunk, denotes that you will soon go on a pleasant trip.

To see the contents of a trunk thrown about in disorder, foretells quarrels, and a hasty journey from which only dissatisfaction will accrue.

Empty trunks foretell disappointment in love and marriage.

For a drummer to check his trunk, is an omen of advancement and comfort. If he finds that his trunk is too small for his wares, he will soon hear of his promotion, and his desires will reach gratification. For a young woman to dream that she tries to unlock her trunk and can't, signifies that she will make an effort to win some wealthy person, but by a misadventure she will lose her chance. If she fails to lock her trunk, she will be disappointed in making a desired trip.

Truss.

To see a truss in your dream, your ill health and unfortunate business engagements are predicted.

Trusts.

To dream of trusts, foretells indifferent success in trade or law.

If you imagine you are a member of a trust, you will be successful in designs of a speculative nature.

Tub.

To dream of seeing a tub full of water, denotes domestic contentment. An empty tub proclaims unhappiness and waning of fortune.

A broken tub, foretells family disagreements and quarrels.

Tumble.

To dream that you tumble off of any thing, denotes that you are given to carelessness, and should strive to be prompt with your affairs.

To see others tumbliing, is a sign that you will profit by the negligence of others.

Tunnel.

To dream of going through a tunnel is bad for those in business and in love.

To see a train coming towards you while in a tunnel, foretells ill health and change in occupation.

To pass through a tunnel in a car, denotes unsatisfactory business, and much unpleasant and expensive travel.

To see a tunnel caving in, portends failure and malignant enemies.

To look into one, denotes that you will soon be compelled to face a desperate issue.

Turf.

To dream of a racing turf, signifies that you will have

pleasure and wealth at your command, but your morals will be questioned by your most intimate friends.

To see a green turf, indicates that interesting affairs will hold your attention.

Turkey.

To dream of seeing turkeys, signifies abundant gain in business, and favorable crops to the farmer.

To see them dressed for the market, denotes improvement in your affairs.

To see them sick, or dead, foretells that stringent circumstances will cause your pride to suffer.

To dream you eat turkey, foretells some joyful occasion approaching.

To see them flying, denotes a rapid transit from obscurity to prominence. To shoot them as game, is a sign that you will unscrupulously amass wealth.

Turkish Baths.

To dream of taking a Turkish bath, foretells that you will seek health far from your home and friends, but you will have much pleasurable enjoyment.

To see others take a Turkish bath, signifies that pleasant companions will occupy your attention.

Turnips.

To see turnips growing, denotes that your prospects will brighten, and that you will be much elated over your success.

To eat them is a sign of ill health. To pull them up, denotes that you will improve your opportunities and your fortune thereby.

To eat turnip greens, is a sign of bitter disappointment. Turnip seed is a sign of future advancement.

For a young woman to sow turnip seed, foretells that

she will inherit good property, and win a handsome husband.

Turpentine.

To dream of turpentine, foretells your near future holds unprofitable and discouraging engagements. For a woman to dream that she binds turpentine to the wound of another, shows she will gain friendships and favor through her benevolent acts.

Turquoise.

To dream of a torquoise, foretells you are soon to realize some desire which will greatly please your relatives. For a woman to have one stolen, foretells she will meet with crosses in love. If she comes by it dishonestly, she must suffer for yielding to hasty susceptibility in love.

Turtle.

To dream of seeing turtles, signifies that an unusual incident will cause you enjoyment, and improve your business conditions.

To drink turtle soup, denotes that you will find pleasure in compromising intrigue.

Tweezers.

To see tweezers in a dream, denotes uncomfortable situations will fill you with discontent, and your companions will abuse you.

Twine.*

To see twine in your dream, warns you that your business is assuming complications which will be hard to overcome.

*See Thread.

Twins.

To dream of seeing twins, foretells security in business, and faithful and loving contentment in the home.

If they are sickly, it signifies that you will have disappointment and grief.

Type.

To see type in a dream, portends unpleasant transactions with friends. For a woman to clean type, foretells she will make fortunate speculations which will bring love and fortune.

Typhoid.

To dream that you are affected with this malady, is a warning to beware of enemies, and look well to your health.

If you dream that there is an epidemic of typhoid, there will be depressions in business, and usual good health will undergo disagreeable changes.

U.

"And Solomon awoke; and, behold, it was a dream."—First Kings, III., 15.

Ugly.

To dream that you are ugly, denotes that you will have a difficulty with your sweetheart, and your prospects will assume a depressed shade.

If a young woman thinks herself ugly, she will conduct herself offensively toward her lover, which will probably cause a break in their pleasant associations.

Ulcer.

To see an ulcer in your dream, signifies loss of friends

and removal from loved ones   Affairs will remain unsatisfactory.

To dream that you have ulcers, denotes that you will become unpopular with your friends by giving yourself up to foolish pleasures.

Umbrella.

To dream of carrying an umbrella, denotes that trouble and annoyances will beset you.

To see others carrying them, foretells that you will be appealed to for aid by charity.

To borrow one, you will have a misunderstanding, perhaps, with a warm friend.

To lend one, portends injury from false friends. To lose one, denotes trouble with some one who holds your confidence.

To see one torn to pieces, or broken, foretells that you will be misrepresented and maligned.

To carry a leaky one, denotes that pain and displeasure will be felt by you towards your sweetheart or companions.

To carry a new umbrella over you in a clear shower, or sunshine, omens exquisite pleasure and prosperity.

Uncle.

If you see your uncle in a dream, you will have news of a sad character soon.

To dream you see your uncle prostrated in mind, and repeatedly have this dream, you will have trouble with your relations which will result in estrangement, at least for a time.

To see your uncle dead, denotes that you have formidable enemies.

To have a misunderstanding with your uncle, denotes

that your family relations will be unpleasant, and illness will be continually present.

Underground.*

To dream of being in an underground habitation, you are in danger of losing reputation and fortune.

To dream of riding on an underground railway, foretells that you will engage in some peculiar speculation which will contribute to your distress and anxiety.

Undress.

To dream that you are undressing, foretells, scandalous gossip will overshadow you.

For a woman to dream that she sees the ruler of her country undressed, signifies sadness will overtake anticipated pleasures. She will suffer pain through the apprehension of evil to those dear to her.

To see others undressed, is an omen of stolen pleasures, which will rebound with grief.

Unfortunate.

To dream that you are unfortunate, is significant of loss to yourself, and trouble for others.

Uniform.

To see a uniform in your dream, denotes that you will have influential friends to aid you in obtaining your desires.

For a young woman to dream that she wears a uniform, foretells that she will luckily confer her favors upon a man who appreciated them, and returns love for passion. If she discards it, she will be in danger of public scandal by her notorious love for adventure.

To see people arrayed in strange uniforms, foretells

---

*See Cars, etc.

the disruption of friendly relations with some other Power by your own government. This may also apply to families or friends. To see a friend or relative looking sad while dressed in uniform, or as a soldier, predicts ill fortune or continued absence.

United States Mail Box.

To see a United States mail box, in a dream. denotes that you are about to enter into transactions which will be claimed to be illegal.

To put a letter in one, denotes you will be held responsible for some irregularity of another.

Unknown.*

To dream of meeting unknown persons, foretells change for good, or bad as the person is good looking, or ugly, or deformed.

To feel that you are unknown, denotes that strange things will cast a shadow of ill luck over you.

Urgent.

To dream that you are supporting an urgent petition, is a sign that you will engage in some affair which will need fine financiering to carry it through successfully.

Urinal.

To dream of a urinal, disorder will predominate in your home.

Urine.

To dream of seeing urine, denotes ill health will make you disagreeable and unpleasant with your friends.

To dream that you are urinating, is an omen of bad luck, and trying seasons to love.

---

*See Mystery.

Urn.

To dream of an urn, foretells you will prosper in some respects, and in others disfavor will be apparent. To see broken urns, unhappiness will confront you.

Usurer.

To find yourself a usurer in your dreams, foretells that you will be treated with coldness by your associates, and your business will decline to your consternation.

If others are usurers, you will discard some former friend on account of treachery.

Usurper.

To dream that you are a usurper, foretells you will have trouble in establishing a good title to property.

If others are trying to usurp your rights, there will be a struggle between you and your competitors, but you will eventually win.

For a young woman to have this dream, she will be a party to a spicy rivalry, in which she will win.

V.

"Where there is no vision, the people perish; but he that keepeth the law, happy is he."—Prov. xxix., 18.

Vaccinate.

To dream of being vaccinated, foretells that your susceptibility to female charms will be played upon to your sorrow.

To dream that others are vaccinated, shows you will fail to find contentment where it is sought, and your affairs will suffer decline in consequence.

For a young woman to be vaccinated on her leg, fore-shadows her undoing through treachery.

Vagrant.

To dream that you are a vagrant, portends poverty and misery. To see vagrants is a sign of contagion invading your community. To give to a vagrant, denotes that your generosity will be applauded.

Valentine.

To dream that you are sending valentines, foretells that you will lose opportunities of enriching yourself.

For a young woman to receive one, denotes that she will marry a weak, but ardent lover against the counsels of her guardians.

Valley.

To find yourself walking through green and pleasant valleys, foretells great improvements in business, and lovers will be happy and congenial. If the valley is barren, the reverse is predicted. If marshy, illness or vexations may follow.

Vapor Bath.

To dream of a vapor bath, you will have fretful people for companions, unless you dream of emerging from one, and then you will find that your cares will be temporary.

Varnishing.

To dream of varnishing anything, denotes that you will seek to win distinction by fraudulent means.

To see others varnishing, foretells that you are threatened with danger from the endeavor of friends to add to their own possessions.

Vase.

To dream of a vase, denotes that you will enjoy sweetest pleasure and contentment in the home life.

To drink from a vase, you will soon thrill with the delights of stolen love.

To see a broken vase, foretells early sorrow. For a young woman to receive one, signifies that she will soon obtain her dearest wish.

Vat.

To see a vat in your dreams, foretells anguish and suffering from the hands of cruel persons, into which you have unwittingly fallen.

Vatican.

To dream of the vatican, signifies unexpected favors will fall within your grasp. You will form the acquaintance of distinguished people, if you see royal personages speaking to the Pope.

Vault.

To dream of a vault, denotes bereavement and other misfortune. To see a vault for valuables, signifies your fortune will surprise many, as your circumstances will appear to be meagre. To see the doors of a vault open, implies loss and treachery of people whom you trust.

Vegetables.

To dream of eating vegetables, is an omen of strange luck. You will think for a time that you are tremendously successful, but will find to your sorrow that you have been grossly imposed upon.

Withered, or decayed vegetables, bring unmitigated woe and sadness.

For a young woman to dream that she is preparing vegetables for dinner, foretells that she will lose the man she desired through pique, but she will win a well-meaning and faithful husband. Her engagements will be somewhat disappointing.

Vehicle.

To ride in a vehicle while dreaming, foretells threatened loss, or illness.

To be thrown from one, foretells hasty and unpleasant news. To see a broken one, signals failure in important affairs.

To buy one, you will reinstate yourself in your former position. To sell one, denotes unfavorable change in affairs.

Veil.

To dream that you wear a veil, denotes that you will not be perfectly sincere with your lover, and you will be forced to use stratagem to retain him.

To see others wearing veils, you will be maligned and defamed by apparent friends.

An old, or torn veil, warns you that deceit is being thrown around you with sinister design.

For a young woman to dream that she loses her veil, denotes that her lover sees through her deceitful ways and is likely to retaliate with the same.

To dream of seeing a bridal veil, foretells that you will make a successful change in the immediate future, and much happiness in your position.

For a young woman to dream that she wears a bridal veil, denotes that she will engage in some affair which will afford her lasting profit and enjoyment. If it gets loose, or any accident befalls it, she will be burdened with sadness and pain.

To throw a veil aside, indicates separation or disgrace.

To see mourning veils in your dreams, signifies distress and trouble, and embarrassment in business.

Vein.

To see your veins in a dream, insures you against slander, if they are normal.

To see them bleeding, denotes that you will have a great sorrow from which there will be no escape.

To see them swollen, you will rise hastily to distinction and places of trust.

Velvet.

To dream of velvet, portends very successful enterprises. If you wear it, some distinction will be conferred upon you.

To see old velvet, means your prosperity will suffer from your extreme pride.

If a young woman dreams that she is clothed in velvet garments, it denotes that she will have honors bestowed upon her, and the choice between several wealthy lovers.

Veneer.

To dream that you are veneering, denotes that you will systematically deceive your friends, your speculations will be of a misleading nature.

Ventriloquist.

To dream of a ventriloquist, denotes that some treasonable affair is going to prove detrimental to your interest.

If you think yourself one, you will not conduct yourself honorably towards people who trust you.

For a young woman to dream she is mystified by the voice of a ventriloquist, foretells that she will be deceived into illicit adventures.

Veranda.

To dream of being on a veranda, denotes that you are to be successful in some affair which is giving you anxiety.

For a young woman to be with her lover on a veranda, denotes her early and happy marriage.

To see an old veranda, denotes the decline of hopes, and disappointment in business and love.

Vermin.*

Vermin crawling in your dreams, signifies sickness and much trouble. If you succeed in ridding yourself of them, you will be fairly successful, but otherwise death may come to you. or your relatives.

Vertigo.

To dream that you have vertigo, foretells you will have loss in domestic happiness, and your affairs will be under gloomy outlooks.

Vessels.†

To dream of vessels, denotes labor and activity.

Vexed.

If you are vexed in your dreams, you will find many worries scattered through your early awakening.

If you think some person is vexed with you, it is a sign that you will not shortly reconcile some slight misunderstanding.

Vicar.

To dream of a vicar, foretells that you will do foolish things while furious with jealousy and envy.

For a young woman to dream she marries a vicar, foretells that she will fail to awake reciprocal affection in the man she desires, and will live a spinster, or marry to keep from being one.

Vice.

To dream that you are favoring any vice, signifies you

*See Locust.   †See Ships and similar words.

are about to endanger your reputation, by letting evil persuasions entice you.

If you see others indulging in vice, some ill fortune will engulf the interest of some relative or associate.

Victim.

To dream that you are the victim of any scheme, foretells that you will be oppressed and over-powered by your enemies. Your family relations will also be strained.

To victimize others, denotes that you will amass wealth dishonorably and prefer illicit relations, to the sorrow of your companions.

Victory.

To dream that you win a victory, foretells that you will successfully resist the attacks of enemies, and will have the love of women for the asking.

Village.

To dream that you are in a village, denotes that you will enjoy good health and find yourself fortunately provided for.

To revisit the village home of your youth, denotes that you will have pleasant surprises in store and favorable news from absent friends.

If the village looks dilapidated, or the dream indistinct, it foretells that trouble and sadness will soon come to you.

Vine.

To dream of vines, is propitious of success and happiness. Good health is in store for those who see flowering vines. If they are dead, you will fail in some momentous enterprise.

To see poisonous vines, foretells that you will be the victim of a plausible scheme and you will impair your health.

Vinegar.

To dream of drinking vinegar, denotes that you will be exasperated and worried into assenting to some engagement which will fill you with evil foreboding.

To use vinegar on vegetables, foretells a deepening of already distressing affairs.

To dream of vinegar at all times, denotes inharmonious and unfavorable aspects.

Vineyard.

To dream of a vineyard, denotes favorable speculations and auspicious love-making.

To visit a vineyard which is not well-kept and filled with bad odors, denotes disappointment will overshadow your most sanguine anticipations.

Violence.

To dream that any person does you violence, denotes that you will be overcome by enemies.

If you do some other persons violence, you will lose fortune and favor by your reprehensible way of conducting your affairs.

Violets.

To see violets in your dreams, or gather them, brings joyous occas..ns in which you will find favor with some superior person.

For a young woman to gather them, denotes that she will soon meet her future husband.

To see them dry, or withered, denotes that her love will be scorned and thrown aside.

Violin.

To see, or hear a violin in dreams, foretells harmony

and peace in the family, and financial affairs will cause no apprehension.

For a young woman to play on one in her dreams, denotes that she will be honored and receive lavish gifts.

If her attempt to play is unsuccessful, she will lose favor, and aspire to things she never can possess.

A broken one, indicates sad bereavement and separation.

Viper.

To dream of a viper, foretells that calamities are threatening you. To dream that a many-hued viper, and capable of throwing itself into many pieces, or unjointing itself, attacks you, denotes that your enemies are bent on your ruin and will work unitedly, yet apart, to displace you.

Virgin.

To dream of a virgin, denotes that you will have comparative luck in your speculations. For a married woman to dream that she is a virgin, foretells that she will suffer remorse over her past, and the future wil' hold no promise of better things.

For a young woman to dream that sne is no longer a virgin, foretells that she will run great risk of losing her reputation by being indiscreet with her male friends.

For a man to dream of illicit association with a virgin, denotes that he will fail to accomplish an enterprise, and much worry will be caused him by the appeals of people. His aspirations will be foiled through unwarranted associations.

Visit.

If you visit in your dreams, you will shortly have some pleasant occasion in your life.

If your visit is unpleasant, your enjoyment will be marred by the action of malicious persons.

For a friend to visit you, denotes that news of a favorable nature will soon reach you. If the friend appears sad and travel-worn, there will be a note of displeasure growing out of the visit, or other slight disappointments may follow. If she is dressed in black or white and looks pale or ghastly, serious illness or accidents are predicted.

Visions.

To dream that you have a strange vision, denotes that you will be unfortunate in your dealings and sickness will unfit you for pleasant duties.

If persons appear to you in visions, it foretells uprising and strife of families or state.

If your friend is near dissolution and you are warned in a vision, he will appear suddenly before you, usually in white garments. Visions of death and trouble have such close resemblance, that they are sometimes mistaken one for the other.

To see visions of any order in your dreams, you may look for unusual developments in your business, and a different atmosphere and surroundings in private life. Things will be reversed for a while with you. You will have changes in your business and private life seemingly bad, but eventually good for all concerned.

The Supreme Will is always directed toward the ultimate good of the race.

Vitriol.

If you see vitriol in your dreams, it is a token of some innocent person being censured by you.

To throw it on people, shows you will bear malice towards parties who seek to favor you.

For a young woman to have a jealous rival throw it in her face, foretells that she will be the innocent object of some person's hatred. This dream for a business man, denotes enemies and much persecution.

Voice.

To dream of hearing voices, denotes pleasant reconciliations, if they are calm and pleasing; high-pitched and angry voices, signify disappointments and unfavorable situations.

To hear weeping voices, shows that sudden anger will cause you to inflict injury upon a friend.

If you hear the voice of God, you will make a noble effort to rise higher in unselfish and honorable principles, and will justly hold the admiration of high-minded people.

For a mother to hear the voice of her child, is a sign of approaching misery, perplexity and grievous doubts.

To hear the voice of distress, or a warning one calling to you, implies your own serious misfortune or that of some one close to you. If the voice is recognized, it is often ominous of accident or illness, which may eliminate death or loss.

Volcano.

To see a volcano in your dreams, signifies that you will be in violent disputes, which threaten your reputation as a fair dealing and honest citizen.

For a young woman, it means that her selfishness and greed will lead her into intricate adventures.

Vomit.

To dream of vomiting, is a sign that you will be afflicted with a malady which will threaten invalidism, or you will be connected with a racy scandal.

To see others vomiting, denotes that you will be made aware of the false pretenses of persons who are trying to engage your aid.

For a woman to dream that she vomits a chicken, and it hops off, denotes she will be disappointed in some pleasure by the illness of some relative. Unfavorable business and discontent are also predicted.

If it is blood you vomit, you will find illness a hurried and unexpected visitor. You will be cast down with gloomy forebodings, and children and domesticity in general will ally to work you discomfort.

Vote.

If you dream of casting a vote on any measure, you will be engulfed in a commotion which will affect your community.

To vote fraudulently, foretells that your dishonesty will overcome your better inclinations.

Voucher.

To dream of vouchers, foretells that patient toil will defeat idle scheming to arrest fortune from you.

To sign one, denotes that you have the aid and confidence of those around you, despite the evil workings of enemies.

To lose one, signifies that you will have a struggle for your rights with relatives.

Vow.

To dream that you are making or listening to vows, foretells complaint will be made against you of unfaithfulness in business, or some love contract. To take the vows of a church, denotes you will bear yourself with unswerving integrity through some difficulty.

To break or ignore a vow, foretells disastrous consequences will attend your dealings.

Voyage.

To make a voyage in your dreams, foretells that you will receive some inheritance besides that which your labors win for you.

A disastrous voyage brings incompetence, and false loves.

Vultures.

To dream of vultures, signifies that some scheming person is bent on injuring you, and will not succeed unless you see the vulture wounded, or dead.

For a woman to dream of a vulture, signifies that she will be overwhelmed with slander and gossip.

W.

"Therefore night shall be unto you, that ye shall not have a vision, and it shall be dark unto you, that ye shall not divine; and the sun shall go down over the prophets, and the day shall be dark over them."—Mich. iii., 6.

Wading.*

If you wade in clear water while dreaming, you will partake of evanescent, but exquisite joys. If the water is muddy, you are in danger of illness, or some sorrowful experiences.

To see children wading in clear water is a happy prognostication, as you will be favored in your enterprises.

For a young woman to dream of wading in clear foaming water, she will soon gain the desire nearest her heart.

Wadding.

Wadding, if seen in a dream, brings consolation to the sorrowing, and indifference to unfriendly criticism.

---

*See Bathing.

585

Wafer.

Wafer, if seen in a dream, purports an encounter with enemies. To eat one, suggests impoverished fortune.

For a young woman to bake them, denotes that she will be tormented and distressed by fears of remaining in the unmarried state.

Wager.

To dream of making a wager, signifies that you will resort to dishonest means to forward your schemes.

If you lose a wager, you will sustain injury from base connections with those out of your social sphere.

To win one, reinstates you in favor with fortune.

If you are not able to put up a wager, you will be discouraged and prostrated by the adverseness of circumstances.

Wages.

Wages, if received in dreams, brings unlooked for good to persons engaging in new enterprises.

To pay out wages, denotes that you will be confounded by dissatisfaction.

To have your wages reduced, warns you of unfriendly interest that is being taken against you.

An increase of wages, suggests unusual profit in any undertaking.

Wagon.

To dream of a wagon, denotes that you will be unhappily mated, and many troubles will prematurely age you.

To drive one down a hill, is ominous of proceedings which will fill you with disquiet, and will cause you loss.

To drive one up hill, improves your worldly affairs.

To drive a heavily loaded wagon, denotes that duty

will hold you in a moral position, despite your efforts to throw her off.

To drive into muddy water, is a gruesome prognostication, bringing you into a vortex of unhappiness and fearful foreboding.

To see a covered wagon, foretells that you will be encompassed by mysterious treachery, which will retard your advancement.

For a young woman to dream that she drives a wagon near a dangerous embankment, portends that she will be driven into an illicit entanglement, which will fill her with terror, lest she be openly discovered and ostracised. If she drives across a clear stream of water, she will enjoy adventure without bringing opprobrium upon herself.

A broken wagon represents distress and failure.

Wagtail.

To see a wagtail in a dream, foretells that you will be the victim of unpleasant gossip, and your affairs will develop unmistakable loss.

Waif.

To dream of a waif, denotes personal difficulties, and especial ill-luck in business.

Wail.*

A wail falling upon your ear while in the midst of a dream, brings fearful news of disaster and woe.

For a young woman to hear a wail, foretells that she will be deserted and left alone in distress, and perchance disgrace.

Waist and Shirt-Waist.

To dream of a round full waist, denotes that you will be favored by an agreeable dispensation of fortune.

---

*See Weeping.

A small, unnatural waist, foretells displeasing success and recriminating disputes.

For a young woman to dream of a nice, ready-made shirt-waist, denotes that she will win admiration through her ingenuity and pleasing manners.

To dream that her shirt-waist is torn, she will be censured for her illicit engagements. If she is trying on a shirt-waist, she will encounter rivalry in love, but if she succeeds in adjusting the waist to her person, she will successfully combat the rivalry and win the object of her love.

Waiter.

To dream of a waiter, signifies you will be pleasantly entertained by a friend. To see one cross or disorderly, means offensive people will thrust themselves upon your hospitality.

Wake.

To dream that you attend a wake, denotes that you will sacrifice some important engagement to enjoy some ill-favored assignation.

For a young woman to see her lover at a wake, foretells that she will listen to the entreaties of passion, and will be persuaded to hazard honor for love.

Walking.*

To dream of walking through rough brier, entangled paths, denotes that you will be much distressed over your business complications, and disagreeable misunderstandings will produce coldness and indifference.

To walk in pleasant places, you will be the possessor of fortune and favor.

To walk in the night brings misadventure, and unavailing struggle for contentment.

*See Wading.

For a young woman to find herself walking rapidly in her dreams, denotes that she will inherit some property, and will possess a much desired object.

Walking Stick.

To see a walking stick in a dream, foretells you will enter into contracts without proper deliberation, and will consequently suffer reverses. If you use one in walking, you will be dependent upon the advice of others. To admire handsome ones, you will entrust your interest to others, but they will be faithful.

Wallet.

To see wallets in a dream, foretells burdens of a pleasant nature will await your discretion as to assuming them. An old or soiled one, implies unfavorable results from your labors.

Walls.

To dream that you find a wall obstructing your progress, you will surely succumb to ill-favored influences and lose important victories in your affairs.

To jump over it, you will overcome obstacles and win your desires. To force a breach in a wall, you will succeed in the attainment of your wishes by sheer tenacity of purpose.

To demolish one, you will overthrow your enemies. To build one, foretells that you will carefully lay plans and will solidify your fortune to the exclusion of failure. or designing enemies.

For a young woman to walk on top of a wall, shows that her future happiness will soon be made secure. For her to hide behind a wall, denotes that she will form connections that she will be ashamed to acknowledge. If she walks beside a base wall, she will soon have run the gamut of her attractions, and will likely be deserted at a precarious time.

Walnut.

To dream of walnuts, is an omen significant of prolific joys and favors.

To dream that you crack a decayed walnut, denotes that your expectations will end in bitterness and regretable collapse.

For a young woman to dream that she has walnut stain on her hands, foretells that she will see her lover turn his attention to another, and she will entertain only regrets for her past indiscreet conduct.

Waltz.

To see the waltz danced, foretells that you will have pleasant relations with a cheerful and adventuresome person.

For a young woman to waltz with her lover, denotes that she will be the object of much admiration, but none will seek her for a wife. If she sees her lover waltzing with a rival, she will overcome obstacles to her desires with strategy. If she waltzes with a woman, she will be loved for her virtues and winning ways. If she sees persons whirling in the waltz as if intoxicated, she will be engulfed so deeply in desire and pleasure that it will be a miracle if she resists the impassioned advances of her lover and male acquaintances.

Want.

To dream that you are in want, denotes that you have unfortunately ignored the realities of life, and chased folly to her stronghold of sorrow and adversity.

If you find yourself contented in a state of want, you will bear the misfortune which threatens you with heroism, and will see the clouds of misery disperse.

To relieve want, signifies that you will be esteemed for your disinterested kindness, but you will feel no pleasure in well doing.

War.

To dream of war, foretells unfortunate conditions in business, and much disorder and strife in domestic affairs.

For a young woman to dream that her lover goes to war, denotes that she will hear of something detrimental to her lover's character.

To dream that your country is defeated in war, is a sign that it will suffer revolution of a business and political nature. Personal interest will sustain a blow either way.

If of victory you dream, there will be brisk activity along business lines, and domesticity will be harmonious.

Wardrobe.

To dream of your wardrobe, denotes that your fortune will be endangered by your attempts to appear richer than you are.

If you imagine you have a scant wardrobe, you will seek association with strangers.

Warehouse.

To dream of a warehouse, denotes for you a successful enterprise. To see an empty one, is a sign that you will be cheated and foiled in some plan which you have given much thought and maneuvering.

Warrant.

To dream that a warrant is being served on you, denotes that you will engage in some important work which will give you great uneasiness as to its standing and profits.

To see a warrant served on some one else, there will be danger of your actions bringing you into fatal quarrels or misunderstandings. You are likely to be justly indignant with the wantonness of some friend.

Warts.

If you are troubled with warts on your person, in dreams, you will be unable to successfully parry the thrusts made at your honor.

To see them leaving your hands, foretells that you will overcome disagreeable obstructions to fortune.

To see them on others, shows that you have bitter enemies near you. If you doctor them, you will struggle with energy to ward off threatened danger to you and yours.

Washboard.

To see a washboard in your dreams, is indicative of embarrassment. If you see a woman using one, it predicts that you will let women rob you of energy and fortune.

A broken one, portends that you will come to grief and disgraceful deeds through fast living.

Wash-bowl.

To dream of a wash-bowl, signifies that new cares will interest you, and afford much enjoyment to others.

To bathe your face and hands in a bowl of clear water, denotes that you will soon consummate passionate wishes which will bind you closely to some one who interested you, but before passion enveloped you.

If the bowl is soiled, or broken, you will rue an illicit engagement, which will give others pain, and afford you small pleasure.

Washer Woman.

A washer woman seen in dreams, represents infidelity and a strange adventure. For the business man, or farmer, this dream indicates expanding trade and fine crops. For a woman to dream that she is a washer woman, denotes that she will throw decorum aside in her persistent effort to hold the illegal favor of men.

Washing.*

To dream that you are washing yourself, signifies that you pride yourself on the numberless liaisons you maintain.

Wasp.

Wasps, if seen in dreams, denotes that enemies will scourge and spitefully villify you.

If one stings you, you will feel the effect of envy and hatred. To kill them, you will be able to throttle your enemies, and fearlessly maintain your rights.

Waste.

To dream of wandering through waste places, foreshadows doubt and failure, where promise of success was bright before you.

To dream of wasting your fortune, denotes you will be unpleasantly encumbered with domestic cares.

Watch.

To dream of a watch, denotes you will be prosperous in well-directed speculations. To look at the time of one, your efforts will be defeated by rivalry. To break one, there will be distress and loss menacing you.

To drop the crystal of one, foretells carelessness, or unpleasant companionship. For a woman to lose one,

*See Wash Bowl or Bathing.

signifies domestic disturbances will produce unhappiness. To imagine you steal one, you will have a violent enemy who will attack your reputation.

To make a present of one, denotes you will suffer your interest to decline in the pursuance of undignified recreations.

Water.

To dream of clear water, foretells that you will joyfully realize prosperity and pleasure.

If the water is muddy, you will be in danger and gloom will occupy Pleasure's seat.

If you see it rise up in your house, denotes that you will struggle to resist evil, but unless you see it subside, you will succumb to dangerous influences.

If you find yourself baling it out, but with feet growing wet, foreshadows trouble, sickness, and misery will work you a hard task, but you will forestall them by your watchfulness. The same may be applied to muddy water rising in vessels.

To fall into muddy water, is a sign that you will make many bitter mistakes, and will suffer poignant grief therefrom.

To drink muddy water, portends sickness, but drinking it clear and refreshing brings favorable consummation of fair hopes.

To sport with water, denotes a sudden awakening to love and passion.

To have it sprayed on your head, denotes that your passionate awakening to love will meet reciprocal consummation.

The following dream and its allegorical occurrence in actual life is related by a young woman student of dreams:

"Without knowing how, I was (in my dream) on a

boat, I waded through clear blue water to a wharf-boat, which I found to be snow white, but rough and splintry. The next evening I had a delightful male caller, but he remained beyond the time prescribed by mothers and I was severely censured for it." The blue water and fairy white boat were the disappointing prospects in the symbol.

Water-carrier.

To see water-carriers passing in your dreams, denotes that your prospects will be favorable in fortune, and love will prove no laggard in your chase for pleasure.

If you think you are a water-carrier, you will rise above your present position.

Waterfall.

To dream of a waterfall, foretells that you will secure your wildest desire, and fortune will be exceedingly favorable to your progress.

Water Lily.

To dream of a water lily, or to see them growing, foretells there will be a close commingling of prosperity and sorrow or bereavement.

Waves.*

To dream of waves, is a sign that you hold some vital step in contemplation, which will evolve much knowledge if the waves are clear; but you will make a fatal error if you see them muddy or lashed by a storm.

Wax Taper.

To dream of lighting wax tapers, denotes that some pleasing occurrence will bring you into association with friends long absent.

---

*See Ocean and Sea.

To blow them out, signals disappointing times, and sickness will forestall expected opportunities of meeting distinguished friends.

Way.*

To dream you lose your way, warns you to disabuse your mind of lucky speculations, as your enterprises threaten failure unless you are painstaking in your management of affairs.

Wealth.

To dream that you are possessed of much wealth, foretells that you will energetically nerve yourself to meet the problems of life with that force which compells success.

To see others wealthy, foretells that you will have friends who will come to your rescue in perilous times.

For a young woman to dream that she is associated with wealthy people, denotes that she will have high aspirations and will manage to enlist some one who is able to further them.

Weasel.

To see a weasel bent on a marauding expedition in your dreams, warns you to beware of the friendships of former enemies, as they will devour you at an unseemly time.

If you destroy them, you will succeed in foiling deep schemes laid for your defeat.

Weather.

To dream of the weather, foretells fluctuating tendencies in fortune. Now you are progressing immensely, to be suddenly confronted with doubts and rumblings of failure.

---

*See Road and Path.

To think you are reading the reports of a weather bureau, you will change your place of abode, after much weary deliberation, but you will be benefited by the change.

To see a weather witch, denotes disagreeable conditions in your family affairs.

To see them conjuring the weather, foretells quarrels in the home and disappointment in business.

Weaving.

To dream that you are weaving, denotes that you will baffle any attempt to defeat you in the struggle for the up-building of an honorable fortune.

To see others weaving shows that you will be surrounded by healthy and energetic conditions.

Web.

To dream of webs, foretells deceitful friends will work you loss and displeasure. If the web is non-elastic, you will remain firm in withstanding the attacks of the envious persons who are seeking to obtain favors from you.

Wedding.*

To attend a wedding in your dream, you will speedily find that there is approaching you an occasion which will cause you bitterness and delayed success.

For a young woman to dream that her wedding is a secret is decidedly unfavorable to character. It imports her probable downfall.

If she contracts a worldly, or approved marriage, signifies she will rise in the estimation of those about her, and anticipated promises and joys will not be withheld.

If she thinks in her dream that there are parental objections, she will find that her engagement will create

*See Marriage and Bride.

dissatisfaction among her relatives. For her to dream her lover weds another, foretells that she will be distressed with needless fears, as her lover will faithfully carry out his promises.

For a person to dream of being wedded, is a sad augury, as death will only be eluded by a miracle. If the wedding is a gay one and there are no ashen, pale-faced or black-robed ministers enjoining solemn vows, the reverses may be expected.

For a young woman to dream that she sees some one at her wedding dressed in mourning, denotes she will only have unhappiness in her married life. If at another's wedding, she will be grieved over the unfavorable fortune of some relative or friend. She may experience displeasure or illness where she expected happiness and health. The pleasure trips of others or her own, after this dream, may be greatly disturbed by unpleasant intrusions or surprises.

Wedding Clothes.

To see wedding clothes, signifies you will participate in pleasing works and will meet new friends. To see them soiled or in disorder, foretells you will lose close relations with some much-admired person.

Wedding Ring.

For a woman to dream her wedding ring is bright and shining, foretells that she will be shielded from cares and infidelity.

If it should be lost or broken, much sadness will come into her life through death and uncongeniality.

To see a wedding ring on the hand of a friend, or some other person, denotes that you will hold your vows lightly and will court illicit pleasure.

Wedge.

To dream of a wedge, denotes you will have trouble in some business arrangements which will be the cause of your separation from relatives.

Separation of lovers or friends may also be implied.

Wedlock.

To dream that you are in the bonds of an unwelcome wedlock, denotes you will be unfortunately implicated in a disagreeable affair.

For a young woman to dream that she is dissatisfied with wedlock, foretells her inclinations will persuade her into scandalous escapades.

For a married woman to dream of her wedding day, warns her to fortify her strength and feelings against disappointment and grief. She will also be involved in secret quarrels and jealousies. For a woman to imagine she is pleased and securely cared for in wedlock, is a propitious dream.

Weeding.

To dream that you are weeding, foretells that you will have difficulty in proceeding with some work which will bring you distinction.

To see others weeding, you will be fearful that enemies will upset your plans.

Weeping.

Weeping in your dreams, foretells ill tidings and disturbances in your family.

To see others weeping, signals pleasant reunion after periods of saddened estrangements. This dream for a young woman is ominous of lovers' quarrels, which can only reach reconciliation by self-abnegation.

For the tradesman, it foretells temporary discouragement and reverses.

Weevil.

To dream of weevils, portends loss in trade and falseness in love.

Weighing.

To dream of weighing, denotes that you are approaching a prosperous period, and if you set yourself determinedly toward success you will victoriously reap the full fruition of your labors.

To weigh others, you will be able to subordinate them to your interest.

For a young woman to weigh with her lover, foretells that he will be ready at all times to comply with her demands.

Well.

To dream that you are employed in a well, foretells that you will succumb to adversity through your misapplied energies. You will let strange elements direct your course.

To fall into a well, signifies that overwhelming despair will possess you. For one to cave in, promises that enemies' schemes will overthrow your own.

To see an empty well, denotes you will be robbed of fortune if you allow strangers to share your confidence.

To see one with a pump in it, shows you will have opportunities to advance your prospects.

To dream of an artesian well, foretells that your splendid resources will gain you admittance into the realms of knowledge and pleasure.

To draw water from a well, denotes the fulfilment of ardent desires. If the water is impure, there will be unpleasantness.

Welcome.

To dream that you receive a warm welcome into any

society, foretells that you will become distinguished among your acquaintances and will have deference shown you by strangers. Your fortune will approximate anticipation.

To accord others welcome, denotes your congeniality and warm nature will be your passport into pleasures, or any other desired place.

Welsh Rarebits.

To dream of preparing or eating Welsh rarebits, denotes that your affairs will assume a complicated state, owing to your attention being absorbed by artful women and enjoyment of neutral fancies.

Wet.

To dream that you are wet, denotes that a possible pleasure may involve you in loss and disease. You are warned to avoid the blandishments of seemingly well-meaning people.

For a young woman to dream that she is soaking wet, portends that she will be disgracefully implicated in some affair with a married man.

Wet Nurse.

To dream that you are a wet nurse, denotes that you will be widowed or have the care of the aged, or little children.

For a woman to dream that she is a wet nurse, signifies that she will depend on her own labors for sustenance.

Whale.

To dream of seeing a whale approaching a ship, denotes that you will have a struggle between duties, and will be threatened with loss of property.

If the whale is demolished, you will happily decide

between right and inclination, and will encounter pleasing successes.

If you see a whale overturn a ship, you will be thrown into a whirlpool of disasters.

Whalebone.

To see or work with whalebone in your dreams, you will form an alliance which will afford you solid benefit.

Wheat.

To see large fields of growing wheat in your dreams, denotes that your interest will take on encouraging prospects.

If the wheat is ripe, your fortune will be assured and love will be your joyous companion.

To see large clear grains of wheat running through the thresher, foretells that prosperity has opened her portals to the fullest for you.

To see it in sacks or barrels, your determination to reach the apex of success is soon to be crowned with victory and your love matters will be firmly grounded.

If your granary is not well covered and you see its contents getting wet, foretells that while you have amassed a fortune, you have not secured your rights and you will see your interests diminishing by the hand of enemies.

If you rub wheat from the head into your hand and eat it, you will labor hard for success and will obtain and make sure of your rights.

To dream that you climb a steep hill covered with wheat and think you are pulling yourself up by the stalks of wheat, denotes you will enjoy great prosperity and thus be able to distinguish yourself in any chosen pursuit.

Wheels.

To see swiftly rotating wheels in your dreams, foretells that you will be thrifty and energetic in your business and be successful in pursuits of domestic bliss.

To see idle or broken wheels, proclaims death or absence of some one in your household.

Whetstone.

To dream of a whetstone, is significant of sharp worries and close attention is needed in your own affairs, if you avoid difficulties.

You are likely to be forced into an uncomfortable journey.

Whip.

To dream of a whip, signifies unhappy dissensions and unfortunate and formidable friendships.

Whirlpool.

To dream of a whirlpool, denotes that great danger is imminent in your business, and, unless you are extremely careful, your reputation will be seriously blackened by some disgraceful intrigue.

Whirlwind.

To dream that you are in the path of a whirlwind, foretells that you are confronting a change which threatens to overwhelm you with loss and calamity.

For a young woman to dream that she is caught in a whirlwind and has trouble to keep her skirts from blowing up and entangling her waist, denotes that she will carry on a secret flirtation and will be horrified to find that scandal has gotten possession of her name and she will run a close risk of disgrace and ostracism.

Whisky.

To dream of whisky in bottles, denotes that you will be careful of your interests, protecting them with energy and watchfulness, thereby adding to their proportion.

To drink it alone, foretells that you will sacrifice your friends to your selfishness.

To destroy whisky, you will lose your friends by your ungenerous conduct.

Whisky is not fraught with much good. Disappointment in some form will likely appear.

To see or drink it, is to strive and reach a desired object after many disappointments. If you only see it, you will never obtain the result hoped and worked for.

Whispering.

To dream of whispering, denotes that you will be disturbed by the evil gossiping of people near you.

To hear a whisper coming to you as advice or warning, foretells that you stand in need of aid and counsel.

Whistle.

To hear a whistle in your dream, denotes that you will be shocked by some sad intelligence, which will change your plans laid for innocent pleasure.

To dream that you are whistling, foretells a merry occasion in which you expect to figure largely. This dream for a young woman indicates indiscreet conduct and failure to obtain wishes is foretold.

White Lead.

To dream of white lead, denotes relatives or children are in danger because of your carelessness. Prosperity will be chary of favor.

White Moth.

To dream of a white moth, foretells unavoidable sickness, though you will be tempted to accuse yourself or some other with wrong-doing, which you think causes the complaint. For a woman to see one flying around in the room at night, forebodes unrequited wishes and disposition which will effect the enjoyment of other people. To see a moth flying and finally settling upon something, or disappearing totally, foreshadows death of friends or relatives.

Whitewash.

To dream that you are whitewashing, foretells that you will seek to reinstate yourself with friends by ridding yourself of offensive habits and companions.

For a young woman, this dream is significant of well-laid plans to deceive others and gain back her lover who has been estranged by her insinuating bearing toward him.

Widow

To dream that you are a widow, foretells that you will have many troubles through malicious persons.

For a man to dream that he marries a widow, denotes he will see some cherished undertaking crumble down in disappointment.

Wife.

To dream of your wife, denotes unsettled affairs and discord in the home.

To dream that your wife is unusually affable, denotes that you will receive profit from some important venture in trade.

For a wife to dream her husband whips her, foretells unlucky influences will cause harsh criticism in the home and a general turmoil will ensue.

Wig.

To dream you wear a wig, indicates that you will soon make an unpropitious change.

To lose a wig, you will incur the derision and contempt of enemies. To see others wearing wigs, is a sign of treachery entangling you.

Wild.

To dream that you are running about wild, foretells that you will sustain a serious fall or accident.

To see others doing so, denotes unfavorable prospects will cause you worry and excitement.

Wild Man.

To see a wild man in your dream, denotes that enemies will openly oppose you in your enterprises. To think you are one foretells you will be unlucky in following out your designs.

Will.

To dream you are making your will, is significant of momentous trials and speculations.

For a wife or any one to think a will is against them, portends that they will have disputes and disorderly proceedings to combat in some event soon to transpire.

If you fail to prove a will, you are in danger of libelous slander. To lose one is unfortunate for your business.

To destroy one, warns you that you are about to be a party to treachery and deceit.

Willow.

To dream of willows, foretells that you will soon make a sad journey, but you will be consoled in your grief by faithful friends.

Wind.

To dream of the wind blowing softly and sadly upon you, signifies that great fortune will come to you through bereavement.

If you hear the wind soughing, denotes that you will wander in estrangement from one whose life is empty without you.

To walk briskly against a brisk wind, foretells that you will courageously resist temptation and pursue fortune with a determination not easily put aside. For the wind to blow you along against your wishes, portends failure in business undertakings and disappointments in love. If the wind blows you in the direction you wish to go you will find unexpected and helpful allies, or that you have natural advantages over a rival or competitor.

Windmill.

To see a windmill in operation in your dreams, foretells abundant accumulation of fortune and marked contentment

To see one broken or idle, signifies adversity coming unawares.

Window.

To see windows in your dreams, is an augury of fateful culmination to bright hopes. You will see your fairest wish go down in despair. Fruitless endeavors will be your portion.

To see closed windows is a representation of desertion. If they are broken, you will be hounded by miserable suspicions of disloyalty from those you love.

To sit in a window, denotes that you will be the victim of folly. To enter a house through a window, denotes that you will be found out while using dishonorable means to consummate a seemingly honorable purpose.

To escape by one, indicates that you will fall into a trouble whose toils will hold you unmercifully close.

To look through a window when passing and strange objects appear, foretells that you will fail in your chosen avocation and lose the respect for which you risked health and contentment.

Wine.

To dream of drinking wine, forebodes joy and consequent friendships.

To dream of breaking bottles of wine, foretells that your love and passion will border on excess.

To see barrels of wine, prognosticates great luxury. To pour it from one vessel into another, signifies that your enjoyments will be varied and you will journey to many notable places.

To dream of dealing in wine denotes that your occupation will be remunerative.

For a young woman to dream of drinking wine, indicates she will marry a wealthy gentleman but withal honorable.

Wine-cellar.

To dream of a wine-cellar, foretells superior amusements or pleasure will come in your way, to be disposed of at your bidding.

Wine-glass.

To dream of a wine-glass, foretells that a disappointment will affect you seriously, as you will fail to see anything pleasing until shocked into the realization of trouble.

Wings.

To dream that you have wings, foretells that you will experience grave fears for the safety of some one gone on a long journey away from you.

To see the wings of fowls or birds, denotes that you will finally overcome adversity and rise to wealthy degrees and honor.

Winter.

To dream of winter, is a prognostication of ill-health and dreary prospects for the favorable progress of fortune. After this dream your efforts will not yield satisfactory results.

Wire.

To dream of wire, denotes that you will make frequent but short journeys which will be to your disparagement.

Old or rusty wire, signifies that you will be possessed of a bad temper, which will give troubles to your kindred.

To see a wire fence in your dreams, foretells that you will be cheated in some trade you have in view.

Wisdom.

To dream you are possessed of wisdom, signifies your spirit will be brave under trying circumstances, and you will be able to overcome these trials and rise to prosperous living. If you think you lack wisdom, it implies you are wasting your native talents.

Witch.

To dream of witches, denotes that you, with others, will seek adventures which will afford hilarious enjoyment, but it will eventually rebound to your mortification. Business will suffer prostration if witches advance upon you, home affairs may be disappointing.

Witness.

To dream that you bear witness against others, signifies you will have great oppression through slight causes. If others bear witness against you, you will be compelled to refuse favors to friends in order to protect your own interest. If you are a witness for a guilty person, you will be implicated in a shameful affair.

Wizard.

To dream of a wizard, denotes you are going to have a big family, which will cause you much inconvenience as well as displeasure. For young people, this dream implies loss and broken engagements.

Wolf.

To dream of a wolf, shows that you have a thieving person in your employ, who will also betray secrets.

To kill one, denotes that you will defeat sly enemies who seek to overshadow you with disgrace. To hear the howl of a wolf, discovers to you a secret alliance to defeat you in honest competition.

Women.

To dream of women, foreshadows intrigue.

To argue with one, foretells that you will be outwitted and foiled.

To see a dark-haired woman with blue eyes and a pug nose, definitely determines your withdrawal from a race in which you stood a showing for victory. If she has brown eyes and a Roman nose, you will be cajoled into a dangerous speculation. If she has auburn hair with this combination, it adds to your perplexity and anxiety. If she is a blonde, you will find that all your engagements will be pleasant and favorable to your inclinations.

Wooden Shoe.

To dream of a wooden shoe, is significant of lonely wanderings and penniless circumstances. Those in love will suffer from unfaithfulness.

Woods.

To dream of woods, brings a natural change in your affairs. If the woods appear green, the change will be lucky. If stripped of verdure, it will prove calamitous.

To see woods on fire, denotes that your plans will reach satisfactory maturity. Prosperity will beam with favor upon you.

To dream that you deal in firewood, denotes that you will win fortune by determined struggle.

Wood-pile.

To dream of a wood-pile, denotes unsatisfactory business and misunderstandings in love.

Wool.

To dream of wool, is a pleasing sign of prosperous opportunities to expand your interests.

To see soiled, or dirty wool, foretells that you will seek employment with those who detest your principles.

Work.

To dream that you are hard at work, denotes that you will win merited success by concentration of energy.

To see others at work, denotes that hopeful conditions will surround you.

To look for work, means that you will be benefited by some unaccountable occurrence.

Workhouse.*

To dream that you are in a workhouse denotes that some event will work you harm and loss.

Workshop.

To see workshops in your dreams, foretells that you

*See Prison.

will use extraordinary schemes to undermine your enemies.

Worms.

To dream of worms, denotes that you will be oppressed by the low intriguing of disreputable persons.

For a young woman to dream they crawl on her, foretells that her aspirations will always tend to the material. If she kills or throws them off, she will shake loose from the material lethargy and seek to live in morality and spirituality.

To use them in your dreams as fish bait, foretells that by your ingenuity you will use your enemies to good advantage.

Wound.

To dream that you are wounded, signals distress and an unfavorable turn in business.

To see others wounded, denotes that injustice will be accorded you by your friends.

To relieve or dress a wound, signifies that you will have occasion to congratulate yourself on your good fortune.

Wreath.

To dream that you see a wreath of fresh flowers, denotes that great opportunities for enriching yourself will soon present themselves before you.

A withered wreath bears sickness and wounded love.

To see a bridal wreath, foretells a happy ending to uncertain engagements.

Wrecks.*

To see a wreck in your dream, foretells that you will be harassed with fears of destitution or sudden failure in business.

*See other like words.

Writing.*

To dream that you are writing, foretells that you will make a mistake which will almost prove your undoing.

To see writing, denotes that you will be upbraided for your careless conduct and a lawsuit may cause you embarrassment.

To try to read strange writing, signifies that you will escape enemies only by making no new speculation after this dream.

Y.

"The Prophet that hath a dream, let him tell a dream."— Jer. XXIII., 28.

Yacht.

To see a yacht in a dream, denotes happy recreation away from business and troublesome encumbrances. A stranded one, represents miscarriage of entertaining engagements.

Yankee.

To dream of a Yankee, foretells that you will remain loyal and true to your promise and duty, but if you are not careful you will be outwitted in some transaction.

Yard Stick.

To dream of a yard stick, foretells much anxiety will possess you, though your affairs assume unusual activity.

Yarn.

To dream of yarn, denotes success in your business and an industrious companion in your home.

------

*See Letters.

For a young woman to dream that she works with yarn, foretells that she will be proudly recognized by a worthy man as his wife.

Yawning.

If you yawn in your dreams, you will search in vain for health and contentment.

To see others yawning, foretells that you will see some of your friends in a miserable state. Sickness will prevent them from their usual labors.

Yearn.

To feel in a dream that you are yearning for the presence of anyone, denotes that you will soon hear comforting tidings from your absent friends.

For a young woman to think her lover is yearning for her, she will have the pleasure of soon hearing some one making a long-wished-for proposal. If she lets him know that she is yearning for him, she will be left alone and her longings will grow apace.

Yellow Bird.

To see a yellow bird flitting about in your dreams, foretells that some great event will cast a sickening fear of the future around you. To see it sick or dead, foretells that you will suffer for another's wild folly.

Yew Tree.

To dream of a yew tree, is a forerunner of illness and disappointment. If a young woman sits under one, she will have many fears to rend her over her fortune and the faithfulness of her lover. If she sees her lover standing by one, she may expect to hear of his illness, or misfortune. To admire one, she will estrange herself from her relatives by a mesalliance.

To visit a yew tree and find it dead and stripped of its foliage, predicts a sad death in your family. Property will not console for this loss.

Yield.

To dream you yield to another's wishes, denotes that you will throw away by weak indecision a great opportunity to elevate yourself.

If others yield to you, exclusive privileges will be accorded you and you will be elevated above your associates.

To receive poor yield for your labors, you may expect cares and worries.

Yoke.

To dream of seeing a yoke, denotes that you will unwillingly conform to the customs and wishes of others.

To yoke oxen in your dreams, signifies that your judgment and counsels will be accepted submissively by those dependent upon you. To fail to yoke them, you will be anxious over some prodigal friend.

Young.

To dream of seeing young people, is a prognostication of reconciliation of family disagreements and favorable times for planning new enterprises.

To dream that you are young again, foretells that you will make mighty efforts to recall lost opportunities, but will nevertheless fail.

For a mother to see her son an infant or small child again, foretells that old wounds will be healed and she will take on her youthful hopes and cheerfulness. If the child seems to be dying, she will fall into ill fortune and misery will attend her.

To see the young in school, foretells that prosperity and usefulness will envelope you with favors.

Yule Log.

To dream of a yule log, foretells that your joyous anticipations will be realized by your attendance at great festivities.

Z.

"Then thou scarest me with dreams, and terrifying me through visions; so that my soul chooseth strangling, and death rather than my life."—Job xvii., 14-15.

Zebra.

To dream of a zebra, denotes that you will be interested in varying and fleeting enterprises.

To see one wild in his native country, foretells that you will pursue a chimerical fancy which will return you unsatisfactory pleasure upon possession.

Zenith.

To dream of the zenith, foretells elaborate prosperity, and your choice of suitors will be successful.

Zephyr.

To dream of soft zephyrs, denotes that you will sacrifice fortune to obtain the object of your affection and will find reciprocal affection in your wooing.

If a young woman dreams that she is saddened by the whisperings of the zephyrs, she will have a season of disquietude by the compelled absence of her lover.

Zinc.

To work with or to see zinc in your dreams, indicates substantial and energetic progress. Business will assume a brisk tone in its varying departments.

To dream of zinc ore promises the approach of eventful success.

Zodiac.

To dream of the zodiac is a prognostication of unparalleled rise in material worth, but also indicates alloyed peace and happiness.

To see it appearing weird, denotes that some untoward grief is hovering over you and it will take strenuous efforts to dispell it.

To study the zodiac in your dreams, denotes that you will gain distinction and favor by your intercourse with strangers.

If you approach it or it approaches you, foretells that you will succeed in your speculations to the wonderment of others and beyond your wildest imagination.

To draw a map of it, signifies future gain.

Zoological Garden.

To dream of visiting zoological gardens, denotes that you will have a varied fortune. Sometimes it seems that enemies will overpower you and again you stand in the front rank of success. You will also gain knowledge by travel and sojourn in foreign countries.